BLOOD, LAND, AND

Blood, Land, and Sex

Legal and Political Pluralism in Eritrea

Lyda Favali and Roy Pateman

INDIANA
University Press
Bloomington & Indianapolis

This book is a publication of
Indiana University Press
601 North Morton Street
Bloomington, IN 47404-3797 USA
http://iupress.indiana.edu
Telephone orders   800-842-6796
Fax orders   812-855-7931
Orders by e-mail   iuporder@indiana.edu
© 2003 by Lyda Favali and Roy Pateman

The paper used in this publication meets the minimum requirements of American National
Standard for Information Sciences—Permanence of Paper for Printed Library Materials,
ANSI Z39.48-1984.

Manufactured in the United States of America

Library of Congress Cataloging-in-Publication Data

Favali, Lyda, date
Blood, land, and sex : legal and political pluralism in Eritrea / Lyda Favali and Roy Pateman.
p.   cm.
Includes bibliographical references and index.
ISBN 0-253-34205-8 (cloth : alk. paper) — ISBN 0-253-21577-3 (paper : alk. paper)
1. Legal polycentricity—Eritrea. I. Pateman, Roy. II. Title.
KRN48.3 .F38 2003
340.5'2635—dc21
2002010945
1 2 3 4 5   08 07 06 05 04 03

To the Eritreans and
others we love

Contents

Preface and Acknowledgments

Eritrea was the last country in Africa to become independent. From 1889 it was occupied in turn by Italy, Britain, and Ethiopia. Eritreans fought Ethiopians for thirty years and overcame their enemy in 1991, when at last they became free to govern their own country. Very few scholars have researched Eritrea since Italian colonization ended in 1941, and the little work that has been carried out has on the whole been Ethiopia-centric or ideologically driven.

Eritrea has many unique features; it is an extremely rare case in Africa in that many of its traditional bodies of rules were written down in the pre-colonial period.[1] This practice was influenced by the availability of canon law codes used in the Coptic Church and written in Ge'ez, its liturgical language. In no other African country, to our knowledge, is such a large, unexplored, and carefully documented body of legal tradition to be found. In the nineteenth century many of these codes were written down and translated into Italian, German, and English, sometimes by the colonial power, sometimes by missionaries. This work continued in the past century in particular during the liberation struggle when it was carried out under the patronage of the Eritrean People's Liberation Front (EPLF) Department of Culture. An especially interesting feature of this body of tradition is that revision occurred at periodic intervals, and the results of the deliberations were meticulously recorded.[2]

Some scholars have cast doubts on the wisdom of using the versions of the traditional laws that were written down during the colonial period on the grounds that the motives of the authorities were questionable, the identity of the scribes was unverifiable and problematic, and by concentrating on a specific text one misses the continual transformation of rules. We do not agree with this argument as far as Eritrea is concerned. Some laws were written down long before the colonial powers arrived in Africa. The Italians, having taken the counsel of some very distinguished figures such as Conti Rossini, were in fact well aware of the difficulties of writing down the codes. They also preferred to use as their main source the people directly involved in deciding upon and administering the laws in a specified area.

Raimond Verdier has pointed out that adaptation and resilience of tradition has been dealt with in the main very superficially and fragmentarily by lawyers.[3] One has to start somewhere and we began by examining some of the huge amount of material available but unused. Much of what we have read shows a contamination with state law; however, it is this very contamination that becomes central to our argument that the bodies that produce law are continually interacting with each other to produce a very rich diversity of rules.

Much work was carried out on African traditional law in the 1950s and 1960s. With the independence of most African countries, interest in the subject waned and work ceased, partly because the new regimes were in general suspicious of traditional law, which was either deemed to be solely responsible for African underdevelopment or at least antithetical to a model of "modernization" so favored by post-colonial rulers.

Our research provides, through the first translations into English of many important Italian texts, a depth and breadth of information about the traditional Eritrean legal system that is almost totally unknown to the English-speaking world. We have made a comprehensive collection of all available traditional codes and religious laws relevant to Eritrea and assessed their importance. The authors have also read, translated, and reworked English and French sources and, with the help of friends and colleagues, materials in German, Tigrinya, Arabic, Saho, and other languages.

We soon discovered that we shared similar beliefs in the value of a pluralistic and multidisciplinary approach, and we have benefited enormously from exposing ourselves to disciplines and languages foreign to our original training, interests, and education. In fact, our book's major contribution to scholarship lies, we believe, in the reinterpretation and analysis of many different types of primary texts and numerous secondary glosses, written in diverse languages at different periods of history. We reach back into the pre-colonial period and bring our study as far as possible right up to the present day.

The topics of Eritrean traditional/customary and religious law have so far not been properly addressed in the studies of the post- or neocolonial state. Ours is the first full-length study to trace the persistence and vibrancy of traditional and religious law in the country since the extensive work carried out by a number of prominent Italian colonial scholars. We are aware that the works of these men is difficult to match for width, depth, and erudition, but unfortunately their work is rarely seen, and is almost never available in English. Unlike our predecessors', our work encompasses more than the major Eritrean group—Tigrinya, which has received the lion's share of attention by researchers to date. We have made every effort—often through personal interviews and building on one of the authors' twenty years of field experience in Eritrea—to obtain information about all the diverse ethnies who inhabit the country. The sources are examined and commented upon in depth in a manner we hope will open up the subject for future research and also serve as a reference tool.

There are no really significant studies on current Eritrean state law, partly because of the language problems; the main documents are in Tigrinya, and very few have been translated officially into English and Arabic. We have commissioned English and Italian translations of some of the most important ones. We have visited Eritrea on many occasions and carried out interviews in the field with Eritreans of different faiths and traditions, other scholars, and government officials, in an attempt to make an objective assessment of the persistence of traditional and religious law. The extent to which these laws have coexisted and conflicted with state and international law throughout an unusually vivid and eventful progress from pre-colonial existence to an independent state constitutes one of the main goals of our research.

In this book we combine theories of legal and political pluralism; this exercise has led to a most productive synergy between the two authors.[4] Our use of legal pluralism in a comparative law perspective is not familiar to many American scholars, and this could open up a new field of research for them. Our interdisciplinary approach makes it useful to different kinds of scholars: comparative lawyers, political scientists, anthropologists, sociologists, historians, public policy and women's studies specialists, and ethnographers. It can form part of the college course for students of law, anthropology, and sociology.

Our work also forms part of a resurgence of a regional and global interest in the subject. For example, the Ford Foundation has funded a large-scale comparative ongoing study based at the University of Cape Town (in which the authors participate) on Islamic Family Law throughout Africa. One of the authors' research agenda priorities has for some years been Islamic law and its diffusion in Africa. The people of the Eritrean coast were among the first Africans to be converted to Islam, and ever since the eighth century Arabic influences and influences from the whole Muslim world have permeated the country.

Legal and political scholars can now learn a number of important lessons from the study of Eritrea. Not only has traditional and Islamic law thrived, but the state appears to realize that it is better to work with traditions as far as possible rather than try and suppress all of them. We report ancient traditions as we find them in the original sources and colonial texts. The reader may find some of them "curious." We are certainly not implying that they have remained unchanged over the past hundred years.

Some of this book started its life in papers written for various solo or joint presentations over the past few years. *Land Tenure* was given in its first form to the Forty-first Annual Conference of the African Studies Association in Chicago in November 1998, and was subsequently published in the *Proceedings of the Conference*. We expanded our discussion to include land disputes and presented it to the Horn of Africa Research Group at the J. S. Coleman African Studies Center, UCLA Los Angeles, also in November 1998. The *Legacy of the Common Law in Eritrea* was prepared for presentation to the Legacy of the Common Law Conference, IPSA Research Committee on Comparative Judicial Studies in London in July 1999. A much shorter version of *Female Genital Surgery in Eritrea* was presented to the Forty-second Annual Conference of African Studies Association meeting in Philadelphia in November 1999, and was subsequently published in the *Proceedings of the Conference*. The essence of chapter one was presented to the Forty-third Annual Conference of African Studies Association meeting in Nashville in 2000. Much of the material on Muslim personal law was discussed at the 2nd Symposium on Islamic Law organized by the Center for Contemporary Islam at the University of Cape Town, held in Dakar, Senegal, June–July 2001. All papers have been prepared both in Italian and in English. Almost all of the translations in this book are the work of the authors. We have used Italian, French, and English editions of several classic works. In every case a check has been undertaken for consistency of interpretation of original sources.

We would like to express our thanks to the chairs, discussants, and participants at these panels for their comments and suggestions. Some individuals have been extraordinarily generous with their time, and we have had extensive conversations with them. We would like to mention especially Alexander Naty, Tekle Abraha, Dehab Abraha, Belai Araia, Berhane Abraham—we are especially grateful to these two EPLF fighters for sharing with us some of the thirty thousand pages of transcripts of oral histories collected by the Eritrean Ministry of Local Government over the past twenty years—Yohannes Ghebremedin, Alemseged Tesfai, Nu Nu Kidane, Ghennet Tesfamariam, Zemhret Yohannes, Lidia Teclu Belay, Ibrahim Ismail Maishigho, Mohamed Said Nawed, Asmeron Legesse, Horst Krietch, Michael Mahrt, Roberta Aluffi Beck-Peccoz, Marco Guadagni, Richard Greenfield, Jonathon Miran, and Luca Castellani. The director Azieb Tewolde and her staff of the Research and Documentation Center in Asmara were as always very helpful. Very special thanks go to Pigi Monateri and his "Black Gaius," which helped us to capture, and demystify, Western strategies of supremacy in the field of law.

Lyda would like to thank a number of her colleagues for their conversation, writing, lectures, and support. Rodolfo Sacco, Francesco Castro, Paul Brietzke, Gianni Piccinelli, Gianmaria Ajani, Michele Graziadei, Ugo Mattei, Elisabetta Grande, Alessandro Simoni, and Leonardo Lesmo. We would like to express our appreciation to Bereket Habte Selassie and Beverly Moran, the readers for Indiana University Press, and also Dee Mortensen, Jane Lyle, and Drew Bryan for making the editorial process as pleasant and fruitful as possible.

We collected some of the source material in Addis Ababa in 1997 and would have paid a return visit before now were it not for the war that Ethiopia unleashed on Eritrea in 1998. We could not have managed without the help of Awet Tewelde, who collected materials for us and translated documents from Amharic, Tigrinya and Tigré. We include a glossary of frequently used terms and words in Tigrinya, Tigré, Saho, Arabic, and other Eritrean languages together with a few Latin words and terms together with their English equivalents.

Our own fruitful and enjoyable cooperation (that began with a chance meeting in Asmara in May 1997) has been made possible mainly though the miracle of electronic communication. We have managed to meet on occasions face to face, exchange the rare telephone call, and constantly mail each other papers, ideas, etc. This work would have been impossible (intellectually as well as financially) without e-mail.[5]

Abbreviations

ADR	Alternative Dispute Resolutions
BIA	Board of Immigration Appeal
BMA	British Military Administration
CEDA	Convention on the Elimination of all forms of Discrimination against Women
CPE	Citizens for Peace in Eritrea
DUP	Democratic Unionist Party
EC	Ethiopian Calendar
ECC	Ethiopian Civil Code
ECOSOC	Economic and Social Council of the United Nations
ECRE	Ente di Colonizzazione Romagna d'Etiopia
EDF	Eritrean Defense Forces
ELF	Eritrean Liberation Front
ELF-PLF	Eritrean Liberation Front–People's Liberation Front
EPLF	Eritrean People's Liberation Front
EPRDF	Ethiopian People's Revolutionary Democratic Front
ERA	Eritrean Relief Association
FGC	Female Genital Cutting
FGM	Female Genital Mutilation
FGS	Female Genital Surgery
IDP	Internally Displaced People
IMF	International Monetary Fund
INS	Immigration and Naturalization Service
LAB	Land Administrative Body
LC	Land Commission

MLWE	Ministry of Land, Water and Environment
MTD	Maria Teresa Dollar
NGO	Non-Governmental Organization
NSC	National Security Council
NUEW	National Union of Eritrean Women
OPEC	Organization of Petroleum Exporting Countries
PA	Peasant Association
PFDJ	People's Front for Democracy and Justice
PGE	Provisional Government of Eritrea
RD	Regio Decreto
SPLA	Sudanese People's Liberation Army
TCCE	Transitional Civil Code of Eritrea
TPLF	Tigrayan People's Liberation Front
UNCITRAL	United Nations Commission on International Trade Law
UNESCO	United Nations Educational, Scientific and Cultural Organization
WHO	World Health Organization
WTO	World Trade Organization

BLOOD, LAND, AND SEX

One

Facts and Ideas
The Struggle for Power and Legitimacy

Facts come before ideas.
—Mikhail Bakunin[1]

Facts must be in agreement with words.
—Lucius Annaeus Seneca[2]

Facts do not cease to exist because they are ignored.
—Aldous Huxley[3]

There are no facts, only interpretations.
—Friedrich Wilhelm Nietzsche[4]

Legal Pluralism

Not surprisingly, pluralism has been at the center of the debates of theorists belonging to different disciplines. It can be used to address ethnic, linguistic, political and religious as well as legal issues. Very loosely, we can describe pluralism as a state of society where different ethnic, social, linguistic, and religious groups maintain their culture and special interests within the confines (which are drawn for the sake of convenience and are consequently somewhat arbitrary) of a common civilization or nation-state. Naturally one person can belong to, and usually identifies with, more than one of these groups.[5]

As far as the legal dimension is concerned, scholars have reached a consensus that legal pluralism is not restricted to Africa, and many authors have found it an advanced tool with which to approach some aspects of Western legal systems. Most agree that it is vital to the study of African law,[6] not surprising as state law was generally only introduced to Africa in the nineteenth century as an essential feature of colonialism. In the West, since the birth of modern states, there has been much greater reliance on state-centered law, whereas in Africa, many actors other than the state have continued to play a significant role in producing legal rules; the legal domain was not controlled by the state and remains influenced by factors not controlled by the state.[7] A state-centered perspective, which has been typical of most studies drawing from legal

1

positivism—the theory that emphasizes the conventional view of law as arising only from the state as opposed to natural law theory—has proved completely inadequate to capture African reality.

Among the legion of definitions of legal pluralism, some concentrate on a single, particular issue and describe the essence of pluralism as the coexistence of multiple mechanisms for the settlement of conflicts (or, in other words, multiple legal solutions that apply to the same case).[8] According to other definitions, a pluralistic system exists where a particular category of social relations is "in the field of operation of two or more bodies of legal norms."[9] More radically, other authors suggest the existence of "different social normative systems."[10] This definition does not exclude situations where an individual may be forced to obey, on occasion, more than one legal system, nor does it deny that for each particular case study, different degrees of pluralism may be found.[11]

In this book we adopt a "strong" definition of legal pluralism that postulates, at the macro level, the existence of multiple socio-political bodies, each of which produces law. We call each of these bodies "actors." Legal scholars dealing with pluralism usually concentrate on rules rather than bodies. And they miss an important dimension in doing so. When we speak of pluralism, we do not refer to the existence, alongside state law, of fragments of religious and traditional law (for instance concerning marriage and inheritance matters) that are recognized and tolerated by the state. This is a perfectly legitimate way of looking at it, but its disadvantage is that it puts state law on a pedestal. In other words, this approach is not balanced because it entails acknowledging the supremacy of state law. Therefore, in this book, by legal pluralism we mean the study of the multiplicity of legal actors concurrent with the state. These do not have any need, in principle, to obtain legitimacy and endorsement from the state. We assume that from an analysis of relations of strength, prestige, and legitimacy between these actors/bodies, we can derive useful elements to capture the relations between the legal rules that each of them produces. For each particular legal issue there will be one state rule, one traditional rule, one šarīʿa rule that may—or may not—differ because of a previous divergence between state and ethnic or religious groups.

Just as in politics, law has seen the growing strength of the international actor—this is also something most studies on legal pluralism do not properly address. In the following pages the international actor will be addressed as an autonomous player alongside the state and ethnic and religious groups. Up to some thirty years ago, research on pluralism was restricted, sometimes implicitly, to the nation-state. Most studies had described "local micro-politics," but few scholars had adopted a wider approach taking into consideration how "the political level of the supra-national activity penetrates local life." This "localism" has been linked (among other reasons) with the reluctance of many post-colonial authors to deal with a topic that African governments would have liked to avoid.[12] It is not easy to tolerate a loss of sovereignty.

The tension existing between various actors throughout its history, and the relatively few years it has existed as a unitary state, make Eritrea a particularly interesting case study to examine instances of cooperation and opposition between legitimate actors. Choices made by each of them, far from being totally free and autonomous, are on the contrary deeply influenced by the strength and authority of other actors at the particular moment when the decision is taken.

Individuals are linked to a group—or groups—of which they are a member by a web of relations of subordination. And they obey a certain command only when they perceive it as legitimate (or are "persuaded" that it is legitimate).[13] This is true, in our view, also at the macro level of legal actors: if the effectiveness of each command depends also on its legitimacy, in a case of a conflict between different rules, we can make the reasonable presumption that the rule that, in a particular moment, has the strongest legitimacy will prevail. From now on in our argument we will assume that pluralism is the coexistence over a certain territory—which may be assumed conventionally as corresponding with colonial or post-colonial borders—of differently legitimated social/political/legal orders, each of them an expression of a different actor.[14]

The different legitimacy—political, religious, or magical—of each actor reflects on the role it plays in the pluralistic system. This leads to a dialectic relationship between legal actors. Each of them tries to keep intact the social structure they express, and then to perpetuate this or that particular legal rule.[15] This approach is crucial in helping to explain the re-emergence of tradition in secular states. Practices that were supposedly superseded by the march of evolution have been revived. This can be explained if we discuss phenomena in terms of relations of strength and legitimacy between actors that create a certain rule or set of rules.

Political Pluralism and Level of Analysis

In political science, pluralism has been the dominant ideology throughout the twentieth century, as well as the area of the most intense empirical research. As the twentieth century drew to a close, pluralism has also been a strongly contested ideology, with opposition coming from those who center their approach on the state, representative government, and majority rule and who are deeply suspicious of empowering minorities and individuals. Our approach, on the contrary, is deliberately pluralist.

Minimal pluralism exists only in totalitarian states or rigid theocracies that attempt to force others to adopt a unitary vision of society and/or religion. Most states can be described as limited pluralist; they tolerate or accept to different degrees non-dominant ethnic groups, political dissidents, and minority religions. Fewer countries fall into a third group: comprehensive pluralism. Here the state confers eligibility on all with the rights and obligations appropriate to whatever identity one adopts.[16]

The other major theoretical tool used is the "levels of analysis" approach drawn from international relations; it is inherently pluralistic and embraces actors at all levels. Three levels of international politics are usually covered: the individual, the state, and the international state system; each level captures a different level of causation.[17] The various levels can also be assessed as to their descriptive, explanatory, and predictive capabilities.[18] In a further refinement, another level of decision making can be added, that of the bureaucracy.[19] As some transnational corporations, non-governmental organizations (NGOs), and international regimes are now vastly larger enterprises than many sovereign states, and have a much wider international reach, we argue that a supra level of analysis should be added to deal with the impact of these bodies.

Manifold errors can arise if a decision is analyzed entirely from the perspective of individual actors or nation-states.[20] If we attempt to understand a problem solely by applying a broad systemic theory, we also risk undervaluing the crucial role of individuals. So, at the micro level, individuals, their psychology, and groups need to be investigated; ideas such as groupthink and misperception are significant.[21] Public opinion and argument, at various levels and branches of government, can also fundamentally shape a nation's policies and actions. On the international level, what is important is not only the interaction with other sovereign nation-states, but the relationships of these actors with others that can take on the character of states. This is exactly what we try to do in subsequent chapters as we deal with the intricacies of Eritrean pluralism. In the course of our analysis it will become clear that no one theory is totally adequate, so we use a variety of theories to come up with a satisfactory explanation; we develop this argument at much greater length in chapter 7, when we look at the conflict with Ethiopia as a dispute over land, power, and hegemony.

Synergy in Action

We have argued that a link exists between the different sources of legitimacy, legitimated actors, and the plurality of rules. This argument constitutes the core of our pluralistic analysis both from a legal and political perspective. We now want to highlight the point that relations between actors are never merely static and antithetic, but are dynamically inter-related; social orders influence each other in a circular process.[22] When examining a complex problem at many levels, a cross-disciplinary and multi-dimensional approach is essential.

Gramsci's concept of hegemony, its role in the negotiation of power, and its relation with ideology,[23] provides a useful insight. He argues that hegemony refers to power that maintains certain structures of domination.[24] Hegemony may constitute a basis upon which to depict each social group as carrying out a certain system of values, beliefs, and opinions.[25] The ability of non-dominant groups to resist and contest power demonstrates that they are often able to think about themselves as outside the ideology of dominant groups.[26] The Gramscian model helps us to focus on the "dynamic" aspect of pluralism: power (hegemony) and ideology are first contested, then agreed, and finally reshaped. It provides a guide to explaining how a wide variety of groups—such as traditional and religious orders—develop a crucial political role as a counterbalance to the state.[27] Ideological wars can reshape social relations in various ways. Hegemonic processes and practices of opposition are mutually constitutive and able to change relations between groups.[28]

Other studies on legitimacy and power come to similar conclusions. Earle identifies four sources of power: social, military, ideological and, economic; "the different sources of power are . . . not equivalent and they cannot be conceived to be independent of one another. The political process involves the selective application of power to control access to these power sources and thus to weaken political opposition."[29] Some authors have suggested that we abandon the idea of power as absolute and asymmetric, according to the terms of prevalence of one actor on another, and call for the adoption of a wider approach, one which is able to capture the entire spectrum of the relations of power.[30] A network of exchanges, borrowings, and reciprocated influencing connects hegemonic and subaltern cultures.[31] Relationships between actors are never, then, all one way. On the contrary, "even the most invincible claimants to power depend on others to make them powerful."[32] The weaker actors are always jockeying for power, and in time they may become dominant.

At various times of Eritrean history, different actors have predominated because although the system is currently in equilibrium, it is inherently unstable and changes over time. Relations between various actors, and the dominance of one over another, vary according to the area concerned, to the field of law, to the time, and to the strength of the actors. There is an apt analogy with quantum mechanics theory. Some experiments on light can only be understood if one assumes that light is a particle, while others can only be understood if one assumes it is a wave. A particle and a wave cannot exist together except at nearly the same time. Uncertainty is as inescapable in quantum mechanics as it is in attempting to understand the dynamic interrelationship between legal actors. It is difficult to capture what is happening at any precise moment. No sooner than you think you understand the position, it changes.

Theories of Legal Transplants, Layers, and Formants

Our analysis of how legal actors interact with each other at a certain time will be combined in the following chapters with that of the legal layers (traditional, religious, colonial and post-colonial, national, and international) prevailing during different periods.[33] This approach shows that the more recent layers never fully supersede the previous ones; on the contrary, the earlier layers survive, entirely or partially. For example, some features of traditional belief, such as totem and initiation rites, were not abandoned after the spread of Islam or Christianity. Neither is traditional law ever entirely suppressed by colonial rule. And the latter has also left important legacies, such as the idea of (arbitrarily drawn) colonial borders, to which post-independence frontiers—as a rule—correspond. Moreover, virtually all states have understood the need to leave šarīʿa untouched, at least in the sphere of family law and inheritance. To rule in this area has proved to be dangerous both politically and legally.

Other useful contributions to our meta-theory come from research on legal transplants, in the light of the manifold studies that have been undertaken after Watson's pioneering work.[34] A legal transplant is the transfer of a part of a legal system, for example the civil code, legal institution, or single rules, from one country to another. The development of a legal system has been described as "largely a history of borrowing of legal material from other legal systems."

We want to make three points. Firstly, a transplant is never merely a static experience for the country that receives it, because, "rules are not self-expressive; institutions need to communicate, and so the law needs, in a way, to be wrapped up in narrative."[35] In transplanting, the importing system appraises the model and almost always changes it radically: "the process of the import/export of rules and institutions is an almost 'unconscious' process of plunging them into the ideology" of the borrowing system. Everything depends on the strategies of the latter; it absorbs what it needs, and it uses what it has borrowed in order to cope with its own problems.[36]

Second, legal transplants are not merely a legacy of colonialism. They take place between the capitalist and socialist world and the less-developed countries, and *vice versa* (if infrequently in the second case). They have always existed; the analysis of historical layers of law shows that African societies before colonization were inherently pluralistic, and Europeans were not the first to import foreign rules into Africa.[37]

Third, actors who import or export models are not necessarily states; transplants also take place both between state and non-state actors, and among non-state actors. Eritrean traditional law has been influenced by a number of migrations that, since the sixth century B.C., have occurred in the Horn of Africa, and by the contact of local people, already very diverse, with invaders. For instance, a significant transplant took place, as we will see in the next chapter, when *šarī'a* first came to the area.

Continuing with our exercise in deconstructing the myth of the monolithic nature of each legal system, we assert that every element of this pluralistic system can be subdivided. For many years, comparative lawyers have stressed the need for a dynamic approach to law. We find this in the notion of legal formants, or the multiple components of a certain (state) legal system, that comprise not only state law, doctrine, and case law, but also, at least, elements that are not verbalized, as well as rhetoric, which is frequently used to enforce and strengthen the legitimacy of state rules and rulers.[38]

The legal formants approach combines an external study of legal actors within the state framework with an intensive internal analysis of legal documents of all kinds. Multiple types of texts—coming from many legal actors—are analyzed specifically to look for differences between them.[39] For example, while looking at the state system, judges and legal theorists must be taken into account, not just legislators.[40] This technique, originally devised for state law, can also be applied usefully in the deconstruction of other elements of the pluralistic system, such as traditional and religious law.

Introducing the Actors

At this stage, after having set the scene, we need to introduce the legal and political actors who will be on the Eritrean stage throughout the whole book. Four actors can be identified: state, ethnic groups (producing traditional law), religious groups, and the international/transnational community.[41]

In spite of all the attempts to suppress them, traditional and religious laws have played a major role. For a brief period of seven years after liberation in 1991, state legislation, strongly influenced by political hegemony, seemed to prevail. The war with Ethiopia that re-erupted in 1998 has had the effect of putting most legislation on hold. It is too early to say definitely, but religious and traditional law may experience a resurgence as the Eritrean state seems resigned and willing to allow more space for other legal actors to maneuver. It is also by no means sure at this point whether the state will succeed where previous colonial powers have failed.[42]

Ethnic Groups

There are three main regions in the country. The densely populated highlands make up one third of the total area and are dominated by Coptic Christians; the eastern coastal region, that includes a large area of desert, is populated mostly by Muslims; and the potentially fertile western lowlands are the home for people of a variety of faiths, including some traditional believers, who attribute a living spirit to creatures living or dead, inanimate objects, and natural phenomena; such spirits can either help or harm their interests with the aid of taboos, magic charms, or amulets. According to the Eritrean government, there are nine nationalities: Afar, Bilein, Kunama, Hedareb, Nara, Rashaida, Saho, Tigré, and Tigrinya.[43] We prefer to use the word "ethnie," a more neutral word than "nationality." The latter is still a highly charged term; it was commonly used in the socialist discourse of the 60s and 70s—in which the EPLF actively participated.[44] It was often used in the heated debates on the right of a nation to secede and be independent. Eritrea has followed the path set by other socialist movements that have fought and won independence. Once a movement is in charge of a sovereign state, the last thing it wants to do is encourage its partition into separate micro-nationalist states. Significantly, the Eritrean constitution never mentions the word "nationality," even though the word is still very much used in public rhetoric. There are no sound reasons to accept the statement that Eritrea has only nine ethnies. A good case could be made that there are more, and we develop this further in the next chapter.

Each of the Eritrean ethnic groups has a long and rich body of tradition, custom, and practice to which it is deeply attached. A recent significant example of this loyalty was when the new Eritrean constitution of 1997 was being drafted; apparently, the main concern of ordinary people was that "their religious practices, their favorite customs and customary laws should not be disturbed."[45] There is not a neat division of one ethnie, one tradition. In the case of the largest ethnic group, Tigrinya, for example, there are some twenty codes, each one reflecting the existence of sub-ethnies, and often showing considerable differences from one another. In our analysis we attempt, as far as possible, to deal with all of them.

Religious Groups

Eritrea is fairly evenly divided between Christians, mostly belonging to the Eritrean Orthodox Church, and Muslims (particularly Malēkī) with a declining population of traditional believers. While the role of the Fetha Negest, the "Law of the Kings" that for many years has been considered the main legal (religious) source for the Coptic community, has been disputed and is still unclear (see next chapter), it is certainly true that Islamic law has thrived during both Italian colonial rule and Ethiopian occupation. Present day Eritrea is a secular state.[46] Clearly religious leaders as well as the government realize that a multi-ethnic and multi-religious state could be rendered seriously unstable if one group obtained too much power and autonomy at the expense of the others. At times in the past, Eritrean society was deeply divided on religious grounds and the liberation movements reflected this division. Some of the bitterness this schism caused has persisted to this day and some Muslims have sought support from neighboring Islamic states for their political and religious objectives.[47] However, there are also many instances of Eritreans of different religions coexisting and cooperating over many generations. For example at religious festivals such as the Maryam Darit pilgrimage day both Christian and Muslim Bilein celebrate with songs and dances in their common vernacular language.[48]

In the following chapters we will also discuss the double role of Islam, which not only constitutes a powerful globalizing force, but which also has become a symbol of resistance to national and international neo-colonial forces.

State

A new actor became involved during the hundred years of colonial rule: for the first time, a territory-wide state system was instituted, and a large body of law based on Western models was superimposed upon custom. Artificial borders were created and an attempt was made to incorporate highly differentiated socio-cultural groups into the colonial state. But underneath this façade, the colonial territories remained multi-ethnic societies where local groups fought to keep their own rules and values. This situation persisted in the early post-colonial phase. The new rulers had to try and solve a fundamental question: whether or how far to accept the autonomous lawmaking power of the various ethnies and sub-ethnies. In the name of "the national interest," the independent state pressed for unification and standardization.[49] Conflict was almost inevitable. During the liberation struggle an embryonic EPLF state existed within the shell of the Ethiopian empire. The EPLF moved at night into many towns and villages that during the day were under Ethiopian control. The EPLF had a sophisticated system of administration and law and therefore the civilian population learned to deal with two political and legal masters. Because of the efficient and comprehensive political and legal infrastructure it had established, the EPLF encountered few difficulties in taking over the reins of state government after they occupied the whole of Eritrea in May 1991.

The International / Transnational Actor

The international/transnational actor comprises entities and individuals that are very different from each other. For example, at the macro level, there are international bodies with a legal personality, bodies such as the NGOs that do not have a legal personality, and foreign states acting as donors under terms of political and/or economic conditionality. At the micro level, we consider anyone to be an international actor who is not Eritrean—such as a foreign consultant who is connected to some of the major outside agencies, universities, or corporations.

All of these entities have greatly gained in strength and importance over the last generation, and this development has eroded the positivistic postulate of unity of the legal system. The state is sometimes forced to acknowledge the superior strength possessed by these actors. State supremacy, largely undisputed in the past, is fading, to the advantage of international and transnational actors, at least in some areas of law. "New relations of power and competition, conflict and intersection, take shape between, on the one hand, national states and actors, and on the other hand, transnational actors."[50]

In this context, it is not surprising that the growing body of state law in Eritrea is incorporating eclectically a wide variety of materials from a number of foreign legal systems and models. This follows a worldwide trend and a pattern that has repeated itself in other significant periods of Eritrean history. International legal experts were involved in drafting constitutions and codes in the late 1940s and early 1950s. At present, Eritrea is a signatory to many of the major international conventions and is a member of most of the relevant international and regional organizations. Following the coming into force of some of these conventions and agreements, the country has issued parallel state legislation (see chapter 4).

A new system of alliances and hierarchies is being created, in which almost every state will be bypassed if necessary for the advantage of the transnational entities. Neither do the transnational entities ignore sub-national bodies, such as traditional and religious groups and important elements of civil society. Eritrea is not alone in that some local urban elites have attempted to form alliances with international actors in an attempt to bypass the state bureaucracy. For example, the founder of the Eritrean Relief Association (ERA) used his international contacts after independence to establish a human rights NGO in the capital, Asmara.[51]

Introducing the Chapters

Throughout most of its history Eritrea has been an extremely unequal society. Many ethnies were rigidly divided along caste lines into nobles and vassals, and sometimes slaves. Many individuals were doomed by an accident of birth into a lifetime of menial or pariah jobs such as blacksmith, potter, or leather worker. The church and mosque often exerted a powerful and by no means benevolent tyranny over a largely illiterate and intensely superstitious population. In almost every family, the father wielded almost absolute power, and the sons were well into adulthood before they were emancipated. Eritrean women were the most unequal members of this unequal society.

Each chapter of the book shows how traditional law has shaped this inequality but has also attempted to change it. Religion and the various metamorphoses of the colonial state have significantly affected tradition. With the access to power of the EPLF, some long-standing practices have been suppressed, altered, or reshaped. However, as in many other countries, the interference of the state has sometimes worked against traditions that were efficient and that served the village and the people well.

In chapters 2 through 4, we introduce the reader to the legal sources produced by each actor, and we show how they are interrelated. We start with traditional and religious sources and move chronologically up to the most recent state and international legislation. An analysis of the reaction of the traditional core to the imposition of centralized state law makes Eritrea a paradigmatic case study for comparison with other societies where traditional law is only one of the many legitimate forms of law. We examine the rise of the Western notion of the state, and the extent to which the present Eritrean state legal system is indebted to the civil and common law traditions.

In the remaining chapters we largely limit our analysis of Eritrea's pluralistic system to case studies involving the interconnected and vital issues of blood, land, and sex. We try to observe the system through the lenses of the various actors, all of whom are directly involved in a struggle for legitimacy. Blood issues—vengeance, feud, money, and the settlement of conflicts arising from homicide—together with the traditional system of property rights over land and disputes that arise from it, are critical concerns for a centralized state. Any state can tolerate these practices to a limited degree—only insofar as they do not put at risk its unity and stability. Consequently, much of our discussion will deal with colonial and post-colonial state strategies for hegemony, and resistance to it by traditional and religious actors. These case studies will also deal with the alliances as well as the conflicts that occur between and within ethnic and religious groups.

We start with the pivotal issue of blood (chapter 5). Because of the incapacity in pre-colonial days of any centralized political or legal authority to levy sanctions and rule upon groups and individuals, and in the absence of a special body of law to shape the powers of the state, justice remained a private question among and inside the group. In colonial times, blood became a major concern of the state, which in the interest of stability could not allow individuals or groups to decide on matters of life and death. Blood feuds and feuds over land are closely related, and a greater importance was sometimes attached to land than to a human life. A major issue was the settlement of murders that were a consequence of old grudges over land; in these cases, if the land question was not settled, it was difficult to terminate the blood feud. The complex and varied regimes of rural property rights and disputes over land are dealt with specifically in chapters 6 and 7.

The main purpose of traditional law was the settlement of disputes, and in the past the large majority of cases concerned land. An important part of our work involves the examination of various forms of dispute resolution. Some are solved within the groups, while other involve third parties. If the disputes remain unresolved, an umpire can be called in with the authority to impose a decision. In chapter 7 we also look at the role of international actors in attempting to resolve some long-standing disputes over land.

With regard to marriage, gender, and women's issues, all four actors are usually involved. Islam, as in other parts of Africa, has had a great impact on family law, and colonial and post-colonial states have experienced considerable difficulties in enforcing their rules and values. In

Eritrea the Coptic Church has also played a major, if ambiguous, role. In the last few decades, international actors have come to the foreground, largely through the medium of human rights and economic and political conditionality. These actors play a crucial role in working—often through the lure and power of money—toward the elimination of traditional practices that they deem to be injurious to women's rights as determined by numerous UN and NGO conventions and declarations.

A pertinent example of the significance of international actors concerns the application in 2000/2001 by the Eritrean government for the customary laws of highland Eritrea to be proclaimed by UNESCO as a "masterpiece of the oral and intangible heritage of humanity." The application failed largely because the jury was swayed by an "expert opinion" that the Eritrean traditional law sanctioned the death penalty and female genital mutilation (FGM)—practices that are alien to UN principles. We will see in later chapters that the Eritrean traditional laws contain nothing of the kind. FGM is a particularly interesting case study because it is an almost universal practice in Eritrea. It has also been the stimulus for much international scholarly and polemical research.

The present Eritrean government is composed largely of men, and like male legislators the world over, gender equality is not necessarily high on their agenda. But they are compelled for a multitude of reasons to make encouraging noises and even to act on occasions. They promised equality to women fighters during the liberation struggle and they promise it now to the international community. The major struggle is between traditional and religious law on one hand and international law on the other, with the state in between, trying to compromise between the two.

Two

From Tradition to Globalization

How can we understand each other, sir, when in the words
that I say I put the meaning and the value of things that
are inside myself; while the one who listens to them,
inevitably confers on them the meaning and value that
they have according to him, that of the world how it is
inside him?

—Luigi Pirandello[1]

Tradition and religions have coexisted and merged in Eritrea since time immemorial, and sometimes it is difficult to understand whether a certain rule has a traditional or religious origin. It is easier to isolate the origin of state and international rules because they are more recent and because we have written documents to consult. Moreover, whenever elements of the state system have been imported into Eritrea, they have interacted with previous layers in a circular process.

Identifying Ethnies . . .

The first actors we examine are the groups producing traditional law. We are aware that both terms—"traditional" and "customary" law—have been criticized, the first because of its imprecision and the second because of the colonial implications.[2] A clarification is needed: throughout this book we use, for the sake of simplicity, the words "traditional" and "customary" law synonymously. Some authors have distinguished between customary law, which refers to the law that was applied in local or "native" courts in the colonial period, and traditional law, which is the law that been evolving in pre-colonial societies for many hundreds of years. Customary law used in native courts derived in some degree from traditional law, but it was often an emasculated or greatly simplified version of traditional law; it represented the law that the colonial government could tolerate or allow space for.[3] Indeed, the concept of the invention of tradition has been at the center of debates since the 1970s[4] And an appeal to tradition has often been the only way to legitimize a

14

modification of the status quo in a society where it was neither possible to contest the colonial power nor feasible to simply follow the elders.[5]

We think that the words "traditional" and "customary," stripped of their political implications, can be used as synonyms and in a constructive way. For the limited purposes of this book we accept the classic, broad definition of what is meant by tradition/custom given by Pospisil: "a law that is internalized by a social group," a law that "the majority of the group considers . . . to be binding."[6] This definition has the merit of creating an immediate link between the legal phenomenon and the groups who express it, and it is consequently an appropriate starting point for an analysis of legal pluralism that is centered on power relationships between social and political actors.

Leaving aside for now the theoretical and lexical debate, a much larger problem is that of the size of the relevant groups. The term "kinship" denotes ties larger than the extended family and involves rules of descent, the transmission of group membership, or other rights such as inheritance and property rights.[7] But which kinship unit is implied by the codes? Is it the ethnie, the clan, the lineage, the enlarged family, or something else? This is in fact a three-pronged question: it first involves the precise anthropological meaning of these words; second, their application to the real world of Eritrea, and third, how much this reality is properly described and exemplified by the codes—and by their translations. For reasons of space, only a few remarks are possible; to describe these problems, an entire book would probably not be enough.

Clan is a general term and usually refers to groups organized around different forms of lineage that claim to descend from a common ancestor, who may be a mythical figure. A clan may be endogamous or exogamous, it can be organized on the basis of lineage, it can be spread territorially, or it can constitute a political unity. Anthropologists also identify as particular features of a clan a feeling of "corporateness" within its members, strengthened by rituals, war, political decisions, and land held in common.[8]

A clan can split into lineages, and each of these may subdivide. A lineage can be described as a group "of individuals descending unilineally from a known common ancestor."[9] A subdivision may occur because of a feeling in the village that a lineage has become too big. It could also occur with the migration of a group out of the village, and it may also result from changes initiated from without.[10] When the splitting is carried out so that each lineage corresponds to a territorial unity, the entity becomes autonomous, and it can ally with other entities of comparable size for various purposes. In this case the term "segmentation" is commonly applied.[11]

We are of course aware of the many criticisms made about the theory of segmentary lineage.[12] Holy in particular sees it as an insufficient analytical model, and in a trenchant and convincing paper asks whether we are dealing with a set of ideas or a set of empirical facts.[13] However, we think it constitutes a useful construction with which to investigate Eritrea, as long as it is not used as a rigid framework. We agree with Tronvoll that among the Tigrinya-speaking people of Akele Guzai, the *enda* system (the agnatic lineage he calls *gezauti*—it means 'group of houses') constitutes an "important constituent part of the villagers' image of his/her local community." Far from being an ideal concept that tends to create distortions in reality, the lineage is a cultural notion held by the villagers, and it is also expressed through a rich folk vocabulary.[14] This appears to be true for the other Eritrean ethnies. Among all the ethnies we have investigated, great relevance is given to a kin group of unilineal, patrilineal (with the exception of the Kunama and Nara) descent, with a formalized system of authority, comprising all of the families originating from a single founder, and living in the same village or villages close by.[15]

The terminology used in vernacular languages to indicate divisions among ethnies is often loose and imprecise. Translation into Italian and English has not helped matters. In the absence of any compelling need for precise definitions, and as time passes, a community may split or intermarry, but keep its general name. So, for example, large highland clans, defined as *daqqi* (sons of) or *kebila*—tribe or, more rarely, *enda*—sometimes separate into smaller groups that are usually called *enda*, but sometimes *daqqi* or *bet* (house) followed by the name of the mythical founder of the group. A smaller subdivision is the ʿ*ad* or ʿ*addi* (village) who inhabit a village. Finally the ʿ*ad* is divided into *geza* or *enda*, in this case having the meaning of (sub) lineage, and subdivided further into households.[16]

The household (in Tigrinya *sidrabet*—family house) also plays a "key role both in access to land, and in obligations towards the communal task of the village."[17] Tronvoll draws a clear distinction between a kinship-centered perspective, focusing on the household, and a descent perspective, centering on the lineage.[18] This dichotomy may cause misunderstanding by giving the impression that the two perspectives are radically different from each other, and not mutually coexistent. We suggest that lineage and household are both relevant and serve different purposes: the first is the unit to which—with some exceptions—each traditional code applies; the second is relevant, as we see later in the chapters, for more specific aspects of life within the lineage, such as impediments to marriage, rules relating to the right and duty to exercise a blood feud, and blood money. The problem is that in many instances, in some codes and in some subject matters, it is not clear whether the lineage or the entire clan is involved.

Tronvoll has observed that in the last decades significant changes have occurred both in the form and the function of the kinship unit and the local community. The Eritreans have attempted to adjust to a radical reorganization of the power structure that dates back to the beginning of the war of liberation.[19] But in spite of these challenges, the systems of rights of access to land, family, and blood alliance appear to be still well-grounded in the lineage.

...and Their Traditional Laws

The traditional laws of the Eritrean highlands were formulated in large assemblies, usually by representatives of one or more contiguous *enda*, less frequently by a smaller community on a territorial basis such as a village. Usually, traditional law is presented as having a religious basis. The Berbers of North Africa have been described as an exceptional case of a society possessing secular traditional law.[20] However, this may also be the case with some Eritrean traditional law (see later the codes of *Adgena Tegeleba, Beni Amir,* and *Loggo Sarda*). These rules primarily governed relationships between members of the same *enda* or, on a territorial basis, members of the same village.[21] They were transmitted orally generation after generation, and reaffirmed or revised periodically (usually every three to seven years).[22]

Laws have a consensual basis. In the pre-colonial past (among those societies that had a written language and a sufficient degree of literacy among the elders) there was sometimes a deliberate attempt not to write down the law. The whole community was expected to memorize it and partake in the process of law. The law arises through the consensus of the people and persists because of it.[23] Tigrinya-speaking Eritreans referred to their laws as the *Heggi Endabba,* or "the law of the fathers." All qualified male villagers agreed to them. Normally all women, strangers to the village, and non-emancipated men were excluded, as well as adult males in categories such as blacksmith or goldsmith.[24] The *Endabba* were not only the authors of the laws, but "also the conservators of the book of laws (*tehaz debter*), the legislators who periodically re-wrote the laws (*haggegti*) and the mediators (*shumagulle*) who applied the laws to particular cases."[25]

Eritreans as well as a number of scholars refer to these laws as "codes." Technically speaking they are not codes because they do not contain anything new but merely consolidate a set of rules agreed to

previously by qualified villagers. Usually traditional "codes" focus on
debated points of a certain regime, points that have given rise to disputes in the past, such as rights over land, houses, and livestock, or rules
on vengeance and marriage.[26] The laws have many aspects in common.
But traditions evolve differently as time passes; people belonging to the
same *enda* can live for many years far away from each other (the *enda*
does not constitute—in principle—a territorial unity). People belonging
to various lineages with different laws may live in one village, and it may
happen that in time they will develop similar traditions that in the end
can lead to the elaboration of a common law.[27] Sometimes a political
reason is at the root of the decision to alter a particular code or create a
new one. This may happen when *enda* who have been divided because
of long-term disputes decide to unite in order to form a larger and
stronger group, or to settle the conflict existing between them. The laws
of *Loggo-Chewa* in Hamasien and of *Scioatte Anseba* are examples of
such agreements.[28]

Cross exchanges have occurred between different ethnic groups who
have lived in the same area (or on the rare occasions when they inter-
married). We know, for example, that although the provisions of a particular traditional law have to be respected by all members of a clan
descent group, exceptions have occurred.[29] Some Tigrinya who came to
settle among a coherent and long-established descent group might also,
to begin with, follow their own laws in some matters.[30] When the old,
established laws were next revised, some of the settlers' innovations
could have been incorporated into a new code. Relationships between
Saho and Tigrinya in Akele Guzai, discussed in more detail in chapter
6, show important mingling of traditions. In other cases, controversy
would arise between settlers and the host community, who would typically say that the settlers had no right to establish their law, but should
accept the long-standing law of the territory.

As part of its effort to cement control over their new colony, the Italian government, in the early twentieth century, commissioned the writing down in the vernacular language (Tigrinya, Tigré) and/or their
translation into Italian of some of the highland and lowland traditional
law. A major contribution came from scholars, missionaries, explorers,
and adventurers, who were taking an extraordinary interest in the new
colony. The Italians were galvanized into activity because of a concern
about the Swedish Evangelical Mission, which had opened a school in
Massawa in 1872 and moved to the Hamasien region the following year,
and had begun to develop considerable influence in the fields of health
and law. It possessed three of the five traditional codes of the highland
province of Hamasien and was consulted by the Tigrinya on legal matters. In an attempt to regain control of the situation, the Italian com-

missioner *Governatore dell'Eritrea,* ordered that the laws of the major populations of Hamasien be written down in Tigrinya. In May 1918 (1910 Ethiopian Calendar [EC]) thirty copies of each of the five main traditional laws were printed and distributed to the chiefs involved. This led to protests by the Loggo-Chewa who complained that, according to tradition, two or three chosen representatives of selected villages should take charge of the original manuscript and of all copies made from it. Because of the heated controversy that arose, the Italian government made no further attempt to publish customary laws in Tigrinya.[31] Not all laws were collected, and the texts were not translated into Italian or any other language.[32] However, revisions of the main traditional codes of the three highland provinces were published during the British Military Administration (BMA) of 1941-1951.[33]

It was also the intention of the Italian colonizers to abridge and unify the traditional criminal law of the "Abyssinian" highland nationalities, with the aim of using it as a basis for the judgments between "natives" in front of colonial courts. The limitation to "Abyssinian law" was because Abyssinian law was the most well-known to them; they attempted to make of it a text that could ultimately be translated into other local languages.[34]

It is not possible to ascertain to what extent the written record of traditional law represented the "actual law." The first variable to be taken into account is the possibility of multiple, and sometimes conflicting, interpretations of oral law among the delegates who have been chosen to write it down. There could also be a divergence between what the drafters see as ideal behavior and what actually happens. Therefore the written record might have been, and probably was, inaccurate and incomplete.[35] The codification of traditional law always involved far more than a mere written description of existing unwritten rules. With time, the original meaning of certain rules was lost, and was subject to lengthy and frequently conflicting interpretations. The elders who carried it out were in an extremely privileged position and were free to attach their own meaning to the original text, by work of interpretation. We should not forget that the transcribers of the codes were usually the only literate people in the village and this gave them considerable power.

Traditional rules contain special mechanisms and formulas for their periodic revision. The codes are numerous. In the following pages, we give brief details of the main ones. With the exception of Kemink, this exercise has not been attempted before. Our list, however, is much fuller than hers, and we think it will be of great help for further research.

There has been a great deal of polemical and ideological debate over whether Eritrea is a nation or when it became a nation. The very concept of nationality has been called into question. It is obvious that the nine ethnies currently given official status by the Eritrean government did not exist in their contemporary form in ancient times. On the one hand, there were more ethnies and considerable differences within each of them (for example, the Tigrinya of Akele Guzai were in some respects very different in social and political organization from those living in Seraye and Hamasien), and on the other hand, some ethnies have died out or merged with more energetic peoples over time. However, in order to provide a starting point for our analysis, in this chapter we group the codes according to the classification adopted by the EPLF and subsequently used by the Eritrean state.

For about one hundred years, since the Italian occupation became complete in 1897, Eritrea was divided into eight or nine provinces, but there was no neat division along ethnic lines; most provinces were multi-ethnic. There has been much speculation over the reasons and rationale for this subdivision. Instead of being due to Machiavellian or sinister motives of the Italian colonizers, the reason may lie in administrative efficiency. Each of Eritrea's ethnies has at least one, and in some cases many, traditional codes. Of necessity our analysis will be heavily indebted to Tigrinya sources, not because of a thinly disguised ethnocentric bias on our part, but because the Tigrinya have the largest number of readily accessible codes and they are in fact the most numerous ethnie. We follow the Tigrinya with the Saho, then the Tigré—with most attention being given to the Mensa and Beni Amir—the Bilein, Hedareb, Kunama, Nara, and Afar. We admit we have least information about the Rashaida.

Tigrinya

The most numerous ethnie comprises Tigrinya speakers; they live predominantly on the highland plateau, known as the *kebessa,* and they traditionally comprise the three provinces of Seraye, Hamasien, and Akele Guzai. Some 93 percent of them are Christians, mainly Coptic, with an important sub-group being the Tsenadegle, a Roman Catholic élite who live in the Segeneiti area. The other 7 percent are Muslim Jiberti—comprising local converts to Islam, descendants of Muslim merchants, and Tigrayan immigrants. The Jiberti adopted Tigrinya customs and practices, but maintain aspects of *šarīᶜa* as far as family, marriage, and inheritance are concerned.[36] They have sometimes been considered as a separate ethnie, but they are usually integrated into the wider Tigrinya-speaking community and share its language and—to a large extent—its traditions.[37]

In the past, the Tigrinya formed a highly stratified ethnie, divided into nobles, serfs, slaves, and "inferior" classes such as blacksmiths and potters. The traditional codes contain detailed rules relating to the different status of these various classes; they show a society that was complex and had relations with a central government.[38] The Tigrinya shared strong ties with the highland peoples of Abyssinia. They were the best-educated and wealthiest group in Eritrea and, because Italian rule was concentrated in the highlands, were the most influenced by the colonization. Later on, they formed the leadership of opposition to Ethiopian rule. However, for many years during Italian colonization and Ethiopian domination, a sizable group of Tigrinya worked enthusiastically for union with Ethiopia. To some extent, these different experiences are still the cause of dissension among the ethnie.

Seraye

Of the three highland provinces, this has the most homogenous customary law. Most groups in the province follow one code, the *Adkeme Melega*.[39] It has been argued by Asmarom Legesse that this reflects the conservative tradition of Seraye compared to a more "liberal" tendency of Hamasien and Akele Guzai. The approach of the Seraye elders is that laws are not subject to change, while in the other parts of the *kebessa*, legislative change is an integral part of the tradition.[40]

Three regions, which were transferred from Hamasien during the Italian colonial period, observed the *Loggo-Chewa* code. The Temezza were governed by the law of *Enda Fegrai*—like their kinsmen in Egghelà Hatzin in Akele Guzai. The district of Liban (an ethnically isolated group) created their own law as soon as they came under Italian control.

Adkeme Melega

The rules of the code were laid down during the second half of the fifteenth century (1467–1477) in Mai Ghif by the representatives of clans coming from the villages of Cudofelassi, Adi Mongunti, Bet Gabriel, Chené-Haiela, Adi Heis, Mai Laham, and Areza.[41] Every three to seven years after the founding, selected elders met for one to three weeks in Mai Ghif to reaffirm and, if need be, revise the codes. The Italian colonial legal officer, Ilario Capomazza, was instrumental in getting the notables, elders, and convent chiefs to inform him about the details of the code; he published it in Italian in 1912. A Tigrinya version was not prepared at this time. During the BMA, representatives of the seven clans met once again in Adi Ugri and agreed on a revised law, which was finally published in Tigrinya in Asmara in 1944.[42] In 1949, Duncanson estimated that 70,000 inhabitants observed this law.[43]

The account is in two parts. The first contains the text of the code divided into eighty-four numbered chapters; the second part contains popular proverbs, known to everyone, which are also part of the tradition. As it has been aptly observed, the code "is in fact a vernacular publication that owes nothing at all to European influence exerted even indirectly through the education or specialized training of its authors."[44]

Loggo-Chewa

In three areas of Seraye, Saf'a, Sellema and Liban, the Hamasien code of *Loggo-Chewa* was enforced. See a fuller account under Hamasien.

Liban

This district followed the code of *Habsellus Gebrecristos* until its subjection to the rule of the princes of Hazzega and Tsazzega ended with the founding of the Italian colony. The people then created their own law.[45] It is not clear whether this law replaced entirely or only in some details the law of *Loggo-Chewa*.

Hamasien

Law of Habsellus Gebrecristos

The law dates back to the end of the seventeenth century; the original document was kept in the church of Adi Qontsi. It originally applied to the entire province, but lost its influence in some areas over time.[46] The law has its origin in an edict of Habsellus—master of Tsazzega—and of his son, Gebrecristos. During the nineteenth century, Dejazmatch Hailu ordered its revision and tried to extend its influence in southern Hamasien. After his death, however, the *Loggo-Chewa* immediately returned to the status it had had prior to Hailu's actions and was once again fully observed. During the Italian administration, modifications took place after meetings in Adi Qontsi in 1901 and 1915. However, because some of the districts originally involved were not consulted, they elaborated their own laws.[47] *Habsellus Gebrecristos* was written down in Tigrinya in 1910 (EC) and its fourteen pages deal mainly with betrothal and marriage contracts.[48] In 1949, Duncanson reported that 100,000 Daqqi Teshim villagers followed this code.[49]

Heggi Saharti, Lamzan, Waqarten, Damban

These areas formerly followed the law of *Habsellus*. After they were denied a chance to participate in a meeting at which this law was to be revised, elders met in Methaz Reesom and formulated an autonomous law.[50] It was written down in Tigrinya in 1910 (EC).[51] According to Duncanson, 13,000 villagers observed this law.[52]

Scioatte Anseba

This law is probably the most recent in Eritrea: it was written down in Adi Berhanu on 15 December 1907, and published in Tigrinya in 1910 (EC).[53] It is an interesting example of an agreement which has been reached among people of different ethnies because of a common material and political interest. Scioatte Anseba (the seven of Anseba), is a confederation of seven districts in the northwest of Hamasien. The population comprises peoples of different origins: the Daqqi Sciahai are of Beja origin; the Balau, the Daqqi Dascim, and the Dersennèi appear to have migrated from Akele Guzai. The bulk of the Anseba, made up of Melazzenai, Daqqi Naammén, and Adi Iohannes, may have migrated from Barka to the highlands. Because of its geographical position, Scioatte Anseba would have been the first area to face this wave of migrations. These seven formed a common bloc, and they elaborated a common law. Also interesting is that the law of Scioatte Anseba appears to constitute a passage from less formal laws such as those dealing with pure Tigré and Tigrinya populations.[54] In 1949, Duncanson reported that 14,500 villagers adhered to this code.[55]

Serat Karnesem

This law pertains to sixteen villages in the most fertile region of Hamasien lying north of Asmara on the edge of the highland plateau. It was adopted in the village Zagr and published in Tigrinya in 1910 (EC), presumably because of the initiative of the Swedish Evangelical Mission.[56] The code, 122 pages long, shows striking similarities to *Habsellus Gebrecristos*,[57] perhaps because it was not until the beginning of the twentieth century that the Karnesem ceased to adhere to *Habsellus'* law. According to Duncanson in 1949, 13,500 villagers had adopted this code.[58]

Highi Endaba Dembezan

A sixty-six-page Tigrinya version of this (not dated) deals with the customary law of the historic Dembezan district that lies at the edge of the Hamasien plateau on the road to Keren.[59]

Zemat Tahtay

This code deals primarily with a district in Hamasien.[60] Pollera mentions that at one time the Scioatte Anseba and other people inhabiting the Anseba valley shared it. The Adirba, a Tigrinya tribe who emigrated from Hamasien and whose two villages were under the administration of the Italian regional commissioner in Keren, also adhered to this law.[61]

Warsa Bet

This is a customary law (three pages long) dealing with inheriting possessions, sharing fields, and selling land. Unfortunately, research has not been able to discover which district in Hamasien adhered to the law.[62]

Loggo-Chewa

According to oral traditions, the law of the *Loggo-Chewa* was set down in 1487 (EC). Meetings to revise the code took place in 1650, 1892, and 1935–37, during the BMA.[63] It was published in Tigrinya in 1910 and republished again in 1935.[64] It comprises laws of twelve villages, some of which had already been written down (the villages of Adi Barò, Adi Bezahannes, and Adi Zaul) and others which had not (Himberti, Uoghericò, Adi Ghebrai, Adi Felest, Emmi Zellim, Sciccheti, Abardà, Chitmauliè, and Adi Ras-Gobai-Torat). The law was consolidated by Ras Haderrau of Sciccheti during the reign of Eiasu (1729–1753) and agreed by elders of Loggo-Chewa, Chebesà Ciuà, and Zellimà in Mai Laham.[65] It is an exhaustive account of social, cultural, religious, and economic aspects of village life.[66] In 1949, some 40,000 people recognized this law.[67]

Akele Guzai

Loggo Sarda

The oldest of the laws, it was kept in a gospel book in a church of the village of Sarda in Akele Guzai along with another document that records the donation due to the church from the nine clans of the Loggo Sarda. Conti Rossini claims that this other document dates back to the end of the fifteenth century, while the law is "of much more recent date."[68] This one-page document is very difficult to translate; the Tigrinya is in an archaic form and often uses words in a vastly different sense than they are used today. However, it is clear what it deals with: what is expected for a dowry; what compensation should be paid to a woman who has been kidnapped; land tenure; and assault.[69]

Mehen Mahaza

An assembly of elders from all over Akele Guzai concluded this law by the stream Mehen Mahaza near Kohaito at the beginning of the nineteenth century.[70] According to tradition, it was written down and the manuscript was taken by Ras Sebagadis to a convent in Agame, Tigray, after his short occupation of the province around 1823.[71] A version of this code appears also in *Bullettino Ufficiale della Colonia Eritrea*, of 1903, where further details are given on the procedure of writing down the code. According to this version, at the time of Ras Sebagadis, fourteen elders convened in Mehen Mahaza to draw up a new document. When the draft was completed, all inhabitants of Akele Guzai were asked to meet and approve it. The elders then met Ras Sebagadis, who applied his seal.[72] Capomazza gives us yet another account. He claims that the law dates back to the period when Ras Woldeselassie ruled over the province (1750–1770).[73] The Loggo Sarda later adopted this law by the beginning of the twentieth century.[74]

Law of Haggegti

This comprises modifications to the *Mehen Mahaza*, made by the Haggegti in 1873 and 1904.[75]

Enda Fegrai

The law takes its name from the village where it was created. Elements of two districts (Egghelà Hatzin and Tedrer) were involved at a very ancient and unrecorded time.[76] This law was revised in Adi Goddo in 1905,[77] and it is also followed in the Seraye district of Temezza.[78]

Mai Adgi

It was passed in Mai Adgi, near Corbaria, by representatives of the Egghela, and was observed by the districts of Egghela Hamès, Daqqi Admocom, Daqqi Ghebri, Enganà, and Robrà that surround the town of Decamare.[79] It is a law of a very ancient origin, modified many times during the eighteenth century. Later revisions were made in 1861, possibly at the behest of Negus Tewodros, 1902, and from 1917–1918 (this revision took place at the foot of Mount Masalu). In the 1930s, the district was incorporated into Hamasien.[80]

Zeban Serao *and* Ennadocò

The inhabitants of these two villages from the district of Egghela Hamès were originally immigrants from Agame in Tigray and were excluded from the meetings of the Shum Egghela held to revise *Mai Adgi* in 1902, on the grounds that they did not belong to the same lineage of the people of Mai Adgi. Therefore their representatives met in the vicinity of Ahnei Sipti and laid down an autonomous law,[81] which mainly consists of amendments to *Mai Adgi*.[82] There is an unusual provision denying eldest sons any particular privileges. The British knew this code as the law of the *Igela*.

Arbate Ba Alfan

This is the law of the four groups of the descendants of Ba Alfan, who constitute the population of Meretta Sebene in the northwest of the province.[83]

Adgena Tegeleba

The *Adgena Tegeleba* laws were first formulated in 1831 and put in writing by order of the governor of the province, Ras Sebagadis.[84] At the end of the Italian colonial period twenty-nine district chiefs and eighty-three experts in law selected by the villages from all over the province carried out a revision. They met several times in Adi Keih, Segeneiti, and Senafé under the direction of Ras Tessema Asberom, a renowned fighter for Eritrean independence. After eighteen months of deliberation, they passed a code valid for the entire province. It was published in Asmara on 6 January 1945.[85] A significant number of amendments were made when it was revised in 1951.[86] According to Duncanson, 85,000 inhabitants of the province in 1949 adhered either to this code, *Mehen Mahaza*, or the law of the *Igela*.[87]

Adgena Tegeleba is the main customary code in Akele Guzai. It has been claimed by Duncanson that the compilers of the code made a conscious effort to try to unify Tigrinya customs together with those of the Saho.[88] However, of the 122 people who helped compile the code, only two had Muslim names.[89] Had the Saho traditions been dealt with adequately, it seems likely that more Muslims would have been included in the discussions.

Saho

The Saho are divided into the following major sub-ethnies: Minifere, Haso-Tor'a, Irob, Asaorta, and the two smaller clans of Senafé and Debri-mela.[90] All of the Saho are Muslim, converted from the eleventh century onward, with the exception of some of the Debri-mela, and the majority of Irob, who are Christian. Almost all of them were once seminomadic pastoralists who migrated from the lowlands to the highlands according to the season in search of pastures. Some of them, such as the Minifere, also settled down and became farmers.[91]

The Haso-Tor'a, the largest group, expanded from the lowlands (northern Danakil and Semhar) to the highlands. Up to about 1700, each clan was autonomous, and on this basis, Conti Rossini categorizes the political structure as patriarchal and democratic. As we will see in more detail in chapter 7, conflicts with the Tigrinya over the use of pastures were particularly frequent.[92]

Apart from the Asaorta, we have little written evidence on the law of other Saho. The major sources for the Asaorta are contained in Italian colonial documents written down after an act of submission in 1887.[93] The chiefs reached an agreement with the Italian government that allowed traditional law to remain in operation. Agreement was reached in a solemn assembly (*rachbe*); the deliberations were later incorporated as law in the *Regolamento per i Commissariati e le Residenze*. In religious matters, the assembly agreed to defer to the *qādī* or his delegate, with an appeal to the government admitted. In all other matters, the competence of the *nebara* (deputy chief) was recognized in the first degree and the *resanto* (clan leader) on appeal. In their absence, any "man of honor" could be the judge.[94]

Afar

The Afar are spread across the present states of Eritrea, Djibouti, and Ethiopia. All of them are Muslims, and their ancestry and language are closely related to that of the Saho. After conversion to Islam, for matters of personal status (marriage, divorce, and family relations), they followed *sarīʿa*, but for everything else they followed the old traditional laws. These included trial by fire, which was used to settle especially grave cases where evidence was lacking. The accused was made to hold a red-hot hatchet in his hand; if (when) burns appeared, he was deemed to be guilty.[95] Another ordeal was known as *f'ima*; here a group punished one of its members by hanging him by the feet and ducking him in the crocodile-infested Awash River.[96]

Beni Amir, Mensa (Tigré), and Bogos (Bilein)

The bulk of these three groups converted to Islam during the nineteenth century; they were an oligarchic and aristocratic society with a clear division into (at least) two castes.[97] Their traditional law reflected the division between dominators and dominated, between nobles and vassals. Before the Italian occupation they were ruled in some periods by highlanders (*habesha*), in others by Egyptians.[98] According to Mondaini, their traditions originated in the highlands and were modified under the influence of foreign customs (Beja coming from the north, and Saho from the southeast) and religion (Islam).[99]

Beni Amir (Sons of Amir)

These are a tribal confederation of Beja origin living in the western lowlands, whose members were known to be cattle owners. The Italian government attempted to settle them as farmers. The *Nabtab* formed the aristocracy of the Beni Amir; they had a supreme chief called *Diglal* living in Agordat and spoke a separate language called To-Bedawi or Beda Wiet.[100] In 1937, Francesco Sarubbi recorded some of their traditions with particular reference to those living in Agordat and Tessenei.[101] In 1960, Sheik Hamid Ferej Hamid, delegate of the Beni Amir, compiled a new "customary law code" in English (comprising twenty-five articles), which came about as a result of numerous meetings of the elected representatives of all the confederation.[102] According to Asmarom Legesse, at present, the oral tradition continues to prevail, and this written text no longer plays a significant role in the administration of justice.[103]

Mensa

The Mensa are another important Tigré group, though smaller in number than the Beni Amir. Re-conversion to Catholicism and Protestantism in the twentieth century has resulted in two-thirds of them being Christian. They were divided into three classes: nobles (lords), subjects (vassals), and slaves (serfs). The rulers were required to be Muslim, as were landholders.

Their law, known in the Tigre language as *Kile' Mensa'e: Dighem, wa Fitih, wa'Adotat*, is more commonly referred to as *Fetha Mahari*. It dates back to the first part of the fifteenth century and took its name from that of its compiler, the legendary tribal hero Mahari. The Kantiba Beemnet, chief of the Mensa from 1869, introduced innovations to the law, and Münzinger Pasha made further modifications when he was governor of Keren.[104] The Mensa were divided into different clans, which also observed special traditions besides the *Fetha Mahari*.[105] The *Fetha Mahari* was translated into Italian from Tigré (and also published in Tigré) by Karl Gustav Rodén, head of the Swedish missionary station at Galab, in 1913.[106] The first part of the book contains traditional accounts about the origin of the two Mensa groups, and the second is dedicated to the customary code.

Bilein

The Bilein, whose ancient name is Bogos, constitute the third most numerous ethnie in Eritrea. They are a group of extended families, of which seventy percent are Muslim and the rest Christian. The ruling class of the two main clans, Bet Targe and Bet Tawque, migrated from Lasta in Abyssinia during the tenth and thirteenth centuries. Many Tigré-speaking people in the Bogos area subsequently adopted the Bilein language and ethnicity.[107] The Bet Targe are evenly divided between Christian and Muslim, while the Bet Tawque are almost entirely Muslim.

Their major law is called *Fethesh Mogaresh*, because of the myth that their founder first of all established his home in the plain of Mogaresh. Münzinger writes about their law: "the idea of God, as a principle of law, is not known. A bad action that does not involve a neighbor too closely is not a crime. The family-state does not care about it and leaves the punishment to God. What is against God, relates to God. Law and morals do not have any connection."[108] This seems to be a convincing piece of evidence that traditional law is not religiously based in this area. Mondaini argues that the differences between the *Fethesh Mogaresh* and highland laws are not of great significance. On the whole, traditional law seems to have a stronger influence than Islamic law in the life of the Bilein community.[109] However, in some cases, šarīʿa has modified tradition, often radically. Some of the most ancient aspects, such as vassalage, were entirely replaced with Qurʾanic rules.[110]

Highi Endaba Bet Targe Fit'ha Targe

This is the customary law of the Bet Targe clan. It is fourteen pages long in Tigrinya; the text was edited in this language because Bilein was written down only during the liberation war.[111] The elders finished drafting the law in September 1960, but they still refer back to an un-written law (that seems to predate the *Fethesh Mogaresh*) if the revised code makes no provision for a particular case.[112]

Bet Tawque Daqqi Nebret

Until 1960 the Bet Tawque clan used an unwritten *Daqqi Nebret* law; since then, the two clans have used the *Bet Targe*.[113]

Assertew klte Neged

The "twelve tribes" are a minority population who came to Bogos from other parts of Eritrea and were gradually assimilated into Bilein society. Starting in the 1940s, they used their own laws, which has caused tension between them and the Bet Targe. The Bet Targe assert that the Neged have no right to establish their law on top of the existing laws of the Bilein and on Bilein territory.[114] An interesting provision relates to mixed marriage and may provide a safeguard against potential conflict. If a Neged indicates a wish to marry someone from the other clans, arguments can occur over which law they should adopt. Rather then offending their relatives, the couple may decide to drop Bilein traditional law and in its place adopt a neutral code such as Tigré, Tigrinya, or even state law.[115]

Hedareb

Although recognized officially as one of the nine "nationalities" of Eritrea, the Hedareb are in fact very diverse. For example, they include sub-ethnies such as that portion of the Beni Amir people who have re-tained their use of To-Bedawi, the Beja language. Another group com-prises people related to the Sudanese Hadendowa. They are all Muslim, and many of them speak Arabic. In the past, they were mainly nomadic; they now live in the northwest and northeast part of the country close to the Sudanese border. They are one of the least researched ethnies in Eritrea; however, we discuss a number of their laws in the chapters on blood and gender.

Kunama and Nara

The Kunama, probably the oldest ethnie in Eritrea, inhabit the area be-tween the Gash and Setit rivers; they speak a Nilotic language (the Mara) and are a matrilineal group that includes Muslims, Christians, and traditional believers.[116] The Nara are their neighbors; their Nilotic language is distinct from that of the Kunama. Their conversion to Islam dates back to the nineteenth century, with the Funj invasion. In the past, they were given the offensive name of *Baria,* which means 'slave.' The Nara are also matrilineal.[117] Pollera argues that Kunama and Nara were originally part of the same ethnie and that the Nara intermingled with other neighbors, while the Kunama remained purer.[118] In the past they were known collectively as the Shankalla.[119]

Kunama had no written language until the early twentieth century. In 1873, the Swedish missionary Englund published a grammar, a dictionary, and few texts of the Kunama language (in a Swedish translation). These were the first written documents in this language.[120] Pollera collected their traditions and those of the Nara in 1913 and this is still the most comprehensive and accessible record. From 1982 to 1989 the EPLF repeated much of the same work. That work, however, remains in Tigrinya.

The social organization of both ethnies has been described as egalitarian. They formed "free associations, between free individuals, who, because of the close circle in which they lived, in the end become relatives and friends."[121] Their government comprised an assembly of elders, called *mohaber,* with the eldest as first among equals. An absolute majority of all adult villagers took decisions concerning most important issues. Decisions were based on similar cases adjudicated by the same or other *mohaber.* If a majority could not be reached, the question devolved upon another village assembly. By the late nineteenth century, if a dispute arose over marriage or inheritance, it was not settled as it had been in the past through a community tribunal, but by using the *šariᶜa* court in the town of Haberetta.[122] Blood issues were usually privately settled through retaliation, but the *mohaber* could be requested to settle the dispute peacefully. It also had the power to decide upon matters of peace and war with the neighbors, and also in times of war to nominate the commander of armed forces, the *Massa Manna.*[123]

Rashaida

They are the smallest ethnie in Eritrea, numbering about ten thousand people, descendants of Arabic speakers who migrated from Saudi Arabia and settled on the Eritrean coast about 150 years ago. All are Muslim. Little is known about their traditions, but we discuss some of their practices, including marriage payments, in chapters 8 and 9.

Multiple Ethnies and Tradition

We have mentioned that the government's division of Eritreans into nine nationalities has been carried out on grounds of policy and often bears little resemblance to reality. A number of the ethnies are, as we have indicated, very diverse, forming, in Conti Rossini's terms, a mosaic of people. Mensa, Marya, and Hedareb were under the influence of highland peoples for generations; they lost their original language and traditions, became farmers, and adopted the Tigré language and customs.[124]

The Saho are one of the most diverse. Some of the Irob, who emigrated to Akele Guzai, became largely assimilated with Tigrinya. They converted to Christianity, started to speak Tigrinya, adopted their traditions and customs, and entered into the political life of the ethnie. Other branches that settled in Agame (present-day Ethiopia) were considered in time to be a constituent part of the region; since the eighteenth century they have elected their own chiefs.[125] This indicates that the Saho ethnie is by no means monolithic. On occasion, the Asaorta moved into the highland and dominated groups of settlers, who adopted the customs, religion, and language of the Asaorta. An Abyssinian military colony had been stationed around Irafaile on the coast of Eritrea in order to halt the advance of the Saho; this colony eventually merged with the Saho to form the Minifere—and afterwards they adopted Saho as their *lingua franca*.[126] And of course reverse assimilation has also occurred.[127]

Identities, and alliances, are continuing to change. As a result of years of prolonged exile in the Sudan and the Middle East, some Eritreans have become less and less attached to their "official" ethnie. Many Asaorta fled the country during the war of liberation and still remain as refugees in the Arab world. In the past there has always been a sizeable group of Asaorta who have made strong representations to successive governments to be considered a separate ethnie. The EPLF has consistently refused to consider them as a separate nationality, arguing that all Saho have a common language, a common history, a common cultural heritage, and a common mode of production. In recent years the Asaorta's voice has been heard even more strongly. A number of nomads, pastoralists, and seasonal workers spend a considerable time in neighboring countries such as Ethiopia and Djibouti. Ties with their ethnie in Eritrea tend to weaken over time.

Religious Groups

Coptic Christians and Muslims also produce law but this is of a very different nature from traditional law. Not only is it an instructional guide to most aspects of life but it is also, for many, a source of spiritual inspiration. No single ethnie is entirely Christian or orthodox Muslim.

The most diverse, the Kunama, comprise Coptic Christians, Catholics, Protestants, and traditional believers as well as Muslims. For some ethnies the decision to convert to Islam or Christianity (or to reconvert) was frequently a consequence of the need to find the strongest protector or ally. At times in the past, the Coptic Christian parts of Abyssinia and highland Eritrea have been united by religion, history, politics, and tradition, but have also been separated on the same grounds from the lowlands of both countries. While each ethnie follows traditional and religious law at the same time, the reach of the religious actor is much wider as Islam and Christianity are able and willing to find allies in the neighboring countries and further afield.

The heart of Coptic Christianity from the second to the ninth centuries A.D. was to be found in the Axumite Empire that included some of present-day Eritrea. An important debate has taken place on the practical legal relevance of a major historical source, the *Fetha Negest,* the "Laws of the King." It is the translation from Arabic to Ge'ez of an Egyptian canon compiled by Ibn al-Assal, from 1240 to 1250, on the basis of a more ancient text of Syrian/Roman origin. It consists of a collection that comprises mainly legal texts that traditionally applied in ecclesiastic, civil, criminal, and procedural matters. It was probably introduced in Egypt with the intention of using it in the administration of justice in the Coptic community. It did not have any official legal status.[128]

There is some debate about when it appeared in Abyssinia, and when it was first translated into Ge'ez. The most likely history is that the Arabic version began to circulate in Abyssinia in the middle of the fifteenth century and was translated into Ge'ez at the end of the seventeenth century.[129] However, it is not clear what its real significance or its influence on Eritrean traditional law has been. Some decisions of higher courts make reference to it, and it was most likely employed in complicated or dubious matters.[130] But it has been observed by Costanzo that it lacks an organic structure due to its eclectic nature, and questions have been raised over the practicality of using Egyptian rules in an "Abyssinian" population.[131] After the Italian conquest of Eritrea, the government ordered its translation with the aim of using it in customary matters, erroneously thinking it was a law in force in the highlands.[132]

According to Costanzo's interesting reconstruction, the *Fetha Negest* played a role in the Horn of Africa similar to that performed by the *Corpus Juris Civilis* in Europe. As in Europe it was thought that Emperor Justin had been mandated by God, so in Ethiopia the myth was perpetuated that the *Fetha Negest* fell from the sky and was dictated to

Ibn al-Assal by the 318 fathers of Nicea under divine inspiration. In both cases the prestige of the text depended on the holy nature attributed to it, and this could have contributed to the legitimization of the power of the sovereign who first used it.[133] The political organization of the Abyssinian state was based on the divine origin of sovereign powers and on close links between law and religion.[134] The use of holy texts in the secular administration of justice is evidence of this.[135] In more recent times, the penal code of Haile Selassie referred to the *Fetha Negest* in order to avoid the accusation that he wanted to change, through codification, established religious and traditional rules.[136]

The practical importance of the *Fetha Negest* in Eritrea is, however, disputed. Conti Rossini refers to it as "a melting pot, awfully translated and badly interpreted of canons of the church, biblical precepts and roman laws" and notes that it was used more in declamations as an "ideal expression of a pure and impartial law" than as a law applied in practice.[137] And Duncanson—probably paraphrasing (but without citing) Conti Rossini—observes that the *Fetha Negest* "was no less inept in village affairs for being highly revered by the Abyssinians."[138] Leaving aside its applicability in trials, which seems to have been limited, we think the *Fetha Negest* could have been important as far as the prince or his deputy was referring to it to increase the authority and prestige of his own legal ruling. Obviously, then, the *Fetha Negest* was not traditional law, based as they are on the consent of the community and legitimized through the permanence of this consent. The *Fetha Negest* was the antithesis of tradition; it played a role in legitimizing the authority of the sovereign. Its rules, produced in a religious framework, became effective through the mediation of another source of legitimacy, such as the prince or other qualified person. The religious command was not and could not have been perceived as immediately coercive because most of the people, including the priests, were illiterate. As in the Western civil tradition, where the Catholic Church has legitimized sovereign power by attributing a divine nature to the king, so the Coptic religious tradition has sown into the popular conscience of the highlands people the idea of a rule which comes from far away that must be obeyed because of the status of the actor who seeks to impose it.

Šarīᶜa

Eritrean Islam is orthodox (Sunni). Of the four orthodox schools, only the Hanbalī is not present in Eritrea. A census carried out in 1931 indicated that the Malēkī school attracted the most numerous followers,

65 percent, followed by Hanafī with 26 percent and Shāfiʿī with 9 percent.[139] Within Sunni Islam, there are differences of interpretation of primary and secondary texts among the various schools. These differences have not caused major schisms between the schools because, according to a tradition attributed to the Prophet, "disagreement, *ikhtilāf*, is a symbol of God's indulgence."[140]

Much syncretism and contamination between *sarīʿa* and previous traditions and customs has been observed.[141] The extent of islamization depends upon a combination of elements, such as the period when it took place, the social structure of the groups that received it, and the resilience of traditional beliefs. For example, Afar and Kunama generally adopted only isolated aspects of Islamic culture, including clothes and ornaments, and are as a rule less respectful of Qurʾanic precepts, such as fasting. If a group is structurally more complex, such as the Bilein, Islam can be absorbed more deeply and at a higher level. Deep islamization also occurs in urban centers, where the mosque and the Qurʾanic school constitute the centers of community and cultural life.[142] The multi-ethnic nature of cities has been important in the spreading of orthodox Islam: former village people feel less attached to the original group and its traditions when they become urbanized. Therefore they are more receptive to new ideas.

The large majority of pastoral nomads in Eritrea have adopted Islam, partly because Islam, unlike Christianity, does not need churches or fixed places for prayer. The extensive network of commercial relations with the Arabian Peninsula has also facilitated the spread of Islam. One of the major caravan and sea routes connecting Arabia with the Horn of Africa passes through Adulis and Massawa to the rest of Africa. These routes date back at least to the sixth century A.D. and have continued to this day. In northeastern Africa, Islam took hold rapidly in the tenth century, mostly in the form of individual conversions.[143]

In the nineteenth century, a new wave of islamization followed the Egyptian occupation of the area. This wave radically modified the social and legal structures of the ethnies involved. The Egyptians governed Massawa and much of the western lowlands of Eritrea from 1865 to 1885; the area was ruled as part of the Sudanese state system. Under Khedive Isma'il, the Egyptians dominated much of present-day Eritrea, including the Bogos region around Keren. They attempted to provide the area with a modern judicial system similar to that of Egypt. At the beginning of their rule, the only agency that served as a quasi-judicial body was an ombudsman's office in Kassala. Later on, a council in Massawa was granted jurisdiction over commercial litigation, with an appeal court in Cairo to review cases that could not be settled in Massawa. The highest judicial body was the Egyptian Privy Council, which suggested that all parties make an attempt to settle all disputes out of court.[144]

Islam has sometimes been adopted by ethnies that had been, at least nominally, Christian, such as Asaorta Saho, Habab, and Mensa, following a tendency for individuals and groups to disguise their ethnic identity or adopt another one in order to improve their social, political, and economic status. During the 350 years of Turkish occupation, some Muslims raided the Christian ethnies of the highlands. Many of these Christian ethnies, such as the Marya and the Bet Tawque, decided then to convert to Islam to avoid further persecution. This phenomenon may also be due to the fact that the traditional organization based on the kinship group hinders the development of any wider social structure and makes such a structure unstable. Inability to unite in a larger confederation led, for instance, to the subjection of the Nara and Kunama to raids from the highland peoples from the first decades of the nineteenth century. The most infamous of these raids was held by Ras Alula in 1886. It caused the extinction of two-thirds of the Kunama and the Nara living in the North Gash region.[145]

As strong as orthodox Islam, except in the cities, is the esoteric form of Islam that was spread in the nineteenth century through the Dervish orders, which have drawn upon the mystic tradition of the medieval Sūfī. Such orders are very important in Eritrea, with the Qādiriyya, the Mirghāniyya, the Rahmaniyya, and the Sammaniyya being the most widely spread, the latter predominantly in the highlands. With the exception of the Qādiriyya, these orders developed in the area from the nineteenth century.

Islam as practiced by brotherhoods is connected with the cult of saints, also extremely important in Eritrea. A believer who is searching for communion with God needs to be guided by somebody who has been given a special power by God (baraka) to act as an intermediary between himself and God. This power is transmitted to descendants. Minorities such as Ad Shaikh and Mirghani in the highlands are considered to be saints because they have as a myth of origin a founder who was vested with power. The saint represents a link between God and the material world, and he can then be easily identified with the person blessed by the baraka.[146]

There are also shaman cults, whose central belief is that some individuals are chosen by spirits to communicate with them while in a state of ecstasy, and these individuals perform the functions of an intermediary between the world of spirits and our world.[147] Elders, whose prestige is universally recognized in Africa and who are so important in the drafting and evolution of Eritrean traditional laws, sometimes seem to share these magic powers. Frequently elders have a special relationship with God and on occasion they are uniquely able to discover the truth. Conti Rossini observes that in a highlands customary trial, the testimony given by an individual in a trance is accepted as full evidence.[148] Among some Eritrean Muslims, the drug Chat is used to facilitate communication with the spirits.[149]

Moreover, as frequently happens in Africa, some features of traditional beliefs have been incorporated into Islam and adopted as articles of faith; the inclusion in a more powerful religion ensures their preservation. It is impossible for monotheistic religions to completely dominate a strong traditional culture.[150] The Muslim Haso do not eat an animal which has been killed or wounded by another animal, nor do they eat the head, the tongue, the neck, the liver, or the spleen of animals in general.[151] The persistence of traditional beliefs may be also seen in ritual scars, female genital surgery, and other acts of intervention on the body. We discuss this in a later chapter.

Earlier, we indicated the consensual basis of most Eritrean traditional laws. Later on we will investigate the extent to which religious layers that have been superimposed onto tradition have modified the tradition. From the earliest period of Islam, there have been lengthy discussions as to whether or not custom—ʿurf or ada—may be considered as a source of Islamic law. It can be said that, on the whole, official Islamic law does not recognize custom as a source of law. But in the Muslim world, custom and Islamic law have coexisted, even if outside the parameters of legal theory. Historically, custom has contributed a great deal to the evolution of Islamic law.[152] In family law, the Prophet legalized one of several systems which were known to the Arabs before Islam. In criminal law the whole system of retaliation and the payment of blood money is derived from pre-Islamic society. As Islam spread, everywhere Muslims came into contact with new kinds of customary law, the yardstick for approval was whether these could provide solutions that would satisfy the interests of the community.[153] Although ʿurf could intervene only in actions that were not forbidden or compulsory according to the Qurʾan, the only acceptable way of applying the many rules in the Qurʾan and the sunna that admit of various interpretations is with reference to the ʿurf of the place where it is to be applied, at the time it is applied.[154]

Throughout the predominantly Muslim countries of north and west Africa (where most Muslims also follow the Malēkī school) there is an uneasy integration of Islamic law into traditional law. In Niger, there are multiple and contradicting layers of the judicial system and an ambiguous relationship between custom and Islam.[155] Roberts, writing about the French Soudan at the beginning of the nineteenth century, details the tensions that existed between native courts, Malēkī rites, and local traditions.[156] The family law of the great Mouride Sūfī Brotherhood of Touba Senegal is a complicated synthesis of Muslim family law and Wolof customary law.[157] The customary law in Mauritania makes no provision for polygyny, whereas under the Malēkī school four wives are allowed.[158]

Coda

This chapter has been a series of monologues and dialogues between two actors: ethnic groups and religious groups. In the next chapter, new actors arrive on the scene. Our third actor, the state, begins to play a significant role—although wearing the different costumes of Italian, British, Ethiopian, and Eritrean rulers. We see the state as a mostly cohesive centralized authority that exercises a monopoly over the use of violence, exacts obedience from its subjects, and extracts tribute. The entity we are talking about in the early scenes of the act, set in pre-colonial times, is not of course a fully sovereign state. The fourth actor, the transnational community, becomes increasingly involved as we move through the years.

Three

Changing Leadership, Unchanging Law

Traditional rules have proved remarkably resilient to change, to a large extent remaining valid during the Italian and British administrations.[1] Ethiopia's attempt to weaken local customary laws by introducing uniform state legislation was even less successful in Eritrea than it was in Ethiopia.[2] Even though Ethiopia annexed Eritrea in 1961, its rule prior to its final collapse in 1991 was never complete. Eritrea was at the periphery of the Empire, and many areas were under the *de facto* rule of the ELF (and later the EPLF) and exercised considerable autonomy.[3]

In the pre-colonial period a diversity of political entities coexisted in Eritrea. At the beginning of the sixteenth century the territory was divided into four distinct parts. The Funj, who had originated in Sudan, ruled the western lowlands and northern highlands. The central highland plateau was overseen by the Beja—also from the Sudan—who were in constant battle with Abyssinian kings. The Danakil region was under the control of the Adal Sultan, while the Ottoman Turks and the Naib of Hirgigo governed Massawa and the surrounding coast. The Turks were displaced by Egypt in 1848. By the time of the Italian invasion of 1886, Egypt had conquered much of present day Eritrea and begun the unification of the country, a process that was completed by the Italians.

The Pre-Colonial Period: Kings, Tribute, and Resistance

At various times in the pre-colonial period, tribute was paid by Eritreans to Abyssinian and Ethiopian kings and emperors, to the warlords of

Tigray, and to other temporary rulers. A number of codes show the importance of tribute as a mark of how traditional communities reacted to the attempted superimposition of a centralized structure or state.

A refusal to pay tribute is a typical expression of the defiance of authority. This refusal becomes the mark of the ability of a people to resist stronger foreign invaders. Eritrean ethnies reacted in a number of different ways to the imposition of tribute. In the more populated highlands, the inhabitants were mainly farmers. Their land had considerable value, and therefore the people were less likely to emigrate and much less able to refuse a demand for tribute. One of the major difficulties faced by small and sometimes isolated kinship groups was their inability to create stable alliances with their neighbors so as to resist stronger invaders. Traditional laws of the nineteenth and twentieth centuries clearly reflect this; the family is still "the state, the prince, the legislator" and "it exercises the right of life and death over its members."[4] But kinship ties became weaker because of internal conflicts, allowing a king or other outside rulers to make laws and to judge disputes. Ties became modified (but not replaced) by the intervention of this higher, stronger authority.

Tribute was imposed on villages and districts and divided internally among villagers; following this the major codes contain rules on how to deal with its allocation.[5] Hamasien villagers paid tribute according to their wealth.[6] Akele Guzai reacted strongly to the imposition; it was particularly difficult to exact tribute in the region at least up to the beginning of the nineteenth century.[7] The people on the northern borders of the highlands were nomadic shepherds, who are notoriously difficult to control. According to Münzinger, they would pay a nominal amount for the sake of convenience and as a way of safeguarding themselves and their pastures. But if the rule was too heavy-handed they could easily escape tribute and domination by finding refuge in desert regions, where no army was willing to follow and fight them. Münzinger considers this the primary reason why a monarchy did not take root in this area.[8]

The Bogos used to pay tribute to the emperor in Gondar. For some time the emperor did not intervene in politics and local administration. The tribute and a few gifts to the princes of Hamasien were enough to avoid disputes with highlanders. But in 1844 they were decimated by Dejazmach Wube, master of Tigray (1831–1855), because they refused to submit.[9] The Saho encountered a similar situation. Before the reign of king Yohannes IV (1872–1889) nobody was able to exact tribute from them, with the exception of a nominal levy of five cows per year, given to the "Abyssinian" chief as a sign of good will. A celebrated battle took place between the Saho and Ras Araia Selassie, the chief of Akele Guzai and the Asaorta region, after he had attempted in vain to impose further tribute upon them.[10]

Sometimes tribute was the instrument through which an ethnie became allied with the central power against other ethnies. The Beni Amir's major enemies were the Hadendowa, Nara, and highlanders from the south. To counter them, they strengthened alliances with the Funj and later on with the Egyptians. The ruling class, *Nabtab*, helped the Egyptians collect from their own vassals; as a *quid pro quo* the Egyptians allowed the Beni Amir to exact a further tribute from their enemies. The Beni Amir also acted as intermediaries in collecting tribute from the Nara and Bilein.[11]

Unable to constitute a stronger political union, and periodically raided by Christian highlanders and Muslim lowlanders, the Kunama and Nara were forced, in order to survive, to recognize the supremacy of the closest and strongest neighbor. The payment of tribute—carried out through a representative of villagers recognized by the rulers—constituted the acknowledgment of this supremacy. The Nara started to pay the Funj invaders from the north in the nineteenth century and, later on, paid the Egyptians. As there was no clear demarcation of boundaries, on occasion both highlanders and Egyptians demanded contributions from the same village.[12] According to one source, the raid carried out by Ras Alula (Tigrean overlord from 1885–1889) that ended in the slaughter of the Kunama was due to their refusal to pay tribute.[13]

The Italian colonizers acted the same way as previous temporary rulers had. According to *Adkeme Melega*, written during the first decades of Italian rule (art. 46§9), the village chief exacted the tribute from villagers, according to the division made by village elders (*shumagulles*), and forwarded it either to the head of the province or to the central government.[14] Another record shows that the Italian government delayed imposing tribute on the Saho because of their history of resistance. *Regio Decreto* 20 October 1891 applied to "indigenous peoples of the Eritrean Colony," but nevertheless it was extended to the Saho only in 1894, with *Bando Governatoriale* of 23 October.[15]

The Western Colonial State

With regard to the circulation of Western models, Eritrean legal history can be looked at in the following way. A first period of colonial rule (1886–1941), characterized by the spread of the Italian model (based on French codes); a second period of British administration, from 1941–1952, that basically left the previous system intact as far as substantive law was concerned, but with common law influencing procedure; a third period of federation with Ethiopia that ended with annexation in 1961; a fourth period, which saw an attempt to incorporate Eritrea into Haile Selassie's Empire and the enactment and extension to Eritrea of a new code system written by Western lawyers; a fifth period of liberation war—in the liberated areas a Marxist/Socialist-oriented system was in force; and a transitional period dating from liberation in 1991. This latest period will end when the constitution enters into force and new codes are enacted.

Before we can look at Western influence in these different phases, we need to clarify which of the multiple meanings of the common/civil law dichotomy are used in our analysis. For this chapter, the terms "common law" and "civil law" will be used as synonyms for Anglo/American law versus European continental law.[16] However, during the past two decades, many scholarly works have questioned the totality of a radical opposition between the two traditions.[17] Historical contacts between civil and common law have been re-evaluated, and synchronicities between the lines of development of the two models have been noted (also defined as convergency theory).[18] The legal world is increasingly becoming a world of "contaminations," where areas of uniformity grow and grow, and values are to a large extent becoming common to both families of law.[19]

Thanks to transnational corporations, international banks, international commercial organizations such as the World Trade Organization (WTO), and transnational cartels such as OPEC, new legal models have appeared. Does the law produced by these new actors fit the common versus civil law dichotomy? To what extent, even, is this dichotomy still a viable hypothesis? The answer is probably no if we look at one of the major parameters that can be used to draw the distinction between common and civil law, namely, case law as opposed to statute law. In this instance, there is no real competition, because the prevalence of statute law over case law cannot be seriously challenged. But the answer is yes if we look at the more obvious parameter: the country or area exporting a certain model. When we speak about globalization we mean that certain North American legal practices are being diffused and are becoming dominant throughout the world. This is not just as a result of the U.S. acting unilaterally, but also because of its actions in the UN, the WTO, and the other international regimes in which it plays the dominant role.

From a broader perspective, some scholars assert that attempts to draw a distinction between common and civil law have obscured the complexity of non-Western legal systems, leading to an ethnocentric view.[20] Alternative classifications of the world's major legal systems have been suggested.[21] Legal pluralism, which constitutes one of the key bases of our book, can be seen as one of these.[22]

The Italian Colony: 1886–1941

Colonization brought a massive influx of continental models. For more than fifty years, while Eritrea was under the sovereignty of the Italian Crown, all legislation in the colony was Italian, or had as its model Italian laws, and was promulgated in Italian, the official, administrative, and judicial language of the colony.[23] As a matter of principle, the Italians chose not to adopt a general policy of assimilation. A colonial lawyer asserted that "among the several mistakes made by Italy in its first experiments of colonization, at least one . . . the system of legislative assimilation in the Colony had been avoided."[24] And the principle of personality in the application of the law (see later in this section) could have granted—at least in theory—an appropriate space for traditional law to be effective.

In more general terms, one can observe that colonial policy was that "of recognizing and incorporating into the state legal system parts of the bodies of customary law existing within that state's claimed field of jurisdiction." This is precisely what has been defined as state legal pluralism.[25] It is therefore not difficult to understand why this weak form of legal pluralism that at times appears in the political programs of many post-independent African governments is criticized and labeled as neo-colonial. This critique is linked with the argument central to this book that subsuming customary law within the framework of state jurisdiction parallels the decay of custom.

A hotly debated—but theoretical—problem was over which way to extend Italian legislation, whether the laws of *Regno d'Italia* were immediately enforceable in Eritrea, or if it was necessary to make an *ad hoc* provision and/or promulgation in the colony. A project to draft special codes intended to embrace all the inhabitants of Eritrea started in 1903. Between 1908 and 1909, civil, civil procedure, penal, and criminal procedure codes were drafted and approved, but they never entered into force.[26] The penal code also reached the stage of the publication in Italian (with *Regio Decreto* [hereafter RD] 25 May 1908, 485), but its application was postponed pending the translation into Tigrinya and Arabic. The Italian Parliament (with *Disegno di Legge* 24 January 1911) delayed the application to an undetermined time.[27]

In theory, promulgation by the government was necessary.[28] As a matter of fact, waiting (in vain) for the enactment of codes for Eritrea, the civil and criminal courts of Massawa and the court of Ancona (which had a second degree jurisdiction over Eritrea up to 1901) applied Italian codes.[29] The same approach was adopted by the central government, many enactments of which took for granted the extension of Italian legislation to Eritrea.[30] The question was solved only with the new *Legge Organica per l'Eritrea* of 6 July 1933, 399, that, after the failure of the project of legal reform, expressly extended to the colony Italian codes, but only as far as "conditions of the locality permit and amendments introduced to them by particular laws excepted" (arts. 39–40).

Italians enforced for Eritrea a principle of "personality" in the application of the law, the rule of *doppio binario* (literally "double track"). This principle was carefully observed from 1882 onward.[31] The population was divided into two groups. One group contained Italians, Europeans, and anyone whose standard of "civilization" was considered to be equivalent to European "civilization." The other group included all Eritreans and "assimilated," i.e., people of foreign nationality whose standard of civilization was regarded as equivalent to that of the Eritreans.[32] As a rule, each group was in principle subject to the law of their "country." Italian legislation applied to all disputes where at least one of the contending parties had Italian citizenship; in all other cases, the relevant customary law was applied. *Šarīᶜa* was reserved for matters that related to marriage, family, and inheritance when the contending parties were Muslim (RD 2 July 1908, 325 art. 11).[33] There were two exceptions to the application of traditional law and *šarīᶜa*: if a controversy arose between Italian law and indigenous law, Italian law must prevail (RD 2/7/1908, 325, arts. 9 and 12). Moreover, in accordance with the so-called "repugnancy clause," frequently present in colonial legislation, the customary law of the ethnic group of origin could be applied only insofar as it was "consistent with the spirit of Italian legislation and civilization."[34] In the application of this principle with regard to criminal law, for more important crimes (crimes under the competence of *Corte d'Assise*), Italian law was enforced, even when the crime took place between indigenous people (art. 9 RD cited above).

Each group had to appear in front of a different set of courts. According to *Ordinamento Giudiziario per la Colonia Eritrea* (approved with RD 20 June 1935, 1649), for disputes when at least one of the parties was Italian or a "stranger," the competent judges were: *Conciliatore, Giudice della Colonia, Corte d'Assise*.[35] The administration of justice for "colonial subjects" and the assimilated was devolved to indigenous chiefs in the first degree. *Commissari Regionali* and *Residenti* (Italian officials respectively in charge of each region and district) dealt directly with private and criminal offenses (except for crimes under the competence of *Tribunale di Commissariato e Corte d'Assise*, strictly enumerated by article 34). They handled claims between Eritreans of different religion or communities and functioned as a higher court for disputes between Eritreans of the same religion and community that could not be resolved by clan heads or district chiefs. The governor exercised the review of appeals against decisions of *Commissari, Residenti*, and *Tribunale di Commissariato*. Appeal against *Corte d'Assise* rulings was possible by asking for a judgment of last resort by the *Corte di Cassazione* in Rome. The final decision for disputes among different ethnic groups and communities on property and collective use of land and water, pastures, and tribute lay with the governor of the colony.[36]

As can be observed, the system was not based on a separate hierarchy of customary tribunals, charged with deciding disputes between "natives." Apart from a first degree trial in front of "indigenous chiefs," the competence to settle such matters was always vested in Italian judges, presiding over military courts, and courts of arbitration, at the beginning of the colonial period, and functionaries-judges thereafter (art. 1 RD n.325/1908).[37] To assist these judges, *Regolamento Giudiziario* of 1908 incorporated some features of "Abyssinian" traditional law that were intended to be applied to all nationalities without distinction (see, for example, arts. 73; 140–170 RD cited). Colonial judges were then asked to apply uniform rules and principles (extrapolated in a random fashion from a variety of traditional laws) that were moreover foreign to their legal tradition.[38] There is little doubt that the "indigenous law" that was applied by Italian judges was a new custom created in the colonial context. The government chose a version of traditional law that seemed more in keeping with the "principles of Italian civilization."

Clearly this operation was unsatisfactory because *Ordinamento Giudiziario* of 1935 provided for the inclusion, even if only with consultative vote, of indigenous notables in the courts entrusted to judge according to customary law.[39] And although RD 26 June 1904, 411, article 24, ordered the government of Eritrea to collect and publish traditions in the matter of personal status and criminal law, this was never done. The collections we have are private and do not have any official status.[40] It is also noticeable that case law—which is usually never mentioned as a source in the codes and legislation of civil law countries—was expressly accorded the rank of a subsidiary source, in civil and commercial matters, for disputes between Italians, or between Italians and the indigenous inhabitants, if the dispute could not be resolved by using colonial laws. Statements of both colonial and traditional judges were taken into account (RD 5 May 1892, 270, art. 6 and l. 24 May 1903, 205, art. 2).[41]

The colonial attitude toward *šari'a* was ambivalent. Italy, like England, France, and Holland, tried at first to reduce the impact of Islamic law, which represented a formidable threat to their hegemony. In the end, in the interest of efficiency, most of the Western colonizers left intact the laws relating to subject matters such as marriage, divorce, inheritance, wills, guardianship, maintenance, and charitable endowments. Eritrea was no exception: *šarī'a* was often favored by the Italian as being preferable to customary law, the trial of which could be influenced by magic or ordeal.[42]

In the 1890s, the *šarī'a* courts of Massawa were funded and upgraded, and the great mosque in Asmara was built. The office of Mufti was created to supervise these courts and also the *Beni Awqaf,* which was responsible for collecting and distributing Islamic charity, further integrating Muslims into the state apparatus.[43] *Regolamento Giudiziario* of 1935 provided for two levels of Islamic courts: *qādī* (one judge) and a *šarī'a* court (composed of three judges). These were entrusted to settle disputes that "were not in the competence of indigenous chiefs according to an acknowledged custom": traditional matters of personal status (family, persons, inheritance, *waqf*).[44] The governor appointed all Islamic court judges, thereby ensuring government control (*Ordinamento Giudiziario* 1935).

The British Administration: 1941–1952

The British made few changes to the legal regime of Eritrea. Because their administration was provisional, they felt bound by the terms of the Hague Convention, which denied to an occupant authority the right to change institutions and laws existing in occupied enemy territory. Italian laws, which were in force in Eritrea at the date of the British occupation, remained in place except insofar as they had been suspended were inconsistent with any proclamation or regulations issued by the English authority, or amended by it. An example was a fascist law of 1933 that restricted the rights of indigenous populations on racial grounds. The previous system, on the whole, remained intact.[45] Some change was introduced, but this was "in a piecemeal fashion," partially amending the laws here and there in Italian (for the sake of convenience) and English languages.[46] For example, English criminal procedure and rules of evidence were introduced.

The British abolished Italian military courts—standing military courts, made up of British personnel, replaced them. The jurisdiction of *Commissari* and *Residenti* was replaced by a system of native courts with broad civil but limited criminal jurisdiction. Village headmen and heads of tribal sections acted, in civil cases, where the parties were of the same religion and/or community. District and tribal chiefs were given first instance jurisdiction in other civil matters and also heard appeals from headmen and chiefs of tribal sections. In all civil disputes, they applied traditional law; in criminal cases they applied Italian law as modified by British administrators.[47] Not having enough trained men for the judiciary, the British were forced to appoint in many key places persons who did not possess the qualifications necessary under Italian law, and in general lacked any legal training.[48]

In August 1946 Ibrahim Mukhtar, Mufti of Eritrea, compiled and published rules of procedure for Islamic courts in the province of Akele Guzai.[49] These rules (207 articles in all) were based upon the Egyptian code and envisaged two levels of šarī‘a courts: first degree and appeal. In the court of appeal a president and two members formed a quorum; the first-degree district courts comprised a single qādī appointed by the grand qādī.[50]

The court's jurisdiction included "1. Marriage and matters connected with marriage, such as dowry, trousseau, repudiation, divorce by mutual consent, mutual release on divorce, proof of relationship and separation. 2. Inheritance of all kinds concerning immovable and movable property. 3. Registration of sale deeds of immovable property or other properties; also mortgages, partnership, guarantees, debts and such similar transactions between Mohammedans. 4. Disputes arising out of the above mentioned registrations. 5. Maintenance of all kinds. 6. Guardianship. 7. Gifts. 8. Wakf.[51] 9. Pre-emption. 10. Lost property" (Section IV, part II). In addition to this, section V, part II provided for a more-than-residual competence of the qādī, in all cases between Muslims except those cases that came "under the penal and defamation law."

The Federation: 1952–1961

In 1952, with the creation of a federal system between Eritrea and Ethiopia, a new constitution was ratified. The English language was used in the administration and legislature, and continued to be in force during the different regimes that ruled Eritrea from 1952–1991: the Ethiopia/Eritrean Federation, the Ethiopian Empire, and the "Socialist" Dergue.

At the beginning of the 1950s, on the basis of UN Resolution 390 (5) of 2 December 1950 and of the act of Federation between Eritrea and Ethiopia, the UN commissioner Felipe Matienzo, assisted by an international group of experts, wrote a constitution for Eritrea, which was submitted to England, as the administrator of the territory, and to the

Ethiopian government.[52] The Eritrean constitutional assembly examined the text of the draft 1952 constitution and made a few amendments. The text was then approved by the commissioner, ratified by the
emperor on 10 June 1952, and came into force on 11 September, after
the ratification of the Federation Act according to the UN resolution.

This first Eritrean constitution, based on a Western democratic
model, has been depicted as an "archetype elaborated by the UN Commissioner with a democratic gloss."[53] Another writer says that it was
never felt by many Eritreans to be a truly national constitution. The
procedure that enacted it was "suspicious."[54] Rosen claims that the 1952
constitution had "no roots in the populace."[55] These comments seem to
miss the point. The 1952 constitution was no more grounded in African
values than any other, since it was based, along with the great majority
of the world's constitutions, on Western democratic principles. This
point is uncontested among public comparative lawyers. But the drafting itself had an important educational function and involved consultation with hundreds of Eritreans.[56] And the fact that a constitution is
not fully effective does not mean that it is completely valueless. A few
examples prove our point.

One of the most "startling innovations in Eritrean history" was article 17 of the constitution, which stated that "the Constitution guarantees to all persons the enjoyment of human rights and fundamental freedoms." This article was based upon the UN declaration of human
rights; it "proved in the hands of an independent judiciary to be not a
useless weapon in the defense of liberty."[57] In August 1953, the president of the Eritrean Supreme Court, P. G. Shearer, and a majority of the
bench ruled that the prosecution of the newspaper *Voce Dell'Eritrea* for
seditious libel was unconstitutional.[58] Also, at least to a certain extent, a
separation of powers was granted. In 1956, the chief executive of Eritrea
asked for the election of Sheik Mohameed Omar Ackito to be declared
invalid; the Supreme Court ruled that the decision of the executive (and
the assembly) was one in which they had no jurisdiction.[59] In our view,
the main reason for "the un-workability of the Constitution" was that
Ethiopia had no intention or wish to allow Eritrea to develop any of the
attributes of a sovereign state. This indeed was the fear expressed by a
panel of legal experts who examined the constitution in draft and declared that the United Nations might need to intervene in Eritrea after
the Federation was established in order to maintain the autonomy of
Eritrea.[60]

From the beginning, the implementation of the Eritrean constitution was problematic. The lack of a federal constitution, and of any precise reference to the relations between the Federation and the Eritrean

state, allowed the Ethiopian government to interfere at will in Eritrean affairs.[61] It was extremely improbable that Ethiopia would ever allow the Eritrean constitution to take root. In the period from 1952–1962, Ethiopia made several important legal moves to weaken the government of Eritrea. Some Ethiopian laws were extended to Eritrea, thereby superseding the Eritrean legislative power enshrined in the Eritrean constitution—which the federal act was intended to preserve. The subterfuge was to make these laws of "federal" relevance, thereby allowing their extension to Eritrea. In particular, order 7/52 extended the executive functions of the ministers of Ethiopia and of the council of ministers of Ethiopia to Eritrea.[62]

Proclamation 138/53, "The Federal Crimes Proclamation," took away from Eritrean courts the competence to deal with a number of serious crimes, placing them under the aegis of federal courts.[63] It is interesting to see that the description of offenses and punishments differed markedly from those in the Ethiopian code. Even Nathan Marein, who was an Ethiopian legal specialist and looked at the problem from this perspective, had to admit that this proclamation was made in a hurry, copying here and there from American sources (for example using American terms that had no counterpart in Ethiopian or Eritrean legislation).[64] Legislation on other matters was enacted in Tigrinya and Arabic.[65]

The previous system remained otherwise intact, according to article 96 of the Eritrean constitution, which prescribed that "all laws and regulations which were in force on 1 April 1941 and have not been repealed . . . shall remain intact," unless they were against the constitution. Ethiopian codes replaced Italian codes.[66] In particular, the promulgation of the constitution did not change the relation of state law with *šarī'a* and traditional law. Shortly after the establishment of the Federation, the Eritrean assembly passed a law creating a commission to draft a code of customary law; the body held a few meetings but did not even adopt rules of procedure, let alone start on drafting legislation.[67]

During the federation period, several amendments were made to the structure of the judiciary in Eritrea. The Ethiopian government drafted the administration of justice proclamation in 1962, but immediately suspended it—everywhere apart from Eritrea, where the Eritreans had already made the required changes at considerable expense.[68]

By 1962 the following structure was in force in Eritrea. *Chikka* courts applied customary law. *Meslene* heard a variety of appeals on, for example, land disputes from *chikkas*. Customary, *šarī'a*, and noncustomary district courts heard appeals from *meslene*. The high court heard appeals from district courts. The Supreme Court reviewed appeals from the divisions of the high court and the statutory Muslim and customary courts.[69] In addition, under the Ethiopian legal system, anyone who had been denied an appeal to the Supreme Court or any other court had the right of petition to the Chamber of Appeal within the Emperor's Office (*Zufan Chilot*). This practice continued in Eritrea through the period of the Dergue to 1991. Because of the large number of cases submitted, a final decision on a case could take a lifetime or longer.[70]

The Empire: 1962–1974

On 15 November 1962, Imperial Order (27/3 of 22/3/1962) abolished the Federation. The Ethiopian constitution of 1955 was declared the sole and unique constitution applicable throughout the Empire, including Eritrea. This constitution, drafted by jurists the majority of whom were from the United States, had been enacted in response to the Eritrean constitution of 1952.[71]

In this period, common law influences became more significant in other components of the legal system. During the late 1950s and early 1960s, Ethiopia drafted six codes. In 1954, Haile Selassie appointed commissions comprising three advisors—two French and a Swiss—to prepare new codes. The penal code was completed first and was promulgated on 23 July 1957; the criminal procedure code followed on 2 November 1961. The civil, the commercial, and the maritime codes were promulgated on 5 May 1960, and became effective on 11 September 1960. The civil procedure code was later drafted by Nirayo Esayas, the assistant minister of justice, promulgated as a decree on 8 October 1965, and approved by Parliament in 1967.[72] The 1955 constitution and the criminal and civil procedure codes were all drafted in English, while the substantive codes were in French.[73]

The civil code was a creation of the eminent French comparative lawyer René David.[74] The sources used range from a firm foundation in French and Swiss law, to Israeli, Italian, Portuguese, Yugoslav, and English legislation, not to mention the Greek and Egyptian civil codes.[75] Consequently, it is extremely eclectic; there is some concession to traditional law, primarily in the first three books (persons, family and inheritance, goods). On the other hand, Western influence is evident in areas where traditional law is silent (books IV and V: obligations in general and special contracts), in the chapters on registers of immovable and literary and artistic property (book III). The manner of determining breach of contract damages, the frequent reference to the idea of "reasonable time," the detailed rules provided for specific cases of criminal liability, the provision of a "property with a specific destination," such as trusts and endowments, are inspired by common law.[76]

The Swiss lawyer Jean Graven was entrusted with the drafting of the penal code. He chaired a commission comprising Ethiopian lawyers from common and civil law backgrounds, "thus assuring a balanced recognition of the elements of both tradition and comparative law."[77] The style—each precept formulated methodically, in a way that is easy to grasp, speaking without complicated terms—was inspired by the method of Hugh Bellot (followed in the Geneva constitution of the nineteenth century) and of Eugène Huber and Carl Stooss in the Swiss civil and penal codes. The model is undoubtedly the Swiss code, in some respects abandoned in favor of the "latest contributions of comparative law and criminology."[78] For example, the Swiss bipartite division of penalties between "punishments" and "measures" was superseded by a unitary conception of the offenses. Furthermore, the code brought together military and civilian criminal offenses, instead of dealing with them in two separate codes. Following the example of the Yugoslav code of 1951, military offenses were dealt with in a special title of the penal code.[79]

Sir Charles Mathew was head of the drafting commission of the criminal procedure code. Its model was the Anglo-Indian criminal procedure code of 1861.[80] The civil procedure code was drafted by Graven and was heavily indebted to the Indian code of civil procedure of 1908.[81] Both codes followed the particular version of the common law that was adopted by India during the Raj. Jean Escarra began the draft of the maritime and commercial codes, and he predicted that new commercial law would be accepted more readily than innovation in other areas of private law because of the lack of developed traditional Ethiopian commercial rules.[82] Professor Alfred Jauffret was asked to complete the commercial code, the final drafting of which had been interrupted by the Escarra's death.[83]

All legislation promulgated in Ethiopia was published in both English and Amharic in the *Negarit Gazeta,* the official gazette of Ethiopia, which started publication in 1951.[84] English was never recognized as an official language.[85] The Amharic versions of the codes were the authoritative ones, but the English versions had some official status by virtue of their publication in the gazette, while French had no such status. In some cases, the versions conflicted with one other to a considerable extent.[86]

The applicability of Ethiopian rules to Eritrea was unclear. Actually, article 6 of Order 27/62—ending the Federation and applying to Eritrea the system of "Unitary Administration of the Empire of Ethiopia"—prescribed the continuation of "all enactments, laws and regulations . . . presently in force within Eritrea," but only "to the extent that the application thereof is necessary to the continued operation of existing administration" and until they "shall be expressly replaced and repealed by subsequently enacted legislation."[87] Fasil Nahum made the observation that this provision, written with the aim of avoiding confusion in the legal system during the transitory period, had the effect of making "every legislation in Eritrea suspect," since it was not at all clear which were and which were not the enactments deemed to be necessary to the continuing operating of the existing administration, and who was charged with this evaluation.[88]

Case law had no formal role to play in the legal system.[89] No rules as to the value of precedent, or the existence of *stare decisis* were to be found in the legislation. On the other hand, the civil code and the constitution did not explicitly contain a provision such as the one in article 5 of the French civil code of 1804, where it is stated that "judges are not allowed to decide cases submitted to them, by way of general rule-making decisions." This enabled some flexibility in the use of judicial power.[90] For example, in subsequent years, the Supreme Court sometimes cited previous judgments to support its decisions, and lower court judges usually conformed to them.[91] The courts developed rules of evidence, as a draft for a judiciary code was compiled but never enacted.[92] However, the most serious obstacle to the development of case law was the absence of case reporting: although written decisions were on file in the archives, in practice it was not feasible for lawyers or judges to consult them.[93]

The Ethiopian code system has been justly labeled as "largely ineffective."[94] This possibility was envisaged from its inception: René David assumed that the codes were intended to be applied immediately on the more developed elements of the population, those living in the highlands, but "could not be expected to be applied in the other regions in the near future."[95] In his original draft of the Ethiopian civil code, David included many carefully drawn adaptations of customary law principles and transitory provisions that would have permitted an accommodation to the new law over a period of years.[96] He admitted that in Ethiopia at that time there was insufficient knowledge of tradition, particularly among the Ethiopian lawyers on the commission who reviewed and revised his draft.[97] The project failed, probably because of their lack of concern. Jean Graven shared the same opinion.[98]

Van Doren has argued that the system was built to sustain and legitimize the emperor's power and placate foreign nations. The Ethiopians who advised the drafters represented the supremacy of the Christian and Amharic minority over the Muslim and non-Amharic majority. Codes were the expression of the elite who dominated the political arena of the times. These were men eager to Westernize the system and to change the image of their legal culture from "primitive" to "modern."[99] Once this "make up" operation was completed, the system continued to be governed by landlords and the religious elite, of which religious and traditional tribunals represented the *longa manus*. From our standpoint it seems that the state actors involved here were consummate operators; they were utilizing the power and prestige of international legal experts and of their home states in order to legitimize and consolidate their own hegemony. Rather than the Ethiopian state being a puppet of foreign powers, it was the other way around (see chapter 7).

The Code System, *Šarīʿa*, and Traditions

In the 1960s and 1970s, following the independence of most African colonial territories, the harmonization, unification, and ultimately consolidation of traditional laws into a code was seen by the new leaders and their advisors, who were all believers in the supremacy of state law, as an essential step in eliminating factors that might cause disunity in the fragile new nation-state.[100] Legal reform in Ethiopia followed this pattern. It was argued that because different ethnic, cultural, religious, and land tenure groups had different rules, mostly unwritten, a uniform and impartial system of justice was impossible as long as traditional laws and *šarīʿa* dominated.[101]

Reducing the strength of local traditions and Islamic law became a priority.[102] Following this trend, a crucial article (3347) of the civil code of 1960 stated, "unless otherwise expressly provided, all rules whether written or customary previously in force concerning matters provided for in this Code shall be replaced by this Code and are hereby repealed." For some commentators, this portended the end of traditional law, as it implied the abrogation of any customary statement *contra* or *praeter legem* in any matter regulated by the code. In practice, article 3347 on tradition had a less devastating effect than it might have had. First, rules which were expressly recognized by the code or which were not regulated by it were assured of survival. Second, traditional law directly inspired some provisions of the code. Finally, the ineffectiveness of the entire code machinery ensured a healthy survival of traditions up to present times.[103]

In principle, *šarīʿa* faced the same difficulty as custom, because a literal interpretation of article 3347 could have led to the repeal of any "rule" previously attributed to *šarīʿa* courts. There was a further complication. The original draft of the civil code contained a special section dealing with marriage and divorce among Muslims. This was an attempt to create a regime consistent with the code and applicable to all Muslims within the Empire.[104] But these articles were not incorporated in the definitive version of the code.[105] Special rules and regulations for Muslims would have openly legitimized *šarīʿa* courts and this was certainly not what the rulers desired. This deletion created a gap in the system and made for an extremely confused situation. It was not clear if the lack in the code of any rules pertaining specifically to Muslims meant an explicit repeal of the *šarīʿa* court's jurisdiction and devolution to state courts of disputes among Muslims.[106]

During the days of the Empire, the *šarīʿa* court system of Eritrea remained separate from that of Ethiopia.[107] As far as procedural law in Eritrea was concerned, Mukhtar's rules of procedure stayed in place all during the British administration and the Federation period up to 1974.[108]

It is extraordinarily difficult to understand how any law could have been administered fairly in Eritrea in this period. There was a patchwork of laws stitched together from a number of sources, and riddled with ambiguity. Most likely the Ethiopians found it easier to let Eritrean Muslims and some of the ethnic groups manage the law much as they had in the past rather than face the problems that an attempt to impose centralized control would have certainly caused.

The Dergue, the EPLF, and
the Liberation Struggle

There is no doubt why most Eritreans abhorred the Marxist military Dergue and Chairman Mengistu much more than they disliked the Empire and the emperor.[109] Under the Empire, most people's lives and institutions remained much the same as they had been during Italian colonial rule, while the Dergue tried to govern their lives, minds, and bodies. There were numerous and well-documented atrocities that continued throughout the seventeen years of the Dergue's occupation of Eritrea.[110] The Dergue's policy was to replace customary courts with an elaborate system of "people's justice." The regular court system (including *šarīʿa*) that had existed under the Empire now coexisted with people's judicial tribunals in the peasant associations and urban *kebeles* at the *woreda* and *awraja* levels in the rural areas, and at three levels in the towns. These tribunals dealt with minor criminal and civil matters.[111] In chapter 6 we discuss the impact and failure of the Dergue's land policies in Eritrea.

Whatever the declared policies of the new regime, it is fair to say that not only did the Dergue copy much of Haile Selassie's political style, but also that there were marked similarities between the legal systems of two supposedly radically opposed systems. The laws of the emperor and of the Dergue alike embodied the demands of small and unrepresentative elites.[112] Later on we will also comment on some similarities between the Dergue and the EPLF together with their divergences.

The EPLF, who effectively controlled much of Eritrea from 1970–1991, and all of it after 1991, was a civilian organization with a strong military wing. It was divided into a number of departments that were equivalent to ministries in a sovereign state. At various stages of its development, the ministries of public administration, interior, local government, and justice all concerned themselves with aspects of legal administration and reform, both with regard to the EPLF and peasants living in the base area. One of the first priorities for the EPLF was drafting a marriage law. This was enacted in 1977, and for the first time EPLF members were allowed to marry each other. The law was gradually enforced on the civilian population of the liberated areas. It has been suggested to us that the Chinese law of 30 April 1950 influenced its drafting.[113]

In 1987, the Second EPLF Congress created a Department of Justice, charged with drafting new codes. The department included such prominent EPLF figures as Teame Beyene, the former chief justice. Bills for the civil, penal, civil procedure, and criminal procedure codes were introduced and discussed by the central committee of the EPLF. They were approved but never published nor fully enacted into law.[114] The civil code was devised with the specific needs of the liberated rural areas in mind, and was not intended to be used for the urban population nor in a future fully liberated Eritrea. It dealt primarily with family law and inheritance. The penal code was eclectic. It did not specifically mandate the death penalty for murder apart from the military. There was a lenient imprisonment regime with the maximum sentence allowed being ten years, an acknowledgment that it was difficult to maintain strict prison conditions in a war situation.[115] Considering the background of the drafters of the EPLF laws, it would be surprising if the Ethiopian codes had not been consulted when the Eritrean counterparts were being drafted.

Traditional laws were taken into account provided they did not conflict with the EPLF program. The EPLF partly used the traditional codes as a frame of reference for its administration of justice among the civilian population. They created a standing committee of elders who went from village to village to try and solve problems as they arose.[116] In 1989, EPLF members elected judges. These men were being trained to administer the codes in the liberated areas when the war ended.[117]

It is difficult to overestimate the importance of Western and socialist ideas and ideology on present-day Eritreans (or for that matter, Ethiopians). Most of today's leaders matured in the sixties and seventies and imbibed a heady mix of Marxism and some elements of counterculture. Since independence, the dominant international ideology at work in Eritrea, at least on the surface, has been that of the liberal market, but old habits die hard.

Four

The Transitional Period and Attempts at Legal Reform

The victory of the EPLF brought about some of the most significant changes to the lives of the peoples of the country. After liberation on 24 May 1991, the EPLF formed the Provisional Government of Eritrea (PGE). For the moment a transitional system operated, still largely based on the Ethiopian codes of the Empire, together with the amendments made by the Dergue, by the EPLF during the war, and by the provisional government after independence. The first interventions were proclamations 1–8 on transitional codes, containing provisions for the repeal and amendment of the Ethiopian codes. The texts are only in Tigrinya.[1] With some adjustment, they extended to the new state most of the rules and regulations in force in EPLF-liberated areas before independence.[2] They will be repealed as soon as the new codes come into force. As of 2002, the bulk of the Ethiopian code system still remained in place, a major disappointment to Eritrean elders. They asked, "why should we perpetuate this sad period of our history by keeping in force laws that were imposed upon us by the Emperor . . . laws that were the instruments of our repression?"[3] However, to be fair, since the proclamations were enacted immediately after the liberation, there was no time to draft a radical reform of the Ethiopian system.

State legislation takes the form of proclamations and legal notices. The first are compiled by the National Assembly and signed by the government; legal notices are compiled by a ministry, upon delegation by the National Assembly, and signed by the relevant ministry. Both enter into force from the day of their publication in the official gazette,

Gazeta Awagiat Eritra.[4] As of writing, some 110 laws (proclamations) and some 46 regulations (legal notices) had been enacted. A constitution was approved and ratified by a Constituent Assembly on 23 May 1997, but by 2002 was still not in force—even though the president had asserted in 2000 that it would be implemented expeditiously.[5] Elections for the National Assembly and the president were scheduled for December 2001 but did not take place.

The state legislation drafted in Eritrea since the country won its independence lacks clarity; it is sometimes not clear which is the law pertaining to the matter in hand. Moreover, much of it is not implemented, for example in the crucial area of land reform. A further element that complicates this scenario, as well as a serious obstacle for foreign scholars who try to organize the study of sources, is that laws are drafted in Tigrinya, and for only a few, usually those of special relevance to foreign interests, is either an English or Arabic translation available. This situation does not seem to be compatible with article 4.3 of the constitution that provides for the equality of all Eritrean languages.[6]

One of the most important proclamations issued by the government is not available in English; it establishes the structure and authority of the government of Eritrea in the four years leading up to the promulgation of the constitution (37/93).[7] According to this proclamation, the National Assembly (who chose the president) was made up of the seventy-five members of the EPLF central committee and sixty others; ten of these were women selected by the EPLF and twenty "other nationalities," the other thirty comprised three from each of the ten regional administrations (art. 4). The executive body (Council of Government) was headed by the president; its composition and number was unspecified. The third arm of government was the judiciary, at the peak of which was the High Court, formally independent from both legislative and executive bodies (art. 7).

The validity of the proclamations on transitional codes, as well as that of the transitional government, technically ceased with the ratification of the constitution in May 1997. Since then Eritrea has been in a form of legal limbo because the constitution is not in force. This situation seems to have had an impact on transnational actors, some of which have acted as though Eritrea was not a fully sovereign legitimate state. It is a moot point whether Eritrea would have been regarded in this way if democratic elections had been held in the 1997–1998 period and the constitution put into force. This matter is covered more fully in chapter 7 and in our conclusion.

The New Codes

Ad hoc commissions, appointed by the government and advised by foreign lawyers, were charged with drafting new codes. In Africa as elsewhere in the post-colonial world a general pattern emerged of keeping in the main the legal system inherited from the colonial power. However, the drafters of the new Eritrean codes considered both common and civil law models. Traditional law and *šarīʿa*, following a trend among drafters dating back to the drafting of the Ethiopian codes, received less consideration.

The Center for International Legal Cooperation in Leiden, in partnership with the Ministry of Justice of Eritrea and the University of Amsterdam, assisted in the drafting of the civil code.[8] The government of Eritrea and the United Nations Development Program (UNDP) underwrote the project. The team was given a mandate to rewrite parts of the transitional civil code. The drafters were instructed by the Eritrean government to use the Ethiopian codes as a basis, making necessary amendments, such as those to improve the present unequal position of women.[9] The team started its work in August 1997 and completed its task at the end of 1999. In February 2000 it was assigned an additional task of drafting the remaining titles of the civil code. At the time of writing, this phase is still to be completed.

The Leiden Center was also charged with assisting in the drafting of the civil procedure code. Its partner this time, in addition to the Eritrean Ministry of Justice, was the Catholic University of Brabant, at Eindhoven. The project, financed once again by the government of Eritrea/UNDP, was carried out in a similar manner to the civil code. It began in May 1999 and was supposed to be completed by December 2000. The first draft should have been ready for discussion in May 2000, during a workshop to be held in Asmara.[10] This did not take place.

According to the president of the Eritrean Supreme Court, the penal code had already passed through the drafting stage by 1998, and was waiting to pass though the National Assembly. Judging from the experience with the 1997 constitution, the National Assembly will probably make some amendments, at least minor ones. Three North American lawyers were invited by the UNDP and the Eritrean Ministry of Justice to draft the penal code and the code of criminal procedure. The three members went to Eritrea in August 1997 to be briefed by the minister and a number of lawyers and government officials and were struck by the insistence of the Eritreans that the codes should be "modern and forward-looking." They looked at criminal law in such countries as Greece, Israel, France, Germany, the United States, and the Commonwealth countries. In 1998, the group delivered its final draft to the Eritrean government after making several revisions. A committee of Eritreans worked with the experts and referred to them views based on Eritrean traditional laws as well as on the former Ethiopian penal code.[11] Further consultation on the document was delayed by renewed fighting between Eritrea and Ethiopia. The code of criminal procedure has still to be finalized.[12]

The foreign advisors for the commercial code were also from North America and we can safely assume that in the end it will be U.S.-oriented. Its drafting process is over; along with the redrafted penal code it was given to the Minister of Justice in December 2000.[13] We have no information on the extent of redrafting the maritime code except that it has been accorded the lowest priority of the six codes. One notes here a continuing tradition of using foreign experts. The first instance was in preparing the Eritrean constitution of 1952, and the second was during the drafting of the Ethiopian codes of the 1960s (some of the same legal experts, including Arthur Schiller, being involved in both cases). Foreigners continued to hold important legal positions in the judiciary of the Federation: Judge P. G. Shearer was the first president of the Eritrean Supreme Court and F. F. Russell served as attorney general in 1956.[14] The use of experts legitimizes the entire enterprise and helps it to find favor in international donor circles and among Western economic and political elites.

All of the drafts of the new codes were written in English; they will be translated into Arabic, Tigrinya, and all other Eritrean languages if "capacity permits."[15] After the codes are translated they will have to be discussed by the National Assembly. This will all take considerable time. Choosing one or more official languages is a difficult political decision. Eritrea has tried to evade the problem by not declaring Tigrinya as an official language but nevertheless issuing all proclamation and government documents in it. By no means all documents are translated into Arabic, the second most common language used; even fewer are translated into English. A number of other African states have faced a similar problem. Mozambique chose Portuguese, the language of the occupying colonial power, rather than any of the vernacular languages. In Eritrea, English has been granted a semi-official status, being used in schools and universities; it is a neutral idiom, without any too obvious post-colonial implications. On the other hand, the choice of English could create problems of translation of legal terms and taxonomies. Words and concepts used in civil law countries do not necessarily find an exact counterpart in common law, which may lack the appropriate terminology.[16] An even greater problem is faced with Tigrinya, which does not have, as is also the case with many vernacular languages, a sufficiently well-developed legal terminology.[17] As the government has decided to use Tigrinya, such a terminology must be created as a matter of priority.

The Constitution

The Eritreans' project to devise a constitution began in July 1994 with the creation of the constitutional commission; this process had a deep symbolic value.[18] The constitution can be seen as the climax of consolidation of the legitimacy of the Eritrean government—that is to say of the party that forms the government—for the Eritrean people and the international community. This follows a line that began with the 1993 referendum and passed through the reorganization of the provisional government—with proclamation 37/93, on the basis of separation of powers—and the reorganization of the party, the change of name (from EPLF to PFDJ—People's Front for Democracy and Justice, in 1994), and the party's declaration that it would not interfere with the government.[19]

During the process of drafting the constitution, a stress on popular involvement was important to legitimize the document in the eyes of the people, while a veneer of Western "professionalism," assured by the presence of foreign consultants and Western-trained Eritrean lawyers, was desirable in order to achieve international recognition.[20] The constitutional commission was created with proclamation 55/94 and charged with the drafting of a constitution on the basis of "a wide-ranging and all-embracing national debate and education through public seminars and lecture series on constitutional principles and practices" (art. 4). Members of the commission were chosen to represent a wide cross-section of Eritrean society: urban and rural populations, different ethnies and social groups, former fighters, and refugees. Respect for the principle of sexual equality was guaranteed by the participation of twenty-one women (42 percent of the commission). Moreover, consulting functions were given to an advisory board of forty-five Eritrean elders and religious leaders, and experts in traditional law of various nationalities—a few of these were women.[21] Emphasis was placed on popular participation in the process, and this had to be obtained by a bottom-to-top dialogue.[22]

In July 1996, the draft constitution was distributed for public scrutiny and debate; on 23 May 1997, a Constituent Assembly, comprising 550 people "democratically elected from both inside and outside Eritrea," approved and ratified the new constitution, but it is still not in force. The last two years have seen an unprecedented debate in Eritrea and in the diaspora on political, economic, and security matters. The government has reacted with draconian measures and created an atmosphere in which the implementation of the constitution seems even further distant.

The text of the constitution comprises fifty-nine articles, organized in seven chapters. The most important models of reference were the constitutions of the USA, South Africa, and Namibia. An advisory board composed of fifteen foreign experts from the United States, Europe, Africa, and the Middle East helped in the drafting. Echoes of common law can be seen in articles that recognize the constitution as the "supreme law of the land" and in those dealing with fundamental rights and freedoms, on separation of powers, and on judicial review.[23]

The political system that the Eritrean constitution wants to implement can be depicted as hybrid, but one more orientated toward a presidential model than to parliamentary sovereignty. All citizens who are qualified to vote will elect, by secret ballot, members of the National Assembly (art. 31.1–3).[24] The president is elected by the National Assembly— which constitutes the "supreme representative and legislative body."[25]

In many African states the post-colonial period saw a rapid process of centralizing power in the hands of the president/head of state.[26] Many men became "presidents for life" and ruled with scant regard to the constitution, or they amended it to suit themselves. Following a trend starting with the Eritrean constitution of 1952, the president, who is the head of state and government, and commander-in-chief of the armed forces, appoints many of the most important officers of the state. The president appoints, among others, ministers and judges, the latter upon the nomination of the judicial service commission (art. 42.8–9).[27] The president can remove any person he has been appointed (art. 42.17). He exercises executive power in "consultation" with the cabinet of ministers (art. 39.2).[28]

The presence of impeachment rules is somewhat of a guarantee against presidential excesses. While the practical implementation of such a radical step is a matter of checks and balances between the institutions of the state, at least the constitution contains the theoretical framework for the process. The procedure for impeachment is envisaged at article 41.6: a two-thirds majority vote of all members of the National Assembly is necessary; the reasons for impeachment are strictly defined by article 41 6a–c; and finally, according to article 49.2b the Supreme

Court has the power of sole jurisdiction of hearing and adjudicating the case.[29]

As far as the form of state is concerned, the proposal to create an ethnically based federal state was decisively rejected. An intention to construct a federal system had been voiced at the 2nd EPLF General Congress of 1987, and was partly carried out with the creation in May 1991 of ten "autonomous" regions, each of them governed by a senior EPLF member belonging to the ethnie dominant in the region. At the time, it was stated that the ten regions would be linked under a federal system, with the central government maintaining total control over defense, foreign policy, trade, and coordination between the regions. Regional assemblies were elected, but even for the brief period they existed, exercised little authority.

The choice of a unitary system, already present in the introduction to proclamations 26/92 and 86/96 (on local government), is made clear in article 1.5 of the constitution that defines Eritrea as a "unitary state, divided into units of local government."[30] Rejection of ethnic tribalism and protection of the unitary choice, safeguarding at the same time national peculiarities, is expressed by the slogan "unity in diversity," which is raised to the status of constitutional principle by article 6.1 of the constitution.

The Administration

A new administrative structure was introduced in 1995, ostensibly to "maximize economic development programs by uniting similar ecological and resource bases." In an interview on 3 June 1995, Minister of Local Government Mahmoud Ahmed Sherifo (who, during the transitional period of 1991–1997, was the most senior member of the National Assembly and also the most important political figure in the country after the president) indicated that the new boundaries were designed to "promote stronger ties between the people."[31] The aims of the new structure included creating larger units that in the future process of decentralizing government will be largely financially self-supporting and economically integrated.[32] Decentralization is one of the major priorities professed by the government, but the process has not proceeded very far; at the time of writing only the Ministry of Marine Resources has moved to Massawa and the Ministry of Defense to Embatkala. The macropolicy unit of the president's office—perhaps the most influential body in the country—declared that the country should set up "decentralised and more participatory democratic institutions."[33] It is arguable whether much progress has been made toward achieving these essential goals.

The pre-1995 administrative divisions were drawn up by the Italians and reflected Eritrean ethno-linguistic and cultural differences as seen by the Italians at the time; their intention was to administer each group separately—*divide et impera*.[34] The new structure has ostensibly a very different objective. It is aimed at "blending together culturally different groups, and treating them as equals, both economically and politically," an element which is seen as a step in achieving the basic principle of the constitution, "unity in diversity" (art. 6.1).[35] It is noticeable that the former province of Hamasien has been sundered into five parts. This is the heartland of the Tigrinya ethnie, and the cauldron in which many of the liberation fighters were forged. The purpose of the dispersal may be, on one hand, to send a message to the other ethnies that the Tigrinya will not strive to dominate Eritrean life in the future, and on the other hand, to season the more impoverished regions with an experienced, entrepreneurial, and educated elite (not all of whom are Tigrinya).

Another radical policy move was announced in 1996 when a proclamation was issued establishing an entirely new local government structure.[36] At each level of regional government there are the same three bodies—executive, judiciary, and legislative—as at the national level. At the village level the executive branch is under an administrator, who is nominated to the post by a regional administrator (who in turn is appointed by the president). It is a permanent appointment. He is helped by an executive director, also a permanent appointment, and by committees of unspecified membership. The legislative body in the village is known as a *megabaaya;* it holds meetings every two or three months where it comments on the performance reports of the administrator, a man who chairs the meeting and has very wide-ranging powers. Village courts, *kebabi*, represent the judiciary.[37]

The Judiciary

The judiciary was reorganized by proclamation 1/91.[38] The organization of civil justice is articulated on three levels, which correspond to the three levels of local government: *woreda* (sub-zonal) courts, *awraja* (zonal) courts, and the High Court (art. 4.1.—to be renamed Supreme Court with the entry into force of the constitution). The High Court, located in Asmara, is at the top of the hierarchy and serves as a first instance as well as an appellate court. Minor infractions fall under village and sub-regional courts' jurisdiction. More serious offenses are prosecuted before regional courts, and cases involving murder, rape, and other serious felonies are heard by the High Court. In regional and sub-regional courts a single judge appointed by the Ministry of Justice on recommendation of the president of the Supreme Court renders all judgments (art. 5.1). In the High Court, panels of three judges hear cases (but five judges are the quorum for appeal against its rulings).

Proclamation 25/92 allows *kebabi* courts to use traditional law. There are a thousand of these throughout Eritrea; they started to function in 1995. They are not under the control of the Ministry of Justice, and their expenses are covered through the imposition of fees on those who lose their cases.[39] The judges are appointed by a panel composed of heads of regional courts, the regional prosecutor, and the regional governor, and they have a competence limited to minor offenses. They are chosen from local elders, who rule on the basis of the "customary law of the locality," and cannot impose sentences involving physical punishment. In Karnesem, meetings are held twice a month, on St. Michael's and Be'ale Egziabher day. In Seraye, tribunals are held in seven villages on the Feast of St. Mary. In upper Barka, the tribunal seems to be in continuous session.[40] Proclamation 3/91 provides for a two-tier level of *šari'a* courts, with the Mufti as an appeal judge sitting in Asmara against decisions of local *qādī* having jurisdiction of matters of family and inheritance among Muslims.

State military courts were established by Proclamation 1/91. They are structured on two levels, one dealing with minor matters, the other with more serious offenses. The president of the High Court appoints the chairman. Military courts are competent for military crimes committed by and against members of the armed forces, as well as for crimes committed by ex-fighters during their national service, unless they fall under the jurisdiction of the tribunal against corruption. There is no right of appeal.

In April 1996, a special court "which deals and decides on criminal acts such as corruption, theft and embezzlement" was created (proclamation 85/96).[41] In the words of the government, one of the reasons for its establishment was that the existing legal system was "influenced by tainted thinking." This court bans defense counsel and the right of appeal, allowing the executive branch to mete out punishment without respect for due process. Judges are senior military officers, mostly with little or no legal experience and are selected by the president of Eritrea. The office of the attorney/advocate general decides which cases are to be tried. There is little doubt that the proclamation violates some of the most crucial and long-standing principles of the legal process (enshrined as well in the transitional codes and in the constitution). For instance, article 4.2 provides that this court can review previously decided cases (violation of the principle of double jeopardy); article 5 provides that there is no appeal against its decisions (violation of the right of appeal); articles 3, 4, and 6 provide that judges of this court can give whatever punishment they may deem appropriate and are not bound by the penal and the criminal procedure codes in their adjudication (violation of principles of legality). It is no surprise that Eritrean judges strongly objected to what they felt to be a direct attack on their independence and very existence.[42]

If and when the constitution enters into force, the rules and regulations contained in proclamation 1/91 will have to be read in conjunction with the provisions contained in the constitution. According to the latter, judicial power shall be vested in a Supreme Court, and in such other lower courts as shall be established by law (arts. 48.1; 49–50). On paper, the independence of judges appears to be ensured.[43] However, the constitution is silent over the creation of other special courts. The rule contained in article 17.6, after a series of provisions of guarantee against arrest and unjust detentions, provides for a fair, speedy, and public trial, excluding however the press and the public from all or any part of the trial for reasons of "morals or national security," a clause which also appears to be dangerous.

The constitution provides a mechanism for judicial review.[44] Article 2.3, after stating that "the constitution is the supreme law of the country and the source of all laws of the State," specifies that "all laws, orders and acts contrary to its letter and spirit shall be null and void."[45] Article 49.2a, indicates that "the power of sole jurisdiction of interpreting this constitution and the constitutionality of any law enacted or any action taken by the Government" shall be vested in the Supreme Court.

As of August 1997 there were thirty-two operational courts at the sub-regional level. From 1997, there was a constitutional provision for a Supreme Court, designed to replace the High Court that existed under the Empire. During the transitional period, a college consisting of the president of the High Court and four other judges heard appeals against High Court rulings.

Unofficial Legal Sources

Law professors and judges currently play a marginal role in Eritrea, even though there is no doubt that in a healthy legal system they should be at least as important as legislators. And this is true no matter what choice is adopted, whether case law or a system based on codes.[46] In developing countries, they are "in the front line of the confrontation between new laws and the nation" because "the acceptance and effectiveness of the entire legal order depend in the first instance and for the most part on these men."[47] Legal texts can be applied only after these actors have made them comprehensible to the general public as well as to legal practitioners.

The University of Asmara reopened in 1991. Before 1996, the law school was able to offer only a law diploma. To obtain an LL.B. or superior qualification, Addis Ababa was a necessary destination. A four-year degree course, preceded by a common year of studies, began in 1996. Legal doctrine has to be built up.[48] Cadres are still lacking: the law school at the moment has very few full time professors. University teaching is an occupation far away from political power positions and, at the moment, does not appear to enjoy a particularly high standing.

With regard to professional legal training, there has been a considerable reliance on expatriate professors for teaching law students at the university.[49] An informal requirement before one is allowed to teach is to have obtained either a master's degree or a Ph.D. abroad. As far as law professors coming through international cooperation agreements are concerned, initially lawyers from the U.S. and Italy had the most impact, but some of the influence has been shifted to other countries, in particular India. Many of the textbooks and teaching materials that were created by foreign professors for use in Addis Ababa in the 1960s were still in use in Eritrea in 2001.[50]

In Asmara, teaching is not entirely oriented to civil law: lectures are sometimes freely structured and expose students to practical case law. But at the same time, professors affirm that Eritrea—because of the colonial legacy and also because of the prevailing civil law emphasis given to the legal system by Ethiopian codes—has been and it is likely to remain basically a civil law country. However, university lectures have been given in English since 1964. This decision is reasonable, even if courses are taught in a language which is not the mother language for many of the professors, and all (students as well as teachers) are faced with the problems of translation of rules and taxonomies elaborated within a civil law context. This problem will be multiplied in the future when the new codes are translated and published.

Legal Profession

In civil law countries, the legal profession is frequently based upon the separation of the careers of advocates and judges, while in common law countries judges are usually former advocates at the top of their careers.[51] Eritrea follows the civil law pattern.

The current state of the legal profession in Eritrea is discouraging. At present, judges are not required to have any legal experience, although the Ministry of Justice is providing training ranging from two months to one year. Many judges operating in Eritrea during the Dergue were fired immediately after liberation.[52] Some of the present judges are ex-EPLF fighters; others are civil servants. Since 1997, a number of diploma holders from the University of Asmara have begun to work as clerks and judges. For the moment, the president selects all the important judges. His nomination is relayed to the executive (and also presumably to the party central committee—even if only informally) and endorsed by it and the National Assembly in one of its infrequent meetings.

In 1995, out of sixteen High Court judges, only six had law degrees; the rest had a certificate or diploma. And fewer than ten in the *zoba* or sub-*zoba* district courts and provincial courts had even a diploma in law.[53] In late 1998 there were some ninety-eight judges in Eritrea, about forty of them operating in the High Court. Of these, only 15 percent had an LL.M. or LL.B. In the attorney general's office only four of the seventy-five employees held law degrees.[54] In Mendefera, an important sub-regional center, none of the judges had any legal training; all were EPLF fighters with no previous ties to the district.[55]

The Eritrean system does not officially recognize case law as a source of law, nor is there case reporting. There is little doubt that the absence of case reporting will create problems in the future as the system develops. At the moment, however, this is an academic point. For a number of years after liberation, court facilities were so primitive that judges had to do all the work, even writing rulings themselves by hand. New courthouses were completed in 1998 but further development of the judicial infrastructure was hindered by the conflict with Ethiopia. This caused a considerable delay in the processing of cases.

Proclamation 88/96 gave the Ministry of Justice the power to regulate the practice of law, providing also for the introduction of an "Advocates Association" (art. 32).[56] A legal committee comprising four members is envisaged to control the behavior of advocates. To plead in front of the High Court (Supreme Court) it is necessary to have passed an *ad hoc* examination in a university, college, or other recognized institution. To plead in front of other courts it is sufficient to have a diploma or a certificate in law from an accredited law school. Previous professional experience and legal background are reasons for exemption from these requirements (art. 5).

Room Given to *Šarīᶜa* and Traditional Law by Present Legislation

Post-independence legislation, just as that of previous administrations, studiously avoids any too explicit reference to the position and relevance of traditional law and *šarīʿa*. The same applies to the constitution. There is no doubt that the more any government says or enacts, the more it risks having to deliver on its commitments and face criticism from Muslim and non-Muslim alike. The government encourages and makes a particular point of the presence of Muslims in the party and all branches of the government, but it does not—just as previous governments—officially recognize *šarīʿa*.[57] Article 4.3 of the constitution guarantees "the equality of all Eritrean languages," and this is a new and welcome development because during Ethiopia's rule Amharic was the only official language.[58]

As far as primary legislation is concerned, few provisions referring to Muslim Eritreans are contained in proclamation 2/91 (amendments to the Ethiopian civil code). These articles say that chapters 2, 3, and 5 of book II of the Ethiopian code that relate to betrothal, marriage, and inheritance do not apply to Eritrean Muslims.[59] The most logical inference from this, which however is not expressly stated, is that the competence of the *šarīʿa* courts is recognized in these matters. Rules contained in proclamation 2/91 are not particularly "new"; *šarīʿa* courts have been regarded in the past as competent in such matters.

Legal sources are completely silent on the role to be given to traditional law in the current system. Article 7 of the Ethiopian code has not been repealed. According to Mengsteab Negash the transitional civil code of 1991, like the Ethiopian Civil Code of 1960, severely restricted various local customary laws, leaving little room in areas of private life such as marriage, divorce, and inheritance, where they have been important for centuries.[60] It is obvious that the space given by the state to traditional law will depend on an evaluation that is more political than legal, and will be contingent upon such factors as the strength, legitimacy, and stability of the government, and the beliefs, attitudes, and expectations of individual members of the government. In the past, a number of socialist systems, although in principle opposed to tradition and "backwardness," nevertheless did not attempt to eradicate all features of it. The reason for this lay in their realization that many elements of modernizing and globalizing Western tradition could have posed a much greater threat than tradition to their ability to effectively control the population. Therefore some latitude was given to tradition and *šarīʿa* to reduce as far as possible the attraction and threat of Western models.

The EPLF case is rather similar. Its Department of Justice, during the war, carried out exhaustive studies on traditional law.[61] The emphasis given by the government to traditional conciliation in settling the dispute between Tsenadegle and Tor'a (see chapter 7) leads us to argue that traditional law may play more than a marginal role in independent Eritrea. The government realizes that customs may—if used wisely—represent a powerful instrument of social control.

In our concluding chapter we will show that the Eritrean government seems to be in a period of rethinking about the role of traditional laws. It has been said that informal legal traditions are "timeless information in a world which must be re-born and re-cycled, and not one subject in principle to individual decision-making and market force." Customary law is an aspect of deeply held beliefs, and it is dangerous to try and marginalize it or treat it as unworthy. The risk of driving opposition underground, into exile, or into martyrdom is always present.[62]

International and Transnational Actors

These actors have been very active throughout this chapter, even though they have not been visible all the time. Because of its strategic position, the Horn of Africa is an area of the world that has always attracted the interest of international actors. During the BMA the United Nations was very influential. In 1947 indirect elections were held under the aegis of a four-power commission, and the question of Eritrea was debated at considerable length within the UN. In 1949 a five-nation commission toured Eritrea, and the General Assembly voted on 2 December 1950 to federate Eritrea as an autonomous entity with Ethiopia. The Federation was terminated unilaterally by Ethiopia in 1962. The UN displayed no interest in the fate of the country it had created. During the rule of Haile Selassie, Eritrea increased in strategic importance. The United States gave considerable diplomatic, military, and economic support to Ethiopia, and helped to ensure that the Eritrean liberation movement was not successful. The USSR also accepted this position, especially after the Marxist Dergue seized power in 1974.

In 1993, after the liberation of the country, the UN sent observers to Eritrea to monitor a sovereignty referendum; following an overwhelming vote for independence, the UN, the Organization of African Unity (OAU), and most other states formally recognized the country's sovereignty. In independent Eritrea, international actors have played a very significant role. One of the major priorities of the new leadership concerned economics. Eritrea quickly tried to restructure its economy in line with the current World Bank, IMF, and United States Agency for International Development (USAID) policies. As a consequence of this, substantial loans were given by donor nations on highly concessionary and favorable terms. Attempts were made to attract some major transnational mining corporations through a liberal investment code. Eritrea began to play a diplomatic role in Africa and the rest of the world; it has been particularly active in the Inter-Governmental Authority on Drought and Development (IGADD).

As a consequence of its strategic importance, Eritrea has faced a number of military threats from its neighbors. A dispute with Yemen was eventually settled through legal means with the aid of French and other international mediators. The conflict with Ethiopia has proved more obdurate. At the time of writing a UN force of some 5,000 military and civilian peacekeepers is controlling the border with Ethiopia, and also facilitating negotiations between the two parties. Eventually international bodies will try and cement a permanent peace settlement.

Because of the persistence of a number of practices deemed to be undesirable by the outside world (alleged violations of human rights), strong representation has been made by Amnesty International, Africa Watch, and the U.S. State Department on matters such as capital punishment, child prostitution, persecution of religious minorities, and the establishment of special courts to deal with "economic criminals" and political dissidents. As a consequence of increased repression in Eritrea, EU ambassadors withdrew from the country in October 2001.

We are writing this book at the time when the U.S. has instigated a crusade against "international fundamental Muslim terrorism" in response to an unparalleled attack on the U.S. civilian population. This crusade will obviously last a long time. As the U.S. and its allies search for and destroy terrorists, and launch raids on nations that harbor them, it may not be too long before Sudan also becomes a target. Eritrea has a substantial Muslim population and many thousands more remain as refugees in the Sudan. A number of these long-time exiles have allied themselves with Eritrean jihad forces opposing the Eritrean government. A number of repressive governments all over the world have received favorable treatment from the U.S. as a result of these governments' offering assistance to the U.S. in its campaign; the Eritrean government may seek to distract attention away from its increasingly authoritarian actions by doing the same.

In the chapters that follow we discuss whether Eritrean law and politics are changing because of increasing international pressure. We can anticipate that, like other small and poor countries, Eritrea will not lightly cross powerful regimes such as the IMF and World Bank. Of course, they do not have to obey all the fine print of these agreements, and policies of the agencies change from time to time; those of the IMF have become much more reasonable than in the past.[63] However, it is inevitable that in the future small, impoverished nations will adopt attractive aspects of law from richer and more successful ones or use the increasing number of global regulations, at least in key sectors such as commerce and contract law, to try and gain some competitive economic advantage.

This happens all around the world and not just in Africa or Eritrea. "[T]he world society which, in the wake of globalization, has taken shape in many . . . dimensions is undermining the importance of the national state, because a multiplicity of social circles, communication networks, market relations and life styles, none of them specific to any particular locality, now cut across the boundaries of the national state."[64]

Five

From Blood Feud and Blood Money to the State Settlement of Murder Cases

For a society in which the systems of alliance, the political form of the sovereign, the differentiation into orders and castes, and the value of descent lines were predominant; for a society in which famine, epidemics, and violence made death imminent, blood constituted one of the fundamental values.

—Michel Foucault[1]

Introduction: The Meaning of Blood Feud and Blood Money

According to Eritrean traditional law, a crime against a person gives rise to a private question, which can be solved with *lex talionis* (blood feud), or be settled with conciliation and monetary compensation. The essence of the blood feud–blood money system is that the family of the victim has the right to take satisfaction by itself for the damage suffered, either by inflicting on the offender a punishment comparable to the damage inflicted (retaliation), or through a system of price setting (blood price).[2]

Murder represents the paradigm of this conception. It gives rise to blood feud, *dam* (blood) in Tigrinya, between the lineage of the victim and of the murderer, a legal condition of hostility against the guilty person and those regarded as being jointly responsible.[3] Fear of the cost and damage caused by a feud is a very effective means of intergroup control, and therefore vengeance may be settled through payment of blood money (*gar*).[4]

The mechanism of blood feud–blood money is commonly presented as a major characteristic of small, kin-based societies.[5] With the lack of a centralized political/legal authority—which can provide sanctions to regulate relations between groups—and of a special body of law designed to regulate the powers of this authority, justice remains a ques-

73

tion both among groups and inside the group. A judge cannot impose a solution, but "he has to oblige the parties to find one by themselves."[6] It is a means of settling disputes and of regulating violence through precise rules and procedures.[7] It may be an efficient—in fact the only— way to solve a conflict in a situation where money or other goods are scarce. Evans Pritchard sees in it an important instrument of social control. It is the institution that creates the dynamic of fission/fusion of groups that is typical of segmentary societies. It facilitates equilibrium between segments; a new social order may emerge from opposition and conflict.[8]

For the purpose of this chapter, we assume that the terms revenge and vengeance are, on the whole, synonymous. We define them as institutionalized processes according to which the group (household, lineage, clan) has the right to obtain compensation for one of its members who has been harmed by one or more members of another group. Revenge is a personal question between the family of the victim and the family of the aggressor: the injury has to be vindicated in order to defend the group's honor. This can start a chain reaction, causing a permanent state of hostility between communities or groups, punctured by periodic violent episodes; this is more properly called feud.[9]

It is usually argued that *lex talionis*, establishing equivalence between offense and vengeance, constitutes an improvement on a system of vengeance without limitation, and that the introduction of blood money represents a further evolutionary step.[10] Of course this construct is vulnerable to the same criticism as the broader theory that produced it. Conti Rossini is certainly indebted to this framework. He describes blood feud as typical of "barbaric" pre-state societies, where the settlement of criminal matters is the prime domain and responsibility of the family and lineage. Gradually, the concept of blood money—a more "modern" and "evolved" practice—was introduced. Retaliation would be a way of settling a dispute that inexorably led to the use of violence as a socially acceptable solution.[11] As the act of vengeance opens a new cycle of killing, a vendetta may ensue and result in the complete extinction of a lineage.[12] For this reason, in order to find a satisfactory, bloodless resolution, the intervention of a third party was encouraged. Elders, religious authorities, or someone delegated by the king, all tried to foster the payment of blood money rather than the pursuit of vengeance. But the crime was still between two groups.[13] With the birth of the state and increasing pressure from a central government, it was thought that vengeance would be transformed into punishment, capital or otherwise, under the supervision of the state. In the last stage of "evolution," the state is able to consolidate and dominate exclusively the power of punishment and the exercise of justice.

At the beginning of the nineteenth century the highlands were in an intermediate stage "in which the slain man's kindred are no longer free to accept or refuse compensation at their will, but are expected to abandon the feud . . . on receiving a sum fixed . . . by custom."[14] The nascent state acts as a "night watchman," to borrow Ferdinand Lassalle's celebrated metaphor.

Some historical accounts argue that groups other than the highland ethnies were still at the blood feud stage. Conti Rossini has said that vengeance "absorbed in the past all material and moral energies of the Bogos (Bilein) people." Entire villages were destroyed because of it, and sometimes the cycle of vengeance continued until all the parties were exhausted, often after a period of many years.[15] A pertinent Bilein expression is "blood does not age." In other words, a feud will never die unless it is avenged.[16] Among the Beni Amir, reports Münzinger in the nineteenth century, blood vengeance was commonly practiced, and was seldom substituted by blood money.[17] In Kunama society at the beginning of the last century, there were a large number of blood crimes. The accusation of a woman soothsayer (ascilmina) that a death was due to witchcraft was enough to instigate a feud.[18] Killing was considered to be a mark of honor. A special ornament, called gasciam, was given as a reward to the admirer who had been a killer.[19] Chains of vendettas were also common among the Saho, as well as among the Hedareb. Blood money was paid only rarely in the later ethnie—records show it happening only once during the Italian times, and once when the ELF was active in the area. The Hedareb say that vengeance was preferred because once the murderer is killed, peace can be guaranteed; blood money can initiate a chain of bitterness that can destroy a family, clan, or larger group.[20]

It is noticeable that an identical explanation is usually given to justify payment of blood money rather than vengeance in almost every other ethnie. The fact that both sides use analogous arguments makes us wonder whether the real reason must logically lie elsewhere. Sometimes in the Western world, a judge, in passing sentence, seeks to rationalize *a posteriori* a decision that is carried out primarily for policy reasons. It is possible that we are in the presence of a similar mechanism. A hypothesis might be that, among the Hedareb, there was little or no goods circulating. Therefore, it was much easier to carry out vengeance than be involved in the complicated economic transactions that blood money entailed.

The evolutionary framework used by colonial authors, epitomized by the writing of Conti Rossini, is much debated. Influenced by Darwin, Durkheim, and Weber, scholars have developed an influential paradigm of legal evolution. Durkheim argues that society is first in a state of mechanical solidarity characterized by punitive law and repressive sanctions. A later stage is organic solidarity; here retributive law becomes predominant.[21] Weber sees the "law minded bureaucrat" as an apostle of modernity, striking down the pre-modern intrusive irrationalities of nepotism, social status, and personal exploitation of official position.[22]

Many scholars have challenged these theories. Nonet and Selznick have argued that legal systems can and do move effortlessly from one type of law to another.[23] Maine's monumental work on the development of law starting from the organization of family and kinship has frequently been regarded as a classic of evolutionism. However, as one of his most celebrated commentators pointed out, "not one of his books professed on the face of it to account for the ultimate origin of human laws . . . or to connect the science of law with any theory . . . of social development."[24] He can more persuasively be read in a different way; in his work on the early state he argues that ancient laws sometimes describe "an immense system of money compensation for homicide, and with few exceptions, as large a scheme of compensation for minor injuries."[25] He explains this as a consequence of the lack of distinction in these societies between offenses against the state and offenses against the individual (*crimina* and *delicta*). The injured person can only proceed "against the wrong-doer by an ordinary civil action, and recovers compensation in the shape of money-damages if he succeeds."[26]

Whitman, more recently, also argues that the two systems would have coexisted from early times, and were never mutually exclusive. According to him, the concern of the early state was not first and foremost the control of violence but the control of payments in money.[27] "Some sort of vengeance or vendetta system *must* lie somewhere in the background of our earliest sources; . . . but the truth . . . is only partial."[28] For alongside vengeance penalties, the archaic sources also establish monetary penalties, at least as "a ransom option."[29] We can observe, moreover, that capital punishment may actually represent the most efficient way, in terms of rapidity and exemplary action, of settling conflicts in a system that has not developed a penitentiary system and in which the lack of security and openness of traditional houses (*hudmo/tukul*) rendered detention practically impossible.[30] Posner claims that a transition from retaliation to compensation is simply because of growing wealth. A system of compensation needs to operate so that murderers and their kin have a sufficient stock of goods in excess of their subsistence needs to be able to pay compensation for the injuries they inflict on others.[31] Today in some parts of the Arab world traditional pre-Islamic laws relating to blood feud and money are still preserved side by side with *šarī'a* and modern secular law.[32]

As Rubinstein points out, "it is clear that human violence and aggression cannot adequately be accounted for in terms of relatively simple models, and that it is essential to appreciate their complex and multicausal nature." An approach that adequately deals with a problem from the micro to the macro level gives us the greatest understanding. In explaining violence we take into account local, political, social, and cultural factors. We also try to understand how agreement is reached through the interaction of individual actors, and how social orders are all to some degree "negotiated orders."[33]

Murder: The Framework

Using a logical approach, we begin by examining murder through the lenses of the codes we have collected. We use them as a framework, relying on secondary sources only when this is necessary because of the lack of relevant primary material, and only after we have carried out our preliminary analysis. Among the secondary sources, we limit ourselves to those proven to be the result of serious field research and not serving the author's agenda—covert or overt. Only after the examination of historical sources has been carried out will we see if some general conclusions can be drawn.

Traditions differ from region to region, and we deal with several different commentators, who often give conflicting descriptions of the "same" tradition. As far as possible, we try to look for points of agreement, and we indicate when necessary if a tradition is specific to one location. By and large, for the ethnies other than Tigrinya, there is only one code to examine, and usually only two (at most) serious commentators to appraise. So the detailed comparative study that we undertake in the highlands is not feasible for the lowlands.

In a previous chapter we attempted to define the boundaries between groups such as clans, lineages, and households. This is a difficult exercise, bound to be somewhat imprecise. As we have seen, the terminology is not uniform throughout all codes and among all ethnies (sometimes *enda* is used to indicate the lineage, sometimes the entire clan), and the translation of the codes into a Western language by different hands does not help. In blood questions, this distinction is extremely important because the basic ethnic unit usually constitutes the limit to the exercise of vengeance.

A kindred group has been described as "a group within which there is no blood feud. If a man kills one of his own kin, either he is put to death by his own people or he becomes an outlaw."[34] As we detail further on, murder within a kindred group is in some cases fully exempt from punishment. But the problem remains of understanding how large this kindred group is. In particular, the prohibition against carrying on a blood feud within the family sometimes entails a small (nuclear or extended) family, and sometimes a lineage, or even the entire clan. This chapter reflects these difficulties.

As we start our analysis with the codes, it becomes apparent that the right to vengeance is rarely mentioned. This can be interpreted in at least three ways. First, the relative lack of a "right to blood vengeance" stated in the codes can be evidence that money compensation in ancient times was more prevalent than is commonly thought, and indeed could have been the preferred alternative (of course in a system where there were sufficient goods and money to be exchanged). It has been observed that bloodshed would represent the exception in a blood feud system, being necessary only when the system had failed and social norms had not worked.[35] For example, among the Kunama, a lowland ethnie (under continuous attack from highland people) that frequently carried out bloody raids upon enemies, murder was preferably dealt with through blood money and the entire community worked toward a peaceful settlement. In their traditional law, special rules were also designed to avoid a feud. Conti Rossini, at the beginning of the twentieth century, observed that in the highlands, "the old barbaric violence is disappearing and normally the punishment is a [. . .] pecuniary compensation." The decision to exact blood money rather than vengeance is "left by the judge to the offended family."[36] Many other examples will follow throughout the chapter.[37]

Second, the lack of references in the codes to the right of vengeance could have been because a blood feud was openly discouraged by religion and state, two actors that, for much of the period we are discussing, profoundly influenced all ethnies. As a consequence, when the codes were being written down, the practice was beginning to disappear. Conti Rossini recollects that at the time of king Suseynyos, a Father Paez obtained from the king a ruling to stop executions carried out by the family of the victim.[38]

Third, as we mentioned earlier, "traditional codes" usually concentrate on disputed questions. The fact that vengeance is not mentioned in the codes could mean that there was no need to rule on something which formed an important part of everyday life and whose procedure was known perfectly well by all members of the community.

When a Murder Does Not Initiate a Blood Feud: War, Murders Within the Family, and the Relevance of Class

The mechanism of vengeance is activated only when there is a certain social distance between the murderer and the victim. If this distance is too large, a war is possible; if it is too short, usually there is no vengeance.[39] The difficulty for the analyst lies in ascertaining where the line is to be drawn. Anthropologists have created a tripartite distinction between feud and war, both activities being highly formalized and ritualized. But first, with regard to the structural distance between groups, in a feud the ties are close enough to demand revenge in a case of murder, but far enough apart to allow for hostility without a total disruption of social life. Second, in a feud, reconciliation of the parties can occur through the use of arbitration, whereas wars are often a "winner takes all" situation. Third, in a feud, compensation often substitutes for retaliation.[40]

The Kunama and Nara, possibly because they were in a situation of permanent hostility with people of the highlands, and the Beja, have traditions that exemplify quite clearly how the right and duty of vengeance is connected to certain blood relations and not to others. Among them, to kill someone who belonged to the same ethnie or to an allied ethnie gave rise to liability only within the group. To kill an enemy was never a crime, and raids were allowed and encouraged. In the past, they were ordered by the *mohaber*, which also blessed the raiders. The operation had to be performed according to rules that were deeply ritualized and influenced by magic. On returning to their village, the raiders were welcomed back as heroes.[41]

Bilein traditions are even more detailed. The ethnie comprised three divisions. The most inclusive tie was composed of all the descendants of Ghebre Terke, the mythical founder; this division was called either ʿad, *idin* (descent) or *faraʾa* and *kaw* (men, people, tribe). They agreed to follow a common law, and did not fight one another, but they were not responsible for each other in blood questions. The second subdivision, called *therk* (meaning blood money), comprised male descendants to the seventh degree. This division is the one that mattered in blood questions and marriage payments. The nuclear family, called *beit* or *ciba*, was composed of father, son and brothers, and formed the third and smallest subdivision. In blood questions each component was considered equal, but crimes within the family were usually exempted from punishment.[42]

Usually, in traditional codes we do not find specific rules on war. This is not surprising since the codes are intended to apply within the ethnie or village; war involves much wider and complex relations. The closest analogue of war is raid, which is dealt with at great length in the *Fetha Mahari*. Unfortunately, the text is sometimes problematic, one example being article 45, which declares that raids are carried out in a "foreign country." It is not absolutely clear whether foreign country refers to land "outside the territory of the Mensa," or any land outside the village.

The raid involved a sophisticated ritual. The paragraphs dealing with the procedure to be followed show that religion and traditions are interacting. The leader turned toward his village and expressed the hope that God and Mary would bless the raid. When the party was close to the village to be raided, its leader announced, "will you raid with the help of God!" When he took the first cow, he cut off the tip of the tail and said, "this is for Mary" (§§2–3).[43]

A full range of rules is dedicated to murder committed "within the family." But again we are not entirely sure what is meant by "family," so we present the sources as we find them, with minimum commentary: when they do not specify, we leave open whether the *enda*, lineage, or family is involved. Murders within the family are usually exempted from vengeance.[44] This is a consequence of the absence of anyone who is entitled to exercise the feud (the perpetrator and the persons offended by the crime are in law the same) and of the need to keep the group intact as much as possible. The family has lost one of its members but the opening of a feud would put the entire community at serious risk.

In the highlands, if a man killed his wife he had no obligation other than paying blood money to her family.[45] The same applied if a father killed his daughter. In theory the mother should exercise the vengeance, but she cannot do it in practice because she is under the authority of her husband. As far as infanticide is concerned, for example to hide the evidence of adultery, this was not punished. The same rule pertained in the case of a voluntary abortion of a fetus conceived as a result of an adulterous liaison. An exception applied in the case of abortion when it was possible to prove it had taken place as a consequence of a poison given to the woman by her lover: this case was considered equivalent to poisoning the woman, and her husband, who is entitled to act for the woman, can kill her lover in the same way.[46]

In the earliest versions of the Bilein traditions, murder within a family could be punished by relatives, but only if the murderer was caught in the act. Later on, consideration was given to whether the deceased had children. If he had children, blood money was paid. If he did not, after a period of exile from the village, the murderer was allowed to return without paying the blood money and could even inherit the deceased's property according to standard rules of inheritance. This ensured that assets remained within the family. At betrothal, a woman entered into the family of the husband, but ties with her blood family were not dissolved completely. As a consequence, if a husband or boyfriend killed his wife or girlfriend, half of the blood money was remitted to the father. Conversely, a father who killed his daughter paid half to the husband or boyfriend.[47]

With regard to the Mensa, the entire clan constituted the unit within which the feud could not be exercised. The feud applied only if the murderer and deceased belonged to different clans, even though there was strong pressure toward social control, perhaps as a consequence of the influence for some centuries of "a head of clan, who is appointed, or at least confirmed by a major foreign power"; this led them to allow his intervention in blood questions.[48]

Blood crimes within the family were rare among the Haso. Whoever killed his father was left without inheritance and banned, but blood vengeance—called *bilo*—could not be carried out. The same punishment was given to a man who killed his son, while if a woman was murdered by her husband, the family of the husband paid to the woman's family half of the blood price.[49] Uniquely among the Hedareb, if a husband killed his wife he in turn was killed. But if either the mother or father killed their children, no action was taken.[50]

Among Kunama and Nara the rule that no vengeance could be exacted if the murder occurred within the family varied significantly from all other ethnies. Immunity was extended to a woman who killed her husband or her son through abortion or infanticide and to the village doctor who provided a woman with traditional medicine with which to abort her fetus.[51] Since the Kunama and Nara were matrilineal societies, the maternal family is the party offended by the crime and therefore the party that has to ask for blood—see the later section.[52]

A significant limitation to the opening of a blood question can be found among ethnies divided into social classes, where usually a murder gives rise to a feud only when the culprit and the deceased belong to the same class, or when the deceased belongs to a class superior to that of the murderer.

We will lay down in detail the rules about the Mensa, which are paradigmatic for these ethnies. "If a noble, with or without premeditation kills another noble, the murder cannot be compensated, and the murderer is strangled" (art. 77§1). The same rule applied if a vassal or a slave killed a vassal (§2). But if a noble killed someone belonging to an inferior class, only the blood price was paid. A distinction in the amount was made if the deceased was subject to him, or to a third person (see below on the amount of blood money). On the other hand, "if a noble kills his vassal or slave, he does not have to pay, because they are his property" (§6). "The slave who murders someone is strangled, but if he manages to escape, his lord is not responsible for the murder the slave has committed" (§5).[53] Article 77§4 of the *Fetha Mahari* deals with the position of a foreigner or stranger who kills a Mensa noble: in this case, "either a vendetta is started between the two groups, or blood money is paid."

From a reading of the article we conclude that murder within the clan could not be compensated with money unless it involved a victim of an inferior class and a murderer of a superior. But if a foreigner or stranger murdered a Mensa noble, compensation rather than blood feud was possible. This could be because of a wish to lessen the risk of future feuds and to avoid the extension of feuds already in progress. Probably here class was the prime factor in determining what action had to be taken.

The rules on murder among the Beni Amir followed the same rationale as the Mensa. Vengeance was carried out only when the offender belonged to the same class as the deceased. The noble who killed someone from an inferior class was originally exempted from any penalty. However, if it was the other way around, the murderer would have been killed, his property would be confiscated, and his family would lose status. Killing a slave was not a cause for blood feud; if a slave murdered someone, he had to be killed by his master.[54]

Blood Feud: Persons Entitled to Exercise It and Legitimate Targets

The right of vengeance (*heniè fadaya*) pertains in principle to each adult male of the lineage of the victim against every adult male of the lineage of the murderer. The existence of someone who has the right or duty of vengeance is of fundamental importance: he is the only man who can legally exercise it without opening a new blood question.[55] There was a perfect correspondence between the members of the lineage who had the right and duty to participate in revenge and those who shared in blood money if one of them was slain.

In the Tigrinya the avenger was selected from males having a blood tie up to seven generations with the victim.[56] There was a hierarchy of entitled men: first in line was the closest blood relative of the deceased; if there were none, the adopted child; and failing this, the servant. Sometimes also the "traveling companion" had this right, or any member of the village, if the deceased had no relatives.[57] In the Mensa, if the vassal or slave did not have a family, his master carried it out.[58] Tronvoll reported in the 1990s that around the town of Segeneiti in Akele Guzai, revenge or payback killing could be carried out only by an emancipated man (*hadaro wetsui*), someone who had been formally freed by his father, thereby becoming a landholder.[59]

The target had to be a male having blood relations with the murderer; he had to be about the same age as the victim. Disabled people could not be targets.[60] If the murderer was unknown to the victim's relatives, it appears that in more ancient times all of the ʿ*addi* of the murderer could have been targeted, either for vengeance or for the payment of blood money. A possible relic of this liability appears to be the following custom, reported by Conti Rossini as still enforced in his time. Soldiers were billeted in the village where the crime had been committed and remained there until the murderer was disclosed. The governor could also ask them to present the murderer within a certain time, warning them that if this did not happen, they would all be obliged to pay compensation. The village—at least in some regions—could be freed from this obligation by making an oath involving seven witnesses, who also had the duty to give to the family of the victim five *ferghi* (home spun cloth) as a kind of indemnity for its lack of vigilance.[61]

Among the Bogos responsibility in the case of blood feud involved *therk*, male descendants to the seventh degree. They were collectively responsible for the murder committed by or perpetrated upon any of them. In the nuclear family, each member was considered equal. If the culprit could not be found, another was taken.[62] In exceptional cases a murderer could be expelled from *therk*, which was a particularly serious punishment in a society where lineage and kinship ties were so powerful; to sever these ties was equivalent to disarming him. A member of *therk* could avoid collective responsibility by attaching his sandals to the point of a spear and declaring that he wanted to be separated from the family. If this occurred, his relatives had no liability for the action if he murdered someone; conversely they had no right over his blood if he was murdered.[63]

If a Beni Amir woman was murdered, vengeance fell to her relatives but not to her husband. It is possible that this rule was a relic of a former matrilineal society.[64] We have found the same rule in the Kunama and Nara. Vengeance could be demanded and performed only by a brother (of the same mother) of the deceased, by his sons, by the son of a sister, or by the uncle and maternal cousins. The rest of the community interfered only insofar as conciliation was involved.[65] If a woman was killed, vengeance was first of all the responsibility of her children, and if she had no children, to her full brother, or to the son of one of her sisters; never to the husband, except when the woman was killed in his presence.[66] The only legitimate targets for vengeance, in addition to the murderer, were relatives of his maternal line to three generations back, including children of both sexes.[67]

In general, women were not allowed to participate in the feud, either as legitimate avengers or targets. For example, according to the *Fethesh Mogaresh*, if a Bilein woman was accused of murder, the person to be targeted was whichever male was her "protector."[68] More complex rules applied to Kunama and Nara, where women, in some occurrences, might be targeted. So, on the one hand, women who entered the family through marriage were excluded because they did not share the same blood. Women who left the family because of marriage were also exempt. On the other hand, unmarried women of the same family as the murderer were responsible.

Another principle is that, as far as possible, the vendetta should be carried out on someone of the same sex as the victim. However, if a Kunama or Nara woman performed the murder, she could be targeted only if she was of the same personal and marital status as the deceased. If her victim was a man, the feud was carried out on one of her male blood relatives. If the woman killed a woman of a different personal or marital status, a relative of the murderer with a status comparable to that of the victim was targeted.[69]

Relevance to the Intention of the Culprit, to Age, and to Other Special Conditions

As a rule, the blood feud system, being interested only in retribution—the equal punishment inflicted by the group offended on the offender and his group—does not take into account either the criminal intent (if the murder is voluntary or not), the age of the culprit, or any special conditions in which the murder has been committed. This appears to be, at least at first sight, the case in most Eritrean traditional laws. In some it is expressly stated that murder, whether intentional or unintentional, is treated in the same way. For example, the law of *Adkeme Melega*, in its version of 1912, states that if somebody is killed "intentionally or unintentionally, the family of the deceased, if conciliation does not take place, has the right to vindicate the death with the blood of the offender" (art. 66§6).[70] Incidentally, the very fact that the two classes are separate from one another indicates that the drafters of the code were aware of a distinction between them.

Also among the Bilein, no relevance was given to the intent of the culprit. For example, if the killing was the result of a gun misfiring, or perpetrated by a mad person or a child, the same rule applied.[71] Among the Hedareb, a person who killed in self-defense was as likely to become a target for vengeance as a willful murderer.[72]

However, other traditional laws do contain a graduation of penalties according to the intention of the culprit and the circumstances in which the death took place. For these instances it would be inappropriate to force tradition into a classical model of blood feud.[73] So, for example, with regard to Akele Guzai, some relevance to *mens rea* is found in *Mai Adgi* and *Zeban Serao Ennadocò* laws. According to article 20 of *Mai Adgi*, "blood money was not due if the deceased went into a house in order to steal." According to article 14 of *Zeban Serao Ennadocò* law, "if the murder was not voluntary, the murderer has the right to ask all of the inhabitants of the village to participate in the payment."[74] Relevance to the intention becomes even more explicit in the recent code of *Adgena Tegeleba* (1954), where article 158 lays down different punishments for intentional and unintentional murder. Moreover, a different penalty was applied in the case of attempted murder (arts. 156–157).

The code of *Saharti, Lamza, Uocarti*, established that "with regard to the liability of the person who has to pay blood money, the age shall be taken into consideration."[75] The logical implication of this rule is that minors were not liable to be targeted, to take part in vengeance, or to pay or receive blood money, or at least that their liability was reduced because of age.

Among the Kunama, no relevance is given in principle to diminished circumstances, because "blood asks for blood and who kills must be killed."[76] However, compensation is obtained more readily if they are present. For example, if the murder took place between children, the *mohaber* had to decide case by case if the culprit had to be considered responsible for his action. If he was deemed not to be liable, no blood price had to be paid. If murder was committed in self-defense, vengeance was not excluded, but in this case it was easier to settle the dispute through compensation.[77]

The Execution

By no means could an execution be carried out without strict observance of the procedure laid down in traditional law. An important principle in the highlands was that the death penalty, inflicted and executed by the relevant authorities, extinguished the blood feud. According to Conti Rossini a sentence of capital punishment was originally imposed by the lineage meeting in a special assembly. Later on its competence was transferred to the head of the ethnie. The government or any third party could not carry out the execution; to do so would have meant that it had entered into a blood question with the family of the murderer.

The culprit was apprehended either by the family of the deceased or by the responsible authority. If the responsible authority found the murder charge to be true, it authorized the family of the deceased to exercise vengeance.[78] The murderer was given the option of requesting that a lottery take place to decide who among his family members was to die, but any of his family members could ask the king to be exempted from the lottery.[79]

In theory, the murderer should have been killed (following a pattern of perfect retaliation) in the same manner as the victim was murdered. But in practice, hanging and strangling were the most common methods. This was because of another principle rooted in traditional law that the feud should not be reopened by the spilling of additional blood. Tigrinya, Bilein, Mensa, Kunama, and Nara followed this rule.[80] For the same reason, in the Kunama and Nara, murder by poisoning could not be punished by blood feud; blood had not been spilled and therefore the murderer had to be poisoned.[81]

If the first attempt at execution failed, vengeance was usually considered to have been satisfied. The same principle applied to executions carried out by a supreme tribunal or by the king (we shall never know which tribunal or king: Conti Rossini relies upon a multiplicity of informants in different periods). There were no time limits for carrying out vengeance.

The treatment of a murderer among the Bogos depended on whether or not he was caught in the act. In the first case, the family settled the matter. In the second, the suspect was taken to the head of the *kaw*, who, after hearing persuasive witnesses and accusers, condemned him to death. The family of the deceased carried out the penalty by hanging the culprit on a tree, and pushing him three times. This act extinguished the feud: if he remained alive, he was a free man. If he managed to escape punishment, a member of his immediate family could be taken instead. No woman could be killed.[82]

An Alternative Path: The Settlement of Blood Disputes through Compensation

The customary laws we have consulted pay special attention to the settlement of disputes through the payment and enforcement of a system of compensation. We will speculate later on in this chapter on the reasons for the presence of so many rules, but we suggest at this stage that they support our view that the systems of feud and money compensation coexisted from early times; they were never mutually exclusive. The elders of the ethnie, and later on the church, would have favored this form of resolution.

To conclude a question of blood, two acts were always necessary: the forgiveness of the crime and the payment of blood money.[83] Possibly a third act, a marriage, would be arranged between a girl belonging to the lineage of the murderer and a man of the family of the deceased.[84] The dispute was sometimes settled through the intervention and mediation of the church.

The initiative for conciliation had to be taken by the murderer's family, who had to contact the family of the victim and ask for pardon. If the victim's family was unwilling to receive them, the church and/or the elders may have attempted to mediate to prevent the feud. If the mediation was successful, the murderer prostrated himself on his forehead before the victim's family and begged to be forgiven. To solemnize the end of the feud, the family of the murderer gave a banquet, and the two families signed an agreement.[85] According to the law of *Adkeme Melega,* the culprit had to surrender himself with rope and knife—the traditional methods of vengeance—to the victim's kin. Seven elders and the priest had to beg for forgiveness on his behalf.[86] Only after the conciliation procedures had been exhausted did the payment of the blood money become possible, and the feud ended.

Multiple sources agree that the Kunama and Nara practiced blood feuds to a lesser extent than highland peoples; vendettas usually did not last for long, and when they took place, to protect the interest of the community, they were treated as a personal affair and could not be carried out in public. A peaceful settlement through reconciliation was favored, and more easily obtained because of the pressure of the entire community.[87] The strong desire of the Kunama and Nara to not be harmed by a long-running dispute is possibly a consequence of their numerical inferiority and continuous exposure to aggression by other ethnies. They needed to be compact and not waste their energies by feuding among themselves.

Another rule designed to limit the feud was the granting of asylum to a murderer. If after the crime the murderer managed to escape to somebody's house, he received protection, and his protectors had to accompany him out of their own territory until he reached safety. Other special places, such as a holy grove, cemeteries, and venues where assemblies were held offered him the same asylum. Whoever tried to follow the murderer into one of these sanctuaries could be murdered by anybody in the community, and no blood feud or money could be demanded in this case. It is interesting here to draw the analogy with the institutions of sanctuary mentioned in Exodus 21:12–14 and cities of refuge in Numbers 35:11–28, that also provide legal protection for one accused of murder. In the medium term, this asylum was extended to relatives of the culprit; they could find refuge in another village to which the community escorted them.[88]

Exile was usually considered to be a sufficient punishment for the murderer.[89] After some years he was allowed to come back home and through the elders ask for mediation with the family of the deceased. This was usually granted and on the settlement day the murderer visited the house of the deceased. Here a sterile cow was sacrificed. The murderer and the legitimate avenger drank beer, ate together from the same dish, and eventually exchanged their clothes. In this way peace was sealed. This practice appears to have the same effect as that of ending a blood feud with a marriage alliance between the families: it creates affinity between the two families.[90]

The above rules applied if the identity of the murderer was known. If the culprit was unknown, the family of the deceased carried out an investigation with the assistance of the village elders. If the clues led them into another community's territory, the entire community was responsible if the murderer was not delivered to the family of the deceased.[91] The rule does not indicate whether compensation was paid in this case. However, an elderly respected authority on the Tigrinya *Loggo-Chewa* affirms that if a wrongful act was committed and the perpetrator was unknown, the village at large was responsible for compensating the victim.[92]

If the identity of the murderer is uncertain, no evidence is admitted apart from a solemn and binding oath. Evidence by witnesses was not legal proof even though in practice occasionally their statements were heard and used.[93] If the murderer was only suspected of the crime, he could prove his innocence by giving a solemn and binding oath. This had the character of a judgment by God and was the only legal evidence admitted in a case of murder, the use of witnesses not being permitted.[94] We find similar rules in the Mensa: "if a man, who had been accused of homicide, did not confess to the crime, he can only be allowed to remain free after giving a solemn oath" (art. 77§8).[95] Conti Rossini adds some further details; he sees the ceremony as a relic of the ancient liability of the group. The chief of the clan asked fifty men and five women of good reputation, including the wife or a relative of the accused, to perform the oath. A delegate of the chief accompanied the group to a priest, who took a member of the group by the hand and stood at the door as witness. The other fifty four oath takers then entered the "House of Mary" and repeated three times a formula of innocence proposed by the accuser. If one of the fifty-four refused to perform the oath, the crime was proven.

In the *Loggo-Chewa*, "if a man is suspected of murder but swears his innocence, he must be compensated with ten *ferghi* by the accuser" (art. 30).[96] This is an example of the immense importance and sacred nature of oath among the Tigrinya: not only does it extinguish the feud—compensation is given to the man who performs it. A similar rule is reported for the Bilein. If a man was only suspected of murder, the family of the deceased could ask him to perform a solemn oath in a trial. If he did this he was free.[97] If a murder took place within the same clan, sixty elders, relatives, and witnesses went to the house of the bereaved in order to settle the case. If the killing involved different clans, 120 elders, relatives, and witnesses were required.[98]

In Bilein society, if magic was used and the victim died, in addition to paying blood money, the murderer and his family were exiled.[99] This indicates the great importance placed on magic. There was considerable fear of magical powers; it was believed that these were shared among certain family circles. The Bilein were concerned that such powers could be used for evil against every other member of the community. Such crimes therefore justified a harsher treatment.

Amount of Blood Money

The number of rules contained in the codes on the amount of compensation shows more concern over the monetary value that should be attached to the human body and its parts than whether a feud should be initiated.[100] The presence of so many rules seems to indicate that compensation at the time, far from being an exceptional occurrence, constituted a concrete alternative to feud.

The older codes of Akele Guzai fixed the amount at 120 MTD, with few exceptions.[101] *Mehen Mahaza* doubled the blood money if a traveler was murdered (see later in this chapter). And *Mai Adgi* specified that it was customary for blood money for a boy to be settled at half of that of a man.[102] Articles 156–162 of the *Adgena Tegeleba* customary law lay down fixed blood money payments for various types of intentional and unintentional homicide.[103] This was the most comprehensive and recent law of the highlands. Attempted murder was punished differently from a consummated murder. Another distinction was drawn between voluntary and involuntary murder. In the first case the blood price was set at 500 MTD, and in the second at 1,000 MTD (art. 158).[104] In Seraye and Hamasien, blood price varied, with the most common measure being 120 *ferghi*, later on commuted into MTD.[105] We can find no reference in the codes to a lesser amount of blood money being paid for the murder of a woman. This is a major difference with *sarīᶜa*, where women invariably are assessed at half the blood price of a man.

According to Conti Rossini, among the Bogos, blood money differed according to the social class of the deceased, but it always had to be given in head of cattle.[106] The compensation to be paid by the murderer of a Bet Targe was 120 head of cattle to the victim's family, half of the cattle being slaughtered for a banquet.[107]

In the Mensa, Pollera alleged that blood money was assessed at a very high level: 800 cows or 1,600 MTD, and that because of the large sum involved, it was often paid over a period of many years.[108] The blood price among the Beni Amir for killing a nobleman was fixed at 200 cows and a horse. The price for other classes was not fixed.[109] In the most recent version of their law of 1960, we find no mention of blood vengeance. Article 1 deals with blood money and reads: "[W]hoever causes the death of a human being intentionally or unintentionally, he shall be bound to pay blood money amounting to Eth. $2600.00 according to the provisions of the Mohammedan . . . law which is in force in the country."[110] This indicates that the colonial powers may have been quite successful in convincing the Beni Amir elders to renounce the blood feud and replace it with monetary compensation. Elsewhere the traditional law of the Asaorta (art. 10) reads, "in the past whoever committed murder was either killed, or blood money was paid in an amount to be determined case by case. The *rachbe* knows that this is not admitted by the Government, and submits to its laws."[111]

Among the Haso clan of the Saho, only on exceptional occasion could blood money be paid. In ancient times it was set at a very high price and comprised seventy-seven cows and considerable other goods and cash. At the time Conti Rossini was writing, an attempt was made to reduce this amount. If a woman was killed, the price was less, but Conti Rossini does not specify the amount. It could be argued that the setting of a very high price in blood money was done deliberately to allow no real alternative to vengeance. Among the Minifere, blood money, set at 100 camels according to Islamic rules, was in practice reduced by half and paid in cash. The blood price paid for the killing of a fellow Minifere was considerably higher than that of killing neighboring Tigrinya speakers.[112]

Very modest, at least when compared to other ethnies, was the amount of blood money to be paid for the murder of a Kunama and Nara. It was fixed in the early 1930s at fifteen cows, ten of which could be "converted" into goats and clothes.[113]

Persons Obliged to Pay Blood Money . . .

As we might expect in a system that gave considerable relevance to compensation, Eritrean traditions contain a number of rules regarding the persons entitled to give and to receive blood money.[114] The codes run the whole gamut from cases where blood money is paid by the whole tribe, a principle followed for example by the Beni Amir and Hadendowa, to the case when only the murderer is responsible for payment.[115]

Between these two extremes, all possible combinations are explored. According to *Enda Fegrai*, "all the lineage of the murderer must concur to the payment" (art. 15§13).[116] It is an obligation that the lineage cannot avoid. The evolutionists would argue that this is the rule predating individual liability. The law of *Adkeme Melega* set a similar liability. Conciliation takes place between the family of the deceased and the murderer, who is expressly given the "right to demand the contribution of the entire lineage" (art. 66§8). The *danya* who is responsible for conciliation receives an honorarium (art. 66§10).[117] This rule shows a situation in which the dispute is settled with the help of a third party, who is paid for his service. Maine has commented on a similar case (with reference to Homer's trial scene in the *Iliad*) where the judge "claimed a share in the compensation awarded to the plaintiff simply as the fair price of . . . [his] time and trouble."[118]

Other laws present a kaleidoscope of rulings that would be tempting to read as a common trend toward personalizing the liability. According to article 14 of *Zeban Serao Ennadocò*, "whoever commits unintentional homicide has the right to ask all villagers to help him pay the blood money."[119] This right is not set for intentional murder, and the whole village is involved, rather than a specific *enda*.

The collective liability of the lineage is matched with a concurrent principle of individual liability for at least a part of the total amount in *Mehen Mahaza* and *Adgena Tegeleba* laws. The *Mehen Mahaza* law provides that of the blood money payable—amounting to 120 MTD—10 MTD should be paid personally (in cash) by the murderer, and "the lineage must help him to make up the difference" (art. 32§7).[120] Article 159 of the *Adgena Tegeleba* code, after stating that the payment for murder is divided between the victim and his family group, gives a different rule in the case of unintentional murder. A guilty person "shall pay out of his own resources 120 MTD and the balance of 380 MTD will be paid by his family group. A person guilty of intentional homicide shall pay 240 MTD out of his own resources and the balance of 760 MTD shall be paid by his family group." This rule looks like a combination of *Zeban Serao Ennadocò* and *Mehen Mahaza* laws: it shares with the first the relevance given to the intention of the culprit, and with the second the separation between the amount that should be paid personally by the culprit and that paid with the help of the lineage.

Mai Adgi law, which is one of the most ancient codes, personalizes the payment. The murderer cannot request any help from the lineage: "all the blood money is paid personally by the murderer" (*Mai Adgi*, art. 20§10).[121] This is clearly a complete contradiction of the evolutionist argument. However, it is important to note that the "original" versions of the highland codes are no longer available. It is obvious that the oldest laws must have been amended many times before they reached the form fixed forever in the written versions that are available to us today. So we have at the moment no way of proving whether one code influenced another and, more importantly, if there is evidence of evolution from one type of punishment to another. It is a typical "chicken-egg" question.

Special rules are contained in *Mehen Mahaza* for women and serfs. We do not know if these rules were an expression of a wider principle that applied in the highlands. "If the murderer is an unmarried woman, the entire blood money is paid by her paternal lineage"; if she is married, "blood money shall be paid half by the paternal lineage . . . and half by the husband's lineage" (§§10-11). This is not surprising: with marriage, the woman enters into the family of the man, who from then on becomes responsible for her actions. The shared payment indicates that she keeps links with her natural family. What is more interesting is that the same rule was extended to serfs: if the murderer was a serf living with his master, the latter must pay half of the blood money; the family of the serf pays the other half "as if the master belonged to it" (§14).[122]

Among the Bilein all adult males of the family paid blood money in equal parts; the murderer was not asked to contribute more than anybody else. The dowry for a girl given as a spouse to end a feud was calculated in the same way.[123] In the Mensa, the payment of blood money was the moral duty of all whose blood relationship to the murderer went back to the seventh generation, and it was divided in diminishing proportion to the degree of kinship.[124] In Rodén the rule is shown very differently: the sons of the same father and their cousins were collectively responsible for the payment of the blood money together with the murderer.[125] If the relatives of the murderer belonged to two different clans, the clan on his father's side paid two-thirds of the blood money, and the clan on his mother's side the rest.[126]

. . . and to Receive Blood Money

As a rule, those in the patrilineal line of descent of the victim had the right to participate in the allotment of blood money, just as they had the right and obligation to participate in the feud.[127] The codes fixed how the sum was to be shared within the family of the deceased. Some traditional laws allocated the money to the entire lineage. For example, in Seraye, according to *Mehen Mahaza* law, blood money had to be paid to the lineage of the deceased, and then shared within the family in the following way: "[T]en dollars must be given in cash to the father, in his absence to the brother, in his absence to the paternal uncle of the deceased. The remaining [which can be in cash or goods] is shared equally among all members of the victim's descent group" (art. 32§5, §9).[128] *Enda Fegrai* gives a different hierarchy of allocation: "[T]o the sons of the deceased; in case there are no sons, to the father; if he is dead to the brothers; and, if there are no brothers, to the next closest relatives" (art. 15§15).[129]

The *Adgena Tegeleba* code tells how the money that has been paid by the murderer (from his resources) is to be shared. The procedure is different from the allocation of the remainder of the compensation that has been contributed by the murderer's family group. "The sum of 120 MTD or 240 MTD that is payable to the nearest relative of the deceased is to be paid firstly to the son, failing this to the father, then to the deceased's brother, and finally to the nearest relative on the paternal side. The balance of the blood money will be divided between the members of the deceased's family group who would have been called upon to share payment of blood-money in the case of homicide" (art. 160). The code does not give any rule for sharing money in a case of attempted murder. Probably the sum should be allocated, with a similar procedure, to the putative victim. Similarly, the law of *Loggo-Chewa* stated that half of the blood price had to be divided among the lineage of the deceased, and the other half given exclusively to close relatives (art. 29).[130] The rules of *Mai Adgi* law were the ones where personalizing was most evident: blood money—paid personally by the murderer— shall also be paid only "to the closest relatives of the deceased" (art. 20§11).[131]

Blood money was assessed in the same way for the murder of men, women, or serfs. But in the latter two categories there were differences about who was entitled to receive the payment. *Enda Fegrai* and *Mehen Mahaza* both contained a distinction based on whether the victim was an unmarried or married woman. In the case of an unmarried woman, the blood money had to be given entirely to the paternal lineage, while if she was married, it should go to the lineage of the husband, entirely (according to *Enda Fegrai*) or partially (according to *Mehen Mahaza*).[132] Among the Bilein, from the day of the betrothal, a woman's blood was divided between the two families: if she was kidnapped or murdered, the blood price went half to the father and half to the boyfriend or husband.[133] With regard to the murder of a serf, the law of *Mehen Mahaza* stated that only if the serf had been living with his master did the master have the right to receive a share equal to that of the family of the serf "as if the master belonged to it" (art. 32§15). The position of women and serfs was similar (see previous section): both categories "enter" into a "new family," which in exchange for protecting them acquires rights over their bodies and substance.[134]

The division into social classes of the Bilein complicates their rules on the allocation of the money within the family. If the deceased was a noble, his father or the closest relative received half, the other half being divided among all adult male relatives. If the victim was a vassal, blood money was shared in three parts, one-third going to his master, one-third to his father or his closest relative, and one-third divided among all adult male relatives. Blood money for the slave was given entirely to the master.[135]

The End of the Feud through Marriage

In addition to reconciliation and payment of blood money, peace was often secured by a marriage between a girl belonging to the lineage of the murderer and a man of the lineage of the victim. In the case of both parties, in principle, the closest relatives available had to be chosen. In practice, the two spouses were frequently selected by lot.[136] In this way, the victim's group could be re-established: a woman was given as compensation specifically so that she might give birth to a child who would replace the victim. The new blood ties prevented the continuation of a blood feud, which could have led to a chain of vendetta killings. The marriage was arranged "to disperse the blood that has been spread."[137] This practice, known in Tigrinya as *menketzdem*, was also common among Tigré, Beni Amir, and Bilein, and we come back to the practice in chapter 8.[138] We know that in order to avoid warfare, the branches of the Bilein were intermixed by various reciprocated marriages.[139] The Saho did not have this tradition, and we have seen no evidence of it taking place among other ethnies.

The Other Actors and Murder

Many of the traditions we have examined above were drawn up before the adherents were converted to Coptic Christianity, Islam, Catholicism, or the various Protestant churches that have established a toehold in Eritrea. The first inhabitants of Eritrea migrated there from the southern Nile Valley; Sabean migrants followed them about 1000 B.C. from the Arabian Peninsula. Later on, Egypt established an important political as well as a religious presence in much of the country from the Sudanese border through Keren to Massawa. All of these people have left traces of their customs, practices, and law. However, the Christian Church and Islam have had by far the major impact.

Pre-Islamic and Islamic culture continuously influenced Eritrea, as well as the rest of the Horn of Africa, just as the existing culture of the region affected local Islam. The customary laws that we have analyzed are versions that were agreed to after the arrival of Christianity and Islam. Since they were being continually revised, they could not have survived in a pristine form. It seems probable that the law of the Kunama prior to their conversion to Islam in the nineteenth century is the closest to the law of "indigenous" inhabitants that we can find.

The Axumite Empire was converted to Coptic Christianity in the fourth century A.D. Catholic missionaries began to play an important role from 1837 with the arrival in the country of Father Giuseppe Sapeto. Swedish Protestant missionaries came in 1872. Christianity and Islam are likely to have had at least an indirect effect on the periodic revision of traditional rules; those regarding blood money seem a paradigm case.

In the following pages we look at the references to blood feud and blood money contained in the Old Testament, the New Testament, and the *Fetha Negest*, as well as those of *šarīʿa*.

The Old Testament, the New Testament, the *Fetha Negest*, and Blood Feud

The God of the Old Testament is an avenging God, who allows vengeance but limits it to precise retaliation.[140] There are a number of biblical passages dealing with this. Just to mention some of the most important: "[A]nd if any mischief follow, then thou shalt give life for life, Eye for eye, tooth for tooth, hand for hand, foot for foot, Burning for burning, wound for wound, stripe for stripe" (Exodus 21:23–25); "he that killeth any man shall surely be put to death" (Leviticus 24:17); "thine eye shall not pity; but life shall go for life, eye for eye, tooth for tooth, hand for hand, foot for foot" (Deuteronomy 19:21). Vengeance in ancient Israelite society was primarily a private matter to be settled between families. Vengeance by the avenger of God of the injured family was the rule in cases of maiming and death, "the revenger of blood himself shall slay the murderer; when he meeteth him, he shall slay him" (Numbers 35:19).

However, sometimes a third party is mentioned. "[T]hen the congregation shall judge between the slayer and the revenger of blood according to these judgements" (Numbers 35:24). A tendency to mitigate these practices by giving authority to God or the king appears in Genesis 4:15 and 2 Samuel 14:1–24. According to Exodus 21:22, "If men strive, and hurt a woman with child, so that her fruit depart from her . . . he shall pay as the judges determine," and Leviticus 19:18 enjoins the people of Israel, "thou shalt not avenge." This is God's law, but the judge determines the punishment. We will see analogous principles operating in the Qurʾan.

In a famous passage, the New Testament states that vengeance should not be carried out by the individual who has been harmed. "[Y]e have heard that it hath been said, An eye for an eye, and a tooth for a tooth: But I say unto you, That ye resist not evil: but whosoever shall smite thee on thy right cheek, turn to him the other also" (Matthew 5:38–39). Saint Paul, in Romans 12:19, envisages that vengeance will be carried out by God: "[D]early beloved, avenge not yourself, but rather give place unto wrath; for it is written, Vengeance is mine; I will repay, saith the Lord." And according to Romans 13:4, a ruler will execute vengeance on God's behalf, "for he is the minister of God, a revenger to execute wrath upon him that doeth evil."

The *Fetha Negest* contains a wider range of circumstances that exclude or diminish liability than is found in the traditional codes.[141] The approach is highly casuistic. Among the exemptions are murders committed by "a person who does not have the use of his reason; someone who is seven years or younger, or someone who was drunk when the crime was committed." These individuals are considered as "not having the use of reason, [and consequently] they could not be killed." Also exempted is a murder committed by someone in self-defense, or by someone who acted on the order of a superior (in this case the superior is liable).[142]

On the other hand, some types of murders that were usually exempted from liability according to traditional law were punished under the *Fetha Negest*, for example, murders within the family. "[W]hoever kills his father . . . son . . . and his closest relatives, shall be handed over to punishment." Also, "if a master kills his serf he shall be killed." If the serf has committed a crime that deserves capital punishment, the master cannot carry out the penalty. If he disobeys, the master, in his turn, is liable to be sentenced to death. The punishment is clearly individualized: "fathers instead of children shall not be killed; the crime of the father has not to be bestowed on the son, nor the son's crimes on their fathers."[143] It is easy to find the source for these rules: Exodus 21:20 for the case of the serf, and Deuteronomy 24:16 for the relatives.

A special rule for murder committed with the use of magic, which we have seen among the Bilein (see the earlier section on the settlement of blood disputes through compensation), finds a counterpart in the *Fetha Negest*: whoever poisons somebody and "whoever invokes demons to kill people, shall be . . . sentenced to death [if death occurred]." However, if the perpetrator did not know that the substance was poisonous, he "will be expelled from the community and by the village, and . . . shall make penitence."[144]

The circumstances in which the murder has been committed and the intention of the culprit also play an important role. Murder with malice and murder without malice are not treated in the same manner: only in the first case is capital punishment applied. "If killing took place with a light instrument, which usually does not cause death, he [the culprit] shall be beaten and exiled." And "whoever beats an animal, and in the process kills a man. . . . his punishment shall be exile." "Whoever wants to kill another person and kills him/her . . . shall be executed, or the family of the victim shall agree on the payment of blood money or on pardon; and if he has not killed voluntarily, he shall be exiled."[145] A person's complicity in the crime is analyzed separately: when an offense is committed by a group of persons, "all shall be killed" On the other hand, "if one man kills a number of people, he shall be the only one to be killed" [and blood feud is superseded].[146]

Vengeance cannot be legitimately carried out by the avenger, but only through the judge. "[W]hoever vindicates a blood debt can not kill his enemy personally, but he shall take him to the judge, in order that the latter could judge him according to his crime."[147]

Rules contained in the highland codes are very similar to those in the Bible and in the *Fetha Negest*: retaliation with some sort of limitation. We leave to other scholars the task of investigating whether the principle of graduated retaliation was also followed for other crimes. We can argue that it is likely that the Bible and the *Fetha Negest* have influenced later versions of the Eritrean traditional law, or at least contributed to the *zeitgeist* of the times.

There are here two separate questions to be faced: that of the time and place where a certain set of rules was "invented," and how they influenced other rules at later times and in other places. Not too much can be said about the first problem; the origins of blood feud and blood money probably lie in a melting pot where many ideas were circulating and used to cope with the practical necessities of life. As far as migrants and settlers are concerned, it is difficult to decide what was the most influential; some ideas may have caught hold just by chance. The traditional way of settling a dispute in a manner similar to that described in the holy books could have existed before they were ever written down, whether in the Horn of Africa, in Arabia, or somewhere else. We could link this argument with the expansion and spread of humans into different continents.

A separate question is that of influences in a later period. We are not speaking anymore of a *zeitgeist* but of a relation between unequals. Traditions could not compete with a powerful alliance between state and church. It seems highly probable that the village priest and deacons in the area would be aware that the New Testament, as well as the *Fetha Negest,* give an explicit command to a ruler (whether the king, the state, or the elders in the *baito*) to execute vengeance on God's behalf. In Ethiopia the emperor was regarded as God's anointed avenger, and this must have had an impact on traditional law. The Ethiopian Orthodox Church would obviously have tremendous authority, perhaps even in some remote areas of the Eritrean highlands that never experienced Ethiopian political or military presence. The church was such an important institution in the daily life of Eritrean villages that, independently of the question of whether the *Fetha Negest* was practically used in trials, it would be surprising if the powerful and simple biblical precepts we have cited above did not percolate universally, and be perpetuated as tradition.

Islam

One of the Prophet's major tasks was how to change the system of private vengeance that was universally practiced among his adherents. In pre-Islamic Arabia, it was thought that if vengeance was not pursued, some form of bloodguilt was bound to fall upon the remaining kin.[148] Any member of the murderer's tribe might be killed in reprisal for the killing. But the immediate kin of the victim—and this is a difference with many of the Eritrean traditional codes we have looked at so far— were always free to choose whether to pursue the blood feud or accept blood money.[149]

The way that murder is dealt with in Islamic law is derived from the pre-Islamic system almost without modification. Murder is included, together with bodily harm and damage to property, in the so-called *ğināyat*, crimes the prosecution of which is left to the injured party: "there is no prosecution or execution *ex officio* . . . [but] only a guarantee of the right of private vengeance, coupled with safeguards against its exceeding the legal limits."[150] The punishment is given at the discretion of the *qādī* (*taᶜzīr* punishment), who can select from a variety of options.

Mohammed encouraged clemency, and the taking of blood money between believers rather than vengeance. The Qurʾan says "and slay not the soul God has forbidden, except by right . . . We have appointed to his next-of-kin authority; but let him not exceed in slaying; he shall be helped" (surah XVII, verse 35).[151] As we can see from this passage, the decision as to what form of vengeance has to be taken, together with the power to execute it, still lay with the individual family.[152] This surah empowers the *malīy al-dam*, the closest relative of the victim among *ᶜasaba* (roughly, the agnates), according to the rules of succession, as avenger of the blood. He is also the person who is entitled to receive blood money.[153] The *malīy* would take a solemn oath. He was obliged to fast, to abstain from wine and perfumes, and not to swear or have sexual intercourse until vengeance had been taken. When striking the mortal blow, the avenger cried out that he was taking vengeance for his murdered kinsman. This was done with the purpose of informing any witness that this was a lawful killing. We will see in chapter 7 that a similar ritual was carried out among some ethnies in Eritrea when land tenure was questioned.

The principle of the right of retaliation and just retribution (eye for an eye) and a penalty that has not to exceed the crime is taken directly from the Bible: "[O] believers, prescribed for you is retaliation, touching the slain; freeman for freeman, slave for slave, female for female. . . . In retaliation there is life for you, men possessed of minds; haply you will be godfearing" (surah II, verses 173 and 175).[154]

On the intention to murder, "it belongs not to a believer to slay a believer, except it be by error. If any slays a believer by error, then let him set free a believing slave, and bloodwit is to be paid to his family. . . . And Whoso slays a believer willfully, his recompense is Gehenna, therein dwelling forever, and God will be wroth with him and will curse him, and prepare for him a mighty chastisement" (surah IV, verses 94–95). This surah has led later jurists and commentators to argue that the Prophet believed that compensation was legally obligatory in certain circumstances.

Islamic law has elaborated a complicated casuistic for different types of murder (*qatl*), according to whether or not the deed was committed deliberately—and distinguishing again among deliberate intent (*ᶜamd*), quasi-deliberate intent (*šibh el-ᶜamd*), mistake (*khatā*), unintentional homicide/indirect causation (*qatl bi-sabah*)—and also according to the sex, religion, and status of the victim.[155] The punishment, which differs according to the category of the offense, could involve retaliation (*qisās*), religious expiation (*kaffāra*), or blood price (*diya*), to be paid by the guilty person or by his *ᶜāqila*.[156] Retaliation is regarded as full amends for intentional homicide; if it does not or cannot take place, *kaffāra* must be performed, and blood money must be paid.[157]

A major difference with pre-Islamic rules is that only the killer can be put to death. Moreover, retaliation is allowable only in the case of intentional murder, and the *walīy* can renounce his right; *šarīᶜa* recommends this solution. Retaliation cannot be applied when somebody, even intentionally, kills his own descendant, if the master kills his own slave, or the slave his own descendant.[158] Execution is carried out with the sword: the rule that blood should not be spilled, typical of the Eritrean highlands, is not present.

If the killer is not known, Schacht tells us that the procedure of *qasāma* takes place. "[T]he inhabitants of the quarter, the owner of the house (and his *ᶜāqila*), the passengers and crew of the boat in which he is found, must swear fifty oaths that they have not killed him and do not know who has killed him. Should they refuse to swear, they are imprisoned until they do. They must, as *ᶜāqila*, pay the blood money." This procedure shows some similarity with that of the Mensa in dealing with the settlement of blood disputes. There is no liability for acts committed upon an unprotected person, such as the *harbī* (enemy alien), or the person wounded or killed in self-defense.[159] The slave is subject to retaliation only if murder is committed with deliberate intent. In the case of *khatā*, the master can choose between surrendering the slave, paying the *arš* (a penalty for wounds), or his value. If he is killed, the same amount of blood money as that of a free man should be paid.[160] It is indisputable that only half of the normal *diya* was paid when the victim was a woman.[161]

Egyptian and Ottoman Rule

A major project of legal reform was initiated by Mahmud II (1808–39). In 1839 his successor Abdulmejid enacted the Imperial Ottoman Decree of Reform or Hatti-Sharif of Gulhane, in which for the first time Muslims and non-Muslims were collectively defined as "subjects." From then the law that applied throughout the Ottoman dominions (including

Massawa, Assab, and the coastal region of Eritrea) included two systems: *šarī'a* and legislation based on Western models. New penal procedure, and the *Majalla*, or civil codes, were enacted. The *Majalla*, which is strictly speaking a secular code, was the first attempt carried out to consolidate and enact parts of *šarī'a* as the law of the state. In 1840, an amendment to an imperial decree provided that if a man had committed murder, he would be imprisoned with hard labor in addition to paying blood money.

The penal code of the Ottoman Empire of 1858 remained in force up to 1918; it was based on the French penal code and provided for the death penalty in case of intentional murder. Homicides were prosecuted in the first instance in the civil *nizam* courts (courts of the Ottoman Empire, opposed to *šarī'a* courts). If the injured party wished to assert his right under *šarī'a*, the case was remitted after sentence to the *šarī'a* tribunal for assessment of *diya*. The award of compensation by this court had no effect upon the execution of the sentence ordered by the *nizam* court.[162] The registers contained records of several murder cases.[163]

The Italian Administration and After

From the start of the colonial period, Italy tried to ensure that crimes against the person became the exclusive monopoly of state law, and they attempted to reduce the incidence of vendettas. We do not know if their attempts were entirely successful. However, a Bilein elder recollected in 1999 that under the Italians, they were forced to abandon the long-established practice of revenge.[164] And Petazzi observes that in his time blood feud was already practiced to a lesser extent "because of the influence of Italian law in the administration of justice among indigenous people."[165]

Falling within the jurisdiction of the *Corte d'Assise*, murder was regulated by the Italian penal code without any distinction made between Italians and "natives" (art. 9, RD 2/7/1908, 325, *Ordinamento Giudiziario dell'Eritrea*). Article 12 of the same law stated that conciliation did not extinguish the criminal action, which persisted and was settled by prosecution in the interest of the state. Here there was a clear conflict between customary and colonial law because, on the one hand the condemnation of the murderer to death according to state law did not extinguish the blood feud that would exist within families if the settlement had not taken place, and on the other hand the settlement of the dispute according to traditional law did not extinguish the criminal action according to state law.

In an attempt to reconcile this conflict, article 161 stated that "conciliation performed with an oath in traditional forms, even after the sentence, can extinguish a criminal action in all cases where the crime is considered to be of a private nature." The same article prescribed also that all crimes committed between natives could be considered to be of a private nature, with consequent application of traditional law, even in the judgments in front of the Court of Assizes, for the evaluation of exempting, mitigating, or aggravating circumstances. This rule was repealed in 1926. What happened in practice was that, in trials for murder, the Italian judge applied the rules of the Italian penal code, taking heed of customary rules for the evaluation of circumstances, and eventually imposing the payment of blood money to enable the settlement of the blood feud among the families.[166]

These rules were mirrored in the traditional laws of the time. In the highlands, conciliation between the relatives of the victim and the murderer usually entails that no further action is taken by the state.[167] However, if the murderer later boasted of his crime, the family of the deceased could resuscitate their right to vengeance and force the murderer to pay a fine to the government "because he has violated the solemn oath of agreement."[168] This is an important example of synergy between state law and traditional law. The state, which is normally the third party in a blood feud, takes over the matter when it seems likely to become a danger to the stability of the community.

Later on, in the Fascist period, according to article 34 of *Ordinamento Giudiziario per la Colonia Eritrea*, approved with RD 20 June 1935, 1649, serious crimes against the state, murders and bodily harm taking place in particular conditions linked to the lineage and the local community blood feuds, slavery, and raids were entirely devolved to *Tribunale di Commissariato* and *Corte d'Assise*, leaving again no room for indigenous law.[169]

During the BMA, interaction between state law and traditional law may be seen if we read the *Adgena Tegeleba* code as amended in 1951: "[W]hosoever by reason of the homicide of a member of his family group has become reconciled, and has received the blood money and taken *fetsmi*, but nevertheless takes revenge by killing another person, shall be punished under the penal code and shall refund the blood money received and pay 1000 MTD laid down for murders"[170] (art. 161).

We have already noted that the Ethiopian penal code of 1957 was extended to Eritrea by a law passed by the Eritrean Assembly on 10 September 1959. The code retained the death penalty, and also included the provision of collective responsibility for certain crimes committed by nomads in the course of raids. Murder was considered an offense against the state, with a limited room for traditional rules to be applied. In a reversal of the 1930 Ethiopian penal code, the 1957 code provided that payment of blood money had no effect on a criminal prosecution, although it might constitute an extenuating circumstance.[171] Traditional rules could be applied in the determination of damages caused to an injured party.[172]

In their turn, in 1987, the EPLF drafted a penal code. This code was never published nor enacted into law, but was used as a basis for the transitional code of 1991. The code did not specifically mandate the death penalty for murder among civilians (although it allowed it for the military).[173] Inevitably the EPLF code and traditional laws sometimes rule in different ways. An example is article 7 of the customary law of the *Loggo-Chewa* that says quite clearly that blood money is payable for causing the death of another during sporting activities. On the other hand, Article 2067 of the transitional penal code says that no liability is incurred.[174] In chapter 4 we referred to the extensive work carried out in recent years by drafters of new penal and criminal procedure codes.

In recent years there have been a number of reports of crimes still being resolved through the blood feud–blood money mechanism. Only in the 1980s among the Bilein was "killing for vengeance being substituted by blood money, or the giving of one of the murderer's sisters or cousins in marriage." But some people objected to the practice, as they disliked being called "eaters of blood money."[175] After liberation, the EPLF attempted to adjudicate in a Saho murder case; it was settled by the payment of blood money.[176] In a conference convened in 1999, a group of elders said they had never come across a case in which the people who agreed to pay *gar* had refused to do so. They always paid in the end mainly because the whole community put pressure on them to fulfill their obligation.

At present, as the state court system is by no means working properly due to the chronic lack of trained persons, traditional law and religious law still play a dominant role. There is an informal division of competence between traditional courts and state courts on cases that have given rise in the past to blood feuds. Cases of murder are usually settled through the payment of blood money, but cases of blood feud are still reported. In the Barka region, the traditional tribunals are fully functional and exercise a great deal of authority. It is known that elders deal with cases of murder and the payment of *diya* and that usually neither at the regional nor at the sub-regional level does the administration intervene in their work.[177]

Afterword

To the superficial observer, Eritrean society is calm, ordered, and stable, and the life of the rural population especially seems not to have changed much, no matter the nature of the actors who claim to rule them, be they Ethiopians, Italians, ELF, or EPLF. On the surface, everything may appear to be calm, but underneath it is anything but. Eritreans have internalized their suffering for so long that their inner anger can now erupt in an instant, and subside just as quickly. This can be observed in common attitudes toward Ethiopian Tigrayans. These people had lived in Eritrea, apparently on harmonious terms with their hosts, for several generations, but any regular visitor to Eritrea knows that on the whole Eritreans look down on people from Tigray. During the recent conflict some of these migrants were unwise enough to openly celebrate Ethiopian victories. The community as a whole suffered hostility because of the actions of these few. Some were dismissed from their jobs and many thousands more were sent back to Ethiopia; several hundred were interned in camps "for their own safety," in the words of the Eritrean government.

The Tigrinya of Ethiopia and Eritrea shared a common origin in the distant past; their common blood ties have been overlaid by the influence of other actors. Tigray was an outlying, despised, and underprivileged part of Abyssinia, whereas the Tigrinya of Eritrea constituted the elite of the Italian colonial domain. As a result of these factors, the two groups are now very different from one another. However, the fact of common blood ties remains a useful tool to use as a smokescreen to simulate sentiments of friendship and participation in front of other actors—state and international. The implications of blood ties in the present day will be discussed in the concluding chapter.

Six

Land Tenure on
the Highland Plateau

The magic of PROPERTY turns sand into gold.
                                    —Sir Arthur Young[1]

In this chapter we look at the long, varied, and frequently contentious history of land. Because the topic is so vast, we have restricted our analysis in the first part to just one of the divisions of highland Eritrea and in particular the region known before the administrative reforms of 1995 as Akele Guzai. This is a particularly illuminating comparative study because two of the largest ethnies, the Tigrinya and the Saho, are involved. Although their land use practices are much different, by and large the two communities have coexisted peacefully for many generations. A traveler writing 150 years ago called it "a most perfect *entente cordiale.*"[2] This may be overstating the case. Over the generations, the Saho undoubtedly have absorbed some traditions from their neighbors, just as the Tigrinya have adopted some of Saho culture, not always voluntarily. The problems that arose were largely due to the encroachment of nomadic Saho onto the land of the settled Tigrinya. For our purposes this forms a useful example of the dynamic interaction of two actors at the micro level.

Collective liability and common ownership over land are among the typical features of small, kinship-based societies.[3] Both are rooted firmly within kinship organization: disputes on land title usually involve descent of one of the litigants, as well as lineage rights and duties. These rights and duties, as we have seen in the previous chapter, are also fundamental in legal relations arising as a consequence of a murder, where the survival of the kin group and its own independence are the main concerns.[4] Nadel has remarked of the African that "he does not possess his land but is possessed by it."[5] That this is particularly true

105

for Eritrea is shown in an old Tigrinya proverb: "property should be defended, women too should fight for it, and even an inch shall never be surrendered."[6] Land dominated people's lives for countless generations, and in the next chapter we discuss some of the numerous disputes this has caused.

We contrast two systems of traditional law, one of which existed in a less centralized and nomadic lifestyle and the other in a sedentary one, and we compare the reactions of two ethnies, both of whom are small, kin-based groups, to the superimposition (or attempted superposition) of centralized colonial and post-colonial structures.[7] This particular case study of traditions in a relatively small area is extremely useful in a wider context. We are indebted to Bohannan, who forcibly argued for a theory of land tenure that fits the African pattern and not one that is crafted in the light of Western concepts and assumptions about property law and land ownership.[8]

Traditional societies can be extremely diversified.[9] Our comparison between Tigrinya and Saho shows differences of language, religion (one ethnie being mainly Christian, the other almost entirely Muslim), and political structure (the Tigrinya in Akele Guzai had a federal republican structure for many generations, while the Saho were more decentralized).[10] The Saho clan is endogamous; each Saho marries a member of the same clan, usually a cousin, whereas Tigrinya are rigidly exogamous.[11] Other differences are analyzed in more detail in the chapter on gender.

As we see in the next chapter, land disputes have frequently been violent and bloody, partly because the Saho, who were originally nomads, have in the past century mostly settled down to a pastoral life of farming and become uneasy neighbors of Tigrinya. Many of them were to be found on transhumance routes as they led their herds to pasture in a good season to the borders of Akele Guzai and beyond. For many centuries they controlled much of the important trade route from the port of Adulis to the Tigray border. The most assertive branch of the Saho, the Asaorta, was especially alienated from Abyssinia (and the Tigrinya) as a result of the repeated raids it suffered.[12] The Asaorta was eventually subdued on behalf of the Italian colonizers by Bahta Hagos, a Tsenadegle Tigrinya from Segeneiti.[13]

Among the Saho, it has been said that there was "no trace of serf and master caste" such as was found in the Tigrinya.[14] In each clan (*are*), an assembly of men elected a *resanto* (chief), and they decided what powers he should have and how long he should rule. Each sub-clan was governed by a deputy (*nebara*).[15] In an attempt to assert their rule, the Italians began to appoint chiefs (*shums*, using the Tigrinya as a model) directly; understandably, this move was never popular with the Saho.[16] In time, the position of *shum* became hereditary, but in spite of this, a commission of elders and spiritual leaders would often act instead of the *shum*, especially in questions of land and intra-clan disputes.[17]

As far as the Tigrinya-speaking people in the province of Akele Guzai were concerned, they differed from those in the other highland provinces of Hamasien and Seraye in having a more egalitarian social structure—at least until Italian times.[18] An assembly composed of elders (*mahber*) selected a leader who remained in office only as long as the community wanted him to.[19] Individual districts were autonomous and came together voluntarily whenever necessary to form a confederation.[20]

The province never readily accepted foreign rule. The inhabitants paid no tribute on a regular basis to either Tigrayan or Abyssinian rulers from the sixteenth to the eighteenth century—we have dealt with this point in chapter 3. In 1893, it was reported that the men of Akele Guzai were not obliged to serve in the Abyssinian army—nor did they pay any taxes.[21] The important town of Segeneiti became the center of Eritrean Catholicism, a religion that often brought its adherents into conflict with the established Ethiopian Orthodox Church.

Although Eritrean land tenure practices were established many generations ago, they have not remained set in stone. As elsewhere, so-called "indigenous" or traditional land tenure systems are not inherently stable; on the contrary, change has been ubiquitous.[22] When the colonial state was established in Eritrea in the late nineteenth century, a new actor appeared, transforming relations between groups and lineages into a more complex system involving them all. All actors had to struggle harder to claim and keep their legitimacy, and they were compelled to make critical choices in order to survive. The full restructuring of social roles and law consequent to the consolidation of power was certainly more dramatic in a power-diffused society than in one accustomed to quasi-central authority.[23]

The Traditional System of
Land Law in the Highlands

A fundamental feature of Akele Guzai society was the long-standing and widespread system of communal land tenure known as *shehena* (called *diesa* in Hamasien and Seraye). Land was, and is, a scarce commodity in the highlands—an area that has been settled for many thousands of years, which has been subject to frequent redistribution, and which has divided and subdivided already small marginal holdings. The

practice dates back to at least medieval times. The traditional laws in
the province provided for a detailed regime of land ownership. Under
shehena tenure, all land was regarded as the common property of the
village, and land use was restricted to individuals living in the village.[24]
Ideally, the villagers redistributed land periodically; this was under the
supervision of special figures, called *akwaro* (usually one for each *enda*
living in the village) or *nabara* (usually one for the entire village).[25] The
practice fell largely in abeyance because of drought, war, and subsequent
upheavals.

Other main forms of land ownership were *resti* (family ownership)
and *gulti* (territorial fiefs or granted land). Individual property and lease
relationships were also present, as well as a separate regime for *tisha*
(land for building a house), urban land, and ruins (*ona*).

Resti is probably the oldest pattern of land ownership; it means literally "occupied land" and refers to the right of first possession, or occupation of a given community or village by the ancestor of the *enda*.[26] In
resti ownership, property rights lie collectively in the lineage or family
constituting the *enda*. *Resti* is full, effective, indefeasible ownership and
refers to land belonging to the ancestor, which has been divided between successive descendants.[27] A secondary division between families
can follow a primary division based on lineage. Descent is patrilineal;
direct male descendants of the first occupant are entitled to full and
entire right of possession.[28] When land is divided, each entitled member
of the *enda* (*ghebbar / restegnat*) is given the same number of plots of land
of the same quality.[29] To facilitate this process, land was classified on
the basis of such factors as cultivation and fertility. The Jiberti were
treated differently from other Tigrinya speakers; a contested law of
Haile Selassie stated they could not obtain *resti* land.[30]

The most distinctive feature of *shehena* is that land title is based on
residence, and not on descent as in *resti:* the right to an equal share in
village land belongs to each permanent male resident and his descendants.[31] The right is temporary and is for three, four, five, or seven years,
depending on the customary law involved. After this period, a new reallocation of land (*warieda*) will take place.[32] Under the supervision of the
chief (*chikka ᶜaddi*), the village priest, and three elders, the villagers
would draw lots for their share of land.[33]

Shehena derives directly from lineage ownership and follows the
transformation of the kinship-based structures into village organization: land belongs at first to the large family, then to the village, and is
vested (in both cases) in those who have to cultivate it.[34] Before the Italians transformed the land tenure system, *shehena* was the most typical
feature of land ownership in the highlands, in particular in the northern

part of Akele Guzai and Hamasien.[35] Nadel agrees that *shehena* is an old institution in the greater part of the Hamasien.[36] Joireman says rather vaguely that communal land tenure was not indigenous to Hamasien but "imposed" by the Italians.[37] As the coming pages will demonstrate, the Italians favored *shehena/diesa* over *resti*.

As a rule, foreigners—*makelay aliet*—had an equal right of access to *shehena* land provided their request was made in due time, that is before a new reallocation, and as long as they paid tribute.[38] Once admitted, they acquired the same rights over land as members of the original lineage. It is probable that they were admitted in order to alleviate the burden of the tribute that was assessed on a village by colonizers.[39] Of particular interest in this regard is article 20 of *Mehen Mahaza*, which, after affirming the right of equal access of foreigners, makes an explicit reference to *Cristianai kab Gonder,* (Christians from Gondar) and *Aslamai kab Mander* (Muslims coming from coastal zones).[40]

As far as the position of women is concerned, this varied according to the locality, but it is fair to say they generally did not have the same rights to land as men had. The only exception to this seems to be widows and unmarried women without brothers; moreover this qualification applied in only a few of the traditional laws. An example from Akele Guzai is the *Loggo Sarda*, where a woman could not legally hold land. If she bought land "she must be given back the price she has paid because she cannot continue to possess it" (§12).[41] Conti Rossini recalls that in the highlands as a whole, it was only after Yohannes IV that widows with children were admitted to a share of communal land.[42]

Originally, *gulti* was the regime applied to conquered territories; the king gave the land as a reward to faithful collaborators *shumgulti* (*gulti* lord).[43] Technically, it was surrender by the feudal ruler of some of his sovereign rights over certain *resti* or villages in favor of an individual family, church, or monastery. There are records dating from the thirteenth century of *gulti* payments to the church.[44] A *gulti* could also include the government over provinces and districts, or a concession given to a lineage to live on a certain land, or the constitution of rent granted by the king over subjects of a certain area.[45] These rights were subject to revocation at any time if the *shumgulti* failed to fulfill his obligations. Like a feudal European landlord, the *shumgulti* had duties of loyalty and protection toward the king; he also exacted tribute and administered justice. Over dependent *resti*, the *gulti* lord had only a formal duty of protection and the right to take for himself part of the tribute.[46] Over time, this regime became common in the highlands, sizes of *gulti* increased, and in some cases the office of *shumgulti* became hereditary.[47]

Sale and Division of
Communally Held Land

A fourth type of land tenure was *medri worki*. This is the land acquired by money (*worki* means gold) and, although the least common, represented the main type of individual land ownership in the highlands.[48] Sale of land usually took place during a village assembly, in the presence of witnesses (the number varies from code to code) and two guarantors (*wahas*), one for each party. Nadel claimed there were three independent witnesses, one must be a Coptic priest, one a Muslim, and the third a blacksmith or goldsmith (neither of the latter classes of artisans being allowed to own *resti*).[49]

That communal land could not be sold is made clear by *Mai Adgi:* "*ghebri* (*shehena*) is the collective property of the lineages, and it cannot be sold, either by the lineage to which it belongs or by a single individual member of it" (art. 16§1).[50] Articles 10–11 of the *Loggo Sarda* reinforce this principle: "whoever has received by allotment common land of *Loggo* to cultivate, cannot sell it."[51] According to one commentator, in theory *shehena* could have been sold with the consent of each lineage in the village, but it is obvious that this condition was very difficult to meet. It may therefore be more appropriate to state that the sale of *shehena* was unknown rather than that land cannot be sold.[52] Joireman cites two cases of "sale" of *diesa* land in Hamasien (each case involving only one-twentieth of an acre). But later on she has to admit that it was possible that the land was not *diesa*.[53]

Resti land could be sold when the holding of an *enda* had been divided between families or individuals, and only after obtaining the consent of the entire lineage.[54] Members of an *enda* were granted a right of pre-emption over *resti* land: they had to be asked if they wished to buy it and, if they declared that they had not been informed about the sale, they were entitled to enforce their right within a year from the date of sale.[55] Similar rules applied to the Mensa. The *Fetha Mahari* lays down a hierarchy of potential buyers of land. It must be offered first to the closest relative and after this to the family, and then to the members of the village or clan. However, land can never be offered to a foreigner (art. 54§2). If all the conditions had been properly met, the buyers were considered to be legal owners to all effects. They could transmit the land to their heirs, sell it to third persons, and make any act of disposal they wished. *Makelay aliet* would acquire the same rights as descendants of the original owners (*daqqi abbat*).[56]

Conti Rossini mentions that when the manuscript of their code was given to him (around 1904) the *Loggo Sarda*, because of an unprecedented economic crisis, were forced to sell communal land (*resti* and *shehena*) to a few buyers.[57] He alleges that in the highlands it was becoming common to divide communal land "at the request of only one of the members of the community." The division was carried out in the following way: land originally belonging to an *enda* or to an *ᶜaddi* was shared among smaller groups such as *geza* and small families. Each *geza* received an equal amount of land—irrespective of the *geza*'s size— and at the request of the individual families the land could be subdivided further. The division was carried out in front of witnesses. This observation—not confirmed by any other source—shows a movement to individual rights over land. It could indicate a breakdown of the communal land system. What is taking place is clearly a division of land and not a sale: the buyer acquired the right to participate in the allotment of the land, and to subsequent division, not a right over a specific parcel.[58]

The *Adkeme Melega* of Seraye depicts a unique type of land ownership, called *medri guaytat*—lands belonging to lords. The three chiefs of the *endas* of *Godofelassi*, *Addi Monguntu*, and *Mai Tsada* had taken over the functions of land division originally exercised by the elders of the community. "At first sight," Conti Rossini says, "it can be argued that these representatives [. . .] were the real owners." They divided the land among people of the same blood as well as foreigners; they paid tribute to the king, who at each succession had to reconfirm them in their right.[59] The source is not detailed enough to clarify that this was in fact a form of land ownership instead of merely a special way of allocation.

Leasehold

Crai is a lease relationship between a *restegnat* and another individual who could be a foreigner or another *resti* holder. The *restegnat* cultivates the land, or uses the pasture, and pays the legal owner a ground rent corresponding to a percentage of the crops for a fixed fee (*meghes* and *metellen*). At one time, *crai* was always revocable by a *restegnat* after giving the leaseholder notice according to the customary time provisions. A form of land use that could transform leaseholders into legal owners was not conceivable, even if the lease lasted for centuries; a lease was always temporary, and could not be transformed into permanent rights over land.

Another form of temporary right over land was *sedbi*, in which owners in general were *gultegnat* or monasteries. Unlike *crai*, it was therefore a relationship based on the superiority of one of the parties involved.

There were other differences between *crai* and *sedbi*. The first regards the payment of the tribute. In *crai*, the *restegnat*—as a legal owner—was the one who had to pay, while in *sedbi*, the *sedbegnat*—the one to whom the land was rented—took upon himself the burden to pay the tribute to the government, in addition to the rent due to the owner.[60] Second, *sedbi* usually referred to holdings of considerable size, and it linked together many families and villages. The contract lasted usually for an indefinite period, but the landlord held the option of ending it, which could leave the *sedbegnat* landless. This enabled rich families to exert considerable pressure over leaseholders.[61]

Land Regime among the Saho

If the land regime among the Tigrinya is complicated by the presence of many possessory rights over the same plot, that of the Saho owes its complexity to the fact that they were migrants. In the highlands, not only did they lease land from the Tigrinya on a number of different terms, but they also claimed land in their own right or acquired it as a result of long residence in the area. In the lowlands, they held pastures and possessed a wide range of rights to cultivated land.

In the highlands, Saho shepherds expanded into Tigrinya land. As they did so, they were frequently subjected to a tribute for pastures called *saari bela*. In some areas of Akele Guzai, the practice of *sedbi* was fairly common. At the time of the original Italian occupation, many villages were abandoned or had been destroyed by war or famine. The owners, for the most part Tigrinya *gultegnat*, were unable to handle, control, and cultivate all the land. For *gultegnat* and *resti* owners, *sedbi* was a way of forging an alliance, cultivating the land, and at the same time avoiding the tribute.[62] Many of these leases involved Saho *makelay aliet*.[63] Land would be leased against one-third of the crops. The tenant had to pay an annual ceremonial visit to his landlord and give him a nominal rent in the presence of guests invited as witnesses to a feast. Most such leases in the village of Mai Weini ceased sometime in the 1970s.[64]

In the Senafé area for many generations, some Saho farmers occupied land on the same terms as their Tigrinya neighbors.[65] They regarded themselves as the original occupants of the land with full rights of ownership. Around Irafaile, a small town on the coast of the Red Sea, a number of Saho became *resti* holders. Such land could not be sold, nor could it be given to a non-descendant.[66] In order for it to pass to a descendant, it had to be proven that the land had been used consistently, and for a long enough time to establish ownership.[67]

For much of the 350 years that the Eritrean coast was under the control of the Ottoman Empire, the *Naib* of Hirghigo collected tribute on behalf of the emperor and spread *šarīʿa* far inland. Only a few rudiments of a general theory of land exist in *šarīʿa*. Rules on this matter vary according to time and place. Muslim jurisprudence drew a distinction between privately owned land, *milk*, possessed by Muslims and by non-believers, and state property that under the Ottoman Empire started to be called *mīrī*.[68] Under the rule of Suleiman during the second half of the sixteenth century, a major reform of state land with the aim of increasing tax revenues and reasserting the right of the state to *mīrī* was carried out.[69] The central authorities granted pasture rights and rights of occupancy to clans or villages. *Mīrī* land was given in usufruct to inhabitants and subject to the issue of a certificate called *tapu*, by which an inhabitant could prove his rights to the *mīrī* land in his possession, and to the payment of tribute.[70] Tribute was not due in the case of *matrūk* (assigned) land set aside for public use as woods and pastures, which could have been entrusted to private citizens or to communities without the payment of an annual rent.[71]

A report issued by an Italian commission in 1891 shows that this reform was enforced in Eritrea. Muslim lowlands were classified in the following way: (a) *milk*, or land in private hands; (b) *mirī*, land in the public domain; (c) *matrūk*, assigned land; (d) *mawat*, or dead land—land which is uncultivated lying fallow and therefore does not belong to anybody; and (e) *mawqūfāt*.[72] *Mawqūfāt* corresponded to *waqf*, of Islamic law, the act of founding a charitable trust and hence the trust itself. The essential elements of a *waqf* are that a person, with the intention of committing a pious deed, declares part of his or her property to be henceforth inalienable and designates persons or public utilities as beneficiaries of its yields. Immovable property may easily be the object of a *waqf*. The beneficiary of a *waqf* can be either persons or public utilities such as mosques and schools.[73]

The above report drew the wrong inference that since there was little land in private hands, land was mostly uncultivated.[74] *Mīrī* land, which as we have seen was usually granted in usufruct for cultivation, was completely forgotten. Interestingly, recent research using the court records of Massawa shows that there were also many land transactions, indicating that a significant amount of land was in private hands.[75] An important point raised by Conti Rossini is that among the Haso, property was never communally owned, but owned absolutely and only individually, perhaps because of their isolation and the necessity to divide into smaller groups as much as possible in order to effectively use scarce pastures.[76]

As far as women were concerned, the Saho followed the *šarīʿa* rules where a woman is only half of a man as far as inheriting land is concerned, but as far as buying and selling property is concerned, she is the equal of a man.[77] Among the Saho, unmarried daughters and divorced girls who moved back home were given a share equal to that of the men and boys.[78] In the Haso, a wife's property was separate from that of the husband; she could leave all her goods to her daughters and exclude her sons from inheritance.[79] Examination of the registers from Ottoman times indicates real estate transactions in which women bought and sold houses and land.[80]

Power, Tribute, and Rights over Land

This might be an appropriate time to come back to the question of tribute and take a brief look at the social structure of Tigrinya and Saho in pre-colonial Akele Guzai. In parts of the highlands, for some periods monarchs attempted to exercise absolute control. A new king had to be legitimized by those who constituted the base of his power. The members of society who were guardians of the group's traditional values, *shumagulle* and *baito* represented a counterbalance to the king's authority. When religious leaders and elders accepted the king as a legitimate chief, tribute was given as a sign of acceptance.[81]

The political structure of Akele Guzai is usually presented as different from the structure of the other regions that constitute the *kebessa*, as being more "democratic" and independent. The democratic nature is inferred from the fact that decisions were taken unanimously after considerable debate by the *baito*; independence is argued because Akele Guzai refused to pay tribute to the king for many years. Power was defined as "federal republicanism."[82] We would like to argue that a "democratic nature and independence" does not exclude the presence of, or at the very least the perception of, a social structure that goes further than the group. On the contrary, clan and state structures do coexist; this is precisely the starting point of any debate on pluralism.

We discussed tribute and its link with religious and traditional law in chapter 3. Here we look at tribute with specific regard to land issues. Tribute (*ghehri*) is a very important test of whether power extends beyond the group. *Seb hara, mariet gebbar* (man is free but land is subjected to tribute). It could be given to a king or *ras*, in both communal forms of land ownership and in *gulti*.[83] It was levied over the entire *enda*, being shared between individual *ghebbar* according to predetermined divisions and allotments. There are detailed traditional rules laying down the correct procedure. We discuss some of them in our next chapter on land disputes because they have given rise to much contention in the past.

In *gulti*, the landlord had the right to keep part of the tribute for himself in recognition of his rights over the land: in this case we see the insertion of a medium in the relationship between king and *ghebbar*. But rights over lands and tribute are intimately connected. The importance of *ghebri* can be seen from the fact that its payment is fundamental in the assessment of *restegnat* rights: if it had not been paid, the title of *restegnat* or *balmeriet* (original inhabitant) could not be used. Conversely the payment of tribute proved legal ownership.

Now, if the tribute is the acknowledgment given to the legitimized ruler, a refusal to pay—far from proving the unawareness of the concept of state—seems only to prove that Tigrayan or Abyssinian rulers were not considered legitimate chiefs, and the Tigrinya-speaking people of Akele Guzai were at times able to be independent of their rule.[84] Their sense of nationality was strong enough: the ability to evaluate a given power's legitimacy, and to refuse to submit to it, clearly presupposes the perception and awareness of the power in question.

As far as the Saho were concerned, it is not overstating the case to say that the first Tigrinya settlers with whom they came in contact regarded them as a subaltern class; only in more recent times did they become partly integrated with the Tigrinya. Moreover, it is a common feature of many sedentary agricultural societies that they experience conflict when nomads arrive among them and try to settle down. And on the other hand, it is difficult for nomads to come to terms with the duties and rules imposed by a central authority. Mohamed Salih has remarked that "the manner in which pastoralists perceive the state and the state's perception of pastoralists are a hindrance to any meaningful communication between the two."[85]

In the conclusion of this book we will discuss the impact of the colonial and post-colonial state on the Saho and Tigrinya, and on the other ethnies of Eritrea. But for the moment we can observe that as soon as Tigrinya and Saho came into contact in Akele Guzai—before the colonial period—relations between the two groups were not always harmonious. Those Saho who decided to settle were *makelay aliet*, and according to some traditional law were equal subjects, with the same rights and duties as the original inhabitants. But contemporary evidence shows that a common arrangement was *sedbi*, a lord-tenant relationship and not one between equals, as *crai* would have been. It is important to stress again that traditional codes usually contain only the problematic aspects of a certain question, the aspects over which there was a dispute.

The Italian Colony: 1869–1941

The Italian government planned originally to make Eritrea a "*colonia di popolamento*," a colony in which to settle the surplus and unemployed Italian population.[86] The land policy constituted a fundamental plank of colonial plans, but many mistakes were made. In the words of one of the most reliable experts on colonial and customary Eritrean law, "we ended up in many cases declaring as public domain, lands which by no means pertained to the state, and by appearing then as treacherous, arousing a suspicion in the minds of the natives that little by little we wanted to deprive them of all their lands."[87]

The origins of Italian colonial land policy date back to *Regio Decreto*, 19/1/1893, 23 (enacted on the basis of law 1/7/1890, 7003), which empowered the king's government to carry on land reform, to grant concessions, and to determine the regime of land rights in the colony (arts. 1–2). In principle, this law was intended to extend public domain over certain categories of land, in particular land previously subjected to Abyssinian and Egyptian state ownership (art. 11), village land abandoned by peasants (art. 12), and *gulti* when the landlord's kinship was extinct (art. 13). The rationale behind this latter rule was to avoid expropriating land that was claimed by traditional groups. However, as a closing rule, the governor had the right to declare any land *demaniale* (government land) if it was in the "interest of the Colony" (art. 15).

The implementation of this regime created general dissatisfaction, not only, as one might expect, among "natives," but also among enlightened colonial lawyers. There was a lack of knowledge and understanding of traditional law, and colonial officers at times made a free interpretation of the instructions they received. As a result, expropriations were frequently carried out without previously ascertaining how indigenous rights over land had been allocated, and there were many legal inconsistencies. The law declared public domain over land, which already obviously belonged to the state (arts. 11 and 13); on the other hand it did not take into account how long ago land had been abandoned or whether the abandonment had been transitory or permanent (art. 12).[88] Public domain was declared in many cases in open violation of *resti* tenure.[89] This was clearly the most serious mistake. Violent expropriations carried out by Italy convinced the Eritreans that in a short time they would be deprived of all their land. With particular regard to the lowlands, commissario Ferdinando Martini wrote in 1913, "all territories belonging to the Muslim tribes for historical and social reasons should be considered directly state lands."[90]

The early years of Italian rule were characterized by famine and epidemic disease, consequently some owners temporarily abandoned large areas of land. The Royal Commission of Inquiry drew an erroneous inference from this and reported that "the attachment between man and land was so weak that, if the indigenous people were to be ordered to leave their land, they could comfortably do so."[91] Therefore much of this land was expropriated, declared to be *terra demaniale*, and granted as concessions to Italian citizens. It is not known if and to what extent those Eritreans dispossessed from their land were compensated. An examination of land rent tax data indicates that some land was leased back to the local inhabitants, but this did not account for more than 3 percent of that expropriated.[92]

In 1894, rebellions erupted in Akele Guzai and Italy had to stop expropriating land.[93] In order to defuse the situation, *Regio Decreto* 2/7/1908, 325 was then enacted. It directly empowered the government "to settle disputes between indigenous people pertaining to collective ownership, pasture land, tributes, cultivation and similar matters" (art. 3).[94] The rationale behind this rule was to avoid a final decision not susceptible to a further appeal—*res iudicata*—on such a sensitive topic, since an administrative measure was always revocable.[95]

Ordinamento Fondiario (Land Law) of 1909, and *Nuovo Ordinamento Fondiario* of 1926 both modified the previous land regime.[96] For the limited purpose of our examination they will be analyzed jointly, and we will give an account only of major differences. In principle, the property of the soil belonged to the Italian state, rights granted or recognized by the government to third persons, and "rights pertaining to indigenous populations over lands enjoyed according to ancient local customary laws" excepted.[97] This had to be combined with the rule of *"doppio binario"* (see chapter 3), that prescribed a different regime for land subjected to Italian rule and land governed by traditional law. The first regime applied to *demaniale* and to land belonging to residents or foreigners and building areas (art. 1), whereas the second to land reserved for local inhabitants.[98]

Compared to the decree of 1893, the list of *demaniale* was redrawn (art. 5) to pay more heed to customary rights. For example, land abandoned by peasants (art. 12 of the decree of 1893) could be taken into the public domain only if the abandonment had taken place more than three years before (art. 5c). Land on transhumance routes was added to the public domain, pasture and water use being provided (art. 5h). *Gulti* holdings were abolished (according to article 13 of the decree of 1893, public domain could have been declared only when *gulti* kinship was extinct), and the right of use was granted to locals (art. 5i). The corresponding article 5 of *Regio Decreto* 269/1926 again revised the list, with a further reduction in the proportion of land that could be declared to be in the public domain.

However, the less-than-successful attempts to colonize the highlands induced the Italian authorities to concentrate on lowland regions, which up to that time had hardly been touched.[99] Italian officials reasoned that since the lowland regions were sparsely populated by nomadic/pastoral Muslim tribes, the declaration of public domain would not affect the rights and interests of indigenous groups. These officials argued that the Italian government had erred by not pursuing this course of action from the beginning.[100] The general principle according to which "land of the western and eastern lowlands not inhabited by resident populations" was considered to be in the public domain was therefore introduced (art. 5e). Land pertaining to the state was destined for European settlement, within the limits imposed by the respect for the local population's use and needs (art. 16).[101]

The same law provided for the creation of a system of land registration (arts. 164–233). As a complement to these rules, a *decreto governatoriale* 21/11/1910, 1247 instituted a central Cadastral Office in Asmara. A system of probatory land registration was followed. The registration of land holdings in special cadastral books, according to article 206, was the only legal proof of the rights over land and their changes in status.[102] With the land law of 1926 this policy was abandoned in favor of a system in which registers were merely descriptive; this was deemed to be cheaper and easier to implement.[103]

In 1935, the government issued a decree making the *shehena* system universal in the southern districts of Akele Guzai.[104] This declaration, far from being inspired by a desire for equality, masked a policy of protecting large estates amassed by collaborating chiefs and large-scale expropriations of village land.[105] It was easier for the Italian government to control villages where *shehena* land was the sole form of land tenure. The government appointed most village heads and through these appointees could administer land distribution and manage conflict. A village largely under *resti* tenure was much more difficult to control, if only for the reason that somebody who does not belong to an *enda* finds it very difficult to discover all the land and family relationships involved.

After the Italian conquest of Ethiopia in 1935, Somalia and Eritrea were merged with the Ethiopian Empire to form *Africa Orientale Italiana*. Tigray was added to Eritrea and the new entity was called *Governatorato d'Eritrea*. The local Fascist party established the Arnaldo

Mussolini farm at Asmara.[106] The Ente di Colonizzazione Romagna d'Etiopia (ECRE) was established to settle farmers from Romagna (Mussolini's home province). Their main area of activity was in the Amhara governorate, but with the defeat of the Italian army in 1941, ECRE moved its headquarters to Eritrea. In 1946 (five years after the start of the British occupation), ECRE members were still operating four estates near Asmara.[107]

The British Administration
and the Federation[108]

The British initially increased the amount of state land in Eritrea and gave some of this land, either freehold or leasehold, as a reward for Eritrean collaborators.[109] The BMA's policy was to encourage the development of individual land tenure.[110] One source estimates that, as a consequence of the administration's actions, 40 percent of the families who were farming communally had lost their land by the end of 1945.[111] This caused considerable discontent and therefore, from 1946 onwards, a portion of the expropriated land was sold or given back to the villages or individuals.[112]

A major feature of the Eritrean Land Tenure Act of 1953 was the change in the terms of redistribution of *diesa/shehena* land—from a seven-year to a twenty-seven-year cycle. At the time there was a great demand for land, and its shortage had led to widows, spinsters, and orphans being given only half a share, rather than a full share, at redistribution.[113] There had already been a considerable number of disputes as a decreasing amount of land was shared among an increasing number of people. For unspecified reasons, the act was never implemented.[114] However, even at this early stage of the Federation, Ethiopia was exerting its strength, and as we have seen in chapter 3, severely restricting Eritrea's ability to enact and enforce legislation.

The Empire

In 1976, Brietzke wrote, "traditional tenures remained largely unaffected by the laws enacted, with great fanfare, from 1944 to 1974."[115] It is generally agreed that Haile Selassie's land policy was largely ineffective. Conscious of the sensitivity of the topic, he tried to balance the expectations of the young elite and international donors on the one hand with large landowners' interest in the conservation of the *status quo* on the other.[116] There is no doubt he ended up on the side of the large landowners. The 1960 civil code provides a detailed regime for immovables into which category land ownership falls.[117] This regime was never implemented.

We remarked in chapter 3 that the code seemed to leave little or no room for traditional law. According to article 3347, all customary rules concerning traditional land law had to be considered automatically repealed, since "land" was a matter expressly ruled by the code. However, a special regulation for customary patterns of land exploitation was contained in articles 1489 through 1500, dedicated to agricultural communities. This regime represented an attempt to frame traditional systems of exploitation within state law and was a case of a lawful custom permitted by the exception contained in the first part of article 3347 ("unless expressly provided"). Article 1489 states that "land owned by an agricultural community such as a village or tribe shall be exploited collectively whenever such mode of exploitation conforms to the tradition and customs of the community concerned." To this end, every community had to draw up a charter detailing its custom (art. 1496). The Ministry of the Interior was entrusted to take steps to ensure that this was done (art. 1490). Land owned by a community could not be acquired by prescription and could not be sold to third parties without the consent of the ministry (art. 1493).

Of course, it is far more difficult to implement a rule than to frame it. Schiller has observed that land continued to be governed by customary law.[118] And even René David indicated shortly after the code came into force that it was aimed primarily at the more developed elements of the population, such as those living in the cities and the highlands, and "could not be expected to be applied in the other regions in the near future."[119] Bilillign Mandefro gives the most exhaustive account of the impact of the civil code on agricultural communities in Tigray and Eritrea. He also reproduces extracts from David's original draft,[120] and quotes Afenegus Kitaw Yitateku, a member of the codification committee responsible for carrying the civil code through the Ethiopian parliament, that the draft was too sophisticated for the communities involved.[121] By 1966 the Ministry of the Interior that had been charged with ensuring that the agricultural communities drew up charters specifying who was responsible for their administration had done nothing whatsoever.[122]

Incidentally, the "Income Tax Proclamation" of 1967, which aimed to rationalize the previous tax system and to introduce a progressive tax on revenue, shared the fate of the civil code.[123] A Parliament composed of large landowners emptied the proclamation of all meaning, "enabling local landowners to assess their own taxes. Corruption and the occa-sional assassination of zealous tax administrators completed the picture on non-implementation."[124]

The Dergue

Aiming at sweeping away all traditional systems of land tenure and laws of the imperial period along with all "reactionary" beliefs, practices, and customs, the Dergue, with proclamation 31/75, nationalized all ru-ral land.[125] A Ministry of Land Reform was empowered to issue regula-tions to implement the proclamation, and newly formed peasant associa-tions (PAs) were given the task of administering and distributing land, as well as of establishing specialized cooperative associations in areas such as labor and credit, pursuant to the directives of the ministry.[126]

In areas which were considered "communal" by the proclamation—corresponding to traditional systems of land use in northern Ethiopia (Eritrea) and central Ethiopia—the PAs were given the task of promot-ing the organization of cooperative farms among peasants. In this case, land was not distributed to individuals, but used in common, and peas-ants were accorded usufructuary rights.[127] In nomadic areas, associations were constituted to foster cooperation, and shepherds were given rights over land customarily used for grazing.[128]

As the government was "reluctant to irritate the volatile . . . Eritre-ans," as one observer commented, Dergue representatives did not always forcefully push land reform in northern areas, thereby tacitly nullifying many provisions of the proclamation.[129] However, all peasants had to pay a multiplicity of taxes, such as land tax, which was levied irrespective of the size of the holding and which increased sevenfold from 1977 to 1984.[130] They also paid income tax and were dunned for "voluntary" payments in cash and labor for public fund-raising campaigns, such as the "call to the Motherland," which helped pay for the Dergue's mili-tary campaigns in Eritrea and Tigray. They were also forced to contrib-ute to PAs, youth and women's associations.[131] It is not surprising, con-sidering the time spent at endless ideological seminars and political meetings, that peasants felt "over burdened and resentful."[132]

In Akele Guzai, as in other areas of Eritrea, PAs never functioned fully. In 1981, the EPLF destroyed the infrastructure of two PAs in Akele Guzai and four in Seraye, and arrested all the officials appointed by the Dergue.[133] During periods of frequent droughts, the PAs were given European Union food aid by the Dergue, provided that they formed an armed wheat militia to "oppose the EPLF."[134]

The Liberation Struggle: 1961–1991

Both the ELF and the EPLF attempted to change some basic aspects of traditional land tenure in the areas under their control. In its National Democratic Program of 1977, the main thrust of the EPLF's agricultural policy (just as the Dergue) was the creation of cooperative and state farms.[135] The EPLF claimed that colonial occupation and war had hampered the *diesa/shehena* system. As a consequence of privileges accorded by the colonial authorities to political appointees, village dignitaries, and churches, their lands were exempted from redistribution and sizably expanded. Feudal relations were even more pronounced in the lowland areas, where the land was in the hands of an aristocratic class of dominant families (*shumagulle* and *diglal*), who exacted heavy dues and services from nomads.[136]

An individual family's share of *diesa/shehena* land typically did not exceed 1.5 acres; continual use of the same land had caused considerable degradation. In addition, some families kept their rural land after migrating to the cities, and the land was consequently not available for redistribution. An equitable redistribution of land and the revival of the *diesa/shehena* system became two of the central themes of EPLF policy. The program of 1977 called for the confiscation of "all land in the hands of the aggressor Ethiopian regime, the imperialists, zionists and Eritrean lackeys," the abolition of feudal land relations, and the redistribution of land as a fundamental prerequisite to building "an independent, self reliant and planned national economy."[137] Another goal of the front was the permanent settlement of nomads, a sensitive and contentious topic to this day. Article 2.A of the 1977 program said that the EPLF would "provide the nomads with . . . agricultural advisors and financial assistance in order to enable them to lead settled lives."[138]

In 1981, the front distributed land to sixty-two landless men and women in the village of Mai-Zila. And in 1982, five other communities in Akele Guzai redistributed land to some 275 peasants.[139] The EPLF attempted to change the discriminatory nature of the previous land systems toward women and strangers. Ownership of land remained communal and subject to the village assembly. Women and young people were recognized as possessors of equal rights of access to the land.[140] Under articles 192 and 193 of the EPLF property law, all heads of households were entitled to a full share of land. Under art. 195, the people's assembly of the village had to keep a land register and issue a certificate to each landholder. Article 203 allowed people who had substantially improved their plots to be compensated before the next redistribution of land.[141]

From 1976 to 1981, the EPLF redistributed land in 162 villages throughout Eritrea. Most had been under *diesa/shehena* tenure, but the twenty-four that had been under *demaniale* were converted to *diesa*.[142] Reform was carried out in the following manner: A "unity of armed propaganda," comprising EPLF cadres, promoted in each village the formation of a peasant's assembly of about ten people.[143] The peasant's assembly, which was convened by traditional chiefs but whose debates were overseen by the EPLF, carried out distribution of land. After the redistribution was completed, the assembly appointed two committees, the first composed of nine members charged with any future redistribution and the second composed of twelve members mandated to run the village from then on.[144]

Four classes of people were excluded from the redistribution. These included "commandos," a special task force of the Ethiopian army composed entirely of Eritreans; people regarded as rich *"compradores"* by the peasant's assembly; those who had not cultivated their land for five years or more; and those who possessed land in other villages. The redistribution of church land was also discussed. In the end, it was decided that priests could take part in the allocation, but unlike in the past, they would not be allowed to possess more land than any other peasant, and they would be compelled to cultivate the land themselves.

ELF land reform policy was outlined in its policy statement, "Building a Democratic Liberation Front," of May 1975. It pledged that land ownership under *diesa* and *resti* "shall be democratized and organized for the realization of social justice and greater productivity."[145] The ELF undertook land reform in some parts of Akele Guzai.[146] We do not know to what extent these attempt were successful. One witness called their attempts in Serage "a complete failure."[147] But more recent research has indicated that there was a measure of success in at least one district.

The Tsilma district of Seraye has been particularly well-documented. In 1974 the Dergue attempted to institute land reform in most of the villages. *Resti* was abolished and women were granted rights over land. Some villages were instructed to amalgamate their land with that of adjacent villages. The reform caused considerable disquiet, and as a consequence, the villagers refused to cultivate the land, frustrating the Dergue's policy.[148] From 1977 until the early 1980s, the ELF controlled the same district. It carried out reform in all but three villages; *diesa* tenure was instituted and women received three-quarters of the share of a man.[149] After their victory in the civil war, the EPLF dominated the district; they instituted land reform in just one village—Adi Kiblo. However, the reform generated much hostility and was not continued.[150]

The land reform policies of the EPLF, ELF, and Dergue had many similarities, perhaps not surprising in view of the indebtedness of all three movements to Marxist and socialist writings. In practice, the Dergue experienced considerable resistance from Eritrean peasants, while the ELF and the EPLF, being national liberation movements, were more welcomed. In the short run, none of the policies were particularly effective. In the case of the EPLF, quite a lot of land was redistributed but was frequently taken back if the Dergue reoccupied the areas.

During the struggle, the National Union of Eritrean Women argued consistently that the EPLF's land reform program should provide that women should have equal opportunity to own land, that in the case of divorce they should receive their share of family-owned land, and that a widow or spinster should have the right to half the family land.[151] This was taken into account when the EPLF drafted their property law and, later on, their civil code.

Liberation

The first intervention of the government of independent Eritrea pertaining to land was proclamation 2/91 containing provisions of repeal and amendment to the Ethiopian Civil Code.[152] Rules relating to land are also contained in the section titled "Amendments dealing with the EPLF Civil Code." Articles 182–213 of the proclamation basically represent—with some adjustment—the extension to the new Eritrean state of rules and regulations that applied to EPLF liberated areas before independence.[153]

The bulk of the reform can be summarized as follows. Village administration was to be carried out by a public assembly (art. 182.1).[154] This assembly was entrusted with the classification of rural land into "arable and non arable" categories (art. 183) and of the appointment of an allocation committee, having the sole task of distributing arable land to the villagers (art. 185).[155] The distribution had to be done equitably, without any discrimination based on race, sex, or religion (art. 186).[156] After land had been allocated, the allocation committee was supposed to disband (art. 190.1).

The right over land was defined as "usufruct," a temporary right, lasting up to a new reallocation (art. 202).[157] The usufructuary must be compensated for improvements (art. 203). Access to land did not give the user the right to dispose of it by sale or succession, or give it to others (art. 201).

It should be noted that a group of rules open up the system with regards to customary rights of access to land. Forests and grazing areas—traditionally "reserved" by custom—are excluded from reallocation (art. 184); a village may administer lands located in different places, for example in the lowlands and highlands (art. 182.3); and a peasant's share can be constituted by land from "two villages which are far away from one to another/for example one on the highland and the other on the lowlands" (art. 204).

One of the first acts of the provisional government was to establish a Land Commission for the revision of property ownership and for the restitution of land nationalized during the period of the Dergue. Its general policy was to reject changes made by the Dergue.[158] However, in some areas such as Ghinda and Dongola, it mirrored the policies of the Dergue in collectivizing agriculture and envisaging state farms.[159] In the event, none of this program was implemented, and in any case it was superseded by the land proclamation 58/94, enacted in accordance with a resolution passed by the Third EPLF Congress.

Recent Eritrean Legislation

The 1994 land proclamation is the most significant legislation enacted after liberation, sweeping away all of the existing land tenure systems and transferring ownership to the Eritrean state.[160] More precisely, the Eritrean government conserved the nationalized status of land that had existed under the Dergue.[161] The proclamation lays out the policy for land reform in the rural areas. It also gives a framework for expropriation processes and establishes the bodies entrusted with the implementation of land reform. Legal notice 31/97 and proclamation 95/97, issued on the basis of proclamation 58/94, provide for a system of management/distribution of rural and urban land, and land earmarked for urban development and expansion, as well as for the implementation of a land registration system.[162]

The major primary sources are only available in Tigrinya; we are working from unofficial translations. The core of the reform is contained in article 3 of proclamation 58/94: all the land is owned by the state (3.1), rights over land may be granted only by the government (3.3), either by the Land Commission or a body delegated by it (3.6). Under the all-inclusive category of "usufruct," three categories of private rights over land are defined: housing land, farming land, and leasehold, ultimately reserved for investment activities.[163] Usufructuary rights

over housing and farming land (4.1 and 4.2) are granted to every Eritrean citizen who is eighteen years of age or emancipated (7.1) pursuant
to government authorization, on an equal basis, and without any discrimination based on sex, belief, race, or clan (4.4).[164] The broad principle laid down in article 4 is subsequently limited by more detailed
rules. For example, for acquiring housing land, Eritrean citizenship is
sufficient, but the right over rural land is restricted to village residents,
and persons whose livelihood depends on land (6.1 and 6.3). On the
other hand, leasehold can be granted to aliens, as well as to businesses
and associations with legal personality (legal notice 31/97, art. 6).

The proclamation did away with the periodic redistribution of land
that was so central to the *diesa* and *shehena* systems. The farmer working
the land is allowed a lifetime usufruct (18.2). Land cannot be sold or
released (24.1). After the death of the usufructuary, the land is restored
to the government, but, subject to certain conditions, priority over the
land held by the deceased is given to the second generation (12.3–4;
24.2–3). Usufructuaries must use the land for the purposes for which it
is granted—to build within three years, or to cultivate within two years
following the grant of the concession—and thereafter the land will re-
vert to the government, unless there is a good cause for the delay (29.4,
13). The usufruct for farming may be converted into lease, the terms
and duration of which are determined by a contract between usufructuary and the land administrative body (LAB) (18.3).

Section three of the land proclamation deals with the regime of expropriation. The government or another appropriate body has the "right
and power" to expropriate, with adequate compensation, lands granted
in usufruct pursuant to proclamation 58/94 "for purposes of various
development and capital investment projects aimed at national reconstruction or other similar purposes."[165] No indication is given as to the
amount of compensation to be paid for land expropriated by the government.

A Land Commission and LABs are the institutions entrusted to implement reform. The Land Commission is directly accountable to the
Office of the President; it has "supreme authority on the matters pertaining to land." It is charged with formulating devices for the implementation of the proclamation, to issue general and special directives,
to coordinate and direct the implementation of the law (57.1–2). LABs
are subordinate executive bodies of the Land Commission; they are to
be established in each sub-zone (legal notice 31/97, art. 5).[166] They are
entrusted with duties of implementation "in the field" of some proclamation articles, among them the classification of land into arable and

non-arable categories and the preparation of details of arable land for purposes of redistribution (9.1–2).

Principles for the planning of rural and urban areas are contained in legal notice 31/97. The Ministry of Land, Water, and Environment (hereinafter MLWE) must prepare a land use plan and an area development plan (legal notice 31/97, arts. 3.1; 3.4). The lack of an efficient system of land rights registration, which is a prerequisite for land reform to be effective, was recognized by proclamation 95/97, establishing a cadastral office under MLWE "to register all land, rights over land and duties that emanate from such rights, and transfer of property through sales, donation, succession or other manner" (58/94, arts. 3.1, 5.1; 95/97, art. 3.1). The proclamation expressly repeals all previous provisions on the matter (95/97, art. 2). All land must be registered even if it had been distributed before the coming into force of the proclamation (95/97, art. 4.2; 31/97, art. 3.14), the registration and allocation of land parcels are prerequisites for the distribution of land (95/97, art. 4.1).[167] The proper administration of this scheme would require a great many more trained bureaucrats than even Eritrea at peace could devote to the task. Because of the conflict with Ethiopia over the past three years and its aftermath, nothing has been done to further this project.

This radical agrarian policy was not universally popular; the academic criticism that has been voiced so far assumes that the EPLF policy of 1977 has been enshrined in Eritrean government legislation. For example, Joireman criticizes it for "failing to ensure grazing rights for lowlanders." She claims that Markakis asserts that it is the Eritrean government's *intention* [our emphasis] to expropriate Muslim pastoralist lowlands for large-scale farming.[168] Actually Markakis says that the government seems to have given "little thought . . . to the obvious impact of such development on the pastoralist mode of production."[169] Tronvoll echoes this attack and adds an unsubstantiated comparison with the ELF. According to him, the ELF "supported the nomad's traditional way of life and defended their rights of livelihood."[170] In fact, ELF policy was outlined in its policy statement, *Building a Democratic Liberation Front*, of May 1975. "The revolutionary state shall settle those sections of the Eritrean population who have been condemned to a lifetime of nomadism."[171]

Wilson uses some primary sources on which to base his critique. He alludes to the "tragedy of the commons," the influential theory of the 1960s that argues that as all those who graze their herds in common areas have an incentive to overstock the land, overgrazing and land de-

terioration is inevitable.[172] Because a number of other developing nations
have attempted to avoid the tragedy of the commons by enticing or forcing pastoralists to settle down to a sedentary life as farmers, Wilson
jumps to the conclusion that this is also the intention of the Eritrean
government.[173] In his words, the fact that the Agricultural Commission
of the EPLF (in a policy statement drafted before liberation in 1991)
does not outline a policy to protect pastoralist rights is an indication
that the EPLF "favors sedentary practices over pastoralism."[174] In fact,
the commission acknowledged that the encroachment of farming into
traditional grazing areas creates serious conflict between agriculturists
and pastoralists. A policy problem then arises on how to resolve this
potential conflict without creating political problems.[175] Wilson also ne-
glects to mention that the tragedy of the commons applies just as much
to communally owned farming land; Girmai Abraham gives a detailed
account of how this theory also applies to *diesa* land.[176]

The situation is more complex than these writers realize, and it requires a much more analytical treatment than it has been given so far.
It receives a critical but more balanced assessment by Kidane Mengisteab.[177] He argues that since land is scarce in the highlands, to grant
land concessions to all commercial farmers and usufructuary rights over
land to all adults over eighteen "is certain to lead to marked encroachment on grazing areas." Of course, as lowlanders are predominantly nomadic shepherds and users of the rangeland, they may suffer most in
this situation because they could lose the land they have used for many
years, land that they regard as their own right. But pastoralism is not
limited to the lowlands; 40 percent of livestock is in the highlands.[178]
Traditional seasonal transhumance—which is actually common to both
Christian and Muslim—may be at risk before a valid alternative has
been created, without "concrete measures to first attract and integrate
them into a different mode of production." The permanent settlement
of nomads is probably the preferred goal of the Eritrean government; as
some key figures in the Land Commission have pointed out, this follows
from the policy expressed by the EPLF during the war.[179]

A sound policy of land reform should balance the interests involved.
It is clear that in emphasizing some issues, others will be sacrificed. On
the one hand, the drafters of the proclamation precisely delineate many
of the deficiencies of traditional land tenure systems.[180] Among these
are: (a) land reallocation after a few years—common to *diesa* and *shehena*
—hampered improvements and long-term investments; (b) the traditional system creates and exacerbates land disputes and friction, especially in densely populated areas and where farmers come into contact
with shepherds; (c) impoverishment of agricultural resources and deg-

radation of the environment due to unplanned and irrational exploitation of resources. On the other hand, the critics of land reform remark that it eliminates many of the roles of the village by allowing the state to take over duties formerly reserved to the village. As the village is no longer the provider of land, its social and administrative functions are unlikely to remain intact.[181] Many positive features of the traditional system will be sacrificed in this process of change, and this will undermine the village before viable alternative institutions are developed—creating a possibly dangerous vacuum.

The land proclamation specifies that to introduce a new system of land allocation, previously existing boundaries shall be invalidated (40). It indicates that "all villages in Eritrea shall, according to local custom, use their own pasture and wood (48.1)."[182] But if the village loses its authority over its traditional boundaries, it will become difficult to maintain land set aside for grazing. Another instance of where the government's land policies reflect a value issue can be seen in the selection of persons eligible to receive land. In this case the basic principle of gender equality voiced by the EPLF before liberation and by the Eritrean government now, but by no means endemic in Eritrean traditional society—clashes with the need to decrease pressure over land.[183] Kidane Mengisteab has pointed out that as long as all adults—male and female—over the age of eighteen have the right to land, the pressure over land will increase. And of course the kinship system will come under relentless attack.[184] We will look further at this issue in our concluding chapter. Another important provision of the land proclamation that has given rise to some debate and opposition is that contained in article 15.2. This gives a woman rights to a house in her home village. In the view of a number of rural people interviewed by Yirgalem Woldegabriel in 1998, this is contributing to the breakup of the family.[185]

There is also another problem. The experience of several other African states that have nationalized land and attempted to introduce a leasehold system has been far from a happy one. In the case of Zimbabwe, Uganda, and Zambia, the state has found it very difficult to take effective control over much of the country. And whenever access to land is a matter of bureaucratic discretion, there is the potential for abuse of office, misuse of influence, and corruption.[186]

It also remains to be seen to what extent legal rules governing the allocation of property rights work in practice. The experience of many post-socialist countries has shown that a gap can arise between a set of rules that allocates property rights equally and the real world where many people are deprived.[187] In the case of Eritrea, where the land belongs to the state, it is important to evaluate the extent to which the principle of equal access to land for Eritreans of both sexes is to be implemented. There is an important proviso in legal notice 31/97.[188] People who have not completed their national service obligations, and the Jehovah's Witnesses who have refused to undertake them, will not be allocated land. We know that a significantly lower proportion of females have completed their national service obligations compared to men; this will skew land allocation in the future in favor of men.

However, as of writing, land reform has not yet been implemented; neither have the LABs started operating, even though many people face an acute shortage of land, and a radical redistribution is long overdue. In 1996, two pilot sites were chosen for a trial run to see how the proclamation would work in practice. In December 1996 a lottery was held by the Land Commission in Adi Guadid to allocate the first parcels of land. There were more villagers than parcels and what happened to those who did not win the lottery is not clear.[189] Pending the implementation of the proclamation (through the issue of a legal regulation), villages continue to use the *diesa/shehena* system. This is the system now practiced by the great majority of Eritrean farmers.[190]

Article 45 of the land proclamation authorizes villages and the government to allocate grazing lands; once again no regulation has been issued.[191] Some 75 percent of the population is either pastoralist or agro-pastoralist, so the preservation of pasture is a priority. Obviously, land will remain a major area of concern for Eritrean governments of the future.

International Actors

At most times in Eritrean history international actors have played only a cameo role in the drama of land reform and tenure. For generations the Ethiopian Orthodox Church was a major landholder. The Italian government later expropriated large areas for plantation agriculture and managed to export produce to the Middle East and Europe. From the time of Haile Selassie onward a multitude of agricultural consultants descended on the country without making much of an impact. Since independence, the Eritrean government has attempted to pursue a strategy of self-reliance, and consultants have largely acted as adjuncts of the state.

Seven

Land Disputes and Conflict Resolution

> Together with *histoires de femmes* land disputes are the
> main issue dealt with by the tribunals.
>
> —A Kobben[1]

The written record and oral history shows that Eritrea has been plagued
by disputes over land since time immemorial. The need for land was at
the root of many of the migrations to the area of present-day Eritrea and
Ethiopia. "Whoever studies the history of Abyssinia, without precon-
ceived and predetermined theories, realizes that this is nothing other
than the history of fights and endless disputes of one group against another."[2]

Eritrea has in proportion to its population an extremely small amount
of fertile land. Over the centuries there have been enormous problems
of land degradation and despoliation as the elements have taken their
toll and warring armies ranged over all the country. The amount of land
available for cultivation or grazing has decreased markedly. These are all
the ingredients for classic battles over land, and it is surprising that
there have not been more clashes. One source claims, citing the Ethiopian Ministry of Land Reform, that in the early 1960s, 30 percent of all
civil disputes in Eritrea concerned *resti*, and these were the most bitter.[3]
In the past years, some 75 percent of civil cases brought to court in
Seraye related to land ownership.[4]

Land disputes are paradigmatic to show how theories of legal pluralism and levels of analysis can enrich and complement each other, and
how by their interaction we come to an improved understanding of particular situations. A number of charismatic individuals are frequently
involved; the sub-national level is always important. When we introduced the actors in the first chapter, we referred to traditional law as a
single subject, with a coherent and unitary body of rules. But as we have

131

seen in subsequent chapters, each ethnie or sub-ethnie has its own rules at the micro level. The same proviso applies to *šarīʿa*—in Muslim communities tradition and religion mix and interrelate. The state also offers its own solutions and tries to impose them. And its interest may be different from that of the other actors. Once again the system is dynamic; equilibrium is fragile, and it changes all the time. The colonial and Eritrean states play vital roles at different periods. Religion and ideology are also crucial. Each of these "levels" expresses a particular set of rules, attitudes, and beliefs; their relationship is never static and varies from case to case. Rules may or may not conflict with each other, but unless we look at a particular dispute we cannot see in practice how they interrelate.

In this chapter we first of all examine a number of the major causes of disputes over land, using the traditional codes as a basis. These include disputes over property rights, pastures, reallocation of *shehena / diesa* land, and boundary problems. Section two contains a number of selected cases arranged in ascending order of complexity. We start with conflicts among individuals and move onto intra- and inter-ethnie disputes. We then look at conflict that has arisen directly out of a ruler's attempt to govern—including that of the colonial Italian state, Ethiopia, and ELF/EPLF, as well as the sovereign Eritrean government. Our analysis ranges over time; one of its goals is to focus on whichever actors are the most important in each particular case—and the roles played by the supporting cast. In the final section we analyze in more detail the actors involved, beginning with those mandated to solve the conflict in various time periods. We conclude with a description of how our case studies fit various models of dispute resolution. A number of cases have proved extremely difficult to resolve; we try to give some explanation for these failures. We also show how five or six conflicts, including the festering Hazamo and Tor'a/Tsenadegle disputes, seem to have been successfully resolved.[5]

A part of the chapter embraces problems in the border areas with Ethiopia. The extreme violence of 1998–2000 cannot adequately be accounted for in terms of a simple model; it is essential to appreciate its complex and multi-causal nature. We examine this "conflict over land" both through the lenses of "our" legal actors, each of whom sees it in a different way, and as a current level of analysis problem. It is dealt with as a land issue in order to demonstrate that conflicts over land are also conflicts over power, hegemony, and legitimacy. Here the two dimensions of state and land coincide: land as communal or private property, and land as part of the territory of the state.

When we look at land disputes as a level of analysis problem, the individual studies are spread across a continuum. A dispute may involve just two individuals arguing over a small parcel of land, or a minor infraction of traditional rules regarding the grazing of pastures. When the number of actors increases, so does the complexity, which makes the resolution of the dispute even more difficult. The most complex case we examine involves vast areas of land and two of the most formidable military powers in Africa. Many international actors have played a part, making analysis as well as resolution almost impossibly difficult.

In the disputes that follow, we look first of all at their causes and the traditional rules that have been devised to settle or to pre-empt them. It is often unclear precisely which area of land is covered by a particular traditional law, whether the law applies to all the population in a particular region or just the dominant ethnie, and whether the inhabitants are governed by other laws. In chapter 2 we gave a number of instances when groups—*enda*, sub-ethnies, and clans—became dissatisfied with rules imposed upon them. They may have broken away from their original *enda* and begun to live in accordance with a new code, and in the intermediate period, they would be governed by two sets of traditional rules until they had sufficiently asserted their complete independence.

We also discuss the role of entities such as the colonial government, church, mosque, occupying force, or liberation movements in attempting to resolve conflicts. Nadel said that "the whole customary law of Eritrea can only be understood as a law which evolved in a society with no special executive body to enforce judicial orders and decisions."[6] Clearly this does not take into account the shifting nature of tradition and its ability to mutate over time as it reacts with other actors. The highland traditional codes show a contamination between *enda* rules and the power of the *Bahr Negash* (lord of the sea, a man nominated by the emperor of Ethiopia to collect tribute) on the one hand and the colonial state on the other. Moreover, colonial authorities played a part in settling disputes, and this process can be seen from the Italians through the British to the Ethiopians.

Of course, success or failure may turn out to be temporary; moreover, what constitutes success or failure? A conflict may appear to have been resolved to the satisfaction of all parties, but then break out again some months, years, decades, or even centuries later, when circumstances have changed or memories may have become confused. Only a foolish analyst would claim that a conflict has been satisfactorily resolved for all time. After all, as a Chinese leader observed when asked what he thought of the French Revolution": "It is still too early to say."

I. Causes of Dispute Seen through the Lenses of Traditional Codes and Commentators

The main purpose of traditional law was the settlement of disputes through reconciliation. There is a long tradition in Africa of reaching decision by unanimous consent. By spending a long time debating a problem, all issues could be raised and minority voices given a fair hearing. Through this decision-making process a person who started out in the minority might be able to convince the other parties of the correctness of an opinion.[7] By taking a long time to reach a decision and examining every side of the issue, there is less chance of an unworkable settlement being railroaded through. This approach differs markedly from Western democracies, which have a built-in risk factor of a permanent minority, which is disenfranchised, discontented, and poses a threat to stability.

Traditional rules were formulated as a result of frequent and prolonged consensual debate. Once a decision had been reached, all participants obeyed it because it was regarded as equitable. If over time decisions became ineffective, they would be revised. From an early age children would be taken to the village assembly to learn and remember the procedures, and build up knowledge of the collective wisdom of the assembly. We agree with Beck that communitarian practices, together with decision making through consensual procedures, permeate the rules of traditional African societies. They are seen as a cornerstone of an African dimension of human rights that emphatically rejects predominant Western conceptions.[8]

We examine the codes in detail in order to determine the major and most common points of contention and potential conflict over land, the overriding concern of all villagers. In this section we deal in passing with rules relating to houses, ruins, and cattle, but only insofar as they relate to land disputes.

Who Is the Legitimate Owner?

We have seen in chapter 6 who is entitled to receive land property. Theoretically, under *shehena / diesa*, disputes over land titles within the village could not arise since all land was owned by the village and not by individuals. However, during the past century land was rarely distributed within the prescribed period; for some villages, fifty years or more had elapsed since the most recent redistribution. Inevitably, some peasants had become particularly attached to "their" plots of land and were reluctant to hand them over. Moreover, a multiplicity of concurrent rights over the same land had arisen because of *gulti, medri worki, crai,* and *sedbi* leases, often involving foreigners; this made the situation much less clear-cut. The same applied to *resti,* where determining who was entitled usually involved complicated rules of inheritance.

As a principle, land should remain with the direct male line of the original occupiers. Whoever was able to prove he was a descendent of a *restegnat* family had a right to a share of land, no matter how long ago he had left the *enda* (*Adgena Tegeleba,* art. 234).[9] In the *Loggo Sarda,* it is clearly stated that the "foreigner who lives among the *Loggo,* cannot buy *resti*" (§9).[10] Conti Rossini explains the rule as a way of preventing the transfer of land to non-qualified descendants, especially foreigners.[11]

The concept of the foreigner, liminary, or stranger is relevant to Africa. Such individuals often enjoyed a privileged social or economic position. Georg Simmel in his brilliant essay *Der Fremde* wrote that the stranger's position in a group was "determined essentially, by the fact that he has not belonged to it from the beginning, that he imports qualities into it which do not, and cannot stem from the group itself."[12] "Tolerance, indifference, and the absence of overt forms of hostility for the most part characterize the attitudes of Ethiopians toward strangers."[13]

Enda Fegrai, after stating that "the same rules apply to the sale of houses [and housing land] as to the sale of *resti,*" differentiated the position of foreigners and family members (art. 8§10). Anyone who belonged to the *Egghela enda* could ask the village for land on which to build a house (art. 8§§1–3). A foreigner did not have the right to a plot, but he could buy an existing house or ask for a ruin that he could rebuild (art. 8§4). Also in this instance, the request was taken into consideration only after all members of the *enda* were satisfied (art. 8§5). If the stranger did not follow this procedure, the sale could be voided at any time (art. 8§6). In light of the above, the position of foreigners appears to be ambivalent. On the one hand foreigners are unable to obtain *resti.* We have seen in chapter 6 that foreigners did on occasion obtain *resti* in order to relieve the burden of taxation on the *enda.*[14] On the other hand, always according to the *Enda Fegrai, ghebri* was a right for each family head of the village—that is to say for each emancipated married man (§§1–2). Foreigners had the equal right to obtain *ghebri* land if they submitted to all contributions made by other villagers (including tribute to the king) (§3).[15]

The *Enda Fegrai* rules in this instance are some of the most apparently contradictory we have seen and must have led to the most extraordinary problems. For example: A villager may have emigrated and been away for decades; when he returns to the village, he may claim to belong to an *enda* and consequently demand his share. Because of the absence of any rule of prescription (statute of limitation) in traditional law, he had this right, whatever time had elapsed. On the other hand, proving this claim could be almost impossible. A clearer rule is present in the *Mehen Mahaza* code, which indicated that whoever asked for a share of land was entitled to it, whether they be members of the *enda* or foreigners (Christian or Muslim), provided they had a guarantor (§§4–5).[16]

The question of who was the rightful owner was made harder by the possibility of coexistence of many rights over the same plot. Dealing with cultivation of land, the *Fetha Mahari* of the Mensa described a situation of scarce resources, where all sorts of agreements between landowners, cattle owners, and cultivators could be reached. It is not difficult to see how disputes could arise in a situation of such complexity. As a rule, the owner of the land had the right to keep for himself the crop.[17] Detailed procedures for dividing produce pertained when cultivation was carried out with oxen belonging to somebody other than the owner.[18] When the land was fallow, the owner could authorize another to use it for pasture and to fertilize it. In this case, crop sharing had to follow particular rules.[19] If the land was given temporarily to a friend or a relative, the owner did not have any right over the crop (§7). A different regime applied when cultivation was carried out without the consent of the owner.[20]

Some codes reserved special land rights to the church (see, for example, *Adkeme Melega* (art. 45§3).[21] Other codes show the existence of a *dominium eminens* of the king, to which land rights of villagers were subordinated. The *Mehen Mahaza*, dealing with the cultivation of someone else's land and its improper use, specifies that "whoever cultivates certain land, and receives intimation in the name of the king or of the government (*zeban negùs* or *zeban mängesti*) to stop cultivation, has to stop immediately and if, having received the intimation he does not obey it, he must pay a fine of 55 MTD" (art. 22§1).[22] The impetus for these rules is always scarcity of resources. That they were laid down so carefully may indicate a situation of latent hostility in which as many details as possible had to be taken into account in an attempt to preempt and cope with future disputes. As we have seen in chapter 6, there is a substantial difference between paying tribute, implying that a superior power such as a king or church is recognized, and claiming ownership. That it is usually the owner who has to pay the tribute over a certain land shows this. But this rule contains exceptions, such as in the case of *sedbi*, where the lessee is the one who has the duty to pay. It is obvious that in such a complicated situation, property rights were not easy to ascertain.

Münzinger depicts an exception to this complicated bundle of rights over land for Kunama and Nara societies of the late nineteenth century. Among them land was abundant and little economic value was attached to it. Neither was there a noble class who could claim to be the first owners. A vacant plot of land belonged to the first who found it, and village property did not need to be demarcated. Anyone could build a house basically wherever they wanted to, and permanently retained the right over land and house.[23] As was the case in pre-colonial Buganda, it was an open society where social ties between the people and *de facto* occupation (possession) of land were more relevant that the ownership of land *per se*.[24]

Reallocation of Shehena/Diesa *Land*

In chapter 6 we briefly discussed how the reallocation of *shehena* land should be performed and which individuals were entitled to a share. We also mentioned earlier how and why disputes over communal land could have arisen. We give here some further details.

Reallocation takes place in the following manner. *Mai Adgi* states that married men and foreigners who wanted to exercise their right to participate in the redistribution had to wait for the special period of the year in which the allotment took place (§§9–10). Whoever was interested in taking part in the allotment had to inform the *nabara* of his lineage (art. 16§§8, 14). After the allotment, the previous holder of a particular plot gave it to the new one, but only after he had harvested two crops (§11).[25] It is unclear what happened if somebody was not satisfied with the arrangement. The *Enda Fegrai* also declares that *ghebri* was divided into equal plots and distributed in a specific period of the year (§§4, 6–8). If the request was late, it was necessary to wait for another five years, unless a plot became available because of somebody else's renunciation (§9).[26]

Under *shehena*, land was divided into fertile, medium, and poor categories. Clearly there would have been considerable arguments at the time of the periodic redistribution if the procedure was carried out unfairly. The codes are largely silent on the procedure to be adopted if the redistribution was not carried out at the specified time intervals or if dissatisfaction was voiced at the mix of land, and we interpret this to indicate that allocation was usually on time and fair. This is not surprising, as the equitable redistribution of communal land is the cornerstone of a successful *shehena* system. It is only with the coming of the colonial rulers that we begin to hear that redistribution was delayed for years or even decades.

The most interesting questions concerned foreigners. As we have seen, the codes in some instances allowed them to cultivate communal land when they were resident in the village, after having obtained the consent of the *enda*. Ostini mentions the case of Muslims in the village of Himberti; decades after they settled, they were allowed to build a mosque and establish a cemetery. Asmarom Legesse says they are called *Himishmish*, outsiders who over time have been tolerated, accepted, and assimilated.[27] They also obtained *ghebri* land for their families. During the BMA, there were many cases involving disputes with village elders who tried to use the powers that had been given to them by the Italians to deny newcomers land, distribute land according to the usual practices, and exclude foreigners from the redistribution.[28]

Transformation in the Status of Land

The process of transformation of land held communally into land held in a few hands (see chapter 6) accelerated in the late nineteenth century, but in all probability it was underway for many years before this. A significant instance of this is to be found in the code of the *Loggo Sarda* that dates back to the fifteenth century. Article 17 stated: "[W]hoever wants to transform common land into hereditary land must be expelled from the village!"[29] The fact that this rule has been specifically included in the code suggests that some villagers must have tried to sell or trade land held in common by the *enda*, family, or village, against the wishes of the majority. The majority still felt that the village was held together through the ties developed over many generations by owning and cultivating land in common. And traditional societies are inherently conservative.

During the latter part of Italian rule, disputes multiplied because of the growing rural population's increased pressure on land. There was considerable unrest in Hamasien concerning the *diesa* system introduced to some areas by the Italians. Inhabitants of at least sixteen villages appealed against this change on the grounds that the land had been *resti tsilmi*. The land had been held within the family for generations. Typically, villagers dislike change, and the prospect of handing over prized plots of land to be redistributed to the entire village did not please them in the least.

From 1930 to 1943, many villagers were jailed for civil disobedience, and a threat was even made to throw one appellant's father into the sea if the village did not accept the change.[30] Discontent continued during the period of the BMA. During 1942, Nadel, who at the time was political officer of Akele Guzai, heard a number of disputes involving land that had been changed from *resti* to *shehena*.[31] Probably as a consequence of this, the *Adgena Tegeleba* code was amended (art. 235 bis, inserted in April 1951). It ruled that "when the *ghebber* of a village decides with *fetzmi* to change their system of land tenure from *shehena* to *resti* or vice versa they must respect such *fetsmi*. They must respect the agreement for a period of 3 years, after which if the villagers are no longer willing to act according to the decision this may be canceled."[32]

Disputes over Land Sold or Given to a Cultivator

In the codes we read that the sale of land is hemmed in with all sorts of restrictions. Only somebody who has a qualified right over land can sell it. This refers to *resti*, *worki*, and *moras* (property obtained by gift), and only very exceptionally *shehena* or *diesa* land.

Article 15 of *Mehen Mahaza* deals with the procedure to be followed in the case of the sale of land and immovable property: "[W]hoever wants to sell inherited *resti*, a house or a ruin (*ona*), must first offer it to the closest relatives, then to other members of the *enda*, and only if all of them refuse, can he sell it to somebody else" (§1). But if the *resti*, house, or ruin is on his property as a consequence of a sale, "he must first of all offer it to the relatives of the first seller, and only if they refuse to buy, is it then possible to sell it to somebody else" (§2).

We find some rule of protection for the buyer here and there throughout the codes. For example, "this right [of family members to repossess the land] lapses if it is not exercised before the *Mescal* holiday in the year in which the sale takes place" (*Mehen Mahaza*, §3). When the sale is between villagers and the seller has misinformed the buyer on the quality of the land, the contract can be rescinded within one year (*Fetha Mahari*, art. 57§2).

This protection is exceptional. As a rule, relatives of the seller could claim back the property at their will, giving back to the purchaser the money paid, provided they were able to demonstrate that they were not informed about the sale (*Mehen Mahaza*, §3). Similarly, the law of *Adkeme Melega* (art. 36§8) states that the "owner of a house or land can still demand his property back no matter how long he has abandoned it."[33] Other laws lay down rather complex procedures. For example, in the case of the Mensa, the sale could be either definitive, or with a right of redemption to be exercised within a certain time according to the agreement, paying to the buyer twice the price paid (§§3–4). In any event the seller has the right to reverse the sale within three days, giving the price back to the buyer (art. 57§1). We find a similar rule among the Kunama and Nara: on the few occasions when land was sold, the sale could be definitive, or it could contain a clause stating that the original owner could claim it back at his will, giving back the price.[34]

It is easy to see how such rules could have given rise to all manner of disputes in the past. They are deeply casuistic and complicated, and slight difference in detail can mean that one rule applies rather than another. Rules no less complex exist for cattle and pastures (on some days land cannot be grazed) and their sale.[35]

The *danya,* guarantor, and witnesses play a vital role in sales of land and in preventing disputes. They record and recollect all the data. Their role was therefore important in a system where there was no land registry. In the *Adkeme Melega,* to be valid, the sale must be performed in front of a *danya* nominated by the parties, and the seller must have a guarantor to affirm that the seller has the property, that he has performed the offer in proper form, and that he will restore the money if the sale is voided. Five other witnesses are also required (art. 37§9).[36] Article 16 of *Mehen Mahaza* covers guaranty and guarantors. A guarantor is necessary for the sale of land, houses, and chattels. In the case of the death of the guarantor, the debt is transferred to the man's relatives (in order: father, children, and widow).[37] According to the *Fetha Mahari,* the sale must be performed in the presence of a guarantor (the brother or son of the seller) and of witnesses, in front of which the price and the terms of the sale must be expressed. If there is no guarantor, the seller can demand the land back at any time, returning the price to the buyer. If there are no witnesses, the contract is invalid (art. 54§§6, 8–9, art. 57§6, and art. 59).

It is clear that these rules were not easy to enforce. In the absence of written records, the details of sale transactions such as date, place, and price are stored in the memory of the people, inevitably creating uncertainty. Moreover, all the figures entrusted by tradition to prevent disputes have limitations; after all, they belong to the *enda* and therefore would protect the latter against any intrusion by a foreigner.

Lease Relations, Sharecropping

In the highlands, it was common for farmers in the case of *medri worki* or among *ghebbar* in the *diesa/shchena* system to lease portions of land in exchange for *meghes* (percentage of the crop) or *metellen* (lump sum). The codes explain how these contracts worked in practice.

The *Mai Adgi* law explains that if the land is leased, the owner cannot rescind the contract before the lessee has collected two crops (art. 16§16).[38] And article 9 of *Enda Fegrai*, relating to *shehena*, points out that land can be leased during the five-year period of allocation. To grant some security to the lessee, the owner cannot take back the land for one to two years. In order to repossess it, the owner must give proper notice before the month of *Gumbot* (roughly May); if he does not, the lessee has the right to keep his lease until *Mescal* (roughly the end of September, §§12–14).[39] According to *Adkeme Melega*, the owner can repossess his land before the termination date, but only under some conditions: at the same point in the crop cycle as when he leased it; after two years in the case of unproductive land, and after three crops have been taken in the case of productive land. The order to leave the land cannot be given from *Gumbot* to *Mescal* (art. 38§§5–6, 9).[40] The *Fetha Mahari* deals with rules in the case of sharecropping: three-quarters of the crop went to the cultivator and one-quarter to the owner. But if the landowner had also contributed half of the seeds and participated in the cleaning of the land, the allocation of the crop was fifty-fifty (art. 55§2).[41]

Reading these, as well as previous rules, one can understand the number of disputes that leasing could have produced because of the presence of so many terms and conditions. But disputes were especially prevalent when leases lasted for decades; the long period of time encouraged leaseholders to claim they possessed a vested interest over land and that this should prevail against every claim of a *restegnat*. Paradoxically, this situation was favored by the new legal regime introduced by the Italian colonial power. According to traditional law, it was inconceivable that the use of land could transform leaseholders into owners, even if the lease lasted for centuries. *Resti* could be claimed back at any time and could not be barred by statute. As a family member possesses land by virtue of a right vested in the family, acquisition of this right (usucaption) from an absent family member is inconceivable. For example, according to the *Loggo Sarda*, "the right to land cannot be forfeited even if it is left abandoned. If somebody else without your authority begins to use the land, to claim back the land all that is necessary is to proclaim your will (shouting loudly) to reclaim your right."[42] With *circolare* 18753, 20 December 1929, the Italian government introduced the rule of prescription: "[T]he action of *restegnatat* against those who possess the land for more than 40 years, provided that the possession has been with no interruptions, continuous, and peaceful, shall be rejected."

This principle was strengthened under the Federation by article 7 of the Act on Administration of Justice of 1953, according to which "no action for the recovery of land or for the enforcement of rights over or in respect of land or other similar rights shall be brought before the courts more than 40 years after such interest or rights is alleged to have arisen." In theory, the situation was clear. The legal owner is the one who pays the tribute to the state: leaseholders cannot raise land ownership claims because they paid *meghes* and *metellen* to *restegnat*, who in turn paid tribute to the state. The use of land against the periodic payment of *meghes* and *metellen* means indirect acknowledgment of the right of the owner: the lessee is not qualified to acquire land by prescription.[43]

As one might expect, a number of problems arose in practice. Already during the BMA, we have evidence of disputes on these matters. To defuse the situation, the chiefs of Akele Guzai decided to defer all *sedbi* disputes until the Second World War was over.[44] Later on, Eritrea experienced massive upheaval during decades of war and famine. Many owners died, were dispossessed, or were exiled. In such situations ownership and occupancy could become equivocal categories in practical and legal terms.

Conflict over Communal Property, with Particular Regard to Pasture Rights

Ethnies have frequently got into disputes over pastures; consequently the codes give the matter great importance. Uncultivated land used for pastures formed the bulk of communal land. Unlike *resti* and *shehena*, which were—even if only temporarily—for the sole use of a family or individual, pastureland was undivided and used by the entire village.[45] A majority of highland codes have detailed rules relating to cattle and the compensation due for theft, grazing infractions, and guardianship of fields.[46] They also deal exhaustively with other communal properties such as forests and trees, the right to collect wood, and water and irrigation rights.[47]

There were fewer conflicts over such communal property since they concern fairly small entities such as clan or villages. The bitterest disputes involved the relations of one community with another community, and these were usually not covered by the codes. Such conflicts included those between Tigrinya from different provinces, districts, sub-districts, villages, and lineage groups; between Saho from various clans; as well as between Saho and Tigrinya.[48] We will mention some of these disputes in the second section of this chapter.

Demarcation of Boundaries

The rules we have found on borders, even if of a smaller local impact, indicate awareness of the need for a proper demarcation of borders at all

levels but within the area defined by the specific code. These rules refer to borders within the village, between villages, between *enda*. For
example, article 31 of the *Scioatte Anseba* deals with land bordering on
the neighbors. The owner of a field which has not been harvested cannot
take his cattle for pasture onto the harvested field of the neighbor: "neither the border, nor the field shall be used for pasture." If he does this,
he has to pay a fine of 2 MTD.[49] The *Adkeme Melega* established the fine
due from an individual who violated the borders between plots of land;
in 1945, it was set at 60 MTD.[50] Disputes between villages over boundaries, such as that between Digsa and Hebo during the Italian period,
were common. Although the Digsa lost the dispute, the arguments continue to the present day.[51]

In this context, the watchman, *zera*, played an important role in enforcing the rules that boundaries should be respected. However, these
rules are of little help in defining the "boundaries" between the community dealt with in a specific code and the "others." Other rules, written and oral, including those pertaining to war and raids, are applied
to solve these problems. However, some of the codes, such as *Mehen
Mahaza*, were clearly intended to cover the whole province.

II. The Dispute: Selected Case Studies

This section is organized in the following way. A clear distinction has
been attempted between disputes among people of the same ethnie, disputes between ethnies, and finally conflicts between states. A selected
number of illustrative case studies are explored to show the great variety
of often complex disputes that have occurred. In section three we examine the resolution or non-resolution of these conflicts and draw some
general conclusions. When we started our research, we did not intend to
deal with the "border dispute" (in fact an extremely vicious war) with
Ethiopia in great detail. But because the issue of land as a cause of the
war has been dealt with so far in a superficial and often misleading way,
we are trying to remedy this deficiency.[52]

Conflicts within the Village and Lineage

We have not found many recorded cases of disputes involving an individual acting on his own against another individual of the same *enda* or
village. Conflicts within the village, clan, and lineage are also little-
documented. Some may find surprising this lack in a country where
records are usually kept with more than meticulous care. And, as we
have seen, these are the issues on which the codes concentrate. The rela-

tive lack of documented legal cases in these areas may be due to two factors that are likely to be interrelated. First, traditional law was usually efficient at preventing and solving conflict at the group level. In the past, "individual" disputes were probably infrequent—or if they occurred they were settled before they reached the trial stage—because the collective dimension of the conflict substituted for and took over from the personal dimension. An individual dispute was a family dispute, to be solved by the head of the family or the oldest male in the *enda*. When a village was entirely comprised of one *enda*, a dispute between villagers was regarded as a family matter, to be settled as a private question. Second, the lack of data about such conflicts may exist simply because the dispute never attained such a "critical level" of importance as to reach an appeals court or to be reflected in traditional laws and commentaries. This shows the ability of the lineage/family/*enda* to negotiate and settle conflicts internally without involving an external mediator or umpire.

In more recent times, there is at least one well-documented instance of a determined individual taking on a power traditionally belonging to the village or another large entity. In 1967, Mengisteab Wolde Kidane asked the Ethiopian government for a concession to plow some 650 hectares of land that had been confiscated by the Italian government and set aside as grazing land. He commenced farming and fenced the land—which included a water hole previously used by all villagers in common. In 1973, elders from the village of Deranto complained about Mengisteab's actions on the ground of their incompatibility with traditional rules on pastures. With the coming into power of the Dergue, the Ethiopian Ministry of Land Reform stated that the use of the disputed land for agriculture might open the door for conflict, so the land was declared to be government property to be used for grazing by the village.[53]

This case is notable as it sheds light on how a determined individual can pursue his own self-interest even though the entire village is against him. If an individual could claim village land, and particularly the water hole, which is traditionally communal land, then the entire system of village solidarity has broken down, or at least has deteriorated. There are no doubt more such cases in the Eritrean and Ethiopian Ministries of Justice archives waiting for researchers to analyze.

Disputes within an Ethnie

Unlike the disputes examined in the previous section, disputes involving two or more *enda* are well-recorded, often notorious, and frequently long-running. Intra-ethnic clashes have often become as bitter as those occurring between ethnies. In 1912, a dispute arose between the *enda* Gebrekristos and the *enda* Ganzay concerning the rights that tenants could claim from *restegnatat*. The traditional rule was that an individual tenant must accept whatever terms the *restegnat* offers him. In 1942, the dispute was submitted to the British court, which upheld this rule.[54] Another case involved the *enda* Belaway Beleza in Hamasien and the *enda* Gumer in Seraye. This concerned a claim for a share of family land based on descent from a man who had lived nine generations or 450 years before.[55] Two different traditional law systems and elders from both regions were involved in the resolution.[56] Clearly, land belonging to different *enda* was contested because the lands had been divided in the past or at least it was alleged that they had been.

Other disputes involved cases of demarcation of contested boundaries, especially when the parties professed different myths of origin. All peoples have these myths which are particular to them; for example, the Saho believe that they are descended from a lion and for this reason they particularly value courage. Some of the Hamasien elite claim they can trace their descent back to the founding fathers of the ethnie.

The two following disputes can be seen as conflicts within an ethnie only according to a particular (and hotly debated) classification of ethnic boundaries. The Asaorta and Minifere Saho would often go to war with one another over territory and control of grazing grounds.[57] When the Dergue came to power in 1974, it exploited this rivalry and offered to consider the Asaorta as a separate ethnie. This offer was made to counter the attraction of the ELF and EPLF, both of which were recruiting many Saho to their ranks. At the same time, the Dergue encouraged Islamic fundamentalism both in Eritrea and in the refugee camps in the Sudan and Saudi Arabia. The Dergue had no desire to settle this conflict; it remained unresolved and is just one of the long-running and nagging problems that the Eritrean government has had to face since it achieved power.

We have framed the following case study as an intra-ethnie conflict because according to the official classification given by the Eritrean government, Marya and Beni Amir are regarded as belonging to the Tigré ethnie, even though there are arguments that they—like the Asaorta—are separate ethnies. The Beni Amir group of Az Ali' Bakit, permanently at war with Marya in a number of districts in Hamasien, had used the pastures of Barka constantly and from time immemorial. The Beni Amir had an interest in these pastures, and this proximity led to a never-ending fight. As is the case with many of the long-standing disputes, the conflict took on a serious violent aspect during the war of liberation from 1961, when some groups allied themselves with the ELF, others with the EPLF, and a third group—even if only by default —with the Ethiopians. Some of the divisions have remained to this day in Eritrea, in the refugee community of Sudan, and in the diaspora.

Disputes between Different Ethnies

These disputes are probably the best documented. This is not surprising; first of all, they involved larger and more powerful actors and therefore had a more than a parochial impact. Second, the Eritrean system of traditional law with multiple codes sometimes covering very small groups was not designed to deal with disputes of this nature. Consequently disputes would often fester for a long time and prove intractable. The most frequent grounds for inter-ethnie conflict were disputes over grazing land (hezaty) and tribute, together with raids.

When the area reserved for pastures exceeded the needs of villagers, highland peoples would lease it to lowlanders, who migrated to the highlands during the big rainy season (kiremti—June to September) to escape the dry season in the lowlands (they stayed in the highlands until the start of the unpredictable rainy season in the lowlands (little rains, belg October to March). As part of the common property of the village, these pastures could not be rented without the consent of the entire community. Moreover, for a fixed period of the year cattle were not allowed to graze on them; a watchman enforced this rule.[58]

Disputes between Asaorta and Tigrinya were particularly intense.[59] An important case concerned three groups who claimed Kohaito, an area a few miles from the town of Adi Keih. Part of this area was under the undisputed ownership of Asaorta, but two Tigrinya groups as well as Saho claimed the other half. After intermittent conflict, the case eventually came to court. Because of continuous military activity taking place in the area (the ELF used the area as a base for its operations in the 1960s and 1970s), the claimants did not want to spend time in court, wasting money to win a piece of ground they might not live on.[60]

If we look at this conflict as a relationship between actors, two ethnies are involved, with the state potentially having the authority to impose a decision. Although the groups often distrusted each other because their interests were frequently opposed, in this instance they decided that the costs of litigation outweighed any benefit that might accrue to them, and therefore it was not worthwhile to wait a possibly long time for a state settlement. In a situation in which power is contested at a higher level (between the state and liberation movements), any decision the state might take is likely to be unattractive and unenforceable.

Another dispute involved the inhabitants of the Engana district (Akele Guzai), who fought a long and seemingly continuous blood feud with Asaorta in colonial times.[61] In particular, this was over the possession of the Ala plateau, which was used extensively by the Asaorta for pasture during the rainy season. At the time of Bahta Hagos's rebellion (December 1894), the *meslene* of Engana put himself at the orders of the Italian government, who took his side.[62] The Asaorta regarded the Tigrinya as puppets of the Italian government, as much later they regarded them as creatures of the Ethiopian government and/or the EPLF during the civil war of the late 1970s and early 1980s.

In the district of Aret, also in Akele Guzai, other conflicts among Christians and Muslims over pasture rights have taken place. In the fall of 1903, the Italian governor visited the area; an official meeting with notables, chiefs, and religious leaders took place in the village of Halai. "As a last resort [the inhabitants] determined to remit their disputes to a supreme judge." The governor ruled that as far as the disputed pastures were concerned, the decision of the notables should be revised, with the revision to be carried out by the *commissario regionale* competent for the area.[63] Unlike the Kohaito case referred to above, here the state settled the dispute, probably because the disputants regarded the colonial power as a stable entity and as a more or less reliable arbitrator.

For some reason that will be worthwhile to investigate further, the level of litigation involving Catholic Tsenadegle farmers living around Segeneiti surpasses that of all other groups. We first find them quarreling with Muslims of the coast because of disputed land in the Hirghigo area, and subsequently with Hadegti for the possession of land close to Agame in Tigray. Vendettas also took place between Tsenadegle and the Saharti in retaliation for old raids, as well as between Tsenadegle and Asaorta. These conflicts ceased after a peace treaty signed in Halai in 1901.

The land dispute between the agro-pastoralist Tor'a, the most northerly Saho clan, and the Tsenadegle is the best documented.[64] It was an especially prolonged and bitter conflict beginning early in the twentieth century when some Tor'a refused to pay tribute to Tsenadegle authorities for the use of pastures. This follows a common pattern in the area. Those who are labeled by the settled inhabitants as foreigners, even if they have been visiting or attempting to live in the area for centuries, have to pay tribute. An Italian court in 1914 ordered the Tor'a to pay, which they did until the Italians were defeated and the British Military Administration took power in 1941. Fighting broke out again in 1946 and lasted until 1951, with the Muslim League (formed in 1946 in Keren to bring together almost all the lowland Muslim communities) supporting the Saho and the Unionist Party (a major political party during the British period and the federation comprising mainly Christian Tigrinya) supporting the Tsenadegle.

In the 1960s, Haile Selassie recruited a substantial number of Tsenadegle to be trained by the Israelis as a counter-insurgency commando force to fight the ELF, which supported the Saho claims. From 1965 through 1967 under Abdelkrim Ahmed, the ELF burned some Catholic villages and exacted tribute from others. Ahmed was ousted from his command in 1968, but these tactics had served to re-ignite the old controversy. From 1970, the Tigrinya wing of the Eritrean Liberation Front–People's Liberation Front (ELF–PLF) supported the Tsenadegle. No resolution of the conflict was achieved before the Dergue occupied the region in 1978. Conflict resumed in 1993; we refer to its resolution in the next section as Tsenadegle versus Tor'a.

The rivalry was manipulated by larger movements with wider aims in the search for alliances. The same also applies to the next conflict, where a larger political actor used ethnic groups for its own purposes. Occasional disputes between other Saho pastoralists and Tigrinya farmers developed into numerous armed clashes in the 1940s. In the 1960s, the conflict became polarized between the ELF, who supported the Saho, and irregular Christian militia units—*banda*—trained by Ethiopia. In two districts of Seraye, the *banda* protected a cordon of Christian villages from the guerrilla activities of the ELF.[65]

Another important conflict involved the Liban, Habela, and Beni Amir. These groups inhabited an area that included both highland and lowland plots. Here we have three feuding groups, two of which were also in conflict with the state. The Liban were an ethnically isolated group of migrants from Agau who settled in Seraye.[66] The Habela were part of the Tigrinya Loggo-Chewa who migrated to Eritrea in the fifteenth century.[67] Both of these groups were farmers and they shared the area with Beni Amir pastoralists. In 1922, the Italian government decided that the Liban and Habela groups should farm land according to the *diesa* system, as part of its general policy of converting *resti* land into *diesa*.

This policy led to some opposition from the farmers. The part of the disputed area that comprised the lowlands was declared to be government land; this move greatly incensed the Beni Amir. The government made some concessions to the Beni Amir with the result that the two farming groups had to get permission from both the government and the Beni Amir before they could farm or graze the lowland. The Beni Amir not only had the ability to enforce their right to the area, but they also received the support of the Italian government. In 1933, the government altered its policy and gave the Habela permission to graze the lowland, a practice that was continued by the BMA. In 1954, the chief executive of Eritrea ordered both the Liban and the Habela not to cultivate the disputed area. In the same year the Mendefera district court, reversing the decision of the Italian government, found in favor of Liban *resti* rather than for Habela.

In June 1956, the Liban fought the Eritrean police in Agordat. Two months later in Mezrah, they were led by *shifta* (bandits) from Tigray. The Eritrean government, following the precedent of last resort set by the Italian government (see chapter 5), stationed some 150 constables in Liban and Habela areas and ordered the villagers to feed them until further notice or until they obeyed government orders. The Habela agreed not to graze inside the disputed area, but the Liban paid a collective fine rather than submit to this ruling. In 1965, the emperor's representative ordered that a high-level committee look at the dispute and that in the meantime grazing was to be allowed and no settlements were to be destroyed. Both Tigrinya communities refused to obey the order. Eventually the Ethiopian police moved out because of security problems caused by ELF guerrilla activities, and the Habela moved back in. In 1967, the conflict flared up again.[68]

Groups against the King, the Church, and the State

In the following cases, the king and/or the state are actively involved in a bilateral conflict and are not merely neutral mediators. We see one of our actors trying to assert its power over the others, and not always succeeding in all of its aims.

The Portuguese historian De Almeida described the Negus as having the ultimate ownership over all lands: *"senhorin solidum de todas as terras que ha em todo o reyno"* [the king has a joint right over all land that exists in the realm]. In theory, the king can do everything because *"iden egrin nay negùs"* [hands and feet belong to the king]. He can also confiscate the *resti:* King Yohannes I [1667–1682] declared that one-tenth of the land in the Tigrinya provinces was to be considered exclusively his own. A corresponding principle is that the king should not abuse his powers: *"medri gabbar sab hara"* [the land is subjected to tribute, men are not]. By imposing tributes over hearth and home, Yohannes IV [1872–1879] violated the terms of his contract with the people.[69] In this context we should probably read article 17 of the *Loggo Sarda* code: "the king who divides Loggo land must be maledicted!"[70] This rule indicates that on occasion the king had attempted to divide the land, presumably granting the land to his collaborators. It is not known if this happened before, but it is certain that if it did, the king's attempt must have been fiercely resisted.

As we have seen in chapter 6, all subsequent regimes in Eritrea, including the present one, tried to emulate the Italian policy of land nationalization. This was probably the major cause of peasant dissatisfaction. The state and ethnic groups are directly opposed to each other. The state tries to justify its policy by claiming that traditional systems allow state exploitation. It argues that the communal system has historically been compatible with the king's ownership of land and therefore state ownership is only substituting one owner for another; moreover, it alleges that peasants were never full owners. As far as we know, peasants never accepted this unsubstantiated line of argument and they contested it on numerous occasions. First of all, peasants are resentful at being dispossessed from their plots of land. Typically, they do not like working in large gangs. Invariably, state farms prove to be economic disasters, and peasants often starve. Because of economic losses and falling food supplies, governments lose political legitimacy, and not infrequently they lose power as well. The following case exemplifies the consequent difficulties.

Ras Michael Suhul transferred the fertile *Halhal* plain in Seraye to the control of the *Naib* of Hirghigo in the mid-eighteenth century. The villagers of Adi Geda farmed the upper portions, but in 1892 the whole plain was confiscated by the Italians and given as a concession to Italian farmers, who farmed it until 1974. The ELF started to operate in the area and Italian farmers abandoned their properties. The ELF administration initially allowed the villagers of Adi Geda back to cultivate the deserted land, but in 1977 attempted to get them to collectivize and operate it as a state farm. This action led to widespread protest. The ELF lost the area to the Dergue in 1978, and the Dergue distributed most of the land to the villagers. In 1993, the Eritrean government— acting in accordance with its policies at the time, which called for large-scale agricultural development—declared the area state land. By legal notice 13/93 of July 1993, the government announced that this land had been illegally distributed by the Dergue, and was thereby taken under the control of the Ministry of Agriculture.

We make further reference to this as the "Halhal case" in the next section, where we look at subsequent developments. The Eritrean government may have learned some lessons from the sorry history of states attempting to rationalize agriculture by aggregating smallholdings into state farms and transforming peasant owner/occupiers into state employees. Nowhere has this process prospered, but several generations of Marxist-Leninist and socialist bureaucrats and *apparatchiks* have continued down the same unproductive path anyway. There is no doubt that in industrialized Western countries agricultural production has typically increased substantially through a growth in farm size and the greater use of inputs such as machinery and fertilizer. But in countries such as Eritrea and Ethiopia, where farm family labor is abundant, the diseconomies of scale far outweigh the advantages of size.[71]

Disputes between Sovereign States: The Role of the International and Transnational Actor

Needless to say, these disputes have always been important. As Lord Curzon remarked, "frontiers are the razor's edge on which hang suspended the issue of war or peace and the life of nations." But particularly with regards to Ethiopia, such disputes have increased in ferocity in recent years. The short period of independence has seen Eritrea engaged in armed conflict with all of its neighbors. All of these, with the exception of the conflict with Ethiopia, have been resolved satisfactorily.

The Hanish Islands

In November and December 1995 Eritrea and Yemen clashed over the Hanish island group in the southern Red Sea. The Anglo-Italian Agreement Regarding Certain Areas in the Middle East, signed in Rome on 16 April 1938, had indicated (art. 4) that the two colonial powers (United Kingdom ruling Aden and Italy ruling Eritrea) viewed the islands as belonging neither to Yemen nor Saudi Arabia.[72] Our reading of this agreement is that Eritrea and present-day Yemen (now including Aden), as powers succeeding the British and Italians, both could claim rights. During the war of liberation, the EPLF forces used the islands. The Eritrean government was of the opinion that all the islands were its sovereign territory, and that maps and treaties confirmed this view. Yemen likewise believed the islands to be theirs and commenced fishing, tourism, and oil exploration. After a brief battle, Eritrea took control of Hanish al Kabir and Hanish as Saghir. International and regional powers put some pressure on Eritrea to commence negotiation with Yemen.

At a meeting in Paris on 21 May 1996, the two countries reached an agreement on the way in which the dispute should be resolved. An arbitration panel was established; it comprised five men—two nominated by Yemen and two by Eritrea, together with an independent president chosen by both parties. The panel eventually granted sovereignty to Yemen, based it seems on opinions that Yemen had been more active on the islands in the 1980s and the early 1990s than either the Dergue or the

EPLF had been.[73] On 1 November 1998, Eritrea evacuated all its troops from the islands and formally handed the islands over to Yemen. On 17 December 1999, the panel delineated the maritime border between the two countries and confirmed Eritrea's fishing rights. Both parties signed an accord, and since then relations have been by and large cordial.

The "Border Conflict" with Ethiopia
Seen as a Land Dispute

After an uneasy period of border conflict, largely arising from economic problems and conflicting claims to hegemony, the Ethiopian parliament formally declared war on Eritrea in May 1998. Planes bombed Asmara, and the Ethiopian armed forces invaded Eritrea at four strategic points. By the time hostilities ceased, Ethiopia was firmly entrenched along the border—at points inside Eritrea to a depth of twenty-five kilometers.[74]

Because of the crucial role played by the USA before, during, and after the conflict, we will first try to make sense of U.S. foreign policy in the region. Until the war began, the United States had very good relations with both countries and placed a great deal of faith in Meles Zenawi and Isaias Afwerki as representatives of a new generation of African leaders, men who it believed were committed to peaceful cooperation, liberal economic development, and eventually full democratization of their countries. Consequently, the USA took the leading role in proposing measures designed to end the war as soon as possible.

Gayle Smith, the senior Africanist at the National Security Council (NSC) formulated U.S. policy. Starting in the 1970s, Smith had gained experience as a journalist and NGO worker in Sudan and Tigray and had developed extremely close links with the leaders of the Tigrayan People's Liberation Front (TPLF)—most notably with Meles Zenawi. After the Ethiopian People's Revolutionary Democratic Front (EPRDF), in which the TPLF was dominant, had seized power in Addis Ababa in May 1991, Smith became an advisor to Meles Zenawi.[75] Smith's superior in Washington was Susan Rice, a young and extremely able African American woman—a protégée of Madeleine Albright. She was relatively new to the position and doubtless wanted to make her mark in an area of Africa of some strategic interest to the United States. These two women wrote and dictated America's policy in the region.

Observation of American position papers and some discussion with Smith and other key players has led us to believe that American policy in this conflict can be summed up by the phrase "keep Meles in power at whatever cost." Consequently, Rice, at an early stage of the war, presented President Isaias Afwerki with the American conditions for a peaceful settlement of the conflict, a document that favored Ethiopia and indeed had received Meles' prior blessing.[76] Susan Rice was extremely annoyed that Isaias rejected this ultimatum, and was also surprised at his less-than-cordial reception of it and of her. Perhaps Rice was guilty of misperception.

Back in Washington, Rice and Smith presented their policy recommendations to the NSC, the State Department chiefs, and the White House, and as so often happens in meetings where very few people have any real knowledge of the subject or interest in it, the view of the "experts" was accepted without much debate.[77] This is "groupthink" in operation. Within a group, pressure for conformity consistently appears. If one member tries to deviate from the group's norms, the rest of the group tries to tone down or change the dissident's views. If this fails, the individual is ignored and not taken seriously in the future. Thus there is a considerable disincentive to putting forward an alternative course of action, let alone pushing hard for it. After Rice and Smith's doctrine had become official U.S. policy, the U.S. position did not change to any marked degree. It clearly was not working, but a policy, once decided upon, frequently proves almost impossible to change. The other important decision makers in Washington, such as the legislative branch, Department of Defense, and the CIA, seem to have made no attempt to alter the decision.

What happened, one might ask, to the broad ideals and strategic objectives that are supposed to guide American foreign policy? The U.S. was acting neither in its strategic national interest nor in accord with its fundamental moral values in pursuing the Rice-Smith policy. First of all, the policy seems to have done little to discourage Ethiopian offensive action. Secondly, the U.S. was pursuing a self-destructive policy in supporting Meles at whatever cost. Meles' hold over his own party, let alone Ethiopia, was tenuous, and it is foolish to place so much reliance on one fallible mortal. There seems to have been little or no attention paid to alternatives to Meles' rule.

As Eritrea seems to have played a minor role in the U.S. scheme of things, the next few paragraphs will examine the conflict from an Eritrean perspective. As Alemseged Tesfai has remarked, incidents and disputes along the border between Eritrea and Ethiopia were not a new phenomenon, but they were never about a boundary. A line drawn in the shifting sand meant nothing to people whose ancestors had lived in the area for centuries and who were related by blood and kinship.[78] The disputes were over access to pastures and the transfer, possession, and use of land, just as they were in villages deep inside Eritrea or Ethiopia.

In the 1950s, during the Federation period, the Ethiopian government issued directives warning authorities close to the border not to attempt to change the old boundaries agreed to in treaties between Italy, the United Kingdom, and Ethiopia in 1900, 1902, and 1908. The boundaries were defined by the wording of the treaties and verbally by the parties. The maps drawn up by the Italians are not precise. Ciampi has argued that this is because in the early nineteenth century the Italians were expecting to expand their borders at the expense of Ethiopia and therefore they were not concerned over an inexact document. The term "border" had a different meaning to the Ethiopians than to the Italians; the Ethiopians did not view the border as an indication of where their sovereignty ended, so in their minds accepting a piece of paper committed them to nothing. The maps were generally accepted throughout the century, but in the view of one cartographic scholar they lack international validity.[79]

The Cairo declaration, adopted by the OAU at its first ordinary session on 21 July 1964, legitimized all existing colonial borders, according to the doctrine of *uti possidetis juris,* the maintenance of the status quo giving precedence to legal title over effective possession. "Member states of the Organization pledge themselves to respect the borders existing on the achievement of national independence."[80] In the Agreement of Friendship and Cooperation that the governments of Ethiopia and Eritrea signed on 30 July 1993, article 12 committed the two parties to "promote cooperation between border regions and provinces."[81] From as early as 1990, when the TPLF took Tigray from the Dergue, border incidents increased in ferocity. The TPLF's tactics were reminiscent of those followed by the old Abyssinian rulers: first of all, it attempted to tax the Eritreans living near the border and force them to pay tribute. When the villagers refused to do so and complained to the Eritrean authorities, the TPLF/EPRDF began to use force.[82]

Eventually a border commission was established to try to mediate the conflict. Before it could begin work in earnest, on 6 May 1998, Ethiopia launched a carefully planned attack on Eritrean armed patrols in the Badme region.[83] The TPLF claim to Eritrean land is not new. During the reign of Haile Selassie, Ras Mengesha of Tigray claimed the Badme area, but the experts and maps consulted by the emperor indicated that Badme belonged to Eritrea, and the claim was dismissed. During the armed struggle, all of this land was under the control of the ELF from 1961 until 1982.[84] After the EPLF had won the civil war with the ELF and driven the remnants of the ELF into the Sudan, the TPLF occupied the area. A fear among Eritrean politicians and intellectuals is that the TPLF has resurrected the dream of a united Tigray stretching to the sea. This dates back at least as far as the reign of Yohannes IV, made a reality during the Italian occupation of Ethiopia, and still exerting siren-like allure on the present-day rulers of Ethiopia.

In spite of clear past evidence of Eritrean sovereignty in the area, Ambassador Shinn and Melvin Foote, the American head of an "independent peace initiative," together with many other senior U.S. officials, persisted in echoing Ethiopian spokesmen in talking about an Eritrean "invasion" of Ethiopian land. Some of the reason for this could be that they accepted the TPLF map of October 1997 that unilaterally redrew the boundary so as to include large chunks of Eritrea in Tigray. In the middle of 2000, both sides stopped fighting and talks to resolve the conflict began. An agreement was signed in Algiers on 12 December 2000, and the initial stages of the peace accord proceeded more on less on track.

III. Resolution or Non-resolution of Land Disputes

In this section we are referring back to the customary process of adjudication and reconciliation and also to the role of the colonial and postcolonial states, together with the role of international/transnational actors in the resolution and non-resolution of conflicts. A number of these conflicts have proven to be very obdurate, and analysis is usually fruitful only if one uses a multi-dimensional and multi-temporal approach. After having indicated the causes of disputes in part I and dealt with selected case studies in part II, we come now to the attempted resolution, and we start with those who were charged with the task from time immemorial.

Who Was Charged with Settling the Dispute
in the Pre-colonial Period?

Traditionally, the jurisdiction in land disputes between individuals from the same village was vested in the *danya*, who was often the village chief (see, for example, art. 23§1 of *Mai Adgi*).[85] The *woreda* chief (*meslene*) would decide disputes between inhabitants of the same village on appeal, and also disputes between villages.[86] The members of the *woreda*, *shumagulle*, and particularly the *akwaro* (see chapter 6) would settle land disputes between *enda* over boundaries.[87]

A land dispute most often started with a formal injunction by the future plaintiff to the future defendant to stop cultivation or grazing. If a matter could not be settled out of court, the plaintiff could compel the defendant to appear in front of the judge by pronouncing the words *zeban mängesti*—in the name of the government, a formal injunction (*gezzi*) that remained in force until removed by the tribunal.[88] Once again we see an appeal to an authority greater than the group who is asked to intervene as a last resort. According to *Adgena Tegeleba*, "in a land case affecting different branches of different families of which some are present and some are absent, if the members who are present have undertaken under *fetsmi* to produce those absent on the day fixed for the hearing and if they are unable to do so, such case shall be discussed by those members who are present at that time" (art. 249).[89]

As a first action, the two parties had each to present a guarantor so that the orders given by the judge would be observed (*Adkeme Melega*, art. 69§2, *Mai Adgi*, art. 23). The plaintiff had to decide the day of the trial and pronounce a *fetzmi* to the judge that he would appear in court on the day established: "if he does not appear he has to give 120 MTD to the state exchequer" (*Mai Adgi*, art. 23§2). In each part of the trial the parties had the right to receive expert assistance (*Adkeme Melega*, art. 69§4).[90] Ullendorff points out two other interesting procedural aspects of trial by customary law. At any stage, the two parties can make a wager (*werdi*) that they will be able to prove the truth of a given assertion, the value of the wager being handed over to the *danya* by the loser. Also, one of the parties can apply for a restraint to be placed on the other to prevent the other party from interfering with witnesses.[91]

Traditional codes place a great deal of emphasis on the procedure to be adopted in trials dealing with land disputes and murder. Blood feuds and land disputes are closely related. A major concern is the settlement of murders that arise out of old grudges relating to land: in this case if the land question is not settled, it is difficult to terminate the blood feud.[92] The importance of land issues is proven by the fact that more witnesses are usually required in such trials. For example, according to *Mehen Mahaza* (art. 25), seven witnesses are necessary to prove an issue in blood and land disputes, instead of the usual three witnesses for other types of disputes. Similar provisions appear in *Mai Adgi* (art. 23§14), *Adkeme Melega* (art. 70§§2–3), *Enda Fegrai* (art. 16§2), and *Adgena Tegeleba* (art. 182).[93]

Numerous categories of witnesses are also excluded: according to *Mehen Mahaza* (art. 25), witnesses cannot all be women or Muslims; according to *Enda Fegrai*, relatives up to the seventh generation of the contending parties cannot be heard as witnesses (art. 16§4); according to the *Adgena Tegeleba* (art. 182), among individuals who cannot be heard as witnesses are those linked by parental ties to the parties up to the fourth degree inclusive, and those who have properties in common with one of the parties (art. 73§2).[94]

In pre-colonial times, if a controversy arose, the use of arbitrators was widespread, and the whole procedure emphasized the restoration of social cohesion after the settlement of the conflict.[95] In the past, many disputes were resolved amicably, or at least fairly conclusively, through a mediator, who tried to balance the interests of the two parties so that in the end there was no winner or loser. The main task of the Eritrean elders was to calm down the passion, emotion, anger, and hostility of the parties by patience and hard work.[96] We find this approach exemplified among the Bilein. In an extended family, the father or the eldest son was the judge. If a question could not be settled within the family it was remitted to the *moheber,* the council of the village. If the council could not solve it, the matter would be passed on to the chief of another village. Alternatively, the contending families could ask for an issue to be settled by a third family. If the question still could not be settled, and war seemed imminent, all the relatives of a certain branch entered into the dispute and worked as intermediaries (*bal mogheb*) to make peace possible. As a last resort, the contending families would ask for a foreign prince to arbitrate the dispute; he made his judgment in accordance with the law of *Mogaresh.*[97] What is particularly interesting in this case is that the foreign prince rules according to traditional law rather than trying to impose his own authority. As far as we know this was a rare occurrence.

And Who Was Charged with Settling the Dispute Later On?

During the Italian period, the most fundamental change to the traditional system was that in many instances Italians officials took over the functions previously exercised by elders and other notables. This followed the typical colonial pattern, whether Italian, British, French, or Ethiopian. The change is evident in some of the traditional laws we have examined. For example, according to the law of *Adkeme Melega,* the government appointed a *restegnat* as head of the village. If the government failed to nominate an individual, all adult male villagers elected one (art. 46§1). The head of the village was the first judge of all disputes between villagers and of disputes where a villager was a defendant (*Adkeme Melega* arts. 46§5 and art. 67§§1–2). Judgments of the second degree were the responsibility of the colonial government (art. 67§3). A *danya* could not inflict punishment directly on villagers, but if villagers committed an offense, he was obliged to refer the matter to the government (art. 46§12). These articles reflect a situation where the state has taken upon itself the authority to inflict punishment, but is still sharing with village chiefs the power to adjudicate disputes. If a villager did not obey the orders of the *danya*, the latter could ask the government to send soldiers to live with the villager until he obeyed the order or nominated a guarantor (art. 46§13). If a village refused to accept the judgment of the governor's court, the governor would billet his guards on the village and extort food and gifts until the village relented (*durgonya* or *ferresenya*).[98]

We see in the latest version of the traditional law of the Asaorta, following their submission of 1887, a similar power-sharing arrangement. A general competence for land disputes was vested in the *shum* or *nebara*, but these officials follow Italian government prescriptions.[99] Under the British administration, quarrels over grazing rights, watering rights, and land disputes between individuals, clans, and ethnies were dealt with by the senior civil affairs (political) officer of the relevant province.[100]

The Dergue's land proclamation of 1974 prohibited land litigation (art. 20). The main effect of this was to reduce the number of cases brought to the regular courts, and since land disputes were the primary source of income for lawyers, there was a reduction in the number of advocates. The use of informal procedures and popular tribunals was encouraged, and this also further reduced the need for trained professionals.[101] The peasant associations were much less effective in Eritrea than they were in Ethiopia. In areas that were controlled by the Dergue during the day and by the EPLF during the night, the PA or village head would try to serve two masters. This was a difficult task and an individual might decide to do as little as possible rather than risk offending either or both parties. Some failed, and in chapter 6 we refer to disciplinary actions taken by the EPLF against people who associated themselves too closely with the Dergue's policies.

It is ironic to note that the EPLF, once in power, tried to enforce a policy similar in a crucial way to that of the Dergue. Its National Democratic Program of 1977 stated that the EPLF would "provide for the peaceful and amicable settling of land disputes and inequality among individuals and villages in such a way as to harmonize the interest of the aggrieved party with that of the national economic interest."[102] However, as we will see later on in some of our case studies, no matter what the EPLF policies were, its practices were a source of conflict.

Bringing this matter of conflict resolution up to date, proclamation 58/94, dealing with land reform, boldly states that "all land disputes among individuals or villages shall be cancelled by this proclamation."[103] The government intends to have the government administrator of a sub-region hear all land dispute claims. The land administrative body has the power to adjudicate. There is a right of appeal to the Land Commission (LC) of the Ministry of Land, Water, and Environment. The decision of the LC shall be final. However, if any person is not satisfied with the decision of the Cadastral Office (see chapter 6), they "may appeal to the court [unspecified] of appropriate jurisdiction."[104] In chapter 6 we indicated our skepticism about the practicality of this facet of the land proclamation. We will come back to this point in our conclusions.

Models of Conflict Resolution

In order to come to a fuller understanding of conflict over land, one must try to develop a typology. Even though the conflicts in Eritrea are some of the most long-standing, complex, and obdurate we have seen, it is helpful to try and locate them in one of three patterns of conflict resolution.[105]

First of all, the disputants may use bilateral negotiation: here the rivals approach each other without the intervention of third parties and try to bring the dispute to an end through discussion. The second form involves the use of a neutral mediator who facilitates communication between the disputants. The mediator may take an active part in pursuing a settlement (this is probably preferable), but does not seek to impose a solution. In the final form, the disputants submit their quarrel to an umpire, who may be an arbitrator, facilitator, or adjudicator, and who has the authority to impose a decision.[106]

Bilateral Negotiation

Here the two litigants discuss the matter without the intervention of third parties. It is generally agreed that third parties can only facilitate agreement when both litigants are ready to settle. Attempts by someone else to resolve a problem frequently make it worse—at least initially. A third party may be able to subdue the conflict for a while, but unless the situation is resolved, it can break out again with redoubled ferocity. Settlement is the second-best solution to winning since it always involves concessions, but if both sides simultaneously think that a continuation of the conflict or armed stalemate will leave them worse off, then the situation may be ripe for resolution (in Zartman's appropriate phrase). Three relevant examples follow. In the first case a conflict between two large *enda* was settled peacefully. There seems to have been no further conflict since then. The resolution of the second case between villages of the same ethnie is of too recent a date for us to pass conclusive judgment. The Chewa community fought the indigenous Loggo people during the fourteenth and fifteenth century until they laid down common rules, the *Loggo-Chewa*, to divide up the land and organize their district.[107] In 1992 the long-standing conflict among villages in the Tsilma district in Seraye was resolved (we referred to the checkered history of land reform in this district in chapter 6). Representatives from twenty-seven villages met to settle the issue and ratify a law to regulate district affairs.[108]

We consider the next case, "the Halhal case," as bilateral negotiation, the two actors involved being the villagers on the one hand and the Eritrean government on the other. We indicated earlier that in 1993 the Eritrean government declared the area state land and attempted to repossess it from the villagers, an act that led to serious protests from the 400 families working the land. In 1997, the government changed tactics and, bowing to pressure which involved delegations from the villages and lengthy discussion, announced plans to develop a village-based cooperative in order to utilize the area's irrigation and dairy potential.[109] The area has enormous commercial prospects; we shall have to wait and see if the conflict has in fact been resolved amicably.

Neutral Mediator

In this model, an intermediary or facilitator is chosen to enable the parties to communicate with each other. In some cases, the parties meet jointly with the mediator; in other cases they communicate through the neutral mediator without face-to-face contact with each other. Sometimes, if the parties cannot agree on one intermediary, two or three may be used. If three are chosen, each side may be allowed to select one without the other being able to impose a veto, but the third must be mutually agreeable to both parties and deemed to be fully neutral. Normally a majority of two is necessary for a decision to be valid, but the details are usually agreed upon in advance. The mediator or mediators should play an active part in pursuing a settlement, but should refrain from trying to impose a solution on either party. Unfortunately, a genuinely disinterested third party is almost unknown. In practice, an intervention usually favors the goals of one of the parties and what seems to be a settlement is in fact a victory for one of them.[110]

With regard to smaller-scale disputes, Eritrea was lucky in the past have some skilled and able negotiators, one of these being Ras Tessema Asberom, who was appointed president of the native court of Akele Guzai in 1947 after he had "become famous for his dispensation of justice and particularly for his settlement of land conflicts including the bitter dispute between the districts of Robra and daqqi Admocom."[111] Many of the cases that were brought to traditional courts in the past fit this pattern of dispute resolution because this was one of the roles of the *danya* in the traditional process, together with adjudication. And also at present, the more than a thousand *kebabi* courts continue to play an absolutely vital and similar role in the Eritrean legal system. In 1999, Seraye elders interviewed said they had settled more than 110 cases through mediation and only five were sent to the courts. Moreover, the parties involved accepted the judgments of the tribunals and did not appeal against them.[112]

Sometimes mediators volunteer their services to the two parties before they ask for assistance. This was the case for much of the Ethiopian-Eritrean conflict of 1998–2000. As we have said earlier, the United States attempted to mediate the conflict, but for reasons already discussed, it was by no means a neutral party. This fact goes a long way in explaining why the conflict was not stopped well before it had caused probably irreparable damage to Eritrea and Ethiopia.

Arbitration—Adjudication

Most of our case studies fit into this model. The two parties submit their quarrel for decision by the arbitrator/adjudicator (umpire). Arbitration or adjudication is usually the final stage in a process which may have initially involved bilateral negotiation, followed by the attempts by a neutral mediator to settle the conflict. The umpire, who has the authority to impose the decision, may be appointed by any of the actors we have discussed so far in this book: individuals, sub-ethnies, ethnies, religious powers, colonial government, liberation movements, the sovereign state, or an international body such as the OAU or UN. For this model to succeed, the two parties must agree in advance to abide by the umpire's decision, no matter how unpalatable it may turn out to be.

The processes of arbitration and adjudication differ in that in arbitration the disputing parties can determine the criteria by which the arbitrator or arbitration panel has to reach a decision. Among the litigious Saho, this was the role of the *resanto* of the village, a *primus inter pares*, first among individuals of equal prestige and dignity. Only since the colonial period, if the complaints were of a serious and persistent nature, he would transmit them to the relevant state court.[113] There are some very interesting instances of arbitration elsewhere in Africa; in Liberia and Sierra Leone, members of a male secret society would act as arbitrators in disguise in disputes between rival chieftains.[114]

Adjudication, on the other hand, is carried out within a court system, which handles the dispute according to established legal procedures and standards. The two parties have little or no control over the process.[115] This is typically the way state courts operate, but it is also the case with *šarīʿa*, and it can be the way of traditional law tribunals if mediation does not work. In addition to arbitration, adjudication was a second important role played by the *danya*, the *meslene*, and other traditional authorities of village life in parts of pre-colonial and colonial Eritrea. Asmarom Legesse refers to adjudication as being used among the Karnesem when mediation had not worked.[116]

On the wider stage, we see an important precedent for the use of adjudication in the peaceful resolution of the Eritrean-Yemeni conflict over the Hanish Islands. The adjudicator decided that some of the islands should go to Yemen. Eritrea accepted the decision, hard as it was. It reacted in the same way to a ruling made by the boundary commission established as part of the Agreement between Eritrea and Ethiopia on Cessation of Hostilities on the final demarcation of the border with Ethiopia. The commission is located in The Hague; its makeup is similar to the body which ruled on the Hanish Island case.

The Tsenadegle–Tor'a conflict has elements of both arbitration and adjudication. It was one of the longest-running and most intractable conflicts; we discussed the early history of it in the previous section. In July 1994, individuals from both communities fought over the old issue at the Waalita rangeland, and three men were killed. The president of Eritrea gathered together the elders and leaders of both communities and told them the area was out of bounds for human and animal use until the communities came up with a satisfactory resolution to the conflict on their own. Troops were garrisoned on the site to enforce the order. This follows an old tradition, as we saw when we looked in detail at the Italian period.

Religious leaders and ex-fighters began to talk urgently about possible means of reconciliation. The community chose a committee. First it mobilized the people in support of reconciliation. The second stage consisted of identifying the points of difference about the rangeland, the people killed, and the livestock stolen. The final stage was formulating a reconciliation agreement and implementing it. A main priority was to restore the stolen livestock to its rightful owners. The families of those killed were implored to forget their grievances and be appeased according to customary practices. The people agreed to let the government decide how the rangeland should be used in the future in accordance with Land Proclamation 58/94. Regulations were agreed on for common resources such as fuel wood, water, roads, and grazing areas, and penalties were enforced in case of trespass. The government was asked to approve these regulations and penalties, and to enforce them.[117] The successful resolution of this conflict may serve as a model for other disputes. The Eritrean government played the role of an arbitrator in a situation where the two parties were not able to find a solution by themselves.

This of course is one explanation and, based on a variety of sources, it may be the closest we can get to the "truth." However, there are other possible readings of this case study, and, acting as devil's advocate and in the spirit of pluralism that informs this book, it is appropriate to offer them. During its long years of guerrilla struggle, the EPLF operated in a classic Marxist fashion. The fighters spent many hours discussing ideology, strategy, tactics, and most aspects of their life in the field. They would pass the results of their deliberation up to the central committee of the party who in turn forwarded them to the Politburo (comprising four men). This group would decide on policy, which might or might not coincide with the wish of the majority of the rank and file. But all members of the front would have to obey the leaders' decision.

The dispute above could be read in a similar way. The two parties to the dispute may have decided that since they could not come to an agreement they would allow the government to impose one. Or the two parties, realizing that the EPLF would decide the policy anyway, did not strive too vigorously to reach an agreement. The government had far more power than either of the two parties. The disputants then played it safe and acted in a way they thought would please the government. They expected some reward for good behavior, and indeed both parties did receive benefits from the settlement.

Closure by State Fiat and Non-settlement

The history of Eritrea shows that actors who try to impose central control with too heavy a hand meet with sustained resistance. This often takes the form of refusing in many different ways to acknowledge the presence and the competence of a central authority. The government loses both its legitimacy and its ability to persuade or force the rural population to do anything. One of the consequences of the authorities losing power is that conflicts can flare up again as soon as the feuding parties get a chance. Then these conflicts are difficult or almost impossible to solve.

As we have seen, few disputes are resolved satisfactorily as a result of unilateral action by a central power. Indeed, many remain unresolved for a long period or prove to be totally intractable. Often with the passage of time one of the parties loses interest or dies and the other party "wins" by default, at least temporarily. Sometimes a more powerful actor is able to impose a solution on the other actors against their will. It is not surprising that such attempted "closures" are bitterly resented by one or both parties. Some of our following case studies illustrate this process.

Arguments over the use and ownership of the arid Hazamo plains along the Mareb River separating Akele Guzai from Seraye have been a constant cause of concern since the beginning of the nineteenth century. Because of the "invasions" and "scourges" of the Asaorta, the Tigrinya *enda* who inhabited the area abandoned it, and the Italians followed the example of Emperor Yohannes IV in declaring the territory to belong to the crown and turning it into state land.[118] This area has remained a contested region.

In the Gundet area of Seraye, the *enda* Zommui and the *enda* Debbas had been in conflict with each other since the seventeenth century. The fighting intensified during Yohannes IV's control of the region. He gave an order that the land be divided between the two *enda,* but this was never carried out properly. The Italian administration re-examined the question and gave each *enda* half. The Debbas contested this division, claiming a larger part of the land, and were unwilling to accept the government's decisions.[119] This case still rankles the Debbas.

In the Liban–Habela–Beni Amir conflict (see earlier, part II), there was no willingness among the three parties to settle the conflict peacefully; no neutral mediator was appointed, and there was no one with the authority to arbitrate decisively. We do not know if these conflicts flared up again in more recent years. The Tsehaflam-Mesfinto village border case and the Addi Gebri Intiterre inter-ethnie dispute are two other important issues that are unresolved.[120]

The present Eritrean government has been no more successful than all previous governments in dealing expeditiously with more than a small fraction of land dispute cases. If the existing legislation or future amendments manage to deal fairly and speedily with the mass of disputes that will continually arise, the government may build upon the legitimacy it largely enjoys in the countryside. Just as in almost all aspects of Eritrean life, the conflict with Ethiopia has certainly set back indefinitely the prospects for real reform—social, political, and legal.

Eight

The Virgin, the Wife, the Spinster, and the Concubine

Gender Roles and Gender Relations

Women are a colonized people.   —Robin Morgan[1]

In this chapter and the one that follows, we look at international organizations and transnational actors working vigorously upon a body of tradition and religious beliefs, with the present state uneasily taking the
middle ground. Religion plays a more pivotal role in marriage relationships than in questions of blood, land ownership, and land disputes.
Family law is one of the areas typically left in the domain of religion
and traditional law. In recent years the international actor has become of
special importance in the fields of human rights and women's rights.
The African state has played a difficult and ambivalent role. In order to
win international legitimacy and all-important aid, it has had at least to
give the impression of being open to suggestions for reform. It has been
compelled to make some decisions which are uncomfortable because of
strong resistance from traditional and religious groups, which in the
main have worked energetically to conserve the status quo.

The Invisible Actor

In Eritrea, we see women first at an early age as betrothed brides, later
on as married women coping with crops and animals and very large
families, and as widows and divorcées attempting to find a place in patriarchal societies. They try to balance the conflicting demands of tradition and religion, coping with the colonial state and liberation movements. They begin to claim social, political, and legal equality. They
reach out to form alliances with international and transnational actors.

But they rarely act together as a group; this may be the main reason why they remain invisible.

"Any act that violates the human rights of women or limits or otherwise thwarts their role and participation is prohibited," states article 7.2 of the Eritrean constitution. According to article 14, "all persons are equal under the law . . . no person may be discriminated against on account of race, ethnic origin, language, color, gender, religion . . . the National Assembly shall enact laws that can assist in eliminating inequalities existing in the Eritrean society."

In spite of the laudable sentiments expressed above, all Eritrean government officials will readily admit that the country is still far from being an equal society. Our chapters on blood and land have shown the grossly unequal position that women held in traditional society. The position of women in some rural areas has not changed much for several hundred years, and the reasons for this are not hard to find. Women have almost no economic power, and in the private sphere they occupy a subordinate position.[2] Some of the reasons for this lie in long-standing pressures from tradition and religion.

In this chapter we concentrate on some of the most problematic aspects of relations between men and women, such as traditional marriage practices, adultery/rape, and prostitution. As usual, we are looking for difficult questions that have been raised, and rulings on these matters, in an attempt to rediscover the really vital points of contention throughout the generations. These issues, along with that of female genital mutilation, which is dealt with in the next chapter, have aroused enormous interest in feminist and Western radical circles. Over the past twenty years or so, some of the most interesting research in anthropology and related disciplines has been concerned with the crucial role that sex and gender play in shaping human social life.[3] Much research tries to find reasons for the wholesale devaluation of women.

In handling African gender issues, a Western observer encounters two major obstacles. The first is that of ghettoizing gender in a Western feminist perspective, or of embracing acritically the discourse of fundamental human rights as they have been developed in Western countries. The second is the temptation to hyper-simplify gender and build the female status as monolithic and independent of social variables and local tradition and practices.

As far as the first problem is concerned, women's issues have for too long been discussed in the rarefied forums of "custom," and of gender studies, according to a misguided cultural approach according to which a person had to fit a special category before being allowed to speak about a certain issue. Making these issues part of a broad feminist agenda had the initial effect of stiffening third world resistance to change. Consequently some feminists became concerned at offending women of color or militant third world males who objected to "white women racists" trying to impose Western values on them and force a change in traditional—often called "cultural"—practices. Some feminists criticized their sisters for making these practices the only point for defining women's oppression in Africa and in the Middle East. In this debate, black feminists faced a particularly awkward dilemma and were concerned that the issues were all too often raised out of context of the important parameters of race, class, and imperialism.[4] The debate was long and acrimonious, and only recently have tempers abated somewhat. The debate is connected with an equally contentious issue—the "real universality" of fundamental human rights. Some scholars see the current stress on human rights as a rhetorical process carried out to hide the fact that rights, as international and transnational actors so often define them, are merely the "rights of white people to export their model of civilization."[5]

As far as the second problem is concerned, much of the classic fieldwork and research on gender relations had been based on the assumptions that the female status is singular and unitary, and that each society has a single gender model.[6] Connected with this approach is the implication that local systems are simply passive, unable to resist the imposition of exogenous socio-economic and political structures. This is clearly very simplistic; emphasis has now, in an encouraging sign, shifted closer to a view that culture and social life are constituted through performances and practices. In this process, the dynamism and vitality of traditional social organizations has been discovered. Chakravorty Spivak points out that the Western intellectual discourse has been in many ways complicit with Western international economic interests. "The masculine-imperialist ideological formation . . . is part of the same formation that constructs the monolithic third world woman." This formation tends to view all "inferior" cultures as simple and unstructured.[7]

We agree that gender relations are structures that are correlated with other axes of social evaluation. Gender, in other words, is not the only axis of social differentiation within a society; there may be important differences between women due to class, race, religion, or ethnicity. By examining traditional Eritrea within this broader framework, we see a varied range of treatments reserved to women, and we realize how inappropriate it is to try to fit them in a unitary and one-dimensional category. To give some taste of the wide range of female conditions that will be analyzed in detail in the text, we can start by mentioning the Bilein proverb, *ogena waka gin*—the woman is a hyena (the hyena being the most despised animal in Africa).[8] Their *Fethesh Mogaresh* allowed the father and the boyfriend-husband the right to sell the woman as a slave, each getting half of the price.[9] According to the *Fetha Mahari* of the Mensa, the father of the girl who has been violated could strangle his daughter, unless she was able to prove that a rape had occurred (art. 76).[10] In both ethnies, women could not ask for divorce, inherit, enter contracts, or act as a witness/guarantor.

In the highlands, there were still serious limitations on a woman's freedom and capacity. For example, an unmarried woman was subject to the total authority of her father. When she married, she passed into the domain of her husband. From then on, apart from ordinary matters, she required her husband's consent in all legal affairs. On the other hand, marriage could be ended by an act of will of the woman alone. In the case of divorce, she acquired the capacity to administer properties and buy and sell goods—trade was usually forbidden to married and unmarried women.[11]

Among some ethnies in the lowlands, women's status was substantially better. According to Conti Rossini, the Beni Amir woman once had "a position in fact and according to the law that can not be found anywhere else [in Eritrea,]" even though at the end of the nineteenth century the situation had changed "because of the long influence of Islam." He adds colorfully that at one time a woman could insult and beat her husband, even in public, without incurring consequences, but if the man performed the same acts, he had to compensate her with presents, and could be obliged to spend the night outside the tent. "The man cannot move a step without consulting the woman, so that he depends completely on the will of the woman."[12] In the Kunama and Nara societies, the woman enjoyed sexual freedom, even after the marriage; her opinion was respected and taken into consideration.[13]

Marriage, Lineage Ties, and Traditional Values

Marriage was originally an agreement between lineages for the exchange of women.[14] The traditional rules we examine show an already altered situation, one in which a relevant role is played by the nuclear family as well as the lineage.

One of the most important residual features was the practice of ending a blood feud with marriage. As mentioned in chapter 5, a blood feud and the subsequent chain of vengeance could be avoided by the marriage of a woman of the culprit's kin to a man of the victim's family. This practice, known as *menketzdem*, was common among Tigré in the Mensa district, Tigrinya, and Bilein. It was unknown in the Saho and other ethnies. Perhaps the most interesting reference to *menketzdem* is contained in the *Fetha Mahari* of the Mensa, whose article 4§2 states "marriage is performed to have children, to cement alliances or to acquire property, or to extinguish a blood feud."[15] The practice is also mentioned in the *Loggo-Chewa:* "the husband of a woman who has entered into the marriage to end a blood feud is forbidden from hitting his wife for any reason. If he does so, he has to compensate her with 30 MTD."[16] This rule is an extremely important safety valve because it is essential for the community to do everything it can to craft procedures designed to prevent either the revival of the feud or continuation of a blood feud.

Another way to obtain women from another lineage was by kidnapping. *Mizeraf* was routinely practiced in the Tigrinya, and occasionally in the Saho and Bilein. It was carried out when the girl's parents had denied a man's request for marriage, when the parents could not afford a dowry, or when the girl was considered to be older than the proper marriageable age. The traditional codes of *Loggo Sarda, Adkeme Melega, Mai Adgi* and *Adgena Tegeleba* explicitly rule on the practice. Without ritual being generally understood and followed, the practice could easily have degenerated into a costly blood feud.[17] Clearly the rule has been devised to justify the practice; over time it has been altered to deal with different contexts and has become part of the ritual. The kidnapper's aggressiveness fits a model of *machismo* enshrined in local law and accepted by the community.[18]

In some instances a girl might implicitly or explicitly comply with the kidnapping. It became necessary, in order to ensure protection of the woman, that the law distinguished between cases of "desired" and "undesired" kidnapping. The *Loggo Sarda* clearly raises the possibility that a woman may be willing to be kidnapped (arts. 5–7).[19] If the woman screamed, this meant she was unwilling to be captured, so those who captured her had to give her ten cows. If she was willing to go, the captor was obliged to give her a guarantee that he would marry her. If the girl had already been criticized because of her "loose behavior," the kidnapper had to give her a *geranna* (measure used for clothes).[20] The customary law of *Adgena Tegeleba* establishes that if a man kidnapped a girl, and later on it was found that he had deflowered her, he had to pay compensation (50 MTD) and the two married.[21]

Exogamy is mandatory in most Eritrean ethnies. A custom, widespread in East Africa, according to which preferred marriage partners are cousins in the paternal lineage, is not as prevalent in Eritrea, with the exception of the Saho.[22] Traditions vary in determining to what extent familial ties constitute a barrier to marriage. In some regions of the highlands, it was impossible to marry someone who belonged to the same *enda*. Usually in the *kebessa*, and among the Christian orthodox Bilein, the ban was to the sixth or seventh degree of relationship from the common ancestor, both in the maternal and in the paternal lines. Among the explanations for exogamy are the desire to establish links with other lineages in order to increase power, and the creation of wider mutual alliances for common defense.

In Hamasien, in addition to the usual ban on marriage between consanguines, it appears that no marriage could be contracted between people who held land in common. This added restriction probably reflects the fear that their relationship may be much closer then the official genealogy indicates. It possibly has been devised to deal with the fact that holding land in common is a major cause of dispute and that marriage between two partners who hold land in common is not as advantageous as that between strangers. In the latter case a new ally can be obtained through the marriage. In the Kunama and Nara societies, marriage was always forbidden in the straight line of descent, legitimate, natural, and adoptive. If the relation was by the maternal side, marriage was banned between brothers and sisters legitimate and natural, uncle and niece, aunt and nephew. Union was also banned between the adoptee and the spouse of the adopter, and between the adopter and the spouse of the adoptee. Neither was it possible to marry anyone belonging to a family with which a blood feud was still current.[23]

The traditional law of the Irob allowed the brother of the deceased to "inherit" his wife. In the Kunama and Nara, the deceased's brother and his widow were preferred marriage partners.[24] In the highlands, the law of *Adkeme Melega* (art. 32) expressly assents to their union, providing that the consent of the woman was obtained. Indeed, a widow who did not marry her brother-in-law could not contract another marriage without the consent of the husband's lineage.[25] The Coptic Church prohibited unions with relatives by marriage, and the *Fetha Negest* reinforced this ban. The conflict between Christianity and tradition on this matter is fully documented, and in Eritrea it was particularly intense.[26]

Marriages were arranged at an early age. In the Mensa and Bilein, children were commonly betrothed when they were babies, or even before they were born.[27] Marriage took place usually when the girl was between twelve and fifteen years of age. According to popular belief, women must be married before menarche. It was deemed to be disgraceful and shameful not to be at least betrothed by this time. Unbetrothed women (*aiam* in Tigrinya) had to wear dresses worn by mature women and they were destined for menial jobs.[28] The two family heads—the wishes of the spouses not being taken into account—arranged the marriage. Only in the Nara and Kunama was marriage the exclusive concern of the couple.[29]

As we will see all throughout this chapter, and particularly in the section on rape, traditional codes placed a high value on female virginity. In ancient times, the bride who had been deflowered by somebody other than her husband could be sent back to her father, with the husband keeping for himself all the bride wealth.[30] At the beginning of the nineteenth century, to receive the payment back, it was enough that the father pronounced the following phrase (regarded as a deadly insult): "my daughter is daughter of Gondar, daughter of Aksum."[31] For most ethnies, pregnancy outside of marriage constituted a great shame. The Bogos, and other aristocratic groups such as the Beni Amir and the Marya, sometimes sacrificed both the illegitimate child and the mother in the name of the honor of the family.[32]

An indemnity, *egghet*, had to be paid to the bridegroom's father if it was found that the bride was not a virgin (*Adgena Tegeleba*, art. 34). In a case of disputed virginity, three elderly women who had no relationship with the bride carried out an investigation. "No further examination of the bride by any other parties is permissible."[33] *Adkeme Melega* lays down a similar stipulation. If defloration occurred as a consequence of rape, "to ensure that the [sexual] violence a girl claims to have suffered is genuine . . . only if they are satisfied that the violence has been proven, will there be a right to compensation" (art. 62§1).[34] The law of *Adgena Tegeleba* was amended in April 1951 to provide for the case when the three women found the girl not to be a virgin but re-examination found that she was still intact (art. 34 *bis*). The first examiners "cannot be held responsible for the erroneous statement they made." P. G. Monateri has remarked that this amendment was necessary because of disputes arising under the old rule. If this special immunity had not been granted, the whole system of independent examination could have collapsed. The amendment seems a highly rational way of avoiding conflict.[35]

We find a very different pattern of behavior in traditional Kunama society, where both men and women, provided that they were pubescent and consenting, could have free sexual relations. A child born from such a union became a legitimate part of the mother's family and was considered to belong to the woman's brother.[36] As the fertility of the woman was given great importance, and pregnancy was an indisputable proof of this, "it frequently happens that only after a period of such [sexual] relations that have given a sure evidence of this fertility the relationship is followed by a formal marriage."[37]

An Insight through the "Codes":
Tradition Reacts with the Other Actors

The codes reflect a situation in which the ancient traditional law has been modified or is in the process of modification by religion (Islam or Christianity), and later by the colonial powers. One instance is the law of *Scioatte Anseba*, containing the following principle: "the rules of the Zamat people were randomly made; we here abolish them and we state that marriage is from now on, performed with a regime of all goods held in common" (art. 3).[38] As indicated in chapter 2, the Zamat were the predecessors of the *Scioatte Anseba* in Hamasien. We see here a cultural clash between two groups, where one, prevailing over the other, chose to adopt a new set of rules.

Another example relates to the rules about *mizeraf*. The codes describe a situation where kidnapping is already unacceptable social behavior and may be subject to a fine. But traces remain of the former time when kidnapping was a legitimate way of obtaining wives from other groups. This is exemplified in the rules that deal with a woman's departure from her father's house during the marriage ceremony. A friend of the husband symbolically kidnapped the woman. He carried the bride on his back out of the house for a few hundred yards, then put her on the ground, uncovered her mouth, and allowed her to say good-bye to the girls of the village, who followed them insulting the man in song. The husband, who was waiting for her in the new conjugal house, performed a war dance (*mazarraf*) in front of his relatives.[39]

In other instances, the conflict is between traditional and religious rules. For example, article 9 of *Scioatte Anseba* contains a clause referring expressly to the possibility of contracting a betrothal according to the *Fetha Negest,* and in this case ". . . the bride shall be fifteen, the groom at least eighteen years old."[40] This indicates that betrothal was usually carried out at an earlier age. Conflict is reflected in the codes only when religion prevails. If the traditional rules show no evidence of religious contamination, we have no way of finding out whether this is because tradition has prevailed or because religious pressure was absent. On the other side of the coin, we are certain that both Islam and Christianity were modified by the customs of the area, but we do not know in each instance the precise extent.

Polygyny was also a source of intense debate. As in almost all African societies, polygyny was common in Eritrean marriages.[41] Cavalli-Sforza and Diamond have observed that an agricultural economy favors an increase in population because more hands are needed to cultivate and because a greater amount of food is available.[42] Women and the rights over them were therefore important commodities for the survival of the group. Unlimited polygyny was common in pre-Islamic Arabia. Islam limited the number of permissible wives to four for the free man and two for the slave, and ruled that it was necessary to treat them equally; the husband should keep a certain number of miles between them.[43]

There is evidence of a similar practice among non-Muslim highland people, where it was common to enter into multiple relationships with women living far away from each other. Ancient chronicles show the king living with more than one wife. In Portuguese accounts of the sixteenth and seventeenth centuries there is mention of attempts to stop the practice. Alvarez, writing between 1520 and 1527, recalled a ban against polygyny, and a law of king Galawdewos in 1543 prohibited bigamy.[44]

The traditional Eritrean codes allowed polygyny, but the practice was moderated both by the influence of the church and by the extra cost of multiple spouses. The Code of *Habsellus Ghebrechristos* and *Daqqi Teshim* says, "the spouse that while legitimately married enters into a relationship with a third person with the aim of marrying her shall give to the betrayed spouse an indemnity of 20 *firghi* from his own property."[45] The text does not properly clarify whether the man was allowed to keep two wives. Polygyny was openly recognized by the Bilein and Mensa. Among the Bilein a man usually had no more than two wives; among the Mensa, the first virgin wife had a privileged position, and was given the title of first legitimized wife (*hema*); the others were adjunct wives (*samar*).[46] Kunama and Nara men could also have multiple wives.[47]

To bring the subject up to our times, according to a survey carried out in Eritrea in 1995, 7 percent of currently married women between the ages from fifteen to forty-nine were living in a polygynous union, and 5.3 percent of married men. There were zonal variations, with, for example, 22 percent of women in the southern Red Sea zone being in polygynous marriages.[48] This reflects the predominance of Islam in the area. The statistics probably underestimate the actual situation because they do not take into account the persistence of the informal marriage arrangements of the highlands discussed later in this chapter.

In Seraye, before the Italian administration, a woman had an almost unlimited right to attribute the paternity of her child to a particular man—even if he had had no sexual contact with her for several years, or may have been dead. Once the claim was made, the man or his family had to provide child maintenance for three years, and then raise the child. As we have seen in many other instances, the rationale behind this rule, which may have also existed in other provinces, was the prevention of conflicts. The certainty of paternity is very important for inheritance and to decide whether a marriage was permitted because of blood considerations.

The Italians forced the inhabitants of Seraye to insert into the *Adkeme Melega* a paragraph to the effect that claims beyond the normal period of pregnancy were not to be allowed.[49] State law, from the Italian period onward, contained the presumption that only children born within a certain time from the dissolution of a marriage were conceived during that marriage.[50] Here is an example of an efficient rule that stretches family linkages to the maximum extent being superseded by an inefficient colonial rule that extends, in the name of the certainty of law, the category of illegitimate children and renders many of them a burden on the state. In Islamic law, these provisions are more elastic; under Hanafī law a child born within two years of the termination of the marriage is legitimate, and under Shāfiʿī and Malēkī it is set at four years and ten months.[51] A similar concern inspired the Islamic rule that children are regarded as legitimate when they are born at least six month after consummation of the marriage and not more than four years after its dissolution.[52]

Eritrean marriage ties were fragile. According to Pollera, writing early in the last century, "marriage, in its varied accepted forms, is nearly always a form of contractual cohabitation, often temporary, which may be easily annulled."[53] It has been claimed that divorce is less frequent in societies that practice bride wealth payments.[54] This does not seem to be the case for Eritrea, where bride wealth as we see later was paid almost universally.

One major instance of conflict between traditions and religion concerns, as could be expected, is the case of divorce. According to traditional law all marriages could end with a relatively easy divorce at the request of either spouse. In past times, a woman's parents could have forced her to break off her union in order to cement a better alliance, or to profit from the division of goods. The ease with which women could sever their marital ties led Conti Rossini to claim that Eritrean women enjoyed a better status than, for example, the Shoa in Ethiopia, and that marriage in the Eritrean highlands could not be conceptualized as "selling the woman. Wherever the marriage has such an aspect, only the husband, that is to say the buyer, has the right to solve it." He draws a parallel with pre-Islamic Arabia, where divorces were also frequent and easy to obtain. He believed that the custom could have circulated from Arabia to the highlands, but of course it could have been the other way around.[55]

In the sixteenth and seventeenth centuries divorce was the object of considerable Jesuit concern and propaganda in Abyssinia; King Susenyos banned divorce, but with the end of the Portuguese influence in the country, it was fully re-established. The Catholic mission in Eritrea also attempted to stop it, with little success.[56] As we see later, a similar policy was carried out during the Federation period.

Types of "Marriage"

In the highlands, there were two forms of marriage. The first, *qal kidan* (covenant), was a solemn alliance between the families of the spouses. Goods were held in common, and in case of divorce they were shared equally between the spouses.[57] It could be performed in one of two ways. The most formal was a religious marriage, the *qal kidan ba-querban* (with Eucharist), indissoluble in theory. It was not widespread, being used mainly for clergy, chiefs, and also as a manner of ending long-running disputes. A non-religious form of *qal kidan* was designed to obviate the need to obtain the consent of a wife in the case of divorce. A *qal kidan ba-querban* might follow, often many years after the first marriage had taken place, but it was not necessary in order to legitimize the union.

The second form of marriage—*dumoz* (compensation)—was a union by contract, limited in time, in which the woman received a regular salary for fulfilling certain marital and domestic duties. The contract could either be arranged by the two spouses, or by the man and the relatives of the woman.[58] Unlike *qal kidan,* where the assets of the two spouses were held in common, in *dumoz* the amount due to the woman was agreed in the presence of guarantors and witnesses, and became her exclusive property.[59] The man was compelled to pay all common expenses; the woman had the right/duty of cohabitation and the duty to take care of the house and food (*Adkeme Melega*, art. 28§§8–9).[60]

The union was essentially transitory, legally ending at the due date; if established by contract it was usually fixed at one year.[61] If no special agreement was laid down, the contract was considered to be for an indeterminate time. This distinction was relevant if the contract was dissolved because of the breakdown of the union.[62] If a term was fixed, the union could legally end when it expired. The contract could also be rescinded before the expiration date by mutual consent or by the will of either of the parties; however, the unwilling party was protected by special rules. These rules did not apply if the contract was for an indeterminate period.[63] The *Loggo Sarda* indicates that the prerogative to breach the contract before the expiration date was given only to the man, who could exercise it by expressly declaring to the woman, in the presence of the guarantor, that he did not want to live anymore with her. Afterwards, they were both free to contract new marriages.[64] In the case of breach of contract before the expiration of the term, the woman kept the sum that had been given to her, or a sum proportional to the time she had spent with the man.[65] Children born from this union were considered to be legitimate. The father was responsible for their maintenance, and when the contract ended they were given into the care of the father.[66]

Dumoz shows considerable similarity with the pre-Islamic *mutʿa* "marriage of pleasure," or temporary marriage. *Mutʿa* was based on the consent of the two parties without needing the intervention of the families, and also involved payment to the woman.[67] The main difference between the two is that in the case of breakdown of *mutʿa*, the children remained with the woman. It is by no means certain if this form of marriage is referred to in the Qurʾan (sura IV, 28), but it is certain that Mohammed allowed his followers to practice *mutʿa*.[68] Temporary marriages are still common among adherents of Shiʾa Islam, but not usually in Sunni. This point is interesting because the vast majority of Eritrean Muslims are Sunni. The origin of temporary marriages can possibly be traced back to matrilineal societies that wanted to keep women within their own groups but nevertheless needed to recruit men to strengthen their fighting forces for a time.[69]

Marriage among Other Ethnies

In this section we give most attention to the Beni Amir, Mensa and Bilein for the obvious reason that their laws are most accessible. It is important to emphasize that all ethnies, including the Tigrinya, contain at least some Muslims. Afar, Rashaida, and Hedareb are entirely Muslim and follow *šarīʿa*, particularly in marriage matters.

The overriding concept of marriage as an agreement between groups for the exchange of women is exemplified by the rule that a marriage obligation does not end merely because of the death of one of the betrothed. If after the formal betrothal, the girl or the boy died, this did not end the commitment of the families. When a Mensa girl died, a sister or a girl of the same lineage was substituted; among the Bilein, it was the closest blood sister, or in her absence the next-born sister, or a paternal cousin. If a Mensa boy died, his brother or closest relative took his place. The man's family, but not the woman's, could renounce the betrothal. Among the Bilein, the father or the brother of the deceased could perform the function.[70]

There were two kinds of marriage. The first was used for girls being married for the first time and it was called *heday walat*. It involved a complex procedure that comprised the "price of the neck" and the exchange of expensive gifts from the betrothed boy or his father to the father and family of the girl. Among the Beni Amir, the "price of the neck" was given for the benefit of the new family, becoming their common property. In the dominant class, the *nahtab*, the bride moved into the husband's house. If he was a serf, the husband lived with the wife's parents until she had given birth to at least two children.[71]

The second type of marriage, one in which gifts were not necessarily exchanged, was the so-called "marriage of a widow" (*heday mober*). This was also used for divorced women and for girls whose families wished to avoid the high costs involved in the other marriage. In all of these ethnies, the parents arranged the marriage, the will of the spouses not being taken into consideration. An exception was made in the case of the Mensa when the groom was already a householder.[72]

We have already mentioned that these ethnies were divided into three classes. There were rules containing various interdictions against marriage between people belonging to these classes; for example when one of the prospective spouses belonged to a slave family, many barriers were raised to prevent the union. A nobleman could marry a woman of inferior class, but a vassal or slave could not marry a "superior" woman.

Divorce conformed largely to *šariʿa*, at times contaminated with tradition. The most frequent way to end a marriage according to *šariʿa* was the repudiation (*talāq*) of the wife by the husband. Both parties could ask for divorce, *tafrīq*, but this had to be pronounced by the *qādī*, either on his own initiative or that of one of the spouses. Divorce involved a more complicated procedure and it was therefore less common than repudiation. The woman was legally entitled to ask for divorce only in the following cases: exercise of her right of rescission on coming of age, her husband's impotence, and, according to some sources, lunacy and the chronic disease of the husband.[73]

In the Mensa, tradition also allowed the woman who wished to separate from her husband to present herself in the village assembly and declare that she renounced all rights toward the husband, or to escape to another clan. In the case of the Bilein, another *denouement* was possible. If the woman escaped three times from the conjugal abode to the family house, on the first two occasions her father returned her to her husband. On the third occasion, the husband forfeited his rights toward her, and she was free to marry again.[74] Among the Beni Amir, a woman could separate from her husband by dismantling the tent and returning to her family, or by accusing the husband of abuse or infidelity.[75] This right given to the woman seems an element of an older tradition in which both spouses likely had the right to break the union. In 1922, Crowfoot observed an instance in which the custom of the area seems to have prevailed over religion. The wedding rites of the Mensa and the Bilein presented a striking resemblance to those of the Sudanese—no matter whether they were Christian or Muslim. One feature was the parading of the bride gifts between the bridegroom's hut and the house of the bride in full sight of all the people.[76]

As far as other ethnies are concerned, the only substantive information concerns the Kunama and Nara. Here marriage took place when both parties were able to bear the financial burden; long betrothals with a partner chosen by the family were unknown. The consent of the woman was always necessary; if it was her first marriage, the consent of her father or mother was also required. Marriage formalities were simple and the ceremony usually took place within a short time after the betrothal. The fathers of the couple formally sealed the contract after killing a cow.[77] Following the conversion of almost all Nara and some Kunama to Islam, marriage as well as inheritance fell under šarīʿa. However, if a husband cut his hair, his wife was still legally entitled to ask for a divorce, and he would lose any claim over his offspring.[78] The reason is obviously connected with magic. Among many cultures, the hair is one of the loci where strength and power lie. This is an interesting case of contamination between šarīʿa and former sacral rules.

Marriage Payments and Their Relevance

In writing this section, we have become even more aware of the difficulties that colonial and later scholars would have encountered in trying to make sense of the diverse practices found in Eritrea and devising accurate terms in Western languages to describe them.

Spiro has distinguished four types of marriage payment. The most widespread of these is bride wealth (also called bride price, "price of the neck," progeny price, and bride gift). It comprises a substantial amount of property, which the groom or his relatives give to the bride's kin. The second most common practice is dowry, gifts given by a bride's family to the groom when she marries. Less common is dower, which consists of property provided by the groom to the wife and is retained by the wife in the event of a divorce. Even less common is groom wealth, which comprises property provided by the wife's family to the kin of the husband.[79] Our research has shown us that many payments in Eritrea cannot be easily slotted into these four categories.

There has been enormous interest over why these payments occur and how they differ from society to society. Their meaning depends upon "the set of organizing principles upon which a socio-cultural sys-

tem is founded." The payments have a different value in different societies even though we give them simple titles such as "bride wealth" or
"dowry." Payment marks a transformation of personal and social status
for the couple and their kin, whose relationship changes because of the
alliance. It is a critical element in classifying whether or not unions are
"valid" and whether or not children are legitimate.[80] Eritrea seems to be
a special case because children became part of the lineage of the father,
even in the case of unions such as concubinage and *dumoz*, where marriage payments are either non-existent or minor.

Several of the founding fathers of anthropology have made gross errors when they have written about marriage payments. For example,
Radcliffe-Brown in 1950 asserted that dowry was absent in Africa.[81]
As we shall see, dowry is almost universal among highland people in
Eritrea. Comaroff says that bride wealth "is usually absent or insubstan-
tial in matrilineal . . . societies."[82] We will see that this comment is also
problematic.

The Price of the Neck

This payment is essential in establishing the legitimacy of a union and
marks the passage of various kinds of rights over a woman and her offspring from family to husband and his kin.[83] Marriage took on the character of a commercial transaction, consisting of an agreement and payment often depicted colorfully as the "price of the neck"[84] With the
agreement of the two families on the price of the neck, the contract of
betrothal was sealed and became inviolable for the parties. After the
marriage, a ceremony would be performed that served to remind the
woman of her subservience to the man. A Mensa man pushed his foot
three times on the neck of the prostrate woman saying: "If her neck is
weak, then mine will be strong!" If he was a Bilein, he stepped over the
neck of the woman and broke a clay pot.[85]

In pre-Islamic Arabia, bride wealth was known as *mahr* (Hebrew
mohar). It was the gift that the bridegroom had to give to the bride when
the contract of marriage was sealed, a gift that became the bride's property. It was given to the *walīy* and was considered a precondition for
marriage, it being considered shameful to be married without it; a relation without *mahr* was considered as concubinage.[86] It was most common
where land was communally owned, and among subsistence pastoralists
with small herds and communally owned pastures and water.[87] Even
though it was usually associated with patrilineal societies and polygyny,
it was practiced widely among all ethnies in Eritrea, including the
matrilineal Nara and Kunama.

Most of the codes deal in detail with bride wealth. In some of them, the price varied according to the social condition of the spouse.[88] Sometimes the amount depended on both the class of the woman and the form of marriage. As we have seen, the Mensa, Bilein, and Beni Amir prescribed different rules for virgins than for other women. For example, among the Mensa the "price of the neck" for the marriage of a Mensa noble virgin was twice that of widows and divorcées. It was even less for the marriage of a girl of the vassal class.[89] We find a similar rule for the Beni Amir. In 1945, the bride price for their serfs (Tigré or Hedarab) was less than one-third of that for their ruling aristocracy, the *nabtab*, and comprised a complex series of gifts and payments.[90] The main departure from the Mensa was that both bride wealth and groom wealth were to be paid, in addition to other substantial gifts divided between the man and the woman, so that the woman's contribution was slightly higher than the man's. All these contributions formed the common property of the two spouses.[91]

In the endogamous Beja Hadendowa, we find an interesting rule that deterred exogamic unions. The further the genealogical distance between the two families, the higher the bride price. A payment in the form of livestock was also made to the bride. This dower was a form of divorce or widowhood insurance.[92] Dower was also found among the Muslim Bilein, Nara, Saho, and Rashaida, where the bride owned the heads of the animals given to her family.[93] The important role played by bride wealth in the life of the lineage is shown by the Afar tradition, in which a portion of the bride wealth was given to the whole lineage *meela* as well as to the bride's paternal uncle and her brother.[94]

In the Kunama and Nara, bride wealth was paid to the father or maternal uncle of the bride. An interesting proviso was that if a woman had children before marriage, the bride wealth was augmented by one or more head of cattle, according to the wealth of the prospective husband. If a man could not afford this price, he was allowed to make symbolic substitutions, on the understanding that he would fulfill the contract later on. When bride wealth involves the presentation of an obligatory gift of symbolic or little value, it is usually referred to as token bride wealth.[95]

The Dowry

Dowry has been regarded as an essential feature of agricultural, monogamous societies with property-owning classes and considerable social differentiation. Families can in effect exchange property for a high status son-in-law, and ensure the security of their daughters and grandchildren (hypergamy).[96] It is a way to entail female property rights; under Greek, Roman, and Jewish marriage laws the husband was required to return the wife's dowry if he divorced her.[97]

Dowry is universal among Eritrean ethnies with the exception of the Kunama and Nara.[98] We find in the Tigrinya that the amount of the dowry was usually determined on the day of the marriage.[99] The father of the bride gave it to a guarantor, who passed it on to the groom's father.[100] Sometimes, if the families were poor, a couple would marry without a dowry. The Coptic Church would not give its approval or allow a marriage in church if a dowry was not paid.[101] This is a case in which a church is working perfectly in accordance with tradition.

Dowry could be given in "participation of the family." This meant that only part of the dowry went to the spouses; the family of the groom—who did not have to give it back in case of divorce—kept the rest. According to our classification, this is technically groom wealth. If the property went entirely to the spouses, it was known as the "privilege of the spouses." Participation of the family was probably the more ancient form, and it is clearly connected with a rationale of marriage as a lineage agreement.[102]

According to Schacht, there was no dowry in the Western sense in marriages according to Islam; while according to Trimingham, in northeast Africa at least, dowry was incorporated into the bride price system.[103] Article 19a of the customary law of the Beni Amir—an ethnie that is entirely Muslim—says, "according to the šari'a, the dowry whether more or little, belongs to the woman who is to be married. Therefore the husband shall have no share in this dowry."[104] As we can see, here the traditional law attributes to Islam a custom which does not appear as Islamic, presumably as a way of legitimizing a more ancient practice.

The System of Gifts

Bride wealth requires substantial return gifts.[105] In the highlands, there is a complex system of gift exchange between the two families at the betrothal, at special events such as Easter and *Mescal*, at the marriage ceremony, at the birth of the first child, and on other occasions throughout the marriage. Some gifts are mandatory: gifts for the nuptial dance (see above); gifts given by the bride's mother when she met the husband after a statutory period of separation; and various jewels given by the groom's father to the bride at the marriage.[106]

The bride's father could also ask the groom's father to collaborate with him in a variety of activities, such as planting and harvesting.[107] We see here an example of what is usually defined as bride service, involving a transfer of labor to the bride's family. It was common in hunting and gathering and small-scale horticultural societies and replaced bride wealth in matrilineal communities.[108] The cost of the marriage ceremony was divided between the two families, with the groom's family paying slightly more than half.[109] Another special gift was the so-called *meftah qenat* (unfastening the belt) or *maqla salaf* (opening the legs). This was given before the marriage was consummated —either by the husband's relatives, the husband, or the guarantor, depending on the codes.[110]

With regard to marriage payments in the case of *dumoz*, apart from the maintenance of the woman and the salary (given only if expressly stated in the contract), there were usually no gifts at the time of the contract. However, when she gave birth, she received gifts "identical, or almost identical, to those given at the birth of a child from a conventional union."[111] This is a logical consequence of the fact that, although the woman did not enter into the husband's family, the children were regarded as legitimate members of the group.

The Mensa and Bilein shared a complicated and similar system of gifts such as clothes and cattle. Gifts called *zekran* by the Mensa were given by the groom, or by his father, to the father and the family of the bride. Gifts of a greater value had to be given to the groom's family by all the recipients before the marriage. These were considered to be legal debts.[112] In the Bilein, the father of the bride committed himself to give back to the groom's father four and half times the value of gifts received by him at betrothal. In addition, the groom or his father gave other gifts to the bride's parents. The exchange of gifts was simpler in the case of the marriage of a widow, where gifts were not compulsory and, if given, did not have to be returned with interest.[113]

In the Kunama and Nara, special gifts (*iso* in Kunama and *iab* in Nara) had to be provided to the groom by his friends. These could be either goats or cash, to be reciprocated when the friend married. The couple's relatives could also provide gifts of cattle; if they were unable to do so, they gave a symbolic gift—figurines in clay representing various animals. The bride's father had to give as a present to the couple two of the cows he received as bride wealth.[114]

The *Cingheret*, the Woman Who Wears the *Helqat* and the *Madamas*

Unlike in Islam, where concubines were invariably slaves, in the highlands the concubine (*cingheret*) was granted an official legal status in traditional law, and in practice concubinage constituted another kind of marital relationship.[115] Taking a *cingheret* was so prevalent in Akele Guzai that the traditional codes have special sections regulating the practice. Perini affirms that, in the highlands, the concubine was given the same respect and consideration as the woman linked by *dumoz*.[116] The many articles that deal with concubinage do not seem to show any particular concern for the "morality" of the practice. As usual, the codes aimed to avoid conflict and, for this reason, the social roles of both wife and concubine were laid down with care.

However, the codes are often confusing with regard to the difference between *dumoz* and concubinage. According to Conti Rossini, concubinage together with *madamismo* was a degeneration of *dumoz*.[117] If true, this implies that concubinage is of more recent origin; this seems unlikely, as *de facto* relationships clearly precede formal ones. Capomazza refers to *dumoz* as concubinage undertaken according to special forms. On balance this seems the most likely explanation.[118]

Enda Fegrai gives further details of the duties of the man toward the concubine and on the agreement of concubinage. "A man who has agreed to give maintenance to his concubine must await her visit, along with her witnesses, to formalize the agreement" (art. 5§10). The entire procedure must be followed exactly. If the money is not asked for in the proper manner (by the concubine) and it is not given at a due time (by the man) this allows the wife to demand an indemnity. A guarantor can be used to fix a monthly salary and maintenance for the concubine.[119]

The only protection that the traditional laws we have examined gave to the wife was a compulsory "compensation for jealousy—*mogono.*" According to *Enda Fegrai*, this consisted of a fixed amount of cereals and butter and a cow, or, alternatively, a certain sum of money. Having obtained this compensation, the wife had to agree to the duties that the husband had toward the concubine. If, having obtained compensation, the wife then asked for divorce, she had to give half the compensation to her children (art. 5§8). Similar rules are also present in the law of *Adkeme Melega* (arts. 28–29).[120]

In the highlands, the situation of legalized concubinage partially eased the "need" for a casual prostitute, *sharmuta*. But at least in Mensa society, the presence of prostitutes is attested and regulated by traditional law. According to the *Fetha Mahari*, "among the Mensa . . . there are no concubines; but there are public women, mostly belonging to the category of slaves" (art. 14§3).[121] Rodén gives some further details about how public women were initiated to their profession. "When a slave reached a marriageable age . . . the master sold her body, keeping all of the proceeds, up to when she was old enough [the age is not indicated] to wear the *helqat* [a silver ornament, whose meaning was that she was to be considered as a public woman]. From then on, the master had the right to take a part of her earnings."[122] During the Italian period, prostitution flourished, particularly in the 1930s when tens of thousands of single Italian men came to the colony. The prostitutes lived and worked in the many bordellos subsidized by the colonial administration.[123]

Iyob highlights the existence of *madamas*, the Eritrean women who were the permanent lovers of soldiers and other Italians during the long colonial period.[124] Even though *madamismo* can be seen as a colonial adaptation of concubinage, *madamas* and concubines have a different status. The system laid down by traditional codes cannot apply to *madamas*, who do not receive even minimal protection from the codes, because the codes are only applicable to members of the same lineage, and not to foreigners. While the colonial government initially adopted a policy of non-interference, possibly because of the absence of Italian women in the colony, fascist legislation first discouraged, and later on proscribed, mixed blood relations on racist grounds. In 1937, during the empire of *Africa Orientale Italiana*, a decree outlawed "relations of conjugal nature" between Italian men and African women. "In other words, madamismo became a crime."[125] This is another example of a cultural clash producing ambiguity and problems in the application of a traditional law that was efficient when it was created.

Prostitution increased again during the Ethiopian occupation, and by liberation in 1991, there were more than 4,000 prostitutes in Eritrea, mostly in the main cities. The EPLF deported half of them, its policy being to "fight to eradicate prostitution." This was announced in the National Democratic Program of 1977 and reaffirmed in 1987.[126] However, so far, the government has not taken any steps to ban the practice. The women are licensed and subject to regular health checks.[127]

The Adulterous and the Violated Woman

Almost all the codes have long and detailed sections on adultery and rape. In the following analysis we will try to draw out the features in common, and the exceptions to the rule. The crimes of adultery, rape, and other extra-marital sexual relations are often lumped together. For example, the *Adgena Tegeleba* code deals with rape under the heading of adultery.[128] In the *Mehen Mahaza* code, carnal knowledge and kidnapping are dealt with under the same rubric (art. 31). The *Mai Adgi* code also conflates carnal knowledge and kidnapping (art. 19).[129] The reason for this is that traditional laws do not need to differentiate; the major category is unlawful "carnal knowledge" (*rukabie saga*), whereby unlawful means any sexual act by a woman, whether or not consensual, that is not within the marriage. Consequently there is no need for different legal terms. If the girl was unmarried, any sexual act was considered to be an offense toward her father, if she was married, toward her husband (*Adgena Tegeleba* art. 62§5). In traditional *habesha* society, "female virginity has very little moral value but a consistent material value, such as the one that can make it easier for the family of the girl to form a union with important families; it is worse to violate a betrothed girl or a wife than to violate a free virgin, because of the disruption that is caused to a settled contract."

Naturally, not all traditional laws rule the matter in the same way, and some laws, usually but not always the most recent, give the woman's will a greater relevance. In only the most recent version of the Beni Amir law have we found that the woman has a right to be personally compensated if she is violated.[130] On the other hand, as we see below, whether the sexual act is consensual becomes relevant if the woman was married, but only insofar as to activate her personal liability toward her husband.

We start our analysis with the rules we have found on adultery. These are perhaps the most straightforward because when such rules are found in a particular code, it means this code has already drawn a distinction between adultery and rape. This happens usually in the most recent laws, such as for example the *Adgena Tegeleba*, where adultery is expressly defined as "voluntary contact" of a married woman with a man other than her husband (arts. 108, 111, 113). According to Petazzi, adultery could be present only in the most formal marriage—*qal kidan*—but because the woman must be faithful also in *dumoz* alliances, effectively the same rules apply.[131]

Adultery was usually settled with compensation given by the man with whom the woman has had sexual intercourse to the husband, and with a punishment inflicted upon the adulterous woman. In the *Adgena Tegeleba*, if the woman had voluntary contact with the man, 55 MTD had to be given to the husband, while the woman "shall receive a quarter of the common property and quit the home" (art. 108). In the *Scioatte Anseba*, the adulterous woman was punished with divorce, expulsion from the conjugal house, and the loss of properties (art. 21).[132] The code of *Mehen Mahaza* added as a further refinement that the husband could cut the hair of the unfaithful woman (art. 4) (for the relevance of the hair, see above).[133] Exceptionally, the *Loggo-Chewa* established as the only penalty a monetary compensation given to the husband by the wife; "the same amount shall be paid by the co-respondent" (art. 25). *Mai Adgi* introduced two limitations to the rule that the payment of compensation by the co-respondent was mandatory. The first of these was that the husband had the right to obtain compensation only if he was able to surprise the couple in the act (§1). Compensation was not due if the husband had surprised the couple in the co-respondent's house; this limitation is presumably out of respect for the principle of privacy. However, in both cases, he could divorce the woman and keep all of her property (§2).

We have discovered relatively few cases where an adulterous husband was punished and the woman received some indemnity. *Adgena Tegeleba* states, "the man shall take a quarter part of the common property and shall leave the home" (art. 109). In *Mai Adgi* if a special clause regarding the husband's infidelity was agreed at the marriage ceremony, the wife had the right to receive one *elchi* (12 MTD) (art. 11§3).[134] This is less than one-third of the sum agreed for a cuckolded husband.

Only one code advocated equal punishment for men and women adulterers. "[I]f one of the spouses linked in a *qal kidan* marriage commits adultery, he/she should compensate the innocent party with 40 *ferghi*" (*Karnesem*, art. 24). Interestingly, we find the same principle of parity in the *Fetha Negest:* "fornication [of men and women] should be punished with the cutting of the hair and of the nose. The married adulterer should be given twelve lashes."[135] The wording of the *Fetha Negest* would have remained the same since it was translated into Ge'ez at the end of the seventeenth century; it is possible that the contemporaneous traditional codes would also have contained similar provisions.

As we have seen in many other instances, the position of Kunama and Nara was quite different from that of other ethnies. After a marriage had taken place, the woman continued to enjoy sexual freedom: "a spear outside of the hut is the sign for the husband . . . that the bed is temporarily occupied."[136] Adultery was not conceivable as an offense to the marriage agreement, but it still had relevance insofar as the dignity and the personal feelings of the husband were involved. In this case, the woman received a reprimand, while the co-respondent was asked not to repeat the act. If he persisted, the husband could take some minor retaliatory actions such as killing a bullock or a few goats belonging to the co-respondent and inviting all of the community to share the banquet.[137]

In most codes, any carnal contact that was not classed as adultery was considered to be "rape." There are a number of references to the procedure to be adopted in the case of rape, and the punishment to be inflicted on the perpetrator. Usually the crime was settled through compensation given to the father if the girl was unmarried, and sometimes to the father and the prospective husband if the girl was betrothed, to the husband alone if she was married, and only to the woman personally if she was a widow or divorcée.

The amount of compensation usually varied according to the status of the woman, the largest sum being given because of the rape of a virgin, especially if she was betrothed. Lesser sums were due in the case of married women, widows, divorcées, *aiam*, and prostitutes.[138] In a departure from the rather shabby treatment that a raped *aiam*, widow, or divorcée usually received, *Loggo-Chewa* is unique in highland codes in that no distinction was drawn as far as compensation was concerned between betrothed girls, non-betrothed girls, married women, or widows (arts. 16–18).[139] The codes usually devalue the violence performed on a prostitute (*Adgena Tegeleba*, art. 62§9; *Mai Adgi*, art. 19§5).

The scale and type of punishment sometimes depended on the religion of the victim and the rapist. The *Habsellus Gebrecristos* laid down that a Muslim paid more compensation than a Christian (art. 12§2).[140] The *Adgena Tegeleba* says that if the assailant was not of the Christian faith, a Christian victim was entitled to double the compensation (art. 105). There was no parallel compensation for a Muslim girl who was violated.[141] Punishment was also sometimes differentiated according to class. The *Adgena Tegeleba* affirms that the rape of a girl of a noble or important family was compensated fivefold that of a girl of a lower class (art. 62§4).[142] If a Tigré noble seduced a young girl—either by rape or consensual sex—and she became pregnant, the couple was usually pardoned, but the child was suffocated. A serf who slept with the daughter of a lord was certain to be killed.[143] If a Hedareb serf raped a girl from a noble family he was killed immediately. However, if a lord raped a vassal, he was not punished.

On a number of occasions a marriage was arranged after a rape had occurred. According to *Adgena Tegeleba*, the girl who had been raped could compel the rapist to marry her "even if this is against his will" (art. 97).[144] If a Tigré girl was violated and was not betrothed, the man's goods were confiscated, and he had to marry the girl after paying the *segada* (bride wealth). If the woman who was raped was a widow or divorcée, the man was obliged to marry her, paying for her the usual bride price (*Fetha Mahari* §5).[145] A marriage plus compensation also settled the matter among the Saho. If the man denied his responsibility, twenty-one men from his clan under oath affirmed whether or not he was the father; if they came to the conclusion the man was guilty, the seducer had to give a mule as a penalty, and after this he had to marry the girl. The Afar culprit not only married the girl who had been violated, but also adopted her child.[146]

In some instances, rape could trigger a blood feud; such as in the Bilein.[147] If another man seduced a bride-to-be, the prospective bridegroom had a right to avenge himself on her father for not guarding her honor adequately.[148] In the 1930s, Thesiger reported that among the Afar if a woman was abducted without permission, a fight ensued, but if the woman had a baby the man could keep her providing he paid four camels to the father.[149] The *Fetha Mahari* gives the fullest account of this matter. If someone raped a girl betrothed to somebody else, her father was entitled to confiscate property of the equivalent value of 120 cows from the rapist. If this was not done, a blood feud could be initiated between the lineages of the girl and of the seducer (§1).[150]

Many laws recognize the importance of proving the offense before compensation could be paid. A complex system was erected to guard against false accusations and most of all to keep peace within lineages. In this system, the oath given by the girl and examination by three expert women played a major role. According to the law of *Adkeme Melega*, if the offense took place outside the village, the woman should immediately announce the fact by crying and shouting (art. 62§2).[151] "If the girl . . . after resisting the man manages to escape and then reports the fact with complaints and tears . . . such evidence is considered sacred" (*Adgena Tegeleba* art. 101). According to the *Mehen Mahaza*, the girl had to be visited by competent persons (art. 31§3). If they verified that the defloration had taken place many days before, she received only the compensation given to an *aiam*. A widow or non-betrothed girl must prove her claim, and if she could not do so, she must also be examined by competent persons (§8). If the violence could not be proved, the widow, the non-betrothed girl, or the *aiam* received no compensation (§9). If the woman was married, or already betrothed, the examiners trusted her words and no further testimony was required from her (§12).[152]

A betrothed Saho girl who had been violated had to perform an oath in front of three witnesses, obliging her seducer to pay blood money in favor of the prospective husband. The prospective husband had the right to the woman and her illegitimate child. When Conti Rossini asked for the rationale behind this custom, he was told bluntly by a local notable, "do you think that if a cow has been inseminated by a bull from another herd, the owner of the cow must give the calf to the owner of the bull?"[153]

After Italian Times

The Ethiopian code of 1960 included a number of important amendments on family law matters. Besides marriage according to the civil code, performed in front of the registrar, marriages according to *šarīʿa* or the traditional law of the locality were allowed and granted equal legal status (arts. 577–580, 625). The technique adopted by the drafters was that of a general referral to custom and *šarīʿa* on these subject matters. To be valid, all marriages had to respect some general provisions contained in articles 581 through 596. Among these, article 581 fixed the legal age of consent in marriage at fifteen for a woman and eighteen for a man, while article 585 banned bigamous marriages (as did the 1987 Ethiopian constitution).[154] Apart from these general rules, no other indication on how religious and customary marriages should be performed was given by the code, leaving the matters entirely to the competence of traditional and religious actors.

The code did not look with favor on a number of traditional marriage practices. It prevented parents from arranging marriages between very young or unborn children by stating that betrothal contracts could not have effect without the personal agreement of the two parties, and were invalid if the couple were not of legal age (arts. 565 and 566.2). Contract marriages and temporary unions that were so common in Eritrea lost their legal status; irregular unions, defined as unions that involved cohabitation without marriage, were also discouraged (arts. 708–721).[155]

With regard to the dissolution of marriage, unilateral repudiation was forbidden, and divorce could be performed only according to the rules of the code, the mutual consent of the spouses being insufficient (664–665). Either spouse could ask for divorce on any ground. However, a "serious cause" allowed the aggrieved party a speedier procedure and more chance of receiving a higher proportion of the divided assets (667, 691–693). Serious causes were adultery of either of the spouses or one of the spouses' leaving the conjugal home for more than two years without the other spouse knowing of his or her whereabouts (669).

Perhaps one of the most startling innovations was the entrustment to family arbitrators, usually the witnesses of the wedding or of the betrothal, of the resolution of a number of disputes arising from marriage. The presence of family arbitrators made the lack of a specific set of rules for Muslims less problematic (see chapter 3). As it was not specified in which way arbitrators had to adjudicate, this opened the door for traditional law and for šarīʿa to be applied in a number of disputes. The decision of family arbitrators was subject to revision in front of state judges in only a limited number of instances, and never because of the merits of the decision. As a matter of fact, Ethiopian judges rejected most appeals on the grounds that they were unreasonable.[156]

Present Times

There have been few more radical plans for transformation in gender relations than the changes that have been envisaged in Eritrea. However, it has proved to be just as difficult to transform gender relations in

Eritrea as in other former socialist and communist countries, where radical policies enjoyed only partial support and short-lived success.

During the struggle for independence, the EPLF consistently spoke of women's rights; women constituted some 40 percent of the EPLF as a whole and almost a quarter of the front-line fighters.[157] At the 1977 organizational congress of the EPLF, thousands of letters were received from fighters wanting to know when new marriage laws would be promulgated by the front. A new law was drafted that banned "feudal" marriage customs, specifically child betrothal, polygyny, and concubinage. Although polygyny was specifically banned among EPLF members, the front did not enforce this interdiction among civilians. Dowry, gifts, and adultery were also prohibited (art. 2).[158] The 1950 Chinese marriage law was the main source of the legislation.[159] The EPLF was somewhat puritanical with regard to sexual freedom in the first decade of its existence, and later on still emphasized stable monogamous relationships as the basis of a family. A number of fighters married, and by the mid 1980s, about 1,500 marriages had taken place in the field.[160]

Change among non-fighters was much slower. In 1977 the EPLF announced that for the first time women could sit in the Decamare *baito*. This radical suggestion was actively opposed by some civilian elements.[161] With the formation of the National Union of Eritrean Women (NUEW) in 1979, a reform of marriage laws and practices was initiated in the liberated areas, and followed the usual EPLF three-stage process. First of all, a rigorous examination of the situation was carried out, assessing the forces for and against change. Second, support was obtained from EPLF cadres, local elders, and religious leaders of all persuasions. Third, change was implemented gradually. One of the most prominent women, Luol Ghebreab, said, "we work with women on differing levels, according to their level of consciousness. We raise issues very slowly. As time goes by the women from the villages take up new concepts themselves, and then they become those who are working for change."[162]

Slowly, the reform began to occur. For example, a hefty penalty was imposed on a man who had sent his wife back to her parents because he found that she was not a virgin.[163] In 1987 the EPLF drafted and circulated another marriage law that was a more-or-less unamended version of the 1977 law. Its article 49/1 specifically prohibits bride wealth and dowry.[164] At least a quarter of the delegates to the 1987 EPLF congress were women, even if only seven were elected to the central committee.[165]

The situation faced after liberation by many women who had often spent years fighting is indicative of the tension between tradition and modernity. A number of marriages contracted in the field ended in divorce or separation when, after the brief period of euphoria that accom-

panied independence, the husband's family found it could not accept
the liberated wife—the antithesis of a traditional submissive Eritrean
woman. And a deserted woman fighter usually found it impossible to
find another mate.

The first statistics available in liberated Eritrea, a survey carried out
by the National Statistics Office in conjunction with an American consulting firm from 1994 to 1995, indicated that a radical change in behavior had apparently occurred since Italian times. A sample of women
aged 20 to 49 were asked the age at which they were first married. Surprisingly the answer was 16.9 years (in other words, at least four years
older than traditional codes would indicate). The median age of first
birth for women aged 25 to 49 was 20.4 years. This is difficult to believe
because it would mean that Eritrean women have their first child at a
much later age than most African women.[166]

A larger program designed to improve the status of women—rights
to equal educational opportunities, equal pay for equal work, and legal
sanctions against domestic violence—has been in force since 1994. At
the PFDJ Third Party Congress, the central committee advocated more
rights for women, including parity in the right to the use of land and
other property, in the spirit of the ideology of the liberation struggle.[167]
The Eritrean government formalized the principle of equality between
man and woman in 1991 with the transitional civil code of Eritrea
(TCCE), and it is now contained in the constitution (arts. 14, 22, 7).[168]

Today, a number of women head important ministries, such as Justice
and Labor. They have been appointed as ambassadors and heads of government departments and other bodies. The mayor of Keren, the third
most important city in Eritrea, is a woman (Zahra Jaffa). Women made
up some 42 percent of the constitutional commission. In the Constituent Assembly that exhaustively discussed the draft constitution clause
by clause, there was a strong contingent of women- -party members,
peasants, and diaspora. The law on inheritance and nationality that unfairly discriminates against Eritrean women who marry non-Eritreans
—they cannot pass their Eritrean citizenship on to their children, unlike Eritrean men who marry foreigners—was discussed at length. The
assembly altered the draft constitution to include a declaration that "any
act that violates the human rights of women or otherwise thwarts their
role and participation is forbidden" (art. 7.2).[169]

In theory, the mass of legislation produced by the government in the
past ten years could form the basis of a radical realignment of gender
relations. But because most of it has not been enforced, it is clear that
the task of reform is likely to be difficult. Some five years ago it was
pointed out that in some parts of Eritrea, "women's rights were still not

protected, especially in the areas of family laws, laws of inheritance, and division of property in the event of a divorce."[170] The transitional codes only take *šarīʿa* into consideration in a marginal fashion. They specify that the bulk of state law on family and inheritance does not apply to Eritrean Muslims; therefore, they leave these subject matters to the exclusive competence of Islamic courts. When the constitution comes into force, the problem of reconciling the freedom of religion (19.4) with the principle of sexual equality will emerge (7.2, 14.2, 22.2).

With proclamation 2/91, a number of amendments were made to the Ethiopian civil code.[171] Prerogatives pertaining to the husband according to the 1960 code were deleted; for example the principle of article 635 ECC, according to which the husband was the family chief and his wife had to obey him, was replaced by an affirmation of the full equality of the spouses. Dowry and *menketzdem* were also expressly prohibited.

The transitional civil code considers the nuclear family as the relevant unit in marriage matters; this centrality is confirmed by article 22 of the constitution, which defines the family as the social unit formed by man and woman through marriage. Consequently the relevance of the enlarged family is bound to decrease. Aspects of this are article 581, which indicates that the only consent relevant in marriage is that of the spouses, and article 607, which raises the legal age of marriage for both spouses to eighteen. In the same vein is the repeal of clauses in the Ethiopian code that empowered the families of the spouses to oppose marriage.[172] Betrothal is defined by article 560 as a private agreement between a man and a woman for a future marriage, thereby excluding the relevance of the will of the families.

The entire chapter VIII of the Ethiopian code dealing with irregular unions was formally repealed.[173] Such a bold step has not proved universally popular. According to present Eritrean law, partners of an irregular union are regarded as if they are completely unknown to one another as far as rights and duties are concerned. Among the Ethiopian rules that have been repealed is that which established a presumption of paternity of children born within such a union. A direct consequence is that thousands of children are at risk of being deprived of rights. As we have seen, traditional law usually gave the mother the power of assignment under oath. The transitional code substituted for this a principle of circumstantial evidence, which complicates the procedure and makes paternity more difficult to ascertain.[174] In general the new Eritrean rules remove even the minimal protection given by the Ethiopian code to the women in irregular unions.

Most communities continue to adhere to their own traditions, even though they may be in conflict with PFDJ policies. For example, in

March 1995 the Asmara Provincial Assembly resolved to enforce the prohibition of dowry, but in spite of this the practice still thrives. We mentioned in chapter 4 that drafters of the new Eritrean civil code were instructed specifically to bear in mind throughout their drafting procedure the principle of equality between the sexes.

One of the most contested issues is the primary role played by family arbitrators—selected and paid by the state in accordance with the transitional civil code of 1991—in attempting to solve marital disputes. There are usually five involved in each case with one of them being neutral. Most of them are male. These arbitrators can use tradition only in recommending the penalties to be imposed. The decision is subject to revision by state court.[175] The transitional system conflicts with traditional law where the parties give prior consent to the *shumagulle* verdict. Arguably, the *shumagulle* are much better qualified to reach a fair consensus than the family arbitrators, who usually lack both the qualities and facilities to be able to adjudicate effectively.[176] One common feature of family arbitrators and *shumagulle* is that they are men and have sometimes exhibited sexist behavior in adjudicating disputes.[177]

The constitution affirms in article 22.1 "the family is the natural and fundamental unit of society and is entitled to the protection and special care of the State and society." It will be instructive to see in a few years' time what lawyers, activists, and politicians make of this, and what it actually implies. Writing in 2003, it is clear that there are some major incompatibilities between the constitution and the transitional civil code. Article 23/1 of the constitution gives a right to dispose of one's property as one desires while the transitional code abolished marriage payments. Moreover, this provision is only applicable to non-Muslims. Muslims are allowed to use *šarīʿa* in such specific matters as betrothal, marriage, divorce, and inheritance, and property matters relating to these. This creates discrimination against non-Muslims and contradicts the principle of equality under the law enshrined in article 14 of the constitution.[178]

Nine

Female Genital Mutilation
Symbol, Tradition, or Survival?

Niemand Lügt So Viel Als Der Entrüstete.[1]

No one is such a liar as an indignant man.

During the last two decades there has been an extensive and often heated debate surrounding female genital mutilation (FGM).[2] Most studies on this subject deal with the situation in Egypt, Kenya, Somalia, Sudan, and Djibouti—the area where the practice of FGM may have originated, and where the most radical form—infibulation—is most prevalent.[3] To our knowledge, so far there have been no comprehensive studies on this subject for Eritrea; and our primary aim is to rectify this omission.

As in the previous chapter, the major actors involved are tradition and religion on one side, which on these issues are allied, and the international/transnational actor on the other. Each one has something to say about the practice and each one has its own reasons to promote or ban it. This is the most contrasting of our case studies, as international debate has been particularly intense. The state has a number of alternative strategies open to it. It may ban FGM or perhaps ban the most radical version, it may expressly condone it, or it may take a neutral stance. A neutral stance might be adopted because of a fear that legal intervention will be counter-productive, or it will be strongly opposed by conservative forces operating within its territory. A state's room to maneuver will be severely circumscribed if it ratifies and starts to put in operation international laws and treaties that restrict or ban FGM. It has even fewer options open to it if powerful states and international regimes threaten or impose sanctions on the state for not enforcing a ban or for not taking the appropriate steps to make it work.

Before we start our analysis we need to point out that none of the more than twenty traditional laws that we examined in print except the *Fetha Mahari* contain any reference to female genital mutilation. The "codes" ruled only upon contentious issues, and FGM was not at all in contention. The community generally accepted it. As we point out later, practically all Eritrean women were operated upon. This is an example of a rule that was not challenged and so central and deeply imbedded in the community that it did not need to be articulated or laid down in the codes.

Between Relativism and Universalism:
Beyond Fundamental Rights?

The term "mutilation" is rejected by the people involved as offensive or injurious. "If we talk about mutilation, people will say that they do not mutilate."[4] There is a contrast between the poles of relativism and universalism, not at all uncommon when one deals with issues that involve traditional thought and customs. Relativists stress the right of each people to keep its own system of values, and of a corresponding "right to be let alone" in its own decisions (to use the Olmstead v. United States terminology).[5] This position—which is usually softened to make it more tolerable to Western sensibilities, was openly expressed by Jomo Kenyatta: "clitoridectomy, like Jewish circumcision . . . is the *conditio sine qua non* of the whole teaching of tribal law, religion, and morality."[6] Smith (arguing from Kenyatta) says that for the Kikuyu the "tribe's distinct values and culture would probably disappear without the circumcision ceremony."[7] Universalists, who now seem to have gotten the better of the argument, oppose the practice. Sexuality, they argue, is seriously impaired by FGM, and the health risks caused by the surgery in the short run as well in the long run make it dangerous and hard to accept.[8] They also argue that cultural relativism and respect for different traditions are a smokescreen behind which to hide inaction.[9]

We agree with relativists on the importance of avoiding an ethnocentric approach to this topic. To proclaim *"j'accuse"* is not useful because it obscures "visions of the multifaceted complexity of those characterized as oppressed 'others.'"[10] However, it is virtually impossible to engage in a critique of a tradition and not be accused *a priori* of being imperialist, or guilty of condemnatory language and action. The difficulties of carrying out a "free minded" study, which is the goal of all research, increase when the topic is highly sensitive and at the cusp of an international campaign and debate.[11] On the other hand, trying to avoid arrogance may indirectly and surreptitiously legitimize a practice which is not rare or marginal, but regular and institutionalized, and which, at least in the more radical forms, causes a permanent and irreparable change to the external genitalia of a woman.

Mutilation in the past and today is a cross-cultural issue, transcending cultural and state boundaries. Men and women in many different parts of the world and at many different times in history have practiced a broad range of bodily mutilations.[12] Such mutilations are not all confined to sexual surgeries. Whitman—exploring a variety of ancient Chinese, Greek, Roman, and German sources—argues that it would be tempting to depict the state of nature as a "sacrifice based religious system" where mutilations "reveal a concern for maintaining proper cosmological order."[13] From an analysis of these sources, he discovers "a complex mental world in which bodily perfection was linked both to central religious ceremonies and some sort of map of the social hierarchy."[14] An analogous concern with linking body and societal order is expressed by Douglas, who asserts that it is not possible to interpret various rituals "unless we are prepared to see in the body a symbol of society, and to see the powers and dangers credited to social structure reproduced in small on the human body."[15] If mutilation is a symbol of a certain society, or if it is linked with the cosmogony of this society, we may infer that it does not have a "one size fits all" meaning. Mutilation—and sexual mutilation as a sub-category of it—gets its meaning only with regard to a definite socio-cultural code.[16] The act of destruction legitimized by the law does not have a belittling connotation; on the contrary it is the symbol of individual and social order.[17]

We use this larger framework as a basis for our analysis, hoping it will be useful for a better understanding of the practice. The chapter is organized as follows: after classifying various forms of FGM, we give some of the multitude of explanations on the diffusion and probable origin of these various practices. We then analyze the Eritrean situation by ethnie, education, and religion, using all pertinent historical sources and the limited statistical data available. We show how the practice has been regarded by church, mosque, and state. We conclude with a discussion of the wider debate that now involves international and transnational actors.

Classification of Female Genital Mutilation

Surgery may be performed in many different ways. Moreover, the terminology used differs from place to place and from author to author. Consequently, for this chapter we have chosen the neutral, official, and medical classification given by a technical working group of the World Health Organization (WHO) in 1995.[18]

After defining female genital mutilations as "all procedures that involve partial or total removal of female external genitalia and/or injury to the female genital organs for cultural or any other non-therapeutic reason," the WHO identifies four types of surgery: type I—excision of the prepuce with or without excision of part or all the clitoris; type II—excision of the clitoris together with partial or total excision of the labia minora; type III—excision of part or all of the external genitalia and stitching/narrowing of the vaginal opening (infibulation); type IV—unclassified: includes pricking, piercing, or incision of the clitoris and/or labia; stretching of the clitoris and/or labia; cauterization by burning of clitoris and surrounding tissues; scraping of the vaginal orifice or cutting of the vagina; introduction of corrosive substances into the vagina to cause bleeding, or herbs with the aim of tightening or narrowing it; any other procedure that falls under the definition of female genital mutilation given above.

This classification needs some elaboration. *Sunna*—excision according to *sarīʿa*—may comprise operations in type I and type II of the WHO classification. In its original form, *sunna* involves cutting of the prepuce according to the tradition of Mohammed. But it may also entail the scarification or partial/total excision of the clitoris and/or all or part of the labia minora (and sometimes the labia majora without stitching).[19] Under the name of "Pharaonic circumcision" or "Sudanese circumcision" is hidden the most radical operation, infibulation, or type III of the WHO classification.[20] In its modern form, pharaonic infibulation involves the same operation with the exception that sometimes the posterior part of the labia majora is left. "It has not been possible to find any references to a general practice of infibulation of a similar scale anywhere in the world but in North East Africa."[21] The word "excision," also frequently employed and which in the WHO classification is used in its literal meaning of "cutting," is also used in some sources to indicate all genital surgeries that are not accompanied by infibulation.[22]

FGM may be performed at almost any time of a woman's life: the post-natal period (including a few days after birth), childhood, adolescence, and the reproductive years; in Ethiopia, it has also been reported among widows.[23]

Where and When Did FGM Start?

In 1998 it was estimated that some 150 million women worldwide had been operated upon.[24] In no other continent did genital mutilation take such hold as in Africa. It is seen in the Middle East, although countries that adhere strictly to Islamic law, such as Iran and Saudi Arabia, seem not to not perform it, but this may also be because these countries have not been surveyed in detail.[25] Genital mutilation has been reported in Asian countries, as well as among some indigenous groups in South America.[26] In the West, notably Great Britain and the U.S., excision was used for the control of "sexual deviation," hysteria, lesbianism, and nymphomania until at least 1950.[27]

It is unknown where and when the practice first originated. There are two hypotheses: independent origin and common origin. According to the latter view, FGM would have originated in the Horn of Africa, Egypt, or in the Arabian peninsula, and from there spread to other regions. Supporters of the independent origin believe that female genital mutilation's broad geographical diffusion is not compatible with a common origin hypothesis.[28] To argue against this second theory, interdisciplinary studies, rooted in genetics and linguistics but integrated with geographic, ecological, archaeological, and physical-anthropological research, point in an opposite direction as far as human evolution is concerned.[29] Humans and their languages would have a common origin, many thousand of years ago, and genetic and linguistic drift accounts for all the differences we see today. The ability of primitive humans to cover long distances in short periods of time has been well argued and demonstrated.[30] It is indeed possible that female genital surgeries are much more ancient than previously thought.

On this point, there are documentary and archaeological sources that prove the existence of two ancient but crowded maritime roads, one connecting India to Egypt and East Africa, and another connecting India to Indonesia.[31] For instance, it has been suggested that infibulation originated in Nubia before the arrival of the Arabs, and spread from there in the Red Sea region and Nilotic areas.[32] The present geographical diffusion of FGM can partially confirm this. This area is where the bulk of FGM, and in particular infibulation, is performed today. According to Nelli, circumcision among Africans dates back 5,000 to 6,000 years before Christ. The origin was therefore in the Neolithic age, and could have been common to all pre-historic humanity.[33] Dieck suggests that there are elements to support the thesis of the existence of this kind of practice in pre-dynastic Egypt.[34] Jews and Arabs could have learned the practice of clitoridectomy and infibulation from the Egyptians. It is thought that the practice was confined at first to ruling classes and was a distinctive mark for women of the royal kin, and for the caste of Egyptian priests. Women were considered to be the unique holders of magic, and FGM would have been a way to keep their powers under control.[35]

The most ancient written evidence of circumcision dates back to the third millennium B.C., and refers to male circumcision in Egypt. Egypt was the center of circumcision rituals according to many historical sources, though there is not agreement on the African or Asiatic origin of the practice.[36] Mentions of female excision are more recent. In Egypt, they date back to the second century B.C.[37] During this time, Agatharchides specifically refers to a Troglodyte population living on the Red Sea's southern coast, probably the ancestors of the present-day Eritrean Afar and Saho.[38] Strabo (the Greek historian and geographer), one century later, resurrected the story and added that Troglodyte women were excised "according to Jewish custom."[39] The interpretation of this fragment has been very much debated since Jews do not excise their women —except the Beta Israel (Falasha) in Ethiopia. Many Arabic sources from the sixth to the tenth century testify to the diffusion and antiquity of excision in pre-Islamic Arabia.[40] There are also references to the Egyptian origin of excision. Among Arab-Byzantine sources, Michael, the Metropolitan of Damietta, mentions excision among Egyptian Copts for the first time in the twelfth century in terms that make reference to the Biblical origin of the practice.[41]

Historical sources seem to indicate that infibulation has a more recent origin, but it is still not easy to prove which practice came first. There are many references to the Horn of Africa. Female infibulation is mentioned for the first time in Maqrizi during the fourteenth century: he refers to the Beja of the Sudan.[42] In East Africa during the sixteenth century, there are two references by Pietro Bembo and Zara Ya'kob.[43] Rodrigo da Castro (1689) gives a description of infibulation "among Arabic Muslims living around the city of Babel Melec," which was probably adjacent to the Bab-el-Mandeb straits, which separate the Red Sea from the Indian Ocean.[44] In 1686, Dapper, in *Description de l'Afrique,* refers again to the practice of excision in Ethiopia and says that it was performed according to a religious precept, and a tradition which refers to a law of the Queen of Sheba.[45]

FGM in Eritrea: Some Statistical Data

Demographic and health survey data on female genital mutilation in Eritrea has become available over the past few years. The practice is almost universal. According to a survey of some 5,054 women aged fifteen to forty-nine, and men aged fifteen to fifty-nine, carried out in 1995 and 1996 by the Eritrean National Statistic Office, 95 percent of Eritrean women have undergone some form of FGM, and 34 percent have been infibulated.[46] This survey showed that women of all Eritrean ethnies have undergone some form of genital mutilation.[47] Other factors considered are literacy, rural or urban residence, region, and religion. Education and residence are not important factors in decreasing FGM, but only in shifting from infibulation to less invasive practices. There is little difference between women with no education, only primary education, or some secondary education; at the same time a decreasing rate of infibulation is observed in more cultivated milieus (46 percent of women with no education have been infibulated; 12 percent of women with primary education; 4 percent of women with secondary education). One should take into account that two-thirds of Eritrean women have never attended school, and only 10 percent have been to secondary school.

As far as residence is concerned, 93 percent of women in urban areas and 95 percent in rural areas have been operated on. However, infibulation occurs more frequently in rural than in urban areas; 44 percent of women in rural areas have been infibulated compared to 13 percent in urban areas. Data on the incidence of infibulation by zone confirms that in the highlands, where the major urban areas are and the most highly educated people live, cases are very rare. Ninety-nine percent of Muslims and 92 percent of Christians have undergone FGM, but only 2 percent of Christians vs. 82 percent of Muslims have been infibulated.[48] The operation is almost always performed by traditional practitioners (95 percent). As far as age is concerned, the majority (44 percent) of females undergo genital mutilation before the age of one, 16 percent between ages one and four; and 12 percent between ages five and fourteen. The median age of cutting is 1.8 months.[49] This particular statistic is problematic because, as we will see in the next section, all evidence shows that the operation is usually carried out at an age even earlier than this.

It is encouraging to find that, unlike many other countries, there is a critical mass in Eritrea supporting change. About four out of ten Eritreans want to see genital cutting discontinued, and opposition is particularly strong among the urban and educated segments of the population.[50] This less favorable attitude toward FGM among the elite may portend a further decline in the practice. Not surprisingly, Muslim women are more likely than those of other faiths to favor continuation, but interestingly, the percentage of opposition to genital cutting is balanced among Eritrean men and women, with a small majority of men opposing it.[51]

Further Data by Ethnie

In this section we collect qualitative data based on a combination of sources. These sources frequently contradict one another in many respects, and the terminology they use may not be precise. Given the impossibility of clarifying the original meaning of each writer or of knowing the reliability and knowledge of the writers or their informants, we have decided to use the terminology of the original writers.

A first group is formed by ethnies such as Tigrinya and Kunama who perform excision (type I and II of the WHO classification). The Tigrinya, including the Jiberti, usually operate seven days after birth.[52] This is a very important ritual; all people who have had sexual intercourse within the preceding twenty-four hours are forbidden to enter the house of the newly circumcised.[53] There is no Tigrinya word for "uncircumcised," which seems to indicate that the practice was universal: a woman is by definition "circumcised." Both Muslim and Christian Kunama are excised but not infibulated. Christians are operated upon at a time depending upon the wealth of the family, but always before the age of seven. The ceremony is a very important event in their lives, and to save money several girls in a family are operated upon at the same time.[54]

Varying percentages of women of all other ethnies undergo infibulation (type III of the WHO classification). According to Hosken, among the Tigré, almost all girls undergo the surgery.[55] The *Fetha Mahari* states that "at the same age [two to eight years, Mensa] women are infibulated, which is . . . an ancient and popular custom, performed with the aim of preserving their virginity."[56] Münzinger says that infibulation was performed by Saho, Beduan (Tigré), and Bilein to protect virginity. In the Bilein it usually took place in the first week after birth for both men and women.[57] Ostini confirms the practice of infibulation among Bilein but remarks that before the ban imposed by Zara Ya'kob, Christian and Muslim alike practiced infibulation.[58]

According to Ostini and Ploss, Beja and Beni Amir also practiced infibulation. For the Beni Amir, the operation was carried out between two and seven years of age.[59] Nadel says that "among the Beni Amer, both [serfs and masters] practice the fundamental institution of the race, male and female circumcision."[60] According to Ausenda, among the Hadendowa Beja of the Gash delta, all the labia majora is excised.[61] Hjort confirms this and says that in the case of the Atmaan-Amar'ar Beja, the operation took place at the time of name-giving, *ti'smaya*, that is at one week of age; the Hadendowa postponed the operation until the girl was five or six years old.[62]

Infibulation is practiced by the Eritrean Afar and Saho.[63] Zaborowski writes that in the Danakil, Massawa, and Beja territory, all are infibulated. Among Danakil Afar, the operation was carried out at three years of age. Thesiger claimed that in this region the operation was usually carried out upon reaching puberty, but could be delayed to just before marriage. The wound is sewn up with long mimosa thorns bound with cotton.[64] The bridegroom de-infibulated the bride; during this usually painful defloration she was held down by two of his friends.[65] After having a baby, she was sewn up again, and this cycle was repeated until she had born three children.[66] Scaramucci and Giglioli claim that infibulation was performed among the Afar when the girl was thirteen.[67] According to De Rivoyre, it was performed on girls when they reached the age of six or seven years. Santelli said that among the Afar, infibulation was frequently done at a very young age, a short time after birth. Courbon gives further details: according to him, on the coastal zones from Massawa to Berbera the clitoris was not cut but the girls were infibulated. Uniquely, Faurot relates in 1886 that infibulation was not performed among the Danakil.[68]

A Multitude of Explanations

Many reasons have been given by those directly involved in the practice. These range from aesthetic and hygienic reasons to moral and religious considerations. Typically, the operation (about which Kenyatta waxed lyrically that it is performed "with the dexterity of a Harley Street surgeon") is performed to initiate a new group of girls and enable them to participate fully in the life of the community. As a result, a woman will become "social, moral, and religious" and be able to play the role expected of her.[69] Mutilations are a fundamental sign that an individual belongs to a certain group (of age, ethnicity, or religion) and not to any other.[70] They strengthen community cohesion and promote identification with a particular culture or lineage group.[71] In many societies, an uncircumcised woman cannot participate fully in religious, political, or social activity.[72]

Many explanations are grounded in aesthetics. One hears such comments as "a vagina without infibulation is ugly, it is like a house without a door," or "there is something superfluous in it that is ugly and not useful." In the highlands, historical sources allege that this "disfigurement" of women made it unpleasant for men to have intercourse with them, and this was the main reason for excision.[73] Decisive demarcation of the sex of men and women is deemed necessary; the clitoris and foreskin are excised to indicate clearly a person's sex. The foreskin is removed because it is regarded as a counterpart of the vulva, and conversely the clitoris is too much akin to the penis. Circumcision deprives man of his female nature and woman of her male nature.[74] This explanation could be connected with the myth that the gods were bisexual, diffused for example in Pharaonic Egypt.[75] To use the words of Eliade, "a man becomes a man only after he has overcome and somewhat abolished the natural humanity."[76] Human beings are by nature imperfect, and must lose aspects of their sexual duality. Only through the rite can they reach a condition of "full humanity." Affirmation of gender identity is reached through sexual alteration.

In addition to aesthetics, strictly functional reasons are given for FGM: it is necessary to remove needless obstacles to penetration, or to induce vaginal tightness and dryness through infibulation.[77] It is relevant that aesthetic and functional reasons appear to be linked together. This seems to indicate a conception of beauty which is at the same time aesthetic, medical, and moral. It is worthwhile to remember that the Tigrinya *tsebuq* and the Arabic *hasan* could be used to indicate indistinctively the concepts of good, perfection, beauty, symmetry, and harmony.[78]

FGM is considered an essential prerequisite to personal cleanliness.[79] Of particular relevance is the presence in many societies of a taboo against menstrual blood, matched with a fear of pollution by genital secretions. The idea of pollution has two dimensions. It can be physical: among the Somali, menstruation is called *wasax*, which means dirtiness; in Egypt the word for uncircumcised girl is *naǧisa*, which means impure.[80] The Arabic word *tahūr*, used for circumcision, also has the meaning of purification. But pollution also means contamination by baleful influences. The Eritrean description of a non-infibulated vulva as "a house without a door" reflects this fear.[81] Among the Tigré in Eritrea, the non-infibulated girl is always given the injurious appellation of *asalat*, which means "a woman with the vulva open as a consequence of multiple deliveries."[82] Perhaps door/woman/land are concepts strictly interrelated in their symbolism. The door has an important meaning in that it symbolizes the separation between an inner space sanctified by man and outside space representing nature and chaos.[83]

FGM is sometimes believed to improve fertility and the chances of becoming pregnant. In some cultures, women are deemed to be naturally sterile; only surgery will make them fertile. There is also a fear that the clitoris could harm the fetus, either physically or spiritually, if it is not removed.[84] Deeply seated in many cultures is the belief that evil lies in the clitoris, so cutting it off will be an act of exorcism.[85] A deeply rooted fear exists that female sexuality is strong, irresponsible, and irresistible. Women are purely erotic creatures and are the source of all men's difficulties.[86] It is alleged that FGM prevents diseases, masturbation, homosexual and adulterous relations, as well as—naturally—fornication. In particular, many sources claim that infibulation is fundamental for the preservation of virginity and chastity.[87] Another alleged reason for infibulation is to protect against sexual rapture; in a popular song, young Somali girls defend the practice on these grounds.[88]

Honor is a crucial component of social identity: a girl's honor is characterized by pre-marital chastity and marital fidelity.[89] Sometimes FGM is a precondition for marriage; among the Berti of Sudan, the marriage of an uncircumcised man or woman is *harām* (ritually forbidden) and therefore invalid.[90] In the past, the ostensible reason for FGM in Eritrea was "to ensure the girl's virginity and then eligibility for a proper marriage." "All Eritrean nationalities, with the exception of the Kunama and the Nara expect a bride to be a virgin at betrothal, and on her wedding day."[91] Among the Tigré, there have been instances where fathers have committed suicide if they are told that their daughters are not virgins on their wedding night.[92]

According to popular belief, courage also plays a part. If the operation is performed when the girl has reached the age of reason, she will remember the acute pain and remember that her suffering was morally and socially necessary. Some women say that because of the ceremony they feel much more in charge of their bodies.[93] One interpretation of the Jewish rite of male circumcision is that it makes "the Israelites as strong as a man wearing a sword, and therefore unafraid of the evil spirits and demons that moved about in the night."[94] Infibulation is an even more severe test of courage and endurance; it is a useful experience for future child bearing.[95]

FGM and Religion

Very frequently, it is alleged that FGM is performed because it follows a tradition rooted in the religion. Many authors have used the prevalence of FGM in Muslim communities as an argument against Islam. But in Eritrea and Ethiopia, excision is widespread also in the Coptic and Catholic Christian community. Moreover, the Beta Israel or Falasha constitute probably a unique example of a Jewish group who practice FGM.[96] Indeed, a Portuguese scholar thought that FGM was of Jewish derivation, even though Zara Ya'kob claimed that it was an Islamic custom which had spread among the Christians of his kingdom.[97] Monotheistic religions at their outset proscribed any attempt to interfere with the physical integrity of the genitalia as a sacrilege against creation. However, as religions developed, sometimes they tolerated the practice, sometimes they enforced it and prescribed a ritualistic way of doing it, such as in the case of Jewish circumcision.

Many passages of the Bible deal with mutilation.[98] In particular, Exodus 21:23-24 contains the following command (specifically related to retaliation, see chapter 5), "And if any mischief follow, then thou shalt give life for life, eye for eye, tooth for tooth, hand for hand, foot for foot." Deuteronomy 23:1 specifically proscribes castration. Any attempt to alter the physical integrity of an individual by mutilation and suicide is banned. There are strict exceptions: among these is the circumcision of a Jew or a proselyte.[99] In Genesis 17:9-14, male circumcision is clearly presented as a symbol of the alliance between God and Abraham. In other passages, it is seen as a rite of initiation to marriage and life in a group (Genesis 34:14; Exodus 4:24-26; Leviticus 19:23).[100] Mutilations are again debated in different passages of the Talmud and Mishnah.[101]

The New Testament rejects blood vengeance—*lex talionis* (Matthew 5:38-39). However, the matter of self-mutilation is raised in various passages of the Gospel according to Matthew (Matthew 5:29-30, 18:8-9, and 19:12), which are very obscure and much debated. The Christian position on mutilation is that it is a usurpation of divine authority. Man is just an administrator of his body and must keep it intact. With regard to sexual mutilation, the position is still ambiguous, because while the history of Christian theology shows acceptance of mystic self-mutilation, it also indicates a ban on any other kind of mutilation, in particular castration.[102]

As far as Islamic sources are concerned, it is necessary to analyze separately the different practices. Infibulation is neither prescribed nor followed by *šarīʿa*, and there is no special name to define it either in Arabic or in Cushitic languages. Most authors agree on this point.[103] More debatable is the issue of whether there are relevant Islamic religious texts in favor of female excision and male circumcision. Circumcision (male *khitān* and female *khifād; tahūr*) is not mentioned in the Qurʾan. Only with a broad "and disputed" interpretation of verses 2:124 and 16:123, containing a rule of referral to the religion of Abraham, is it possible to find a trace of it, but only with regard to male circumcision.[104] The most quoted reference to female excision is the *hadīt* of Umm ʿAtiyyah, where the practice is presented as a pre-Islamic custom which the Prophet tried to limit. The Prophet advised an excisor that she could have continued to practice the surgery, but on the condition that she "scratch but do not overdo it."[105] Differences among various schools of Islam exist on whether the obligation is mandatory or advisable, and whether it refers to all of the clitoris or only the prepuce.[106]

From the analysis of the above sources, it can be argued that both Christianity and Islam gave an *a posteriori* rationalization to the practice. Historical and religious sources both confirm that FGM dates back well before the spread of monotheistic religions. Rather, religion plays a fundamental role in legitimizing the practice and contributing to its conservation.

FGM, State, and Church

According to Forbes, in the highlands, the Coptic Church at one time placed a ban on FGM.[107] Other travelers refer to the practice in the early seventeenth century (de Almeida) and early nineteenth century (Gobat).[108] The first record of an attempt to halt the practice in the highlands seems to have been that of Zara Ya'kob (1434–1468), a stout defender of monophysite Christianity. In the *Mashafa Berhan,* a collection of religious precepts attributed to him, it is reported that the king intimated to his subjects that the practice should be stopped under penalty of excommunication. Infibulation is depicted as a "Muslim and pagan custom which had spread among Christian of the Tigré, without thinking that God has made men in his image, as Genesis (1:27) stated. . . . If you perform this practice, you become liable to the penalty of the law and you rebel against God who has created you."[109] Nevertheless he agreed that excision could take place.[110]

Under the empire of Claudius (1540–1559), the issue of circumcision was raised in conjunction with a fight, fomented by the Portuguese, between the local Coptic Church and Catholic proselytes. The Coptic Church claimed the practice was traditional and should not be banned.[111] The Catholic Church's campaign had some success, but men refused to marry non-excised Catholic girls and consequently conversion fell off. The College of Cardinals in Rome sent a medical mission to the region, which affirmed that excision was sometimes necessary because of anatomical reasons. The excised woman and her parents had to declare that the practice was not performed because of Jewish custom but out of anatomical necessity.[112]

To the best of our knowledge, no significant steps toward abolition were taken until the period of the liberation struggle against Ethiopia. Shortly before independence, the EPLF embarked on a campaign based on educating women about the negative aspects of FGM. The aid of religious leaders was enlisted in informing them that the practice did not have a religious basis.[113] According to Mary Dines, the EPLF during this period "categorically and successfully forbade genital mutilation and forced marriage."[114] However, in a thirty-page booklet on *Women and Revolution* published by the Eritrean Women's Association in Europe in 1979, there is no mention of FGM. At that time, the EPLF Health Department merely expressed the hope that mutilation would eventually die out "in the context of wider changes taking place in people's attitudes to women in Eritrean society."[115] Lightfoot-Klein stated that all the young girls from the Sudanese border area joined the EPLF; when they returned to their villages they all refused to be operated upon, and that within five years, the practice was totally eradicated in the area.[116] She gives no source for this claim, but there is some corroborating evidence from Rora Habab, an isolated mountain plateau in the north of Eritrea. During the struggle it was home to some 2,000 Muslims who practiced FGM. A nurse from the local health center lobbied men and women in a largely successful campaign to discontinue the practice.[117]

The policy of the present government on this topic has so far been equivocal. On the one hand, the Ministry of Health and the NUEW have expressly discouraged FGM.[118] This is a part of a larger program to improve the status of women; on this point, resolutions were passed at the 1993 PFDJ congress, and legislation was enshrined in the transitional civil code (see the previous chapter). On the other hand, the government has drafted no specific legislation on FGM and has taken no legal action against those who perform the operation.[119] If the government eventually gives this matter a higher priority, two points of the constitution are relevant. Article 7.2 contains a direct reference to women's rights, providing that "any act that violates the human rights of women or limits or otherwise thwarts their participation is prohibited," while article 16.2 prohibits torture and "cruel, inhuman or degrading treatment or punishment."[120] Moreover, Eritrea has ratified the Convention on the Elimination of All Forms of Discrimination against Women (CEDAW), which specifically asks states to take all appropriate measures "to modify the social and cultural patterns of conduct of men and women, with a view to achieving the elimination of prejudices and customary and all other practices which are based on the idea of the inferiority . . . of either of the sexes" (art. 5.a).[121]

FGM and the Transnational Actor

The issue only came to the center of international debate and became an intensely argued matter at the state level as a consequence of Western feminist theorizing and activism. Many people took up this campaign, and their tactics and strategy changed markedly during the course of the years. Western feminists launched the initial attack. This concentrated on the extremely deleterious and well-documented health consequences of FGM, and they hoped to convince attorneys and legislators, who of course were mainly male, of the need to craft legislation banning

FGM on medical grounds, as well as a deprivation of human rights. There was an immediate and intense reaction. After all, FGM is a topic that African women usually only talk about with the utmost discretion, and they certainly do not rush their thoughts into print or perform on a public platform. Feminists were criticized for putting such a contentious and sensitive topic—which had been used in the past by racists and imperialists to stereotype the third world, particularly black African culture, as "backward" and "barbaric"—firmly on the agenda.[122]

The heat generated by this topic placed activists in a dilemma. How could they justify practices that they would never allow to be performed on themselves or their girl children? Not surprisingly, the arguments for and against it became extremely convoluted and sometimes far removed from reality. Some feminists criticized their sisters for making FGM "the only point for defining women's oppression in Africa and the Middle East." A well-known activist and writer on the subject, Fran Hosken, was pilloried (albeit incoherently) because she "exotifies [sic] Egypt and the subject in general."[123] James tackled this squarely and cautioned us to be aware of the sin of "arrogant perception" when dealing with the issue of genital mutilation.[124] Mohanty wrote that it was not helpful to base an analysis on "the privileged premise" that FGM was entirely a matter of men trying to diminish or obliterate the sexual pleasure and satisfaction of woman.[125]

However, activists persisted in raising the issue, and eventually it was taken up by other activists fighting for a different agenda and by bureaucrats who did not usually share the same liberal sensitivity to criticism by the third world. For bureaucrats at the international level, it became a fairly painless way of diverting criticism, placating liberal and feminist activists and also annoying and pressuring third world leaders. They had nothing to lose, and in the end they could only gain from pursuing the issue, as it distracted the opposition's attention away from hard strategic and economic problems. It was soft politics—a sideshow. Here we have a transnational ideology elaborated by a largely middle-class Western female elite which, after some gross political mistakes, formed alliances with African feminists, male politicians, and NGO bureaucrats.

The issue was eventually taken up at the level of international organizations. After a long and often acrimonious debate, a consensus developed within the specialized agencies of the United Nations that FGM had to be abolished.[126] The major breakthrough occurred at the 1993 UN First World Conference on Human Rights, in Vienna, where sexual discrimination, and in particular FGM, was recognized as violence against women, and therefore as a violation of fundamental human rights.[127] Human rights of women were recognized as an "inalienable, integral and indivisible part of universal human rights" (18, 21, 37, 42). At the Beijing Fourth World Conference on Women (1995), "FGM and other traditional practices harmful to women" were specifically mentioned as forms of violence against women that impairs or nullifies the enjoyment by women of "human rights and fundamental freedoms."[128] A formal ban against FGM was announced as the strategic objective I.2, 232.h, that prohibits "female genital mutilation wherever it exists" and matches the objective with "support to efforts among non-governmental and community organizations and religious institutions to eliminate such practices."[129]

At present, the debate has shifted from the issue of whether the practice is legitimate to how to eradicate it.[130] FGM can be seen as a violation of the most fundamental of human rights.[131] As far as the women's rights dimension is concerned, the most important document is the Convention on the Elimination of All Forms of Discrimination against Women (CEDAW).[132] On children's rights, the UN Convention on the Rights of the Child is aimed at protecting children from harmful traditional practices.[133] Another instrument with the same aim is the African Charter on the Rights and Welfare of the Child adopted by the OAU in 1990.[134]

Many states agreed, often reluctantly, to these declarations, and under increasing pressure enacted laws conforming to them. Some states even enacted legislation and prosecuted anyone performing the operation, profiting from it, and even in some cases having undergone it.[135] In the case of a number of states, however, nothing much changed; although a state might accede to international law, it did nothing to enforce a ban on FGM. Therefore a new wave of activism ensued. *Ad hoc* alliances of international bureaucrats and feminists worked more effectively and sensitively with religious and traditional leaders, both men and women, to try from a grass-roots level to discourage and extirpate the practice. Moreover, the threat of economic sanctions from big actors such as the U.S. and the EU were often sufficient to encourage governments to take some steps toward abolition of FGM. A lot of the stick and a little of the carrot worked wonders in changing some governments' attitudes and practices.

What's Next?

Assuredly there will be many steps backward on the long path to total abolition. Legislation in itself has little value if it is only on paper and stays at the level of theoretical declamation and honest intentions for the future. We are only at the beginning of what it is likely to be a long road before the practice disappears, and it is naive to expect immediate results. One should not underestimate the importance of inertia in the conservation of a certain rule. As far as FGM is concerned, many individuals are interested in its preservation. These include traditional operators, who would lose a respected profession and a steady source of income; families, who may not want to risk their daughters becoming unsuitable partners for marriage; individuals who are the custodians of traditional rules and culture such as the elders, who would have to justify changing their minds on this issue.

Marx highlighted a significant fact: sometimes individuals or groups that objectively have a reason to change a certain rule are the very people who are its staunchest supporters. This may help to explain why women, who are the ones who suffer from FGM, who are the strongest supporters and the most resistant to its abolition. Inherently conservative, they are terrified of change. In this way, and for these reasons, social, religious, and legal rules may last and be enforced indefinitely. This has been true of civilizations in the West and the East as well as in Africa, but the phenomenon is even more apparent in culturally and physically isolated traditional societies. However, even the most remote community can be galvanized into change. This is usually because a new rule, more prestigious, more legitimized, or simply enforced by a more powerful actor, begins to circulate and gain acceptance. This seems to be precisely what is occurring with the issue of FGM.

One of the most encouraging features is that some influential religious leaders have now embraced the cause. For a long period, Islam was considered, erroneously, as solely responsible for the introduction and persistence of FGM; thankfully this canard has been laid to rest. In this regard, a most significant event in recent years was the assurance given at a Banjul conference that "FGM has neither Islamic or Christian origin nor justification." This declaration released many women from their firmly held belief that they were fulfilling a religious obligation.[136] Another development is that abolition of FGM is being used as a new conditionality governing the granting of loans and assistance. In the U.S., for example, since 1996, the Female Genital Mutilation Act, after criminalizing genital surgeries performed on females under the age of eighteen in the U.S., stipulated that "[t]he Secretary of the Treasury shall instruct the U.S. Executive Director of each international financial institution to use the voice and vote of the U.S. to oppose any loan or other utilization of the funds of their respective institution, other than to address basic human needs, for the Government of any country which the Secretary of the Treasury determines: 1) has, as a cultural custom, a known history of the practice of female genital mutilation; and 2) has not taken steps to implement educational programs designed to prevent the practice of female genital mutilation."[137] A similar path seems to have been taken by UNESCO. In 2001, the Eritrean government asked that the highland traditional laws be declared a "masterpiece of the oral and intangible heritage of humanity." Among the reasons for the rejection of this proposal was that recognition by the international community of the laws would perpetuate women's inferiority and would specifically condone FGM.[138]

What are the options for the Eritrean government in this new international and transnational legal environment? Traditional rules, not necessarily inefficient in the past, have been questioned and tested and are now severely problematic. The costs of continuing with the practice may very well outweigh the benefits to be gained from it, particularly because its continuation will penalize Eritrea's economic profile and international image. If Eritrea does not give at least the impression of sincerely supporting the abolition, it risks losing even the marginal support —economic, diplomatic, and cultural—it has won in the past ten years.

Ten

Creating Space in a Changing World for Traditional and Religious Law

> The ultimate end of all revolutionary social change is to
> establish the sanctity of human life, the dignity of man,
> the right of every human being to liberty and well being.
> —Emma Goldman[1]

In our role as actors we enter from stage left and admit that since we discovered Eritrea—at very different times and circumstances—we have both been passionately involved and interested in the country. This love affair may be used by our detractors to devalue or deprecate our work as "idyllic," "non-objective," or a host of other epithets. Leaving aside the question of whether "scholarly objectivity" is ever possible in research carried out by a human being, or if the product of such anemic work is ever worth reading, we try to do our best to be judicious. Luckily, over the past four years we have been able to rein each other in and keep each other from being carried away on too great flights of fancy. And we are consoled by the fact that no book worth reading has ever been written by a non-compassionate, bloodless observer.

We can say honestly that neither of us has pre-judged the issues. In the introduction, we promised the reader that we would demonstrate the value of a pluralistic multi-disciplinary approach to a number of important concerns, at the legal, political, and social level. We have dealt at length with the three fundamental issues of blood, land, and sex/gender. We feel that we have shown the value of our research in reaching a deeper understanding of what has gone on over the past few centuries in Eritrea. Different issues have been deconstructed and reassembled according to our lights; others may approach the puzzle in a different manner and come to different conclusions. Our analysis is constructive but not bloodless, and although we have left much unsaid, as the confines of this book do not allow us much more time, we confidently ex-

212

pect that it will form a useful basis for further research both on our part
and on the part of other scholars.

To continue with our analogy drawn from Pirandello, the actors are
waiting in the wings to continue the play; some of them do not know
their lines very thoroughly so they will improvise.[2] We give some of the
closing lines, or broad conclusions, following the format of the preceding chapters. So we deal with issues of blood, land, and sex in that order.

First of all we look at the international and transnational actor, because after a performance, the actors usually take their bows in reverse
order.

International and Transnational Actors

We started this book talking about the origin many centuries ago of
traditional and religious law in Eritrea. We end the book at a significant
time in Eritrea's history. The country is poor, vulnerable, and endeavor-
ing to recover from a devastating war. It is particularly susceptible to a
new, powerful, and in many observers' eyes dangerous actor, that of the
new world order envisaged by globalization. Large and rapacious transnational corporations (TNCs) are constantly searching for areas of the
world where labor costs are low, labor organizations weak, and health
and safety regulations lacking in punch. They are also looking for the
most favorable investment climate, fiscal system, and infrastructure,
and they want to be sure they are able to repatriate the vast bulk of their
profits. Eritrea could be a tempting venue. The current president domi-
nates the political and economic landscape of the country. It is really
only he whom the TNCs need to bring on board in order to ensure
profitable operations.

In the domain of law, globalization has made legal transplants such as
a code, a legal institution, or single rules appealing for reasons that did
not exist in the past. During the colonial period models were imposed.
After decolonization, either the *status quo* before colonization was kept
or transplants matched political alliances.[3] During this period of upheaval, Eritrea against its will was the remotest province of Ethiopia,
and therefore missed this important development. In theory, Eritrea can
now choose. However, legal reform has become compulsory for another
reason; it is now a necessity for a country that desires to be regarded as
"modern" and therefore eligible to receive preferential international
support and consideration. Legal reform has become a saleable commodity.

At first sight, it might appear that globalization has enabled states to select from an increased menu of legal choices—such as a single or group of rules, a law on a certain subject matter, or a code—trawled from all around the world. This is an illusion; globalization is creating a system which is pluralist only on the surface but which offers less choice than before. English is the language of globalization, and transnational corporations are mainly American. The UN system, through its specialized agencies, spreads Western legal culture and values. Law is becoming increasingly subordinate to the rich and powerful elites.[4] In many ways Eritrea has few alternatives to becoming part of the new order even though the country cannot expect any rich pickings as a consequence of becoming a part of the liberal market regime. The devastating cost of the war has resulted in an impoverished country, which is not an ideal place for conventional investors, either Eritrean or non-Eritrean.

In this book we have paid little attention to Eritreans forming the diaspora, which is becoming an increasingly important political actor straddling the state and international domain and mirroring Eritrean state and society. Much of the impressive development that took place from 1991 to 1998 was financed in large part by remittances sent to Eritrea by them. They contributed even more during the war, but now have less impetus and also little left to give. The omission from this book is partly deliberate because the diaspora's influence on law, although vital in the drafting of the constitution, is now at best indirect as intellectuals are marginalized and play no significant independent role. The diaspora is not a unitary actor and includes Eritreans of many different beliefs, political persuasions, and expectations. The Eritrean Jihad, a group primarily devoted to a violent overthrow of the secular Eritrean government and its replacement by a narrowly based fundamentalist government, is one of its most disturbing elements. However, others are equally partisan EPLF supporters.

State

At the moment Eritrea appears to have a hybrid and stratified legal system, one in which current borrowings from civil and common law coexist with elements of the colonial and pre-colonial period, the BMA, and Ethiopian rule. In the sixties, a team of comparative lawyers were involved in the drafting of new codes for the Empire. The new codes were a feature of a previous wave of globalization that began at the turn of the last century and also strongly influenced economic, political, and social development strategies in the whole post-colonial period. The codes were a major breakthrough for both Ethiopia and Eritrea, not so much, we argue, because of the extent to which they were enforced, but because they were a very persuasive model of what an "ideal state" should have.[5] Since then, choosing a code system rather than one based on case law is no longer an issue.

These codes continue, beyond the rhetoric of the present government, to form the basis of Eritrean state law. This, although denied for political reasons, applies both to the transitional codes, that only merely amended the Ethiopian codes, and to the new codes, whose drafters were told to follow the outline of the previous codes. It is inevitable that they will pick up new ideas and solutions from a wide variety of sources, following the worldwide practice of contamination between legal systems, which forms an important part of a recent, transcolonial, new wave of globalization.

Implementation will be a major task. A legal text, even if imported, is seldom inherently efficient. But legal rules are often able to cope quite easily with historical, social, and political environments that are radically different from where they originated and evolved. Legal enforcement requires both technical skill and political will. Experience has shown that the surest way to abort a reform is to label it as inefficient or unworkable. The Eritrean government has to build a legal system appropriate to the society it envisages. Advocates, judges, and professors will carry out the spadework, giving meaning to imported law and institutions. The application and interpretation of the new codes will be largely determined by the quality of the legal education these actors receive. It is therefore disturbing to learn of a public perception among ordinary Eritreans of "a corrupt and inefficient judiciary in place."[6] It is also unfortunate that university training depends so much upon the uncertain loyalty of foreign professors connected in the main with the UN and Western aid agencies.

In any legal reform process, a major role ought to be played by the constitution. As Eritrea's is not yet in force, we cannot say whether or not its promise of fundamental freedoms and separation of powers will become a reality. It is to be hoped that the constitutional future of Eritrea will not mirror the past of Ethiopia, where all constitutions of the past hundred years have been essentially irrelevant.[7] The major reservation, which we raised in chapter 4, is that the Eritrean constitution, like so many in Africa, gives wide-ranging powers to the president. At the moment this point is academic because there is no sign of the constitution's coming into force, and the president is playing all the major roles and some of the subordinate ones in this production, which shows no signs of ending its run.

Another important aspect of legal reform concerns the drastic redrawing of long-standing internal boundaries. In the long run this seems likely to create some major problems. It cuts across the *enda* kinship system that has been and is still such a vital part of Eritrean life. A new infrastructure, including not only roads and power supplies, but also courts, schools, and local government offices, has to be put in place to serve the new divisions adequately. The Ethiopian occupation of parts of Eritrea in 2000 was accompanied by a systematic destruction of all new construction, power plants, bridges, and dams. One consequence of this has been that international NGOs, who by and large had left the country in the 1990s as Eritrea pursued a militant self-reliant mode of development, have been invited back into the country as the massive and urgent rebuilding necessary was beyond the resources of the Eritreans. International actors seem destined to play an even larger role over the next few years, particularly because of the need to rehabilitate hundreds of thousands of internally displaced people (IDP) and returnees from the Sudan.

We referred in chapter 4 to the government's express commitment to decentralize economic and political power. However, it seems highly unlikely that any real power will be given to any form of autonomous authority until national and *zoba* elections have been held. The government will want to weigh the implications of allowing voters to choose independent or non-PFDJ party members to represent them. Until then, local government will be carried out much as the central government desires and directs.

As long ago as 1991, President Isaias Afwerki expressed to one of the authors his personal preference for a multi-party system, but added that Eritreans at that time did not have the necessary background for a fully functioning liberal democracy.[8] All of his statements over the past ten years show that he has not changed his views. Indeed, he has become even more autocratic, concentrating in himself and his office more and more power. Obviously, there needs to be regular change among the leadership and an injection of new blood into both the PFDJ and the government.[9] Unfortunately, as some recent incidents have shown, the president's response to criticism is not to engage in debate, but to silence his critics through prison, solitary confinement, and intimidation.[10] As a consequence, he has lost much legitimacy in the eyes of the international community and the Eritrean intelligentsia. He probably still has the support of the bulk of the population, especially women.

Whatever the prospects for the present leadership, in order to survive, the country will have to remain a unitary state. If the government continues the long-established EPLF practice of coordinated decentralization, there will be in time a comprehensive administrative structure stretching from the central ministries run by the executive branch through the regions and sub-regions, down to the remotest villages and farthest settlements of the country.[11]

A defining characteristic of the independent Eritrean state that has been evolving since the 1960s has been the cohesiveness of the EPLF, and in particular of the central committee. These men and women acted as a kin group bound together by sacrifice, a shared life of extraordinary spartan closeness and intensity, and an ideology that replaced the myth of a common ancestor—the defining feature of other kin groups.[12] Through our research, we have come to realize that the EPLF shared another characteristic of kin groups, namely, its members acted together in cases of bloodshed. All members of the group regarded themselves as of one blood. If one murdered another, he was either executed or became an outlaw. If a member of the group was slain by an outsider, a blood feud arose at once, and the martyr could be avenged by any of the group. It was a point of honor never to leave a wounded or dead comrade on the battlefield. Casualties in the thirty-year war of liberation, and during the 1998–2000 Ethiopian offensives, were very large in comparison to Eritrea's small population, and few families have not lost at least one of their children. The preamble to the Eritrean constitution starts with these words: "With eternal gratitude to the scores of thousands of our martyrs." Eritrea is a small country, and death on such a large scale impinges on the lives of everyone. In a sense the whole country becomes one kin group.

By the end of 2000 it was becoming clear that the monolithic coherence of the EPLF was breaking down. For the first time senior members were prepared to admit that the front was fundamentally divided on most important issues. The implications of this are far-reaching. Whenever a blood group starts to disintegrate, feuds become more common and the rhetoric of retaliation re-emerges.[13]

Traditional and Religious Law

Traditional law and šarīʿa continue to be observed in everyday life. There is no one universal traditional law, rather there are more than twenty separate written codes, all very different from one another. The ones we have seen are just the tip of the iceberg; we have seen scattered allusions to many others that have existed in the past and may still be found in obscure and isolated places.

The large body of tradition has three components. The first comprises the written documents, the ones that we have mainly worked upon being the most accessible. There is a second, much larger group of rules which is the main oral and impenetrable for a number of reasons, including language, the senility of some of the custodians, and the remote areas where the rules are found. This is the case with the rules on FGM, which are usually not mentioned in the codes. There is no need to do so, because the surgery takes place according to well-understood and undisputed procedures transmitted verbally generation after generation, procedures that for many years were not an issue for traditional law. Finally, there is a third body of unrecorded legal rules that are deeply rooted in a particular system, which is sometimes not even accessible to the people who practice it and live under its umbrella. These are rules that constitute the mentality, the way or reasoning about the law, the way of building a legal rule. These rules cannot be verbalized. They form part of an unrecorded and unexpressed background that an outsider cannot understand, and certainly cannot supplant. This is one of the main aspects of a legal tradition. Tradition is not something that has been built or invented overnight. Certainly it cannot be abolished or curbed on short notice.

Traditional and religious laws are deeply imbedded in people's minds; everybody is supposed to memorize them. Most Eritreans are illiterate; their knowledge of the traditions, as well as the Qur'an, is through constant rote learning. In this regard, the dominant role is played by respected elder members of the community. These two bodies of law have coexisted for a long time, and the relationship on the whole has been one of harmony. Neither of the two bodies of law pretends to have exclusive knowledge and power. *Šarī'a* is traditionally distinct from *siyāsa*, the art of government, which is left to the prince and temporal ruler. State law is incomprehensible to them because it speaks a different (in the past Amharic, Arabic, Italian, English, and now Tigrinya) and specialized language. State legal actors are remote, far distant from their villages and frequently different in status and ethnicity.

How the Actors Regard Each Other

We drew our case studies from the areas of blood, land, and sex, where traditional law has been most influential through the centuries. The codes rule comprehensively on all these matters. Only with the advent of the colonial state did issues of blood move out of the domain of the *enda* to the realm of the state. As far as land tenure and land disputes are concerned, in the colonial period a lot of space was left for the community to administer its own law. These remarks are even more pertinent if we consider the rules concerning marital and extra-marital unions; these the colonial rulers left by and large to the domain of traditional and religious law.

What we are seeing at present is that the state is interfering more and more in all three areas. Traditional and religious groups understandably regard this as a threat to their autonomy and very existence. They are prepared to tolerate state legal reform provided it does not run against their own rulings or at least against some of the well-established agreements they have created. One of the most significant examples is the matter of tribute, which we have examined in our case study on land. The Tigrinya were helped to accept the idea of sovereign power via the role played by the Coptic Church in legitimizing the power of the king and other rulers. There was usually general acceptance to pay, but only insofar as the rulers did not demand too much power in the community or become too invasive. The central powers who survived best were those who were not too greedy, satisfied with what they received, and involved themselves no further in the social, political, and legal life of the village.

During the long debate over the 1997 constitution, an elder remarked, "the government needs a strong hand to be able to govern, but it must be harnessed by the *lugam* (bridle) of the law."[14] However, the problem, as we have seen all through this book, is that there is not just one law. Besides state law, traditions and religious laws are also offering their own solutions to particular problems, and these solutions do not necessarily match with the brand-new rules created by the state.[15] Any state that embarks upon an ambitious scheme of legal reform must expect the sometimes vehement intervention of non-state actors. The success of any reform depends ultimately upon the interplay between the state and ethnic groups, the state and religion, and the state and international/transnational actors.

Paradoxically, a state may find it much easier to deal with other sovereign states than with the traditional and religious groups living within its territory. States speak the same political and legal language, as a result of the efforts of professional elites who have received comparable scholarly training. The same obviously does not apply when the state has to engage in dialogue with *šariʿa* and with more than twenty traditional laws working in competition with its own—laws that by no means all rule the same way on any particular point. Every secular state sees traditions and particularly *šariʿa* as a potential threat to its own unity and stability. Most attempts to best *šariʿa* have failed almost everywhere else in the world. *Šariʿa* might eventually be harnessed, but the state has to take an extremely subtle approach. Islam is feared because it is an extremely powerful actor, able to form links with actors even from the remotest areas. It is a formidable counterbalance to Westernization; šariʿa has been and remains a globalizing force, able to create a Muslim identity that transcends geographic, ethnic, class, and gender divisions. At present, in its "fundamentalist" form, it is militantly opposed to Western modernity.[16]

The contest between state and tradition is fought on unequal grounds. Traditional law and Islam are both flexible and able to adapt to changing situations, while state written law is in principle fixed until amended, even though the interpretive work of judges and professors can in time initiate radical changes. The state has to embark on the daunting task of opening a dialogue and minimizing the almost inevitable frictions deriving from it, and of finding the right equilibrium of checks and balances needed to avoid and, if need be, to ameliorate conflict. This is the crux of the struggle between our actors.

And we come here to a point which is particularly important in our work: the room that has been given in the past, or that may be given in the future, to traditional rules, and the degree to which the state will allow groups and their laws to survive beside state law. These two aspects should not be confused. They represent two separate levels of pluralism—weak and strong. Elsewhere in the world, there have been two very different approaches to traditional law. The first is a radical attempt that involves their almost complete abolition; this was followed, at least in theory, by Ethiopia in the 1960s. The alleged rationale behind this is that customary law would impede development and would be inappropriate for a "modernizing" society; indeed it has been said that traditional law, practices, and customs are primarily responsible for the underdevelopment of a would-be modern society.[17]

A second approach to legal reform is to work in close conformity with traditional law wherever possible.[18] This approach seems to have been taken, at least in part—and we cannot yet assess whether at a declamatory or operational level- -by the Eritrean government. In 1998, a workshop was organized to collect all relevant data on traditional law in the area of environmental protection and management, the aim being to use the information to draft a national environment law.[19] The Ministry of Justice initiated a comparable project in 1999. It commissioned the anthropologist Asmarom Legesse and his team from Citizens for Peace in Eritrea (CPE) to talk with the elders of each Eritrean nationality and establish what customary laws existed in the past and at present. Many hours of testimony were recorded and transcribed.[20]

Some of the actions taken by the Eritrean government in the past ten years show some sensitivity toward preservation of aspects of traditional law. Many legal cases have lingered for five years or more, as untrained and inexperienced officials battle to cope with difficult and often impossible legal questions and demands. Therefore, in an attempt to deal with the backlog, traditional practices are being used to settle disputes.[21] It is certain that until a body of state lawyers is trained, customary and *šarī'a* law will continue to be used, particularly in the fields of conciliation and arbitration. If the constitution ever comes into force, article 10.4, according to which "the State shall encourage equitable out-of-court settlement of disputes through conciliation, mediation or arbitration," may be used as a basis for the incorporation of "elements of traditional law which are compatible with the principles of the governing party into the new state legislation."[22] However, a major omission in most legislation is a statement of any specific place for *šarī'a*. As we have pointed out, this is a continuation of a practice that started during the imperial period. The state's position could be read as an implicit acknowledgment that the Muslim communities will continue to be governed by *šarī'a* in matters traditionally reserved to it. This follows the well-known technique of saying something but never too much, and not writing anything down, because *verba volant, scripta manent* [spoken words fly away, written words remain].

Coming back to traditional law, it appears quite obvious that to be used by the state, traditional law should be thoroughly understood by whoever is charged with law reform. It is probably less obvious that if this knowledge is lacking, customary laws may become difficult for state officials to control. It is difficult enough for new legislation to be applied when its meaning is certain, or at least probable. It is an impossible task when it is not, when legal actors have to rely on uncertain data. It is not therefore clear which traditional law, if any, among the twenty or thirty versions of it will be used and who will be asked and trained to enforce it. The vast majority of present-day Eritreans are unaware of the traditional law of any area different from their own, not to mention that of other ethnies. The same certainly applies to the knowledge of non-Muslim Eritreans about *šarī'a*. There are also many important local differences in the observance of *šarī'a*. It is impossible to forecast what will be the outcome.

On the other hand, if the Eritrean government's project is carried out successfully, it will be a singular and important achievement. Up to now in Africa, laws and customs have always been killed off in the process of state building. It has been said innumerable times that the customary law of a given ethnie or sub-ethnie usually reflects the needs of its members far more closely than does legislation at the national or sub-national level.[23] And this is even more so when we look at the impact of international law on small groups.

We do not use these arguments to advocate a paternalistic return to an idealized past. Traditional rules on substantive and procedural matters may be difficult to graft onto modern law, but it is certain that when state laws depart too much from tradition, they are unlikely to be followed freely or enthusiastically.[24] Moreover, the sudden imposition of an entire body of state rules upon a largely illiterate people in a rural area has frequently caused serious social upheaval.[25] Radical changes in long-established traditions such as blood feud are bound to be difficult to administer as societies regard the punishment levied by the state as something extraneous, something to be opposed. In the end a choice has to be made by the government in accord with other state legal actors. They all are charged with the uneasy and sometimes unwelcome task of finding a balance between state and non-state rules. They are surely aware that to apply traditional rules may be dangerous because the state risks ceding legitimacy, but it is just as dangerous to ignore or to attempt to suppress them.

We should recollect that what is under discussion in this section is state pluralism or a weak version of pluralism, and that the recognition of the principle of coexistence of different non-state actors alongside the state, and not subordinate to it, is another matter. The struggle between actors for legitimacy has been our major goal throughout this book. In particular, in our chapter on land disputes, we have seen that some actors succeed by force of arms, some by persuasion and force of argument, and others through the mediation of respected judges (elders, qādī, or state). Some prevail through a consensus reached between contending parties, some through the payment of fines, and some by default.

However, even the most committed government will never go so far as to accept other actors as equal partners. It could not be expected to do so, since this would be diametrically opposed to its own interest and survival; it would mean to openly recognize a situation in which its own supremacy is contested and downgraded. The most it would do would be to delegate competence to tradition and religion in certain subject matters, but under strict control. However, if we look at this situation objectively, we can see that this approach, understandable as it may be and even commendable in a few instances, is fraught with risks for the survival of tradition. The history of land reform exemplifies this very well. Elsewhere in Africa the most serious challenge to the survival of traditional land tenure practices came when the state gave formal recognition to them. The state was then able to demarcate the areas where tradition was to be allowed to prevail. The consequence in several west and southern African countries was that large areas of tribal lands were created. Recognition of traditional practices by the colonial masters was in fact the first step in a process of cooptation that eventually rendered local authorities less powerful than they had been in the past.[26]

Unfortunately we do not possess the magic formula to make Eritrean pluralism feasible and workable. We can only indicate some of the major difficulties that past efforts have created and make some recommendations for the future. In particular, we observe that on land issues, the Eritrean state has most singularly failed to take even a marginal step toward recognition of the role of traditions. The government policies on land might be summarized as too radical, too unpopular, and unworkable. The main implication of land nationalization is that in the future there will be little or no room for traditional law. This will lead inevitably to the breakdown of the complex network of lineage and village relationships that is built upon it. Therefore any change will certainly engender a major opposition. The government may find it impossibly difficult to impose the rigid central control that is implicit in the policies it has drafted since independence. Just one example is that it would undoubtedly take many years, if it could ever be done, for the Land Commission to draw up a precise register of land holdings and distribute the land to a plethora of applicants. In the end the speed and success of Eritrea's development will depend upon the slimming down of the vast majority of subsistence-level or below subsistence-level farmers. In order to break out from a cycle of grinding poverty, Eritrea must industrialize quickly and equitably, and develop a more efficient commercial agriculture. The country may find that a land system that grants full possessory rights to farmers will be more efficient than one where all land is owned by the state.

The Invisible Actor Revealed

A declared priority of the present government is to redress the inequality of women. The government has to tread very carefully on this issue, because although ignored by colonial and post-colonial states, women's inequality has in recent years been a major concern of many international actors. However, the path to permanent improvement is likely to prove to be a long and difficult one. There can be no more illustrative example than the campaign to abolish FGM.

The present Eritrean president is a man, almost all senior party and government officials are men; they make the important decisions on all issues. By and large they are motivated to improve the position of women only if it is to their advantage to do so. Because FGM is not directly related to the political economy or the defense of the country, many of them do not see why it deserves a high priority on the agenda.

On the other hand, this topic is one where international and transnational actors seem to be determined to make an inroad upon traditional values. But yet again, even though these actors have on the surface argued strongly for the total abolition of FGM, other issues, such as the institution of a market economy, independent press, and a multi-party electoral system, still seem to be of much higher priority.

It will be instructive to see who will be the eventual victors and vanquished in this confrontation. One wonders if pressures from the transnational community are sustained enough to raise the issue to the level of the highest priority, one of those priorities which are worth fighting for, or whether women will be used as pawns in a complex exchange of favors at political and economical levels between powerful lobbies and African states. It is only to be hoped this trial of strength will not see Eritrean women once again behind the scenes, watching men taking decisions over their heads.

Afterword

One of the consequences of the military and political reverses in the war with Ethiopia in 1999 and 2000 has been a willingness of Eritreans to raise sensitive and controversial issues for the first time. Elsewhere we have mentioned the presence in Eritrea of a "conspiracy of silence," as Ruth Iyob has termed it. Both in Eritrea and in the diaspora, presidential decisions have been challenged openly and trenchantly. The so-called Berlin group of thirteen, comprising some leading Eritrean academics and professionals, wrote a pertinent letter to the president apprising him of their great concerns over recent developments in the country. Among other proposals, they urged him to implement the constitution immediately, so that Eritreans could enjoy their rights. They also asked him to abolish the special court against corruption.

A feature common to much of Africa is that most people prefer to remain in the majority whatever the cost. This is a pragmatic view; if you are in the minority you lose *a priori* any possibility of changing the situation and improving the prospects for you or your family. The minority is always seen as a perpetual loser; this makes the chances of forming a serious viable political opposition even less likely. It is far better to practice a qualified opposition within the majority. Eritrea is the only country in Africa with no independent press; it is also the one with the least exposure to the Internet. Eritreans therefore lack the vital safety valve of free access to the media that is open to individuals in other countries. Without such outlets, movements to form the loyal opposition so necessary to the development of a viable democratic society cannot develop. The Tigrinya elite has always preferred to pursue its political opposition through the medium of underground cells, usually comprising groups of three, five, or seven operating independently. Any future highland opposition to the present government is almost certain to follow this pattern; a number of Muslims seem likely to gravitate to the outlawed and exiled offshoots of the ELF and Eritrean Jihad.

The Eritrean government and people have embarked upon a long and difficult struggle to win the peace. We trust they will approach this task with the same determination, stamina, and ingenuity they applied to winning a long war against an enemy some twenty times their size. They are attempting to change ancient communities, and in the process are making many mistakes. We hope they will learn from the experience of other post-colonial African states. In all of them, traditional institutions and values provided legitimacy for the leaders of the pre-colonial societies. The modern state has often severed this link with the past and has not been able to act as an adequate substitute. Our exhumation and analysis of the rich body of traditional law may constitute a small contribution to their attempt to integrate the past with the present, and to ensure a bright future.

Glossary

Vernacular	Language	English
ꜥad	Bilein	descent
ꜥad (ꜥaddi)	Tigrinya	village
ꜥāda	Arabic	custom, habits
adera	Bilein	patron/lord
adjr (aǧr)	Arabic	reward
aiam	Tigrinya	unmarried woman
akwaro	Tigrinya	village committee to settle land disputes
ama	Arabic	slave girl
amanzara	Tigrinya	adulterous woman
ꜥamd	Arabic	deliberate intent
amets (ꜥamäṣ)	Tigrinya	rape
ꜥāqila	Arabic	lineage, blood kinship
are	Saho	clan—Asaorta
arš	Arabic	penalty for wounds
ꜥasaba	Arabic	agnatic relatives
asalat	Tigré	non-infibulated
ascilmina	Kunama	soothsayer
asker	Bilein	protected persons
awraja (awräǧä)	Tigrinya	province
Bahr Negash (Bahr Näguš)	Tigrinya	Lord of the Sea
baito	Tigrinya	assembly
bal mogheb	Bilein	intermediaries in disputes
ballabat	Ge'ez	original inhabitant

227

Vernacular	Language	English
balmeriet (balmäryet)	Tigrinya	original inhabitants/land holders
banda	Italian/Tigrinya	irregular armed forces
baraka	Arabic	special power/blessing
Baria	Tigrinya	Nara (formerly slave)
beit	Bilein/Tigré	house
belg	Tigrinya	little rains
berchi	Tigrinya	garment worn at a solemnized marriage
bet (biet)	Tigrinya	house
bilo	Saho	vengeance
bir	Bilein	vengeance
cahabò	Tigrinya	measure of cereals of about 5 kilograms
cerhi	Tigrinya	Asmara's red light district
chat	Somali/Amharic	narcotic plant
chikka ᶜaddi	Tigrinya	village chief
chikka sum	Tigrinya	village chief—colonial period
ciba	Bilein	family
cingheret	Tigrinya	concubine
crai	Tigrinya	lease
dam	Tigrinya	blood
dam	Tigré	blood feud
dāmīn	Hebrew	blood/price/money
danaili	Saho	arbiters
danya (daña)	Tigrinya	Judge
daqqi	Tigrinya	sons of/people
daqqi abbat	Tigrinya	descendants of original owners
debtera	Tigrinya	cultivated man
dekkibat	Tigrinya	first inhabitants
Dergue	Amharic	committee
diesa	Tigrinya	commonly owned land
diglal	Beni Amir	supreme chief of Beni Amir
diwan	Arabic	records of the tribunal
diya	Arabic	blood money
dumoz	Tigrinya	compensation—type of marriage
durgonyu	Tigrinya	billeting troops in a village
egghet	Tigrinya	indemnity
elchi	Tigrinya	equivalent to 12 or 18 MTD
enda	Tigrinya	descent group
enficti	Tigrinya	measure
entalam	Tigrinya	measure
faraᵓa	Bilein	men, people, tribe
ferghi	Tigrinya	home spun cloth

Vernacular	Language	English
ferghi gibri	Tigrinya	half share
ferresenya	Tigrinya	billeting troops in a village
fethesh	Bilein	law
fetsmi	Tigrinya	oath
futa	Tigrinya/Saho	garment, dress
gabi	Tigrinya	garment
gaisha	Saho	clan—Haso
galamota zamawit	Tigrinya	prostitute
gar nefsi	Tigrinya	blood money
geranna	Tigrinya	measure of cloth
geza	Tigrinya	gift
gezauti	Tigrinya	group of houses
gezmi	Tigrinya	bride wealth
gezzi	Tigrinya	injunction
ghebbar	Tigrinya	one who pays tribute
ghebetà	Tigrinya	measure of cereals of about 20 kilograms
ghebri (gäbri)	Tigrinya	tribute
gherazit	Amharic	female exciser
ǧināya (pl. *ǧināyat*)	Arabic	crime
gulfare	Tigré	vassal
gultegnat	Tigrinya	tenant of *gulti* lord
gulti	Tigrinya	tribute land
habeas corpus	Latin	requiring a prisoner to be brought to court
habesha	Tigrinya	Abyssinian
hadaro wetsui	Tigrinya	emancipated man
hadd	Arabic	special punishment for crimes prohibited by the Qurʾan
hadīt	Arabic	a tradition of the Prophet
haggegti	Tigrinya	laws/legislators
harām	Arabic	ritually forbidden
harbī	Arabic	enemy alien
hasan	Arabic	good, beauty, perfection
hazu	Tigrinya	forbidden or reserved pasture
heday mober	Bilein	marriage of a widow
Heggi Endabba	Tigrinya	law of the fathers
helqat	Tigré	silver wedding ornament
heniè fadaya	Tigrinya	vengeance
hezaty	Tigrinya	pasture
hudmo (tukul)	Tigrinya	house
iab	Nara	gifts
idin	Bilein	descent

Vernacular	Language	English
ikhtilāf	Arabic	disagreement
iso	Kunama	gifts
jelli baho	Afar	God-given child
kaffāra	Arabic	religious expiation
kantiba	Tigrinya	district political leader
kaw	Bilein	villages, people, tribe
kawn are	Saho	the five clans
kebabi (*käbabi*)	Tigrinya	village/neighborhood
kebele	Amharic	association
kebessa (*käbässa*)	Tigrinya	highland plateau
kebila (*qabīla*)	Tigrinya	tribe
kerai	Kunama	paid laborer
khamsa	Arabic	five, kin group
khatā	Arabic	unintentional murder
khifād	Arabic	female circumcision, reduction
khitān	Arabic	male circumcision
kiremti	Tigrinya	big rains/rainy season
kirma	Bilein	price of the neck
lex non scripta	Latin	unwritten law
lex talionis	Latin	retaliation
longa manus	Latin	the long arm of the law
lubale	Saho	lion
lugam	Tigrinya	bridle of a horse or mule/harness
madama	Italian	Eritrean mistress of an Italian Man
mahber	Tigrinya	elder
mahr	Arabic	bride wealth, price of the neck, dower
makelay aliet	Tigrinya	foreigner
maqaderai	Tigrinya	man who cuts the uvula
mara	Kunama	blood/leader/language
marbata	Kunama	vengeance
marda	Tigrinya	silver necklace
matlot	Tigré	marriage gifts
matlu	Bilein	marriage gifts
matrūk	Arabic	assigned land
mawqūfāt	Arabic	trust land
mazarraf	Tigrinya	war dance
meʾdabo	Tigrinya	committee dividing land
medri guaytat	Tigrinya	land held by lords
medri worki	Tigrinya	land bought with gold
megabaaya	Tigrinya	village assembly
meghes	Tigrinya	percentage of the crop paid by lease-holder
meghezza	Tigrinya	measure
mehaber	Tigrinya	gatherings/association

Vernacular	Language	English
mekinshab	Tigrinya	circumcision (male and female)
mekneyat	Tigrinya	marriage by contract
melechet	Tigrinya	musical instrument
menketzdem	Tigrinya	giving a daughter of a murderer to the son of the victim
mens rea	Latin	criminal intent
meret terrado	Tigrinya	communal sharing (EPLF)
meslene	Tigrinya	district chief/representative
metellen	Tigrinya	fixed lump sum fee paid by lessee
milk	Arabic	privately owned land
mīrī	Arabic	state land
mizeraf	Tigrinya	kidnapping of a woman for marriage
mogono	Tigrinya	compensation for jealousy
mohaber	Kunama	assembly of elders
mohar	Hebrew	bride wealth, price of the neck
moheber	Bilein	gathering
morus	Tigrinya	property by gift
muluie gibri	Tigrinya	full share
mutᶜa (nikā al-mutᶜa)	Arabic	marriage of pleasure, temporary marriage
nabara	Tigrinya	deputy clan leader
naga	Rashaida	price of the neck
nağisa	Arabic	uncircumcised girl
nebara	Saho	notables elected by enda
nebari	Bilein	custom
nefqi	Tigrinya	measure of cereals
ona	Saho	clan leader
ona	Tigrinya	ruins of a building
praeter legem	Latin	beyond the law
qabila	Tigré	tribe/clan/ethnic group
qādī	Arabic	Islamic judge
qadra	Tigrinya	virgin land/unfarmed land
qal kidan	Tigrinya	covenant—type of marriage
qasāma	Arabic	compurgation
qatl	Arabic	murder
qatl bi-sabab	Arabic	unintentional homicide
qisās	Arabic	retaliation
rachbe	Saho	assembly
res iudicata	Latin	a judicial decision to which there is no appeal
res nullius	Latin	something belonging to no one
resanto	Saho	leader
restegnat (pl. restegnatat)	Tigrinya	entitled to property/inheritors

Glossary

Vernacular	Language	English
resti	Tigrinya	occupied land
rim	Tigrinya	benefit/entitlement
rukabie saga	Tigrinya	unlawful carnal knowledge
saari bela	Saho	tribute for pastures
sadāq	Arabic	dowry
sargo arbaa	Tigrinya	special indemnity
šarīᶜa	Arabic	system of Islamic law
sciumaghilli	Bilein	elders
sedaq	Hedareb	price of the neck
sedbegnat	Tigrinya	leaseholder
sedbi	Tigrinya	lease
segada	Tigré	bride wealth
selmat	Tigrinya	bride wealth
sembil arare	Tigrinya	breach of marriage promise
semmai madharata	Tigré	price of the neck
shabia (ša ᶜbīya)	Arabic	people's/popular
sharmuta	Tigrinya	prostitute (pejorative)
shehena	Tigrinya	commonly owned land
shellʾkiru	Nuba	cutting the clitoris
shifta	Tigrinya	bandit
shum	Tigrinya/Tigré	chief/office holder
shumagulle	Tigrinya/Tigré	village chief
shumgulti	Tigrinya	*gulti* landlord
šibh el-ᶜamd	Arabic	quasi deliberate intent
sim	Bilein	chief
simeghel	Bilein	firstborn
siyāsa	Arabic	politics, government
stare decisis	Latin	case law
šughūl šaytān	Arabic	Devil's work
Sunna (of the Prophet)	Arabic	second source of Islamic law after the Quʾran
sunna	Arabic	tradition
sūq	Arabic	market
tafrīq	Arabic	divorce
tuhūr	Arabic	purification, excision/circumcision
talāq	Arabic	repudiation
tapu	Turkish	certificate relating to *mīrī* land
tarq	Bilein	blood money
tašrīᶜ	Arabic	Islamization
taᶜzīr	Arabic	punishment
tegadelti	Tigrinya	liberation fighters
tehaz debter	Tigrinya	book/holder of the laws
tescar (täzkar)	Tigrinya	deceased, commemoration of
tisha	Tigrinya	right of habitation

Vernacular	Language	English
ti'smaya	Beja	name giving
tsebuq	Tigrinya	good, beauty, perfection
tsilmi	Tigrinya	land tenure based on passing rights to the next generation
ʿumda	Arabic	leader, village head
ʿurf	Arabic	custom
wad galamota	Tigrinya	son of a prostitute (insult)
wad sahsam	Tigrinya	son of a prostitute (insult)
wadjib	Arabic	compulsory
wahas	Tigrinya	guarantor
walīy al-dam	Arabic	avenger of the blood
waqf	Arabic	religious endowment
wasax	Somali	menstruation
wedebat	Tigrinya	descendant of common ancestor
werdi	Tigrinya	wager
wocho	Tigrinya	mantle/black cloth blanket
woreda (wärädä)	Tigrinya	district, land
zamut (zamät)	Tigrinya	adultery
zarafa	Tigrinya	riches
zeban mängesti	Tigrinya	in the name of the government
zekran	Tigré	gifts
zemawi	Tigrinya	adulterous woman
zemewti	Tigrinya	adulterous couple
zera	Tigrinya	watchman
zoba	Tigrinya	zone/region
Zufan Chilot	Amharic	Chamber of Appeal

Compiled from several sources

Notes

Preface and Acknowledgments

1. Another interesting exception is shown in Albania: the "Kanun di Lek Dukagjini"—Canon of Alexander, Duke of the Giny. Alexander the III, comrade in arms of Scanderbeg, commissioned the writing down of Albanian traditional codes during the fifteenth century. On this point, see Salvatore Villari, *Le consuetudini giuridiche dell'Albania* (Rome, 1944).

2. In other areas of Africa, traditional law was written down and translated, but only during the colonial period. See, for example, Isaac Schapera, *A Handbook of Tswana Law and Customs* (London: Oxford University Press, 1938). For French West Africa, see *Coutumiers Juridiques de l'Afrique Occidentale Française* (Paris: Larose, 1939). These attempts have been much criticized; see chapter 2.

3. Raimond Verdier, "Coutume et loi dans le droit parental et foncier (Afrique de l'Ouest francophone)" in Gérard Conac, ed., *Dynamiques et finalités des droits africains* (Paris: Economica, 1980), 309.

4. One of our strengths, we have found, lies in our differing political backgrounds. This has forced us to question for ideological bias anything we have written.

5. For purposes of attribution, Lyda Favali is the author of chapters 2, 3, 4, 5, 8, and 9. Roy Pateman wrote chapters 6 and 7. The preface and chapters 1 and 10 were written jointly.

1. Facts and Ideas

1. Cited by Peter Marshall, *Demanding the Impossible: A History of Anarchism* (London: Fontana, 1993), 303.

2. Lucius Annaeus Seneca, *Epistulae Morales ad Lucilium*, Libri XX

[Seneca's Letters to Lucilius, letter 20], trans. E. Phillips Barker (Oxford: Clarendon, 1932).

3. Aldous Huxley, "A Note on Dogma," in *Proper Studies* (London: Chatto & Windus, 1927), 247.

4. Friedrich W. Nietzsche, *Nachlass* (Frankfurt am Main: Fischer Bücheri, 1959), 318.

5. In the case of Eritrea, someone might identify himself or herself as Eritrean, as Muslim or Christian, as a member of the Jiberti or Tigrinya ethnic group, as merchant or farmer, as ex-fighter, or any combination of these. And no doubt other identities might be adopted during life.

6. The phenomenon is widely acknowledged by legal theorists. Among these, see Jacques Vanderlinden, "À propos des familles de droits en droit civil comparé," in *Hommages à Renée Dekkers* (Brussels: Bruylant, 1982), 363; Filip Reyntjens, "Note sur l'utilité d'introduire un système juridique 'pluraliste' dans la macrocomparaison des droits," *Revue de Droit Internationale et Droit Comparé* 68 (1991): 41; Sally Engle Merry, "Legal Pluralism," *Law and Society Review* 22, no. 5 (1988): 869; Sally Engle Merry, "Anthropology, Law, and Transnational Processes," *Annual Review of Anthropology* (1992): 357; Warwick Tie, *Legal Pluralism: Toward a Multicultural Conception of Law* (Brookfield, Vt.: Dartmouth, 1999).

7. Our view is shared by John M. Van Doren, "Positivism and the Rule of Law, Formal Systems or Concealed Values: A Case Study of the Ethiopian Legal System," *Journal of Transnational Law and Policy* 3 (1994): 165–204.

8. This definition is given by Jacques Vanderlinden, "Le pluralisme juridique: essay de synthèse," in *Le pluralisme juridique,* ed. John Gilissen (Brussels: University of Brussels, 1971), from which many other definitions have originated. For an overview of these definitions, Marco Guadagni, "Legal Pluralism," in *The New Palgrave, a Dictionary of Economics and the Law,* ed. Peter Newman (London: Macmillan, 1998).

9. Gordon R. Woodman, "Legal Pluralism and the Search for Justice," *Journal of African Law* 30, no. 2 (1996): 152. In the same vein are Kurt Nickerson Llewellyn and Edward Adamson Hoebel, *The Cheyenne Way: Conflict and Case Law in Primitive Jurisprudence* (Norman: University of Oklahoma Press, 1941), 53; Leopold Pospisil, *The Anthropology of Law: A Comparative Theory of Law* (New York. Harper and Row, 1971), 105.

10. Henry F. Morris and James S. Read, *Indirect Rule and the Search for Justice: Essays in East African Legal History* (Oxford: Clarendon Press, 1972), 45. For a similar approach, H. Patrick Glenn, *Legal Traditions of the World* (Oxford: Oxford University Press, 2000).

11. On the distinction between a subjective and an objective aspect of pluralism, Jacques Vanderlinden, "Return to Legal Pluralism: Twenty Years Later," *Journal of Legal Pluralism* 28 (1989): 149. This is related to the notion of a semi-autonomous social field given by Sally Falk Moore, *Law as a Process: An Anthropological Approach* (London: Routledge and Kegan Paul, 1978), 29–30,

57–58. See the distinction between strong and weak pluralism in John Griffiths, "What Is Legal Pluralism?" *Journal of Legal Pluralism* 24, no. 1 (1986); Gordon R. Woodman, "Ideological Combat and Social Observation: Recent Debate about Legal Pluralism," *Journal of Legal Pluralism* 42 (1998): 21–59.

12. Falk Moore, *Law as a Process*, 114, 116.

13. Laura Nader, "Controlling Processes: (Tracing the Dynamic Components of Power)," *Current Anthropology* 38, no. 5 (1997): 711. See also Rodolfo Sacco, "Perché l'armato ubbidisce all'inerme (Saggio sulla legittimazione del diritto e del potere)," *Rivista di Diritto Civile* 1 (1997): 1–18; Rodolfo Sacco, *Il diritto africano* (Torino: Utet, 1995).

14. It is clearly a convention, because the acknowledgment of state borders recognizes the superiority of the state, whereas according to a pluralistic viewpoint each legitimized subject has equal dignity. See Falk Moore, *Law as a Process*, chapter 2.

15. For a similar approach see Duncan Kennedy, *Legal Education and the Reproduction of Hierarchy: A Polemic against the System* (Cambridge: Afar, 1983).

16. Michel Rosenfeld, "A Pluralist Critique of the Constitutional Treatment of Religion," in *The Law of Religious Identity: Models or Post-Communism*, ed. Andras Sajo and Shlomo Avineri (The Hague: Kluwer Law International, 1999), 44–45.

17. Kenneth N. Waltz, *Man, the State, and War* (New York: Columbia University Press, 1959).

18. J. David Singer, "The Level-of-Analysis Problem in International Relations," in *The International System: Theoretical Essays*, ed. Klaus Knorr and Sidney Verba (Princeton, N.J.: Princeton University Press, 1961).

19. Robert Jervis, *Perception and Misperception in International Politics* (Princeton, N.J.: Princeton University Press, 1976).

20. Kenneth N. Waltz, "Anarchic Orders and Balance of Power," in *American Foreign Policy: Theoretical Essays*, ed. G. John Ikenberry (New York: Longman, 1999), 67–90.

21. Irving L. Janis, "Escalation of the Vietnam War: How Could It Happen?" in *American Foreign Policy: Theoretical Essays*, ed. G. John Ikenberry (New York: Longman, 1999), 533–560; Robert Jervis, "Hypothesis on Misperception," in *American Foreign Policy: Theoretical Essays*, ed. G. John Ikenberry (New York: Longman, 1999), 483–504.

22. Francis G. Snyder, *Capitalism and Legal Change: An African Transformation* (New York: Academic Press, 1981), 47: "plural normative orders are part of the same system in any particular social context and are usually intertwined in the same social micro-processes."

23. Antonio Gramsci, *Quaderni dal carcere* (Torino: Einaudi, 1948–1951), 51; Antonio Gramsci, "Osservazioni sul folklore," *Letteratura e vita nazionale*, (Torino: Einaudi, 1950).

24. Susan F. Hirsch and Mindie Lazarus-Black, *Contested States: Law, Hegemony and Resistance* (New York: Routledge, 1994), 6-7.

25. For a fuller study, see Jean Comaroff and John L. Comaroff, *Of Revelation and Revolution: Christianity, Colonialism, and Consciousness in South Africa,* vol. 2 (Chicago: University of Chicago Press, 1991), 24-28.

26. James C. Scott, *Domination and the Arts of Resistance: Hidden Transcripts* (New Haven, Conn.: Yale University Press, 1990).

27. Daniel Miller et al., "Introduction," in *Domination and Resistance,* ed. Daniel Miller, Michael Rowlands, and Christopher Tilley (London: Unwin Hyman, 1989), 11-12.

28. Hirsch and Lazarus-Black, *Contested States*, 9.

29. The author applies this structure to offer a model for the evolution of complex societies focusing on the political processes. Timothy Earle, "Political Domination and Social Evolution," in *Companion Encyclopedia of Anthropology,* ed. Tim Ingold (London: Routledge, 1997), 955, 951.

30. Anthony Giddens, *Central Problems in Social Theory* (Berkeley: University of California Press, 1979), 88-94.

31. Luigi M. Lombardi Satriani, *Antropologia culturale e analisi della cultura subalterna* (Messina: Pletoriana, 1968).

32. Hannah Arendt, "Communicative Power," in *Power,* ed. Steven Lukes (New York: New York University Press, 1986), 62.

33. This approach is due in Italy to Rodolfo Sacco and Marco Guadagni. See, for example, Rodolfo Sacco, *"Il Diritto africano"*; Antonio Gambaro and Rodolfo Sacco, *Sistemi giuridici comparati* (Torino: Utet, 1996), 543-544.

34. Alan Watson, *Legal Transplants: an Approach to Comparative Law* (Edinburgh: Scottish Academic Press, 1974). The word transplant is more commonly understood in its medical usage—the transfer of a healthy organ into a diseased body. This metaphor only partially captures the reality; legal transplants are not always one-way and the body is not always diseased. Since Watson the literature on legal transplants has grown much larger. See, among recent contributions, Gianmaria Ajani, "Legal Transplants and Economic Performance," in *New Trends in International Trade Law*, ed. Gianmaria Ajani and Giuseppe Porro (Torino: Giappichelli, 2000), 1-16; Daniel Berkowitz, Katharina Pistor, and Jean-François Richard, *Economic Development, Legality, and the Transplant Effect*, 39 CID Working Papers on Law and Development (Cambridge, Mass.: Center for International Development at Harvard University, 2000).

35. Pier Giuseppe Monateri, *The Weak Law: Contaminations and Legal Cultures, Italian National Reports to the XVth International Congress of Comparative Law* (Bristol, 1998), 84-85.

36. Monateri, "The 'Weak' Law," 95, 107.

37. In the same sense, see Clifford Geertz, *Local Knowledge: Further Essays in Interpretive Anthropology* (New York: Basic Books, 1983), 226; Martin Chanock,

Law, Custom and Social Order: The Colonial Experience in Malawi and Zambia (New York: Cambridge University Press, 1985).

38. Rodolfo Sacco, "Legal Formants: a Dynamic Approach to Comparative Law," *American Journal of Comparative Law* 39 (1991): 343; Pier Giuseppe Monateri and Rodolfo Sacco, "Legal Formants," in *The New Palgrave Dictionary of Economics and the Law*, ed. Peter Newman (London: Macmillan, 1998), 531.

39. Rodolfo Sacco, *Introduzione al diritto comparato* (Torino: Utet, 1994), 43–63.

40. Raoul Charles Van Caenegem, *Judges, Legislators and Professors* (New York: Cambridge University Press, 1987).

41. Lyda Favali, "La legittimazione e i suoi protagonisti (una premessa allo studio delle fonti in Eritrea)" in *New Law for New States*, eds. Lyda Favali, Elisabetta Grande, Marco Guadagni (Torino: L'Harmattan, 1998), 159–182.

42. The tensions between traditional and state law did not abate with the end of colonialism. For some fascinating examples see Leon Shaskolsky Sheleff, *The Future of Tradition: Customary Law, Common Law, and Legal Pluralism* (Ilford: Frank Cass, 2000).

43. We use Smith and Hutchinson's definition of ethnie as "a named human population with myths of common ancestry, shared historical memories, one or more elements of common culture, a link with a homeland and a sense of solidarity among at least some of its members." John Hutchinson and Anthony D. Smith, eds., *Ethnicity* (Oxford: Oxford University Press, 1996), 6.

44. Roy Pateman, "Liberté, Egalité, Fraternité: Aspects of the Eritrean Revolution," *The Journal of Modern African Studies* 28, no. 3 (1990): 457–472.

45. Bereket Habte Selassie and Richard R. Rosen, "The Eritrean Constitutional Process: An Interview with Dr. Bereket Habte Selassie," *Eritrean Studies Review* 3, no. 1 (1999): 158.

46. When the constitution was being drafted from 1994 to 1997, the Mufti of Eritrea informed the constitutional commission chair (Professor Bereket Habte Selassie) that he wanted Eritrea to remain a secular state. Bereket Habte Selassie and Rosen, "The Eritrean Constitutional Process," 167.

47. Baudouin Dupret, Maurits Berger, and Laila al-Zwaini, *Legal Pluralism in the Arab World* (The Hague: Kluwer Law International, 1999).

48. Abebe Kifleyesus, "Bilin: Speaker Status Strength and Weakness," *Africa* LVI, no. 1 (2000): 83.

49. Merry, "Legal Pluralism," 871.

50. Ulrich Beck, *What Is Globalization?* trans. Patrick Camiller (Cambridge: Polity Press, 2000), 21.

51. The government speedily closed it down but in recent years we have seen less formal contacts succeed.

2. From Tradition to Globalization

1. *E come possiamo intenderci, signore, se nelle parole ch'io dico metto il senso ed il valore delle cose come sono dentro di me; mentre chi le ascolta, inevitabilmente le assume col senso e col valore che hanno per sé, del mondo come egli l'ha dentro?* Luigi Pirandello, *Sei personaggi in cerca d'autore* (Firenze: Bemporad, 1921).

2. See, for example, Pascal Boyer, *Tradition as Truth and Communication: A Cognitive Description of Traditional Discourse* (Cambridge: Cambridge University Press, 1990).

3. Raimond Verdier, "Customary Family Law," *International Encyclopaedia of Comparative Law*, ed. René David et al. (Tübingen: J. C. B. Mohr, IV, 1983), 11.221–289.

4. Elisabeth Colson, *The Social Consequences of Resettlement* (Manchester: Manchester University Press, 1971); Eric Hobsbawm and Terence Ranger, eds., *The Invention of Traditions* (Cambridge: Cambridge University Press, 1983); Benedict Richard O'Gorman Anderson, *Imagined Communities: Reflections on the Origin and Spread of Nationalism* (London: Verso, 1991).

5. John Arundel Barnes, "Class and Committees in a Norwegian Island Parish," *Human Relations* 7, no. 1 (1954): 39–58.

6. Leopold Pospisil, *The Anthropology of Law: A Comparative Theory of Law* (New York: Harper and Row, 1971), 196.

7. Austin L. Hughes, *Evolution and Human Kinship* (New York: Oxford University Press, 1988), 62; Alan Barnard, "Rules and Prohibitions: The Form and Content of Human Kinship," in *Companion Encyclopedia of Anthropology*, ed. Tim Ingold (London: Routledge, 1999), 786, 794.

8. Alfred Reginald Radcliffe-Brown, "Introduction," *African Systems of Kinship and Marriage*, ed. Alfred Reginald Radcliffe-Brown and Daryll Forde (London: Oxford University Press, 1950), 39–43.

9. On this see, naturally, Edward Evan Evans-Pritchard, *The Nuer: A Description of the Modes of Livelihood and Political Institutions of a Nilotic People* (Oxford: Clarendon Press, 1940). For a similar approach see Pospisil, "Anthropology of Law," 190.

10. Jack Goody, *Literacy in Traditional Societies* (Cambridge: Cambridge University Press, 1968), 2.

11. Ugo Fabietti and Francesco Remotti, eds., *Dizionario di antropologia, etnologia, antropologia culturale, antropologia sociale* (Bologna: Zanichelli, 1997), 416.

12. E. L. Peters, "The Proliferation of Segments in the Lineage of Bedouin of Cyrenaica," *Journal of the Royal Anthropological Institute* 90 (1960): 29–53; M. G. Smith, "On Segmentary Lineage Systems," *Journal of the Royal Anthropological Institute* 86 (1956): 9; Ladislav Holy, ed., *Comparative Anthropology* (Oxford: Blackwell, 1987).

13. Ladislav Holy, "The Segmentary Lineage Structure and Its Existential

Status," in *Segmentary Lineage Systems Reconsidered,* ed. Ladislav Holy (Belfast: The Queen's University of Belfast, 1979), 1.

14. Kjetil Tronvoll, *Mai Weini: A Highland Village in Eritrea* (Lawrenceville, N.J.: Red Sea Press, 1998), 127.

15. It is interesting to look at the definition of the Roman *gens* given by Jhering. This constitutes a model for kinship-based societies, is comparable with *enda* and *gaisha,* and gives a perfect idea of the nexus between family ties and power. *Gens* has been defined as "daß die Gens die Identität der Familie und des Staates ist, sich, wie man will, als eine Familie mit politischem Charakter und als eine politische Verbindung mit familienartigem Charakter bezeichnen läßt." ("Identity of lineage and state with the lineage having a political character where the political influences the lineage just as the lineage influences the political.") Rudolph von Jhering, *Geist des römischen Rechts* (Leipzig: Breitkopf und Härtel, 1878), 184. Similarly, the head of the village/head of the *enda,* assisted by the council of elders, has powers going further than the ones he has over families. We can find similar forms in other patriarchal farming societies—Semitic or non-Semitic—such as pre-Roman *gens,* Germanic *vicus,* Celtic clan, Longobard *fara,* Scottish highlanders, Iranian *vic,* Russian *mir.*

16. Carlo Conti Rossini, "I Loggo e la legge dei Loggo Sarda," *Giornale della Società Asiatica Italiana* XVII Firenze (1904): 15 16 The work of this meticulous and cultivated scholar has never been matched and still forms the basic source for any serious research on Eritrean traditional law; Belai Araia and Berhane Abraham, personal communication, Asmara November 2000.

17. Tronvoll, *Mai Weini,* 73–74.

18. Tronvoll, *Mai Weini,* 100. In the Bilein the head of the family is the father or the first-born son. He is called *simeghel.* The chief of a branch is the eldest son, in direct line from the first-born to the first-born.

19. Tronvoll, *Mai Weini,* 102, 128.

20. On this point see Rodolfo Sacco, "Di alcune singolari convergenze fra il diritto ancestrale dei Berberi e quello dei Somali," *Africa* 44, no. 3 (1989): 341.

21. In the Mensa, art. 64 of the *Fetha Mahari* states: "the law is not equal for everybody. The law is different for people who belong to the same village and for foreigners. Each is judged according to his status." Karl Gustav Rodén, *Le tribù dei Mensa—Storia, legge e costumi, Traduzione italiana dalla lingua Tigré* (Stockholm: Nordiska Boktryckeriet, 1913).

22. Marco Guadagni, "Note sulle fonti del diritto etiopico, con particolare riferimento all'istituto del divorzio," *Africa* 28, no. 3 (1973): 369; Giuseppe Aurio Costanzo, *Le fonti del diritto abissino delle popolazioni cristiane,* (Rome: Ferraiolo, 1940), 124.

23. T. W. Bennett and Jan Vermeulen, "Codification of Customary Law," *Journal of African Law* 24, no. 2 (1980): 207–208, 215.

24. It has been said that in Seraye the *Adkeme Melega* law gave equal rights to women from its initial drafting in the thirteenth century. Bocresion Haile,

The Collusion on Eritrea (Asmara: Bocresion Haile, 2000), 16. This is overstating the position.

25. Asmarom Legesse, *Customary Law and Alternative Dispute Resolution (ADR)* (Asmara: Ministry of Justice, 1999), 3–4.

26. *Eritrea Profile*, "Eritrean Traditions and Customs," 4 October 1997.

27. Carlo Conti Rossini, "Lo statuto degli Scioattè Ansebà (Eritrea)," *Scritti Giuridici in onore di Santi Romano*, III (Padova: Cedam, 1940): 347.

28. Costanzo, *Le fonti*, 128–129.

29. Gennaro Mondaini, *La legislazione coloniale italiana nel suo sviluppo storico e nel suo stato attuale (1881–1940)*, I (Milan: Istituto per gli Studi di Politica Internazionale, 1941), 128.

30. Friederike Kemink, "The Tegreñña Customary Law Codes," *Paideuma: Mitteilungen zur Kulturkunde* 37 (1991): 57.

31. Kemink, "The Tegreñña," 60–61.

32. Conti Rossini, "Lo statuto," 348.

33. Kemink, "The Tegreñña," 54.

34. This was in the minds of Ercole Petazzi, *L'odierno diritto penale consuetudinario dell'Hamasien (Eritrea)* (Asmara: Fioretti, 1937), 1–7; Carlo Conti Rossini, *Principi di diritto consuetudinario dell'Eritrea* (Rome: Ministero delle Colonie, Tip. Unione Ed., 1916), 16 (who spoke largely of the possibility of codifying all Eritrean highland laws to "counterbalance the influence of Islam"); and Caffarel, who in the beginning of the nineteenth century delineated a general scheme of criminal legislation for indigenous tribes of the Eritrean colony (Schema generale di un progetto di legislatura penale per le tribù indigene della Colonia Eritrea.) See Ferdinando Martini, Relazione sulla Colonia Eritrea per gli esercizi 1902–7, Allegato 20, II, Tipografia della Camera dei Deputati, Roma, 1913.

35. Simon Roberts, "The Recording of Customary Law: Some Problems of Method," in *Folk Law: Essays in the Theory and Practice of Lex Non Scripta, 1*, ed. Alison Dundes Renteln and Alan Dundes (New York: Garland, 1994), 331–337.

36. *Jiberti* is the general Arabic term used to describe Muslims in East Africa.

37. Martino Mario Moreno, "Le popolazioni dell'Eritrea," in *L'Italia in Africa, I, Il territorio e le popolazioni* (Rome: Ministero degli Affari Esteri, n.d.), 121.

38. Ilario Capomazza, *Istituzioni di diritto consuetudinario del Seraé—La legge degli Atchemè-Melga* (Macerata: Stabilimento tipografico Giorgetti, 1912), arts. 47–53, 90–97, 99–100.

39. Alberto Pollera, *The Native Peoples of Eritrea*, trans. Linda Lappin (Asmara: University of Asmara, 1996), 83.

40. Asmarom Legesse, *Customary Law*, 20–21.

41. Capomazza, *Istituzioni di diritto*, 9–11.

42. Kemink, "The Tegreñña," 67. An English translation was made by Tesfatzion Medhanie in Addis Ababa, and is available for consultation in the Law Library of the University. Bilillign Mandefro, "Agricultural Communities and the Civil Code," *Journal of Ethiopian Law* VI, no. 1 (1969): 198.

43. Dennis J. Duncanson, "Sir'at 'Adkeme Milga'-A Native Law Code of Eritrea," *Africa* XIX, no. 2 (1949): 142.

44. Duncanson, "Sir'at 'Adkeme Milga'," 149.

45. Pollera, *The Native Peoples*, 85.

46. Asmarom Legesse, *Customary Law*, 6.

47. Petazzi, *L'odierno diritto penale*, 24–25; Conti Rossini, *Principi*, 67.

48. Research and Documentation Center, Asmara, *Sir'at nay Habslus, nay GhebreKristos nay DegiTeshim*, Document 00494, Asmara 1910.

49. Duncanson, "Sir'at 'Adkeme Milga'," 142.

50. Petazzi, *L'odierno diritto penale*, 27; Kemink, "The Tegreñña," 62.

51. Research and Documentation Center, Asmara, *Highi Dehartyn Lamzan Weqertyn Damban*, Box 4/07006.

52. Duncanson, "Sir'at 'Adkeme Milga'," 142.

53. Research and Documentation Center, Asmara, *Wa'ela Shewa'te Anseba*, Box 4/07006.

54. Conti Rossini, "Lo statuto," 348–350.

55. Duncanson, "Sir'at 'Adkeme Milga'," 142.

56. Kemink, "The Tegreñña," 63.

57. Research and Documentation Center, Asmara, *Sir'at Karneshim*, Document 00492.

58. Duncanson, "Sir'at 'Adkeme Milga'," 142.

59. Research and Documentation Center, Asmara, *Sir'at Dembezan*, Box 4/007008.

60. To be found in *Highin Siratin Nay MeretAdebo: Codes and Bylaws of Eritrean Regions and Countries*, comp. and pub. ZeraYacob Estifanos, Wolde-Mariam Abraham, and Gherima GhebreMeskel (West Germany, 1990).

61. Pollera, *The Native Peoples*, 75–77.

62. Research and Documentation Center, Asmara, *Warsa Bet*, Document 00534, n.d.

63. The Ethiopian calendar is seven or eight years behind the Western calendar.

64. *Highin Siratin Nay MeretAdebo*.

65. Petazzi, *L'odierno diritto penale*, 26.

66. Research and Documentation Center, Asmara, Sira'at LogoChewa, Tigrinya, 1935, Document 00502. An English translation by Yohannes Habte Sellasie may be consulted in the law library of the University of Addis Ababa. Bilillign Mandefro, "Agricultural Communities," 198.

67. Duncanson, "'Sir'at 'Adkeme Milga'," 142.

68. Conti Rossini, "I Loggo," 9–10.

69. Carlo Conti Rossini, *Ricordo di un soggiorno in Eritrea* (Asmara: Tipografia della Missione Svedese, 1903). Pollera claims—we do not know on what grounds—that Tigrinya and Tigré (the two mostly widely spoken languages in Eritrea) were not written down until around 1880 when Catholic and Protestant missionaries applied Amharic Ge'ez characters to the spoken languages. Pollera, *The Native Peoples*, 18.

70. Duncanson, "Sir'At 'Adkeme Milga'," 142.

71. Kemink, "The Tegreñña," 65.

72. *Bullettino Ufficiale della Colonia Eritrea*, n.47, Asmara, 21 November 1903, 2.

73. The law was formulated by chiefs and elected representatives of Liksait (of the Attehò Mellasc') and Serait (of Mai Gund Mellasc) and others from Akele Guzai. In 1937, it was still observed in the relations between the following districts: Scimezana, Tsenadegle, Haggegti, Daqqi Dighna; Daqqi Zeresennai; Mezhé, Dericièn, Aret, Zebaonti, Daqqi Tehextà, Merettà Sabené. Ilario Capomazza, *Il diritto consuetudinario dell'Acchele-Guzai* (Asmara: Fioretti, 1937), 57–58.

74. Conti Rossini, *Ricordo di un soggiorno*, 61; Conti Rossini, "Lo statuto," 347–348; Kemink, "The Tegreñña," 64.

75. Conti Rossini, *Principi*, 63.

76. Capomazza, *Il diritto*, 60.

77. Kemink, "The Tegreñña," 66.

78. Pollera, *The Native Peoples*, 85.

79. Solomon G/Khristos, *Highi Engana's; Sira'at Astmi Harmaz*, March 1993.

80. According to Capomazza, *Il diritto*, 58, this law was observed by inhabitants of the following districts: Egghelà Hamès, Daqqi Admocom, Daqqi Ghebri', Enganà, Robrà. See also Kemink, "The Tegreñña," 65.

81. Mondaini, *La legislazione*, 141.

82. Capomazza, *Il diritto*, 59; Conti Rossini, *Principi*, 64; Kemink, "The Tegreñña," 65–66.

83. Pollera, *The Native Peoples*, 82–83.

84. Law of *Adgena Tegeleba*, English translation on file at Haile Selassie University, Addis Ababa, 1951, Chapter XI, arts. 156–162. This was partially translated by Alemseged Tesfai. Bilillign Mandefro, "Agricultural Communities," 198.

85. Kemink, "The Tegreñña," 66.

86. *The Code of Customary Law of Acchele Guzay*, April 1951, Asmara, 44–47.

87. Duncanson, "Sir'At 'Adkeme Milga'," 142.

88. Duncanson, "Sir'At 'Adkeme Milga'," 148.

89. Tekle Abraha, personal communication, 1998.

90. Ioan M. Lewis, *Peoples of the Horn of Africa: Somali, Afar and Saho* (London: Haan Associates, 1994), 174–175; Ilario Capomazza, *L'Assaorta-Saho* (Naples: Società Africana d'Italia, 1914), 6.

91. In the northeast of the Schimezana region in Akele Guzai, for example, there were some villages of Minifere Saho farmers. Carlo Conti Rossini, "Al Ragali," in *Estratti dal Bollettino della Societá Italiana di Esplorazioni Geografiche e Commerciali, anni 1903–1904* (Milan: Stabilimento Tipografico Bellini, 1903), 35–37.

92. Conti Rossini, "Al Ragali," 40–43.

93. Numbers 45, 46, 47, *Bullettino Ufficiale della Colonia Eritrea*, 1903.

94. *Bullettino Ufficiale della Colonia Eritrea*, Asmara, 14 November 1903, n.46, arts. 1–2.

95. Pollera, *The Native Peoples*, 156.

96. Asmarom Legesse, *Customary Law*, 13.

97. The Tigré speak Eritrea's second most widely used language, Tigré, but many of them are bilingual with either Arabic or Beja as their other language. Another pastoral sub-ethnie is the Marya, originally Coptic Christian but converted to Islam from 1600 onwards.

98. William Caffarel, "La legislazione dell'Eritrea," *L'Eritrea Economica* (Novara Rome: De Agostini, 1913), 467.

99. Mondaini, *La legislazione*, 138.

100. Caffarel, "La legislazione," 169.

101. Francesco Sarubbi, "Di alcune consuetudini delle popolazioni del bacsopiano occidentale in Eritrea," *Atti del terzo congresso di studi coloniali*, III, Section II, Firenze-Roma: Centro di Studi Coloniali, Istituto Coloniale Fascista, 1937, 297.

102. Eritrean Assembly, *New Customary Law of the Beni Amer Tribes*, Asmara, 1 June 1960.

103. Asmarom Legesse, *Customary Law*, 45.

104. The Swiss adventurer and scholar played a crucial role in the Egyptian conquest of large areas of Eritrea.

105. Pollera, *The Native Peoples*, 106.

106. Shlomo Raz, *Tigré Grammar and Texts* (Malibu: Undena Publications, 1983), 1–2. For a fuller description of the Mensa, see Ferdinando Martini, *Nell'Africa italiana* (Milan: Treves, 1892).

107. Werner Münzinger, *Dei costumi e del diritto dei Bogos. Traduzione dal tedesco a cura di A. Ostini*, con prefazione di I. M.Ziegler, Ministero degli Affari Esteri (Ministero degli Affari Esteri: Rome, 1891), 42–44.

108. Münzinger, *Dei costumi*, 39.

109. Mondaini, *La legislazione*, 136.

110. Pollera, *The Native Peoples*, 99.

111. *Highi Endaba BetTarge Bogos*, Research and Documentation Center, Asmara, Document 4/07007, no date indicated.

112. Ghebil Temnewo, "Murder and Blood Money under the Fit'ha Megarh"

(LL.B. senior thesis, University of Asmara, 1999), 4; Pollera, *The Native Peoples*, 99.

113. Ghebil Temnewo, "Murder and Blood Money," 5.

114. Asmarom Legesse, *Customary Law*, 17–18.

115. Medhanie Habtezghi, "Customary Marriage and Divorce in Blin Society" (LL.B. senior thesis, University of Asmara, 1999), 51.

116. Pollera argues, from the names of their ancient kings, that they were exposed to Judaism around 1000 B.C. Alberto Pollera, *I Baria e i Cunama* (Rome: Reale Società Geografica, 1913), 13–15.

117. *Eritrea Profile*, "Eritrean Traditions and Customs," 15 November 1997, 7.

118. Pollera, *I Baria e i Cunama*, 9.

119. Ghada H. Talhami, *Suakin and Massawa under Egyptian Rule, 1865–1885* (Washington, D.C.: University Press of America, 1979), 51.

120. Pollera, *I Baria e i Cunama*, 34, 37.

121. Pollera, *I Baria e i Cunama*, 98.

122. Werner Münzinger, *Studi sull'Africa Orientale-Traduzione dal Tedesco per cura del Corpo di Stato Maggiore* (Rome: Voghera, 1890), 398.

123. Pollera, *I Baria e i Cunama*, 100–108.

124. Conti Rossini, "Al Ragali," 42–43.

125. Conti Rossini, "Al Ragali," 46–47.

126. Carlo Conti Rossini, "Schizzo etnico e storico delle popolazioni eritree," ed. Ferdinando Martini, *l'Eritrea Economica* (Rome, 1913).

127. According to one legend, the Loggo Sarda were also of Saho origin, but Conti Rossini denies this. Conti Rossini, "Al Ragali," 48–49.

128. Costanzo, *Le fonti*, 33–36.

129. Costanzo, *Le fonti*, 39–41.

130. Costanzo, *Le fonti*, 63.

131. Costanzo, *Le fonti*, 49.

132. The translation was by Ignazio Guidi, *Il Fetha Nagast o Legislazione dei Re. Codice ecclesiastico e civile di Abissinia*, Pubblicazioni scientifiche del R. Istituto Orientale di Napoli (Rome: Tipografia Casa Ed. Italiana, 1897).

133. Costanzo, *Le fonti*, 69–70.

134. See Alberto Pollera, *Lo stato etiopico e la sua chiesa* (Rome-Milan: S.E.A.I, 1926).

135. Costanzo, *Le fonti*, 67.

136. Costanzo, *Le fonti*, 30–31, 63–66.

137. Conti Rossini, "I Loggo," 1.

138. Duncanson, "Sir'At 'Adkeme Milga'," 141.

139. The Malēkī school is dominant in northwestern Eritrea—Beni Amir, Kunama, Nara; the Hanafī in eastern Eritrea, among Afar, in the city of Assab and the coast, in the Dahlak islands, in Massawa, and among Saho. There

are Shāfiʿī communities in the Afar of Assab and Somali. Alberto Pollera, *Le popolazioni indigene dell'Eritrea* (Bologna: Manuali Coloniali, 1935), 285–286.

140. All of the schools transmit God's will as it is expressed in the Qurʾan and the *sunna*, and consequently all their interpretations are deemed to be equally valid. Each Muslim can adhere to any one of the orthodox schools and can also choose another school insofar as a single legal act is concerned. This reciprocal acknowledgment did not exclude a strenuous theoretical debate among the schools. Joseph Schacht, *An Introduction to Islamic Law* (Oxford: Clarendon Press, 1964), 67–68.

141. Mondaini, *La legislazione*, 133–134.

142. J. Spencer Trimingham, *Islam in Ethiopia* (London: Oxford University Press, 1952), 269–275.

143. D. C. Cumming, "The History of Kassala and the Province of Taka," *Sudan Notes and Records* XXI (1937): 6.

144. Ghada H. Talhami, *Suakin and Massawa*, 93–95, 227.

145. Pollera, *I Baria e i Cunama*, 34–37, 53.

146. Trimingham, *Islam in Ethiopia*, 233–247.

147. Ioan M. Lewis, "South of North: Shamanism in Africa: A Neglected Theme," *Paideuma Mitteilungen zur Kulturkunde* 35 (1989): 187.

148. Conti Rossini, *Principi*, 561.

149. Norman J. Singer, *Governmental Recognition of Non-governmental Laws and Legal Institutions in Ethiopia*, manuscript, Law Library, Haile Selassie I University, Addis Ababa, n.d., 10.

150. For example the *sheikh* takes over the powers and functions of the shaman who presided over the village in olden times.

151. Conti Rossini, "Al Ragali," 42–43.

152. Schacht, *An Introduction*, 62.

153. Mohamed El-Awa, "The Place of Custom ('urf) in Islamic Legal Theory," *Islamic Quarterly* XVII, no. 3 and 4 (1973): 177–179.

154. Mohamed El-Awa, "The Place of Custom," 180–182.

155. Barbara Cooper "Ambiguities of Laïcité: Reflections on Women and the Christian Minority in Colonial and Post-Colonial Niger," paper presented to the Second Symposium of the Islamic Law in Africa Project, Dakar, Senegal, 29 June 2001, 8–11.

156. Richard Roberts, "Custom and Muslim Family Law in the Native Courts of the French Soudan, 1905–1912," paper presented to the Second Symposium of the Islamic Law in Africa Project, Dakar, Senegal, 30 June 2001, 15–32.

157. Cheikh Gueye, "Règles de succession dans l'Islam et dans la société mouride: des articulations complexes et des effets stimulateurs de l'urbanisation toubienne," paper presented to the Second Symposium of the Islamic Law in Africa Project, Dakar, Senegal, 1 July 2001.

158. Yahya Ould El-Bara, "Le statut personnel de la femme entre droit musul-

man et droit coutumier dans la Mauritanie post-coloniale," paper presented to the Second Symposium of the Islamic Law in Africa Project, Dakar, Senegal, 29 June 2001.

3. Changing Leadership, Unchanging Law

1. Friederike Kemink, "The Tegreñña Customary Law Codes," *Paideuma: Mitteilungen zur Kulturkunde* 37 (1991): 54.

2. Steven Lowenstein, "Ethiopia," in *African Penal Systems*, ed. Alan Milner (New York: Praeger, 1969), 55.

3. Roy Pateman, *Eritrea: Even the Stones Are Burning* (Trenton, N.J.: Red Sea Press, 1998).

4. Werner Münzinger, *Dei costumi e del diritto dei Bogos. Traduzione dal tedesco a cura di A. Ostini,* con prefazione di I. M.Ziegler, Ministero degli Affari Esteri (Ministero degli Affari Esteri: Rome, 1891), 39–40.

5. Carlo Conti Rossini, *Principi di diritto consuetudinario dell'Eritrea* (Rome: Ministero delle Colonie, Tip. Unione Ed., 1916), 123, 132.

6. Some figures, because of their special status, were exempted; these included the head of the village, the priest, the blacksmith, the musician, and the man who cut the uvula.

7. After this time only a gun and a carpet a year was given to the Negus as acknowledgment of his sovereignty. According to another source, which appears too detailed to be unreliable, tribute was in fact paid, even if not on a regular basis. At the time of Negus Iasu, each adult male contributed half an MTD (this tribute was called *ghebri azie Iasu*). From 1825 to 1850, the part of Akele Guzai that was under control of Dejazmach Wube paid a tribute of 5,000 MTD per year. Ras Alula increased this to 7,900 MTD. Under kings Tewodros and Yohannes, the *fesses* (*fasas*—tribute in kind) and contributions in various kind were added to the tribute. The Italians decreased the tribute, and in 1903 it was reported that it was not difficult to collect. *Bullettino Ufficiale della Colonia Eritrea,* 14 November 1903, 3.

8. Münzinger, *Dei costumi,* 3, 39–40; Werner Münzinger *Studi sull'Africa Orientale-Traduzione dal Tedesco per cura del Corpo di Stato Maggiore* (Rome: Voghera, 1890), 230.

9. Münzinger, *Dei costumi,* 25.

10. *Bullettino Ufficiale della Colonia Eritrea,* 7 November 1903, 4.

11. Münzinger, *Studi sull'Africa,* 229–232.

12. Alberto Pollera, *I Baria e i Cunama* (Rome: Reale Società Geografica, 1913), 34–37.

13. According to another source, the reason was that he wanted to destroy a region which constituted the border between the Christian highlanders and Dervishes, thinking in this way to stop the advance of Mahdism among the Kunama and Nara. Pollera, *I Baria e i Cunama,* 54.

14. Ilario Capomazza, *Istituzioni di diritto consuetudinario del Serae—La legge degli Atcheme-Melga* (Macerata: Stabilimento tipografico Giorgetti, 1912), 88–89.

15. *Bullettino Ufficiale della Colonia Eritrea*, 7 November 1903, 4.

16. René David, *Les grandes systèmes de droit contemporain* (Paris: Précis Dalloz, 1992); Arthur R. Hogue, *Origins of the Common Law* (Bloomington: Indiana University Press, 1966). Inside the tradition of Anglo-American Law, it can be seen as opposed to equity on one hand and statutes on the other. On this point, see Ugo Mattei, *Common law-Il diritto anglo-americano* (Torino: Utet, 1992), 83–99.

17. The starting point of this debate can be found in Harold Joseph Berman, *Law and Revolution: The Formation of the Western Legal Tradition* (Boston: Harvard University Press, 1983). See also James Gordley, "Common Law v. Civil Law: una distinzione che va scomparendo?" in *Scritti in onore di Rodolfo Sacco* (Milano: Giuffré, 1994), I, 559; and Frank Lawson, "A Common Lawyer Looks at Codification: Further Reflections on Codification," in Frank Lawson, *Selected Essays*, 1997, I, 48 and III, 96.

18. See Mathias Reimann, ed., *The Reception of Continental Ideas in the Common Law World 1820–1920* (Berlin: Duncker and Humblot, 1993).

19. See Antonio Gambaro and Rodolfo Sacco, *Sistemi giuridici comparati* (Torino: Utet, 1996), 19; Ugo Mattei and Pier Giuseppe Monateri, *Introduzione breve al diritto comparato* (Padova: Cedam, 1997), 52.

20. Because the traditional dichotomy veils the complexity of legal phenomena that are outside it, the historical focus on the antithesis between common and civil law was joined to the systemic approach based on the superiority of the Western legal tradition over "other conceptions of law." In this way, African law was relegated, along with Hindu, Chinese, and Japanese systems, into a "family by default." The critique has been wide and consistent: see, for example: Jacques Vanderlinden, "À propos des familles de droit en droit civil comparé," *Hommages à René Dekkers* (Brussels: Bruylant, 1982).

21. On this point see Ugo Mattei, "Three Patterns of Law: Taxonomy and Change in the World's Legal Systems," *American Journal of Comparative Law* 45 (1997): 5–44.

22. In an attempt to avoid legal ethnocentrism, the school of comparative law of the University of Trento, in Italy, has suggested a grouping of the major world legal systems on the basis of the prevalence of law (rule of law), that of politics (rule of politics), and that of tradition (rule of tradition). All of these have the same weight. This classification identifies common law, civil law, post-socialist, and Islamic legal systems, in addition to a pluralistic legal system such as is present in Africa.

23. Fasil Nahum, "The Enigma of Eritrean Legislation," *Journal of Ethiopian Law* 9, no. 2 (1973): 310–311.

24. William Caffarel, "La legislazione dell'Eritrea," in *L'Eritrea Economica* (Novara-Rome: De Agostini, 1913): 487.

25. Gordon R. Woodman, "Legal Pluralism and the Search for Justice," *Journal of African Law* 30, no. 2 (1996): 158.

26. Gennaro Mondaini, *La legislazione coloniale italiana nel suo sviluppo storico e nel suo stato attuale (1881–1940)*, I (Milan: Istituto per gli Studi di Politica Internazionale, 1941), 23–25, 218–226.

27. See *Atti Parlamentari, legisl.* XXIII, sess. 1909–1911, docum. n. 756.

28. According to a law of 1 July 1890, n.7003, art. 1, 2. This principle was reinforced by *Regio Decreto* 5 May 1892 n.270 (arts. 5–6) and by arts. 2–3 of *Legge Organica* 24 May 1903, n.205 that prescribed an *ad hoc* promulgation in the colony by the government, both for laws enacted after the colonial occupation and for those already in force before this period. Mondaini, *La legislazione*, 102.

29. Mondaini, *La legislazione*, 112–114. However, according to Irma Taddia, *L'Eritrea-Colonia 1890–1952* (Milan: F. Angeli, 1986), 67, the new penal code for Eritrea received an informal application in Eritrean courts, in place of the Italian code.

30. This regime was left intact by the law that created *Africa Orientale Italiana* (AOI—Law, 11 January 1937, n.285) that ultimately extended Eritrean and Somali legislation to newly conquered territories. Mondaini, *La legislazione*, 43, 109–126.

31. With law 5 July, n.857. This solution, which was also adopted in the French colonies of Tunisia and Morocco, was explicitly restricted to Eritrea by the Italians. For the different regimes of *Somalia Italiana* and Libya, see art. 1, RD 8/6/1911 n.695 and art. 5 of RD 26/1/1913 n.48.

32. Nathan Marein, *The Ethiopian Empire: Federation and Laws* (Rotterdam: Royal Netherlands Printing and Lithographing Company, 1954), 371. For the definition of "assimilated," see art. 2, *Ordinamento Giudiziario*, approved with *Regio Decreto* 20 June 1935, n.1649.

33. Gerald Kennedy Nicholas Trevaskis, *Eritrea, A Colony in Transition: 1941–52* (Westport, Conn.: Greenwood, 1975), 27.

34. Art. 9, RD 2/7/1908 n.325, *Ordinamento Giudiziario dell'Eritrea*.

35. Mondaini, *La legislazione*, 160–163.

36. *Ordinamento Giudiziario* of 1935, arts. 53–4; Mondaini, *La legislazione*, 166.

37. Giuseppe de Stefano, *I costumi penali abissini ed il Fetha Neghest* (Firenze: Bemporad & Figlio, 1906), 6; F. F. Russell, "Eritrean Customary Law," *Journal of African Law* 3, no. 2 (1959): 99.

38. Massimo Colucci, *Sistemi di accertamento e di pubblicitá dei diritti fondiari nelle Colonie*, Estratto dagli *Atti del secondo Congresso di Studi Coloniali*, Napoli, 1–5 October 1934, 16.

39. The *Tribunale di Commissariato* constituted the *Commissario Regionale* and two members selected from among civil servants or the army. The governor could also appoint two indigenous notables, with a consultative vote. The *Corte*

d'Assise comprised a judge and four indigenous notables, also with a consultative vote. Notables and *qāḍī* could also assist *Commissari* and *Residenti*, always with a consultative vote. Mondaini, *La legislazione*, 164–166.

40. Mondaini, *La legislazione*, 127.

41. Mondaini, *La legislazione*, 108–109.

42. J. J. Gow, "Law and the Sudan," *Sudan Notes and Records* XXXIII, no. 2 (1952): 304.

43. Tom Killion, ed., *Historical Dictionary of Eritrea* (Lanham, Md.: Scarecrow Press, 1998), 266.

44. For Ethiopia, see *Governatorato di Addis Ababa, Ordinamento della giustizia*, 1936, art. 5.

45. Trevaskis, *Eritrea*, 24–26; Fasil Nahum, "The Enigma," 310–311; Marein, *The Ethiopian Empire*, 389.

46. Nahum, "The Enigma," 311.

47. Marein, *The Ethiopian Empire*, 378–385; Trevaskis, *Eritrea*, 31.

48. Marein, *The Ethiopian Empire*, 383, 385–386.

49. Ibrahim Mukhtar saved from destruction some thirty records from the *šarīʿa* court in Massawa dating from 1603. As the history of Islam in the region is obscure, these court records are especially valuable. They show which school of Islam was followed and in which areas traditional law was taken into consideration in the decisions. They also served informally as an official gazette: sometimes government edicts or translations of official letters were copied. Jonathan Miran, "Islamic Court Records: A Source for the Social and Economic History of Massawa in the Nineteenth Century," paper presented at the First International Conference of Eritrean Studies, Asmara, 22–26 July 2001, 3.

50. *Procedures and Rules, Shari'a Courts of Eritrea*, n. 2 of 1946, on file in the Attorney General Office, Asmara, 1997.

51. *Waqf*—religious endowment—is a very important issue decided by Muslim courts.

52. The legal instrument that formed the basis of the Federation was Resolution n.390 (V), 2-12-1950 that was ratified by Ethiopia and Eritrea. See Order n 6, 1952, *Negarit Gazeta*, 11 September 1952. This resolution was called the Federal Act. It is published in Department of Public Information, UN, *The United Nations and the Independence of Eritrea*, with an introduction by Boutros Boutros Ghali, The UN Blue Books Series, XII (New York, 1996), 94. For a comment on the Eritrean constitution and its relation with the Ethiopian constitution, see Trevaskis, *Eritrea*, 81; Amedeo Giannini, *Nuove costituzioni di stati del Vicino Oriente e dell'Africa* (Milan: Giuffré, 1954), 73; Haile Semere, "The Roots of the Ethiopia-Eritrea Conflict: The Erosion of the Federal Act," *Journal of Eritrean Studies* 1, no. 1 (1996): 1–18. Federal Incorporation and Inclusion of the Territory of Eritrea within the Empire of Ethiopia Order, 11-9-1952, *Negarit Gazeta* 12th Year, n.1; A. Arthur Schiller, "Legislation," *The*

American Journal of Comparative Law 2 (1953): 377–380. Schiller served as a legal adviser to the United Nations Commissioner in Eritrea.

53. Giannini, *Nuove costituzioni*, 73.

54. Haile Semere, "The Roots," 4.

55. Richard A Rosen, "Constitutional Process, Constitutionalism and the Eritrean Experience," *North Carolina Journal of International Law and Commercial Regulation* 24, no. 2 (1999): 283.

56. Schiller, "Legislation," 378.

57. Clarence J. A. Smith, "Human Rights in Eritrea," *Modern Law Review* 18, no. 5 (1955): 484–486.

58. See Ruling of Supreme Court, 19 August 1953. We are very grateful to Alemseged Tesfai for bringing this, and other cases, to our attention.

59. See Ruling of Supreme Court, 12 February 1957.

60. Schiller, "Legislation," 380.

61. The UN resolution provided for the creation of "federal institutions" that had to have Eritrean participation; these institutions were largely inoperative according to most writers. Moreover, the Imperial Decree n.6 of 11/8/52, promulgated on the same day that the Eritrean constitution was ratified, stated that in Eritrea, the Ethiopian constitution, laws, and regulations applied.

62. See "Designation and the Extension of Functions of Our Federal Minister Orders, 1952," *Negarit Gazeta*, 11 September 1952.

63. In *Negarit Gazeta*, 25 September 1953 (13th Year, n.2.)

64. Marein, *The Ethiopian Empire*, 423.

65. The two official languages according to art. 38.1 of the Eritrean constitution of 1952.

66. The Ethiopian penal code of 1957 was extended to Eritrea with a law adopted by the Eritrean Assembly on 10 September 1959, and promulgated on 12 October 1959. See "The Penal Code (Extension) Act," in *Eritrean Gazette*, XXI, 1959, n.12. Notice found in Fasil Nahum, "The Enigma," 6. The text of the "Extension Act" is available in Italian in appendix IG, 60–61. In 1961, when the new Ethiopian code was enacted, it was immediately extended to Eritrea.

67. Russell, "Eritrean Customary Law," 100, 104.

68. Thomas Geraghty, "People, Practice, Attitudes and Problems in the Lower Courts of Ethiopia," *Journal of Ethiopian Law* VI, no. 2 (1969): 451. The alleged reason for the suspension of the proclamation in Ethiopia was "a widespread belief" that the lower level courts were not competent and organized enough to be able to cope with the extra legal burden that the proposed restructuring would entail. Probably more important was the opposition from provincial governors to the abolition of courts they dominated and used to perpetuate their privilege. On this point, see Robert Allen Sedler, "The Development of Legal Systems: the Ethiopian Experience," *Iowa Law Review* 53, no. 3 (1967): 615.

69. Geraghty, "People, Practice, Attitudes," 450.

70. Teame Beyene, "The Eritrean Judiciary: Struggling for Independence," paper submitted to the International Conference of Eritrean Studies, Asmara, July 2001.

71. The Ethiopian constitution of 1931 took as a model the Japanese constitution of 1883. See John M. Van Doren, "Positivism and the Rule of Law, Formal Systems or Concealed Values: A Case Study of the Ethiopian Legal System," *Journal of Transnational Law and Policy* 165, no. 3 (1994): 182.

72. Penal Code of Ethiopia, published in proclamation n.158, 1957, *Negarit Gazeta*, 16th Year, Extraordinary Issue n.1; maritime code of Ethiopia, in proclamation n.164, 1960, *Negarit Gazeta*, 19th Year, Extraordinary Issue n.1.; civil code of Ethiopia, in proclamation n.165, 1960, *Negarit Gazeta*, 19th Year, Extraordinary Issue n.2; commercial code of Ethiopia, in proclamation n.166, 1960, *Negarit Gazeta*, 19th Year, Extraordinary Issue n.3.; criminal procedure code of Ethiopia in Proclamation (without number) 1961, *Negarit Gazeta*, 21st Year, Extraordinary Issue n.1; civil procedure code of Ethiopia, in Decree n.52, 1965, *Negarit Gazeta*, 25th Year, Extraordinary Issue n.1.

73. Fassil Abebe and Stanley Z. Fisher, "Language and Law in Ethiopia," *Journal of Ethiopian Law* V, no 3 (1968): 553.

74. Civil code of the Empire of Ethiopia, proclamation n. 165 of 1960, published in a special number of *Negarit Gazeta*, 19th Year, n.2, Addis Ababa, 5 May 1960.

75. Jacques Vanderlinden, "Ethiopia," in *National Report E/F of the International Encyclopaedia of Comparative Law*, I, ed. Viktor Knapp (Tübingen: J. C. B. Mohr, 1973), E.28.

76. René David, "Les Sources du Code Civil Ethiopien," in *Revue de droit international et droit comparé* (1962): 497–506; Vanderlinden, "Ethiopia," 29.

77. Jean Graven, "The Penal Code of the Empire of Ethiopia," *Journal of Ethiopian Law* I, no. 2 (1964): 280.

78. Graven, "The Penal Code," 282.

79. Graven, "The Penal Code," 285–287.

80. Yohannes Ghebremedin, personal communication, 1999.

81. Vanderlinden, "Ethiopia," 33.

82. Jean Escarra, "Exposé des Motifs," unpublished typescript, Law Faculty Library Haile Selassie I University, 1954.

83. Graven, "The Penal Code," 279.

84. Jacques Vanderlinden, "An Introduction to the Sources of Ethiopian Law from the 13th to 20th Century," *Journal of Ethiopian Law* III, no. 1 (1966): 239.

85. Vanderlinden, "An Introduction," 240.

86. Fassil Abebe and Fisher, "Language and Law," 553.

87. In *Negarit Gazeta*, 22nd Year n.3.

88. Nahum, "The Enigma," 316–317.

89. This is also the situation—in theory at least—in civil law countries. On the contrary, the practice of many national courts (the Supreme Italian and French courts in particular) shows a great respect for the judgments of previous judges, even if precedents are not accorded binding force. In general, the dichotomy between the "code system and the court system"—or written vs. unwritten law—where the code is regarded as peculiar to the civil law system and case law as peculiar to common law systems, has been justly criticized as unable to adequately describe the complexity of each national system. Written law is not anymore the only source of law in a civil law system, and case law shows an increasing strength in civil law countries. Moreover, in many common law countries *stare decisis* is intended as an elastic rule. See Frank Lawson, "A Common Lawyer," I, 48, III, 96.

90. Vanderlinden, "An Introduction," 246.

91. Van Doren, "Positivism," 176; Vanderlinden, "Ethiopia," 26.

92. Graven, "The Penal Code," 279.

93. Van Doren, "Positivism," 178.

94. Marco Guadagni, "Eritrean Law Between Past and Future: An Introduction," in *New Law for New States: Politica del Diritto in Eritrea,* ed. Lyda Favali, Elisabetta Grande, and Marco Guadagni (Torino: L'Harmattan, 1998), 15; of the same opinion is Van Doren, "Positivism," 179–180.

95. René David, "A Civil Code for Ethiopia: Considerations on the Codification of the Civil Law in African Countries," *Tulane Law Review* 37 (1963): 202.

96. A. Arthur Schiller, "Customary Land Tenure among The Highland Peoples of Northern Ethiopia: A Bibliographical Essay," *African Law Studies* (1 June 1969): 1–2.

97. John H. Beckstrom, "Paternity Claims in Ethiopia: Ten Years after the Civil Code," *African Law Studies* X (1973): 61–62.

98. Graven, "The Penal Code," 288–291.

99. Van Doren, "Positivism," 178.

100. Obeid Hag Ali, "The Conversion of Customary Law to Written Law," in *Folk Law: Essays in the Theory and Practice of Lex Non Scripta, 1,* ed. Alison Dundes Renteln and Alan Dundes (New York: Garland, 1994), 355.

101. Paul Brietzke, "Private Law in Ethiopia," *Journal of African Law* 18, no. 2 (1974): 156.

102. Steven Lowenstein, "Ethiopia," in *African Penal Systems,* ed. Alan Milner (New York: Praeger, 1969), 55, 30.

103. For the opinion that the field of application of customary law was "severely or strictly limited," see George Krzeczunowicz, "Code and Custom in Ethiopia," *Journal of Ethiopian Law* II, no. 2 (1965): 425–429; George Krzeczunowicz, "Putting the Legal Clock Back? The Law and Its Sources," *Journal of Ethiopian Law* III, no. 2 (1966): 623–625; George Krzeczunowicz, "A New Legislative Approach to Customary Law," *Journal of Ethiopian Law* I, no. 1 (1964): 117. For a contrary opinion, see Vanderlinden, "An Introduction,"

244–245; Jacques Vanderlinden, "A Further Note on an Introduction to the Sources of Ethiopian Law," *Journal of Ethiopian Law* III, no. 2 (1966): 636–637. For the opinion that it was undesirable to keep a system of traditional law separated from the state system, see Kenneth R. Redden, *The Legal System of Ethiopia* (Charlottesville, Va.: The Michie Company, 1968), 72–81.

104. Chapter III, title XXI, consisting of thirty-three articles. See further: Abdul Wasir Yusuf, "The Legal Status of the Shari'a Courts in Ethiopia," senior paper, Addis Ababa, 1971, 56–63.

105. Zaki Mustfa, "The Substantive Law Applied by Muslim Courts in Ethiopia," *Journal of Ethiopian Law* IX, no. I (1973): 142.

106. Redden, *The Legal System*, 82.

107. In the rest of the empire there were three levels: *naiba, qāḍī*, and court of *šarī'a*. On this point see Musa Naib, "The Applicability of the Civil Procedure Code to the Muslim Courts" (senior thesis, Addis Ababa University, 1974), 11.

108. As a matter of fact, *šarī'a* courts also continued to work after 1960 in Ethiopia. Their elimination would have caused a great deal of dissatisfaction among Muslims. The courts were recognized in 1964, in circular n.1/F/4721 of the Ministry of Justice, which provided that *šarī'a* courts could continue with their jurisdiction as stated in the proclamation of 1944. Geraghty, "People, Practice, Attitudes," 450.

109. In September 1974, the Provisional Military Administrative Council (PMAC) took power in Ethiopia, deposing the emperor, dissolving the Parliament, and suspending the Revised constitution of 1955 (see proclamation n.1/1974, published in *Negarit Gazeta*, 34 year, n.1). From 12/9/1974 to 12/9/1987 Ethiopia—as well as Eritrea—did not have a written constitution. For further reference, see Belayneh Mamo, "Constitution as a Supreme Law with a Special Reference to the Constitution of the PDRE," senior paper, Addis Ababa University, 1988; Fasil Nahum, "Socialist Ethiopia's Achievements as Reflected in its Basic Law: The Law Making Process in Ethiopia Post 1974, Part One," *Journal of Ethiopian Law* 4, no. 1 (1989): 122–127.

110. Mary Dines, "Ethiopian Violation of Human Rights in Eritrea," in *The Long Struggle of Eritrea for Independence and Constructive Peace*, ed. Lionel Cliffe and Basil Davidson (Nottingham: Spokesman, 1988), 141.

111. Kenneth Robert Redden, "Ethiopia," *Modern Legal Systems Cyclopedia, V 6A part II* (Buffalo: William S. Horn, 1990), 6.190.4, 6.190.10.

112. Paul H. Brietzke, *Law, Development, and the Ethiopian Revolution* (East Brunswick, N.J.: Associated University Press, 1982), 179.

113. From a source who does not wish to be cited. A number of senior EPLF leaders received military training in China in the 1960s. Many more of them had read Maoist texts and were inspired by the success of the Red Army.

114. See, for example, Yohannes Habteselassie, member of the Department of Culture during the liberation war, personal communication, 1997.

115. Internal EPLF Document, Ministry of Justice, The Field, 1988.

116. Asmarom Legesse, *Customary Law and Alternative Dispute Resolution (ADR)* (Asmara: Ministry of Justice, 1999), 17–18.

117. Tzehainesh Tekle, "Prime osservazioni sul sistema giudiziario eritreo: la fase della transizione," in *New Law for New States: politica del diritto in Eritrea*, ed. Lyda Favali, Elisabetta Grande, and Marco Guadagni (Torino: L'Harmattan, 1998), 185.

4. The Transitional Period and Attempts at Legal Reform

1. Proclamations n.1–8/91 contain amendments on the administration of justice, civil code, civil procedure code, penal code, criminal procedure code, commercial code, and the maritime code. In *Gazeta Awagiat Eritra*, n.1/91. These were followed by proclamations n.12–15/1991, containing further amendments to civil code, civil and criminal procedure codes, and penal code; proclamation n.25/1992, *Amendments to Proclamations 1/91; 3/91; n.5/91*, in *Gazeta Awagiat Eritra*, n.2/92; proclamation n.42/1993, *Amendments to Proclamation n.8/91*, in *Gazeta Awagiat Eritra*, n.3/93; proclamation n.85/1996, *Proclamation enacted to establish special court which deals and decides on criminal acts as corruption, theft and embezzlement*, in *Gazeta Awagiat Eritra*, n.6/96.

2. Tekle Abraha, personal communication, 1999.

3. Asmarom Legesse, *Customary Law and Alternative Dispute Resolution (ADR)* (Asmara: Ministry of Justice, 1999), 2.

4. *Gazeta Awagiat Eritra* superseded Ethiopian *Negarit Gazeta* with effect from proclamation n.9/1991.

5. Interviewed by *Eritrea Profile*, August 2000.

6. Art. 4.3 "Equality of all Eritrean languages is guaranteed."

7. We are greatly indebted to Nu Nu Kidane for translating this proclamation from Tigrinya for us.

8. See web page of Peter Winship, http://www.smu.edu.

9. Gerard René de Groot, University of Maastricht (a member of the drafting team), personal communication, November 2000.

10. Web page of the Center for International Legal Cooperation, http://www.CILC/IIOME/PROJECTS/LIST.

11. Teame Beyene, "Interview," *Eritrean Profile*, 14 November 1998.

12. Bronwyn Chester, "When the UN Comes Calling," *McGill University: Public and Media: McGill Reporter*, 24 February 2000, http://www.mcgill.ca/public/reporter/11/healy.

13. Web site of Peter Winship, http://www.miami.edu; Teame Beyene, "Interview."

14. F. F. Russell, "Eritrean Customary Law," *Journal of African Law* 3, no. 2 (1959): 101.

15. Teame Beyene, "Interview."

16. For a general overview of these subjects, see William Twining and Jennifer S. Uglow, eds., *Legal Studies in Small Jurisdictions*: *A Report of a Conference Held at Osgoode Hall Law School*, York University, Donsview, Ontario, 1978.

17. See, for example, as far as the Ethiopian Penal Code was concerned, Jean Graven, "The Penal Code of the Empire of Ethiopia," *Journal of Ethiopian Law* I, no. 2 (1964): 284.

18. See proclamation n.55/1994, "A Proclamation to Establish the Constitutional Commission," *Gazeta Awagiat Eritra*, n.4/1994. On this point see Ugo Mattei, "Patterns of African Constitution in the Making," paper presented at the International Conference on African Constitutions held at the University of Bologna, Italy, 27 November 1999, 1.

19. On the Eritrean referendum, see different positions and judgments of Roy Pateman, *Eritrea: Even the Stones Are Burning* (Trenton, N.J.: Red Sea Press, 1998), and Kjetil Tronvoll, "The Eritrean Referendum: Peasant Voices," *Eritrean Studies Review* 1, no. 1 (1996): 23–67. These themes are developed in Lyda Favali, "La legittimazione e i suoi protagonisti (una premessa allo studio delle fonti in Eritrea)" in *New Law for New States*, eds. Lyda Favali, Elisabetta Grande, Marco Guadagni (Torino: L'Harmattan, 1998), 162–164. And significantly, during the war with Ethiopia (1998–2000), the name commonly used to indicate the party was again "EPLF," which proves the successful—and then reversible—identification of the front with the government.

20. Mattei, "Patterns," 2.

21. The constitutional commission was formed by a council of fifty and an executive committee consisting of ten members of the council, including a president, vice president and secretary. Under the supervision of the executive committee, four committees were charged with study and research, and a permanent committee was charged with the civic education and public debate in Eritrea and abroad. See Constitutional Commission of Eritrea (CCE), *Information on Strategy, Plans and Activities*, Asmara, October 1995.

22. The political declaration shows its approval for a constitution that comes from the free will and freedom of citizens and that reflects Eritrean history and traditions. Pamphlets issued by the constitutional commission of Eritrea—see, for example, *An Introduction for the Constitution* and *An Introduction for the Constitution in Cartoons*, Asmara, 1995.

23. Contained in chapter 3 (fundamental rights, freedoms, and duties), at arts. 14–29; in chapter 4 (the National Assembly) at arts. 30–38; in chapter 5 (the executive) at arts. 39–47; and in chapter 6 (the administration of justice) at arts. 48–54.

24. The National Assembly will stay in office for five years. The first session of the National Assembly shall be held within one month after a general election (art. 31.5.)

25. More specifically, by an absolute majority vote of its members that involves at least 20 percent of all members of the National Assembly (art. 41.1). See art.

39.1. The term of office of the president shall be five years (art. 41.2) and a president cannot hold the office for more than two terms (art. 41.3).

26. Rodolfo Sacco, *Il diritto africano* (Torino: Utet, 1995), 217–220.

27. For a comparison with the Eritrean constitution of 1952, see Tzehainesh Tekle, "Eritrea: il processo di formazione di uno stato africano," in Elisabetta Grande, ed., *Transplants Innovation and Legal Tradition in the Horn of Africa* (Torino: L'Harmattan, 1995), 216–217. Appointment of ministers and judges of the Supreme Court require also the approval of the legislative body (art. 42.7 and 8). This approval is not necessary for judges of the lower courts (art. 42.9).

28. According to art. 47 (1), the ministers are individually accountable to the president—as chief of the executive—for the administration of their own ministries (hierarchic liability), and collectively responsible to the National Assembly, through the president, for the administration of the work of the cabinet. It is not clear if the liability of ministers toward the National Assembly involves the president in his capacity as chief of the executive.

29. (a) violation of the constitution or grave violation of the law; (b) conducting himself in a manner which brings the authority or honor of the office of the president into ridicule, contempt, and disrepute; (c) being incapable of performing the functions of his office by reason of physical or mental incapability. Definition of procedures for the election and removal of the president from office is left to the National Assembly (art. 41.7.)

30. For a more detailed description, see Roy Pateman, "Structure and Functions of the Eritrean Government," paper commissioned by, and on file at, Eritrean Institute of Management, Embatkalla, 1997.

31. Mahmoud Ahmed Sherifo, "Why a New Administrative Structure?" *Eritrea Profile* 2, no. 1 (June 1995): 3.

32. The regions (*zoba*) are as follows: Region 1—the Southern Red Sea. *Debubawi Keyh Bahri* has the sma. :st population of any region. It includes three districts of the former Danakil, including the port of Assab. Most of it is semi-desert, and the majority of the inhabitants live on the coast as fishermen. However, it is known that the area contains unexploited minerals, and possibly oil. Region 2—the Northern Red Sea. *Semenawi Keyh Bahri* absorbed eastern Akele Guzai (the Irafaile district) and has some 13 percent of the nation's population. It includes the main port of Massawa, Bore, and the Dahlak islands. It also includes *Semenawi* and *Debubawi Bahri* from Hamasien. Region 3—Anseba. It is very mountainous, but well-supplied with water; in time it could be irrigated and therefore much more productive. It includes parts of the Dembezan district of Hamasien. Region 4—Gash Barka. This also includes part of the former Hamasien district of Anseba. There are five ethnic groups living here, and the harmonious relations that have existed between groups in the Anseba Valley for generations bode well for future cooperation. Region 5—the Southern Zoba. Debub contains most of Akele Guzai and Seraye as well as southern Hamasien—Lamza-Sahrati and Loggo-Chewa. Incidentally, with an estimated population of 550,000 it is the most populous region; most of the

inhabitants are farmers. This particular redistribution was not popular with many people. The town of Mendefera is now the center of Debub, while Adi Keih, which had been the center of Akele Guzai, is now of much less importance. Region 6—Maakel. This is the central region and includes Asmara and ten surrounding villages.

33. The Government of the State of Eritrea, *Macro-policy*, November 1994, 36.

34. Irma Taddia, *L'Eritrea-Colonia 1890–1952; paesaggi, strutture, uomini del colonialismo* (Milano: F. Angeli, 1986), 63.

35. Tekle Abraha, personal communication, 1998.

36. *Proclamation for the Establishment of Regional Administrations* no.86/1996, Government of Eritrea, Asmara, 15 April.

37. Kjetil Tronvoll, "The Process of Nation-Building in Post-war Eritrea: Created from Below or Directed from Above?" *The Journal of Modern African Studies* 36, no. 3 (1998).

38. Proclamation n.1, *Transitional Administration of Justice*, in *Gazeta Awagiat Eritra*, n.1/1991.

39. Tzehainesh Tekle, "Prime osservazioni sul sistema giudiziario eritreo: la fase della transizione," in *New Law for New States: politica del diritto in Eritrea*, ed. Lyda Favali, Elisabetta Grande, and Marco Guadagni (Torino: L'Harmattan, 1998), 185.

40. Asmarom Legesse, *Customary Law*, 7, 5.

41. Proclamation n.85/96, In *Gazeta Awagiat Eritra*, n.6/96.

42. Teame Beyene, "The Eritrean Judiciary: Struggling for Independence," paper submitted to the International Conference of Eritrean Studies, Asmara, July 2001.

43. Art. 48.2 states, "In exercising the judicial power, courts shall be free from the direction and control of any person or authority. Judges shall be subject only to the law, to a judicial code of conduct determined by law and to their conscience"; art. 48.3: "a judge shall not be liable to any suit for any act in the course of exercising his judicial function." Art. 52 provides for conditions of removal from office: before the expiration of his tenure, a judge may be removed by the president only, acting on recommendation of the judicial service commission, only for "physical or mental incapacity, violation of the law or breach of judicial code of conduct."

44. After its first "invention" in the U.S. with the case of Marbury v. Madison, in Europe, the principle of judicial review was introduced, after World War II, under the influence of U.S. constitutional thought.

45. The Constitution of Eritrea, ratified by the Constituent Assembly on 23 May 1997.

46. Raoul Charles Van Caenegem, *Judges, Legislators, and Professors* (New York: Cambridge University Press, 1987).

47. John H. Beckstrom, "Transplantation of Legal Systems: an Early Report

on the Reception of Western Laws in Ethiopia," *American Journal of Comparative Law* 21 (1973): 561.

48. On legal education in countries in transition, and with particular reference to the reform of the law curricula, see Gianmaria Ajani, "Legal Education in Russia: Present and Future—An Analysis of the State Educational Standards for Higher Professional Instruction and a Comparison with the European Legal Education Reform Experience," *Review of Central and East European Law* 23 (1997): 267–300.

49. According to Yohannes Ghebremedin, personal communication, 1999.

50. Thomas R. French, "Legal Literature of Eritrea: A Bibliographic Essay," *North Carolina Journal of International Law and Commercial Regulation* 24, no. 2 (1999): 431–432.

51. Van Caenegem, *Judges*.

52. Yohannes Habtesellassie, personal communication, 1998.

53. Tzehainesh Tekle, "Prime osservazioni," 186.

54. Ministry of Justice, *Human Resources Development Strategies Report*, Asmara, Eritrea, December 1998.

55. Michael Mahrt, personal communication, Asmara, 2000.

56. "The Advocates Proclamation," *Gazeta Awagiat Eritra* 6/96, n.4, Asmara, 30 April. Incidentally, an advocates association was established by the British Administration in the 1940s.

57. Eritrean People's Liberation Front, *"A National Charter,"* 19; *The Constitutional Commission of Eritrea. Information on Strategy, Plans and Activities;* Asmara, October 1995, 1.

58. This arises from attempts made by the EPLF during the first war of liberation to conserve ethnic languages. Cadres started to write down some of these languages in order to preserve them. They chose to use the Latin alphabet in order to bypass potential religious conflicts between Christians and Muslims. For example, a question was posed for the Bilein at the beginning of the nineties. The adoption of Ge'ez or of Arabic would have created conflicts between Islamic and Christian communities. Bilein Muslims wished to use the Arabic alphabet, and Christians the Ge'ez alphabet. So the decision of the Ministry of Education to use Latin diction, phonetics, and grammar is both neutral and political. At present, the first six years of obligatory schooling are given in the language of the dominant ethnicity, and afterwards in English.

59. Respectively, pages 18, 19, 26 of the proclamation (articles are not numbered).

60. Mengsteab Negash, "Investment Law in Eritrea," *North Carolina Journal of International Law and Commercial Regulation* 24, no. 2 (1999): 339.

61. These studies, in Tigrinya, are on file in the Research and Documentation Center, Asmara. In summary form, they are periodically published (in English) in the local weekly newspaper, *Eritrea Profile.*

62. H. Patrick Glenn, "The Capture, Reconciliation and Marginalization of Custom," *American Journal of Comparative Law* 45 (1997): 620.

63. Richard Sklar remarks in this context that "the idea of foreign domination by proxy, through the medium of a clientele or puppetised upper class, is controverted by a large body of evidence. In many post-colonial and newly developing countries, governments, businessmen, and leaders of thought regularly defy the demands and frustrate the desires of their counterparts in the industrial countries." Richard L. Sklar, "The Nature of Class Domination in Africa," *The Journal of Modern African Studies* 17, no. 4 (1979): 531.

64. Ulrich Beck, *What is Globalization?* (Cambridge: Polity Press, 2000), 4.

5. From Blood Feud and Blood Money to the State Settlement of Murder Cases

1. Michel Foucault, *The History of Sexuality, Volume I: An Introduction*, trans. Robert Hurley (New York: Random House, 1990), 147.

2. Carlo Conti Rossini, *Principi di diritto consuetudinario dell'Eritrea* (Rome: Ministero delle Colonie, Tip. Unione Ed., 1916), 435–436. The author also says specifically that crimes against the state were excluded. They were punished by the state: "[D]eath, usually by hanging; exile, banishment, confiscation of properties, loss of feudal benefits are the penalties for these crimes." The aim of the state, when it is strong enough to impose the penalty, is to deter others from committing the same crime in the future. We have already seen in the introduction to this book that imprisonment was not feasible in most of Eritrea because of the lack of suitable prisons.

3. Corresponding to the *faida* of barbaric European law of the Middle Ages.

4. Felice Ostini, *Trattato di diritto consuetudinario dell'Eritrea* (Rome: Officina Grafica-Corriere Eritreo, 1956), 30–31; Conti Rossini, *Principi*, 435–437. However, it is important to note that both Conti Rossini and Ostini introduced an exception for crimes against the state, the king, the state religion, and some crimes against property: these types of crimes could not be settled with a private vengeance system. We can assume that since the two authors are dealing with common principles of Eritrean traditional law, they had to summarize, and the exception in fact relates to the traditional laws of Seraye and Hamasien, where a central authority was already present. Moreover, because of the colonial period when their books were written, the authors may well have conflated custom and colonial law with regard to these matters. See also Giuseppe De Stefano, *I costumi penali abissini ed il Fetha Neghest* (Firenze, 1906), 56–57; Ercole Petazzi, *L'odierno diritto penale consuetudinario dell'Hamasien (Eritrea)* (Asmara: Fioretti, 1937), 30–32.

5. John Middleton and David Tait, *Tribes Without Rulers: Studies in African Segmentary States* (London: Routledge & Kegan Paul, 1958), 12, 19. They remark that exercise of self-help can be found in many centralized states, "but it

is there under the control of the chief, who makes use of it as a means to enforce his judgments."

6. Ugo Mattei and Pier Giuseppe Monateri, *Introduzione breve al diritto comparato* (Padova: Cedam, 1997), 140.

7. Raimond Verdier, *La vengeance: études d'ethnologie, d'histoire et de philosophie* (Paris: Cujas, 1980).

8. Edward Evan Evans-Pritchard, *The Nuer: A Description of the Modes of Livelihoood and Political Institutions of Nilotic People* (Oxford: Clarendon Press, 1940), 160–161.

9. Ugo Fabietti and Francesco Remotti, eds., *Dizionario di antropologia, etnologia, antropologia culturale, antropologia sociale* (Bologna: Zanichelli, 1997), 788.

10. Leonard Trelawny Hobhouse, *Morals and Evolution: A Study in Comparative Ethics* (London: Chapman and Hall, 1951), 99–102.

11. Fabietti and Remotti, *Dizionario di antropologia*, 734.

12. Ostini, *Trattato*, 30–31; Conti Rossini, *Principi*, 435–450.

13. Conti Rossini, *Principi*, 435–436.

14. Frederick Pollock, "Introduction," Henry Sumner Maine, *Ancient Law: Its Connection with the Early History of Society and its Relation to Modern Ideas* (London: John Murray, 1930), 419.

15. Conti Rossini, *Principi*, 671–676.

16. *Eritrea Profile*, "Eritrean Traditions and Customs," 14 June 1997.

17. Werner Münzinger, *Dei costumi e del diritto dei Bogos, traduzione dal tedesco a cura di A. Ostini*, con prefazione di I. M. Ziegler, Ministero degli Affari Esteri (Rome: Ministero degli Affari Esteri, 1891), 255. In passing we should note that the most recent codification of their law does not mention blood vengeance at all (see later, in the section that deals with the amount of blood money that has to be paid.)

18. Alberto Pollera, *I Baria e i Cunama* (Rome: Reale Societá Geografica, 1913), 134–135.

19. Pollera, *I Baria e i Cunama*, 140–141.

20. *Eritrea Profile*, "Eritrean Traditions and Customs," 12 July 1997, 7.

21. Philip Selznick, *Law, Society, and Industrial Justice* (New York: Russell Sage Foundation, 1969), 19.

22. Selznick, *Law, Society, and Industrial Justice*, 94.

23. Philippe Nonet and Philip Selznick, *Law and Society in Transition: Toward Responsive Law* (New York: Harper & Row, 1978), 26.

24. Pollock, "Introduction," XIV.

25. Henry Sumner Maine, *Ancient Law: Its Connection with the Early History of Society and Its Relation to Modern Ideas* (London: John Murray, 1930), 392.

26. Maine, *Ancient Law*, 391.

27. James Q. Whitman, "At the Origins of Law and the State: Supervision of Violence, Mutilation of Bodies, or Setting of Prices?" *Chicago Kent Law Re-*

view 71, no. 1 (1996): 79–83. Interestingly, he claims that mutilation was once only applied to members of the servant and slave classes, and made its way into general criminal law; only then was it applied to free and noble persons.

28. Whitman, "At the Origins of Law," 43.

29. Whitman, "At the Origins of Law," 71.

30. The infrequency of detention in the highlands is confirmed by De Stefano, *I costumi penali*, 12–13, and Conti Rossini, *Principi*, 193.

31. See Richard A. Posner, *The Economics of Justice* (Cambridge, Mass.: Harvard University Press, 1983), 192–193.

32. Michael James Langley Hardy, *Blood Feuds and the Payment of Blood Money in the Middle East* (Leiden: E. J. Brill, 1963), 75.

33. Robert A. Rubinstein, "Collective Violence and Common Security," in *Companion Encyclopedia of Anthropology*, ed. Tim Ingold (London: Routledge, 1997), 995–996.

34. W. Robertson Smith, *Kinship and Marriage in Early Arabia* (Oosterhout, The Netherlands: Anthropological Publications, 1966), 25.

35. Thomas Acton, Susan Caffrey, and Gary Mundy, "Theorizing Gypsy Law," *American Journal of Comparative Law* XLV Spring (1997): 241.

36. Carlo Conti Rossini, "I Loggo e la legge dei Loggo Sarda," *Giornale della Società Asiatica Italiana* XVII (Firenze, 1904); 48–49; Conti Rossini, *Principi*, 435.

37. Pollera, *I Baria e i Cunama*, 143, 146–147.

38. Conti Rossini, *Principi*, 440.

39. The ambiguous concept of distance was memorably used by Simmel; we are using it here to refer to the degree of emotional attachment between the actors. Donald N. Levine, "Simmel at a Distance: On the History and Systematics of the Sociology of the Stranger," in *Strangers in African Societies*, ed. William A. Shack and Elliott P. Skinner (Berkeley: University of California Press, 1979), 29.

40. Fabietti and Remotti, *Dizionario di antropologia*, 297.

41. Pollera, *I Baria e i Cunama*, 141–146.

42. Münzinger, *Dei costumi*, 42; Conti Rossini, *Principi*, 644.

43. Karl Gustav Rodén, *Le tribù dei Mensa—Storia, legge e costumi. Traduzione italiana dalla lingua tigré* (Stockholm: Nordiska Boktryckeriet, 1913), 274–282.

44. Conti Rossini, *Principi*, 441, 443, 449–450, 679.

45. Siegfried Frederick Nadel, "Land Tenure on the Eritrean Plateau (Conclusion)," *Africa* XVI, no. 2 (1946): 106.

46. Conti Rossini, *Principi*, 449–450.

47. Conti Rossini, *Principi*, 678–680.

48. Conti Rossini, *Principi*, 608–612.

49. Carlo Conti Rossini, "Al Ragali," in *Estratti dal Bollettino della Società*

Italiana di Esplorazioni Geografiche e Commerciali, Anni 1903–1904 (Milan: Stabilimento Tipografico Bellini, 1903), 52.

50. *Eritrea Profile*, "Eritrean Traditions and Customs," 5 July 1997, 7.

51. Pollera, *I Baria e i Cunama*, 148–151.

52. Conti Rossini, *Principi*, 782.

53. Alberto Pollera, *The Native Peoples of Eritrea*, trans. Linda Lappin (Asmara: University of Asmara, 1996), 113–114.

54. Conti Rossini, *Principi*, 738.

55. Conti Rossini, *Principi*, 439.

56. *Eritrea Profile*, "Eritrean Traditions and Customs," 8 March 1997.

57. Conti Rossini, *Principi*, 438–439.

58. Conti Rossini, *Principi*, 738.

59. The father must give him a third of his grain and agricultural equipment, including a plow, before access to *shehena* land is granted to a new household. Kjetil Tronvoll, "Mai Weini: A Village in Highland Eritrea" (M.A. thesis, Oslo University, 1996), 282.

60. *Eritrea Profile*, "Eritrean Traditions and Customs," 8 March 1997.

61. Conti Rossini, *Principi*, 447–449.

62. Münzinger, *Dei costumi*, 42.

63. Conti Rossini, *Principi*, 671–673.

64. Conti Rossini, *Principi*, 738.

65. Werner Münzinger, *Studi sull'Africa Orientale—Traduzione dal tedesco per cura del corpo di stato maggiore* (Rome: Voghera, 1890), 412–413; Conti Rossini, *Principi*, 782.

66. Münzinger, *Studi sull'Africa*, 404.

67. These rules do not apply if the killer's clan was a long-time enemy. In this case the whole village to which the victim belonged had to participate in vengeance and any member of the clan of the murderer could be targeted. Conti Rossini, *Principi*, 781–782; Pollera, *I Baria e i Cunama*, 141.

68. Conti Rossini, *Principi*, 646.

69. Münzinger, *Studi sull'Africa*, 412, 416; Conti Rossini, *Principi*, 782–783; *Eritrea Profile*, "Eritrean Traditions and Customs," 2 August 1997, 7.

70. Ilario Capomazza, *Istituzioni di diritto consuetudinario del Serae—La legge degli Atcheme-Melgà* (Macerata: Giorgetti, 1912), art. 66, 113–115.

71. Conti Rossini, *Principi*, 673–674.

72. *Eritrea Profile*, "Eritrean Traditions and Customs," 5 July 1997, 7.

73. Petazzi, *L'odierno diritto penale*, 30–32.

74. Ilario Capomazza, *Il diritto consuetudinario dell'Acchele-Guzai* (Asmara: Fioretti, 1937), 159, 173.

75. Petazzi, *L'odierno diritto penale*, 28–29.

76. Münzinger, *Studi sull'Africa*, 412, 415.

77. Pollera, *I Baria e i Cunama*, 150–151.

78. Conti Rossini, *Principi*, 438.

79. Conti Rossini, "I Loggo," 49.

80. Conti Rossini, *Principi*, 610, 674.

81. Conti Rossini, *Principi*, 789–790.

82. *Eritrea Profile*, "Eritrean Traditions and Customs," 21 June 1997, 7.

83. In the past, transgression against the codes was settled by payment in kind. Among measures used were the *elchi*, equivalent to twelve MTD (eighteen MTD in *Adkeme Melega*). When money was scarce, various goods could be substituted. Among these were *ferghi*, a length of cotton of indigenous production of twelve cubits in length, *ghebetà*, a measure of cereals of about twenty kilograms, and the *cahabò*, another measure of cereals of about five kilograms in weight. The payment of money as indemnity is of recent origin. Carlo Conti Rossini, "Lo statuto degli Scioattè Ansebà (Eritrea)," *Scritti Giuridici in onore di Santi Romano*, III (Padova: Cedam, 1940): 349–350.

84. Ostini, *Trattato*, 31.

85. *Mehen Mahaza*, art. 32, Capomazza, *Il diritto*, 107–108; *Eritrea Profile*, "Eritrean Traditions and Customs," 1 March 1997.

86. Dennis J. Duncanson, "Sir'at 'Adkeme Milga' A Native Law Code of Eritrea," *Africa* XIX, no. 2 (1949): 147.

87. Münzinger, *Studi sull'Africa*, 415–416: Conti Rossini, *Principi*, 785–787.

88. Pollera, *I Baria e i Cunama*, 146–147.

89. Münzinger, *Studi sull'Africa*, 415–416: Conti Rossini, "Principi," 785–787.

90. Münzinger, *Studi sull'Africa*, 413–414; *Eritrea Profile*, "Eritrean Traditions and Customs," 23 August 1997, 7. A slightly different, but not contradictory, account is given by Pollera, *I Baria e i Cunama*, 148–150.

91. Conti Rossini, Principi, 788–789.

92. The centenarian Tsegai Gudum of Debarwa, cited by Amanuel Tesfai, "Comparative Analysis of the Loggo-Chiwa, Adghene-Tegheleba, and the Transitional Civil Code of Eritrea with Particular Reference to the Law of Torts" (senior LL.B thesis, University of Asmara, 1999), 36–37.

93. Conti Rossini, *Principi*, 613.

94. To begin the process, he spends four days in the village of the victim accompanied by men of his village. If the relatives of the victim remain quiet in their huts, on the fourth day, the matter is closed, and the accused is recognized as being innocent. If the victim's relatives are convinced that the man is guilty, they come out of their huts—accompanied by all the men of the village—to meet the suspected murderer and his entourage. If the latter run away, their behavior is considered as evidence of guilt, and the suspected murderer and his closest relatives can be killed. But if they stay quiet, and do no try to run away, this is considered as evidence of innocence, and the elders of the village inter-

Notes to pages 88–89

266

pose themselves between the two parties to settle the dispute. Münzinger, *Studi sull'Africa*, 413.

95. Rodén, *Le tribù*, 305.

96. Petazzi, *L'odierno diritto penale*, 38.

97. Conti Rossini, *Principi*, 678.

98. *Eritrea Profile*, "Eritrean Traditions and Customs," 14 June 1997.

99. Conti Rossini, *Principi*, 679–680.

100. This casuistic mentality is not at all exceptional. For a description of a similar attitude in Western thought, see Caroline Walker Bynum, "Material Continuity, Personal Survival, and the Resurrection of the Body: A Scholastic Discussion in Its Medieval and Modern Contexts," in *Fragmentation and Redemption: Essays on Gender and the Human Body in Medieval Religion* (New York: Zone Books, 1991), 253. See also Albert R. Jonsen and Stephen Toulmin, *The Abuse of Casuistry: A History of Moral Reasoning* (Berkeley: University of California Press, 1988).

101. Regolamento Giudiziario per la Colonia Eritrea, enacted with Decreto Governatoriale 11 July 1908, n.756, approved with Regio Decreto 11 July 1909, n.620, art. 112, extended this to the entire plateau. Petazzi, *L'odierno diritto penale*, 38, lamented that in practice the blood price still differed in various customary laws.

102. See *Enda Fegrai*, art. 15§12; *Mehen Mahaza*, art. 32§5 and 16; and *Mai Adgi*, art. 20§8, Capomazza, *Il diritto*, 206, 106–108, 159.

103. Research and Documentation Centre, Asmara, *Code of Customary Law of Acchele Guzai "Adghena Tegheleba"* 1954 English, Document 138300.

104. Two cases of attempted murder are mentioned in the code. "[W]hoever administers herbs or other drugs with the object of causing a death, and fails in this intent . . . shall pay 250 MTD" (art. 156). And, "whoever tried to push another down a precipice, [in a] ditch or into a lake," with the same intent, without causing death, shall also pay 250 MTD (art. 157). *Code of Customary Law*, 23.

105. More precisely, the law of *Adkeme Melega* in its version of 1912, fixed the blood price at 120 *ferghi*. In a more recent version from the 1940s, the blood price was 250 *ferghi* (in this version one *ferghi* is equal to two MTD) and 250 MTD (art. 75). At the time this sum was the highest applied in Eritrea. In Hamasien, the *Loggo-Chewa* fixed the blood price at 120 *ferghi* in addition to other measures of goods (art. 29); in the *Habsellus Gebrecristos*, gar is 120 *ferghi* (art. 28); for the *Saharti, Lamza, Uocarti*, art. 31, it is 240 MTD in addition to a girl (see later) (art. 31). In the *Scioatté Ansebà*, it was set at 120 MTD. This code actually has no specific rules relating to homicide, but we can reconstruct the amount with the help of article 64 (rules pertaining to bodily injuries), which states that damage to both of the eyes, or both feet or hands will receive blood money as though it involved a death (art. 66§8). Capomazza, *Istituzioni*, 113–115; Duncanson, "Sir'at 'Adkeme Milga," 147; Petazzi, *L'odierno diritto penale*, 37–39, 41; Conti Rossini, "Lo statuto," 364.

106. Conti Rossini, *Principi*, 677.

107. *Eritrea Profile*, "Eritrean Traditions and Customs," 14 June 1997, 7.

108. Pollera, *The Native Peoples*, 111.

109. Münzinger, *Dei costumi*, 255.

110. Eritrean Assembly, *New Customary Law of The Beni Amer Tribes*, Asmara, 1 June 1960.

111. *Bullettino Ufficiale della Colonia Eritrea*, Anno XII, Asmara, 14 November 1903, n.46, 2, art. 10. See also Conti Rossini, "Al Ragali," 52.

112. Tekle Abraha, personal communication, 1998.

113. Pollera, *The Native Peoples*, 149.

114. See art. 13, *Enda Fegrai;* art. 14, *Zeban Serao Ennadocò;* art. 32, *Mehen Mahaza;* art. 20, *Mai Adgi;* Capomazza, *Il diritto*, 204, 173, 106, 150. See also arts. 156/162 *Adgena Tegeleba* code, "Code of the Customary Law of Acchele Guzay," 23.

115. J. Spencer Trimingham, *Islam in the Sudan* (London: Frank Cass and Co., 1965), 14, 27.

116. Art. 15, Capomazza, *Il diritto*, 206.

117. Capomazza, *Istituzioni*, art. 66, 113–115.

118. Maine, *Ancient Law*, 398.

119. Capomazza, *Il diritto*, 173.

120. Art. 32, Capomazza, *Il diritto*, 106–108.

121. Art. 20, Capomazza, *Il diritto*, 159.

122. Art. 32, Capomazza, *Il diritto*, 106–108. For the case when the serf was the victim, see the next section.

123. Conti Rossini, *Principi*, 677–678.

124. *Eritrea Profile*, "Eritrean Traditions and Customs," 3 May 1997, 7.

125. Rodén, *Le tribù*, art. 77 (murder), here §10, 305.

126. *Eritrea Profile*, "Eritrean Traditions and Customs," 3 May 1997, 7.

127. Art. 20, *Mai Adgi*, Capomazza, *Il diritto*, 159; art. 15, *Enda Fegrai*, Capomazza, *Il diritto*, 206; art. 32, *Mehen Mahaza*, Capomazza, *Il diritto*, 106; art. 160, *Adgena Tegeleba*, 23.

128. Art. 32, Capomazza, *Il diritto*, 106–108.

129. Art. 15, Capomazza, *Il diritto*, 205–207.

130. Petazzi, *L'odierno diritto penale*, 38.

131. Art. 20, Capomazza, *Il diritto*, 159.

132. More precisely, according to *Enda Fegrai*, the money must be given "to the paternal family, if the deceased was a man or unmarried woman, or to the husband if the deceased was a married woman" (art. 15§12). In this latter case, "her husband, after he has deducted from the sum of 120 MTD the amount that he has expended for the *tescar* [commemoration of the deceased], must divide the remaining sum with the sons, or with any others having a right" (art.

15§16). *Mehen Mahaza* law established that if a married woman was killed, blood money was equally shared between the paternal lineage and the husband (art. 32§12). If a widow with children was killed, the blood money went half to her father and half to her children (art. 32§13). Art. 15, *Enda Fegrai*, Capomazza, *Il diritto*, 205–207; art. 32, *Mehen Mahaza*, Capomazza, *Il diritto*, 106–108.

133. Conti Rossini, *Principi*, 653.

134. The same code also deals with the situation of the traveler: "[I]f a traveler accompanied by attendants is killed, the murderer, in addition to the blood payment to the family of the deceased [120 MTD,] shall pay 60 MTD and a horse to the value of 60 MTD to the attendants." The total blood money is therefore 240 MTD (art. 32 §16). If one of the attendants (and not the traveler) was killed, only the blood money was due [of 120 MTD, payable to his family] (art. 32§17). Art. 32, Capomazza, *Il diritto*, 106–108.

135. Conti Rossini, *Principi*, 677–678. Münzinger, *Dei costumi*, 57–62, mentions two classes of "protected" persons, for whom a different regime of blood feud applied. The first included a group of Tigré of Ethiopian origin; they agreed to be subject to the Bogos in exchange for their lives. A rule according to which the patron had the right to keep for himself a third of the blood price if "his" Tigré was murdered was applied to them. A second class of protected people comprised the *asker*. Negotiating with the Bogos, they asked for a patron and were allowed to stay in the country provided they paid him for protection. The patron had the right to exercise vengeance if "his" *asker* was killed.

136. Petazzi, *L'odierno diritto penale*, 38–39.

137. Eritrean saying, recorded by Conti Rossini, *Principi*, 442.

138. Münzinger, *Dei costumi*, 255.

139. Münzinger, *Dei costumi*, 24.

140. In Hebrew, *dāmīn*, blood, also means money. Paul Lawrence Rose, *Revolutionary Antisemitism from Kant to Wagner* (Princeton, N.J.: Princeton University Press, 1990), 316.

141. Ignazio Guidi, *Il Fetha Nagast o Legislazione dei Re. Codice ecclesiastico e civile di Abissinia*, Pubblicazioni scientifiche del R. Istituto Orientale di Napoli (Rome: Tipografia Casa Ed. Italiana, 1897), 494–508.

142. Guidi, *Il Fetha Nagast*, 495–496.

143. Guidi, *Il Fetha Nagast*, 497.

144. Guidi, *Il Fetha Nagast*, 498.

145. Guidi, *Il Fetha Nagast*, 499, 501–504.

146. Guidi, *Il Fetha Nagast*, 503.

147. Guidi, *Il Fetha Nagast*, 506.

148. Hardy, *Blood Feuds*, 16.

149. Joseph Schacht, "Notes sur la sociologie du droit musulman," *Revue Africaine* 93 (1952): 311.

150. *Ǧināyat* differ from crimes against religion; these are actions expressly prohibited or punished by the Qur'an, to which a special punishment, called *hadd*, applies. Joseph Schacht, *An Introduction to Islamic Law* (Oxford: Clarendon Press, 1964), 175, 177–178.

151. Arthur J. Arberry, *The Koran Interpreted* (New York: Macmillan, 1955), 114.

152. Hardy, *Blood Feuds*, 29–30.

153. Schacht, *An Introduction*, 181, 184.

154. Arberry, *The Koran Interpreted*, 51.

155. The distinction between deliberate intent and quasi-deliberate intent is according to whether the culprit has employed a deadly implement or not. Of course in practice it is not always easy to ascertain whether an implement is deadly or not. *Khatā* is present, for example, if the culprit wanted to shoot at a target but accidentally killed a man. Indirect causation implies liability only when the act in question was not authorized. If a man fell from a bridge that has been built on public property, no liability arises. Schacht, *An Introduction*, 181–183.

156. After Mohammed, the ʿāqila becomes the relevant entity to pay blood money. It consisted of "those who, as members of the Muslim army, have their names inscribed in the list *(diwan)* [records of the tribunal] and receive pay, provided the culprit belongs to them; alternatively, of the male members of his tribe . . . or the nearest related tribes . . . ; alternatively, of the fellow workers in his craft or his confederates." However, the whole institution fell into disuse in an early stage in the development of Islam. Schacht, *An Introduction*, 186.

157. Schacht, *An Introduction*, 185.

158. Schacht, *An Introduction*, 182, 185.

159. Schacht, *An Introduction*, 184.

160. Schacht, *An Introduction*, 186–187.

161. Hardy, *Blood Feuds*, 101; Schacht, *An Introduction*, 185.

162. Hardy, *Blood Feuds*, 48–51.

163. Jonathan Miran, "Islamic Court Records: A Source for the Social and Economic History of Massawa in the Nineteenth Century," paper presented at the First International Conference of Eritrean Studies, Asmara, July 22–26, 2001.

164. Ibrahim Mohamed, cited by Ghebil Temnewo, "Murder and Blood Money under the Fit'ha Megarh" (LL.B. senior thesis, University of Asmara, 1999), 8.

165. Petazzi, *L'odierno diritto penale*, 71.

166. See also Petazzi, *L'odierno diritto penale*, 37.

167. Ostini, *Trattato*, 33.

168. Conti Rossini, *Principi*, 442.

169. Gennaro Mondaini, *La legislazione coloniale italiana nel suo sviluppo sto-*

rico e nel suo stato attuale (1881–1940) I (Milan: Istituto per gli Studi di Politica Internazionale, 1941), 165.

170. Capomazza, *Il diritto,* 107–108.

171. Robert Allen Sedler, "The Development of Legal Systems: The Ethiopian Experience," *Iowa Law Review* 53, no. 3 (1967): 600.

172. Jean Graven, "The Penal Code of Ethiopia Part 1," *Journal of Ethiopian Law* 1, no. 2 (1964): 289.

173. Internal EPLF Document, Ministry of Justice, The Field, 1988.

174. Amanuel Tesfai, "Comparative Analysis," 16.

175. *Eritrea Profile,* "Eritrean Traditions and Customs," 14 June 1997.

176. Tekle Abraha, personal communication, 1998.

177. Asmarom Legesse, *Customary Law and Alternative Dispute Resolution (ADR)* (Asmara: Ministry of Justice, 1999), 12, 15; AbdulNasser Abdella, "The Institution of Family Arbitration in Eritrea" (senior LL.B. thesis, University of Asmara, 1999), 48; Adhana Mengisteab, personal communication, Asmara, November 2000.

6. Land Tenure on the Highland Plateau

1. Arthur Young, *Travels in France,* ed. Matilda Betham-Edwards (London: Bell, 1892), 109.

2. Mansfield Parkyns, *Life in Abyssinia, II* (London: John Murray, 1853), 116.

3. Ugo Mattei and Pier Giuseppe Monateri, *Introduzione breve al diritto comparato* (Padova: Cedam, 1997), 136–137; Bairu Tafla, "La notion du pouvoir dans l'Afrique traditionnelle: le cas de l'Éthiopie," *Introduction à la culture africaine* (Paris: Les Presses de l'Unesco, 1977): 183–184.

4. The literature on kinship is vast. For an introductory approach, see Alan Barnard, "Rules and Prohibitions: the Form and Content of Human Kinship," in *Companion Encyclopedia of Anthropology,* ed. Tim Ingold (London: Routledge, 1997), 783–812; Ladislav Holy, *Anthropological Perspectives on Kinship* (London: Pluto Press, 1996), both with an extensive and useful bibliography. See also Linda Stone, *Kinship and Gender: An Introduction* (Boulder, Colo.: Westview Press, 1998).

5. Siegfried Frederick Nadel, "Land Tenure on the Eritrean Plateau," *Africa* XVI, no. 1 (1946): 1.

6. Ambaye Zekarias, *Land Tenure in Eritrea (Ethiopia)* (Addis Ababa: Institute of Ethiopian Studies, 1966), 7.

7. For the analogous case of the gypsies, see Thomas Acton, Susan Caffrey, and Gary Mundy, "Theorizing Gypsy Law," *American Journal of Comparative Law* XLV (Spring 1997): 238.

8. Paul Bohannan, "Land, Tenure, and Land-Tenure," in *African Agrarian Systems,* ed. Daniel P. Biebuyck (London: Oxford University Press, 1963), 103–105.

9. Evans-Pritchard highlighted three main types and, for each of these, several sub-types. Adopting his categories, Tigrinya and Saho societies can be included in the so called segmentary decentralized societies, where the word "segmentary" indicates that relations between groups are characterized "by their being in a state of segmentary opposition."

10. William Caffarel, "La legislazione dell'Eritrea," in *L'Eritrea Economica* (Novara-Rome: De Agostini, 1913), 462–463.

11. This can be because of Islamic influence on the former; pre-Islamic exogamic Arabia became endogamous with the rise of Mohammed. Abdul Kader Saleh Mohammed, "Die Afar-Saho Nomaden in Nordost-Afrika" (Ph.D. dissertation, Universität zu Münster, 1984), 100.

12. Richard Caulk, "Bad Men of the Borders: Shum and Shefta in Northern Ethiopia in the 19th Century," *International Journal of African Historical Studies* 17, no. 2 (1984): 225.

13. Yemane Mesghenna, *Italian Colonialism: A Case Study of Eritrea, 1869–1934—Motive, Praxis, and Result,* (Lund: Skrifter utgiva av Ekonomisk-historiska föreningen i Lund, LVIII, 1988), 98–101; Roy Pateman, *Eritrea: Even the Stones Are Burning* (Trenton, N.J.: Red Sea Press, 1998), 52–53

14. Stephen H. Longrigg, *A Short History of Eritrea* (Westport, Conn.: Greenwood, 1974), 61.

15. J. Spencer Trimingham, *Islam in Ethiopia* (London· Oxford University Press, 1952), 177.

16. Gerald Kennedy Nicholas Trevaskis, *Eritrea: A Colony in Transition, 1941–52* (Westport, Conn.: Greenwood, 1975), 15.

17. Abdul Kader Saleh Mohammed, "Die Afar-Saho," 98.

18. Siegfried Frederick Nadel, *Races and Tribes of Eritrea* (Asmara: British Military Administration, 1944), 67.

19. Alberto Pollera, *L'ordinamento della giustizia e la procedura indigena in Etiopia e in Eritrea* (Rome: Tipografia Bertero e C., 1913), 81–82.

20. Friederike Kemink, "The Tegreñña Customary Law Codes," *Paideuma: Mitteilungen zur Kulturkunde* 37 (1991): 63–64.

21. James T. Bent, *The Sacred City of the Abyssinians: Being a Record of Travel and Research in Abyssinia in 1893* (London: Longmans Green, 1896), 206–207.

22. John W. Bruce, "A Perspective on Indigenous Land Tenure Systems and Land Concentration," in *Land and Society in Contemporary Africa,* ed. R. E. Downs and Stephen P. Reyna (Hanover, N.H.: University Press of New England, 1988), 28

23. For a distinction between centralized and decentralized societies, see particularly Meyer Fortes and Edward Evan Evans-Pritchard, *African Political Systems* (London: Oxford University Press, 1958), 5.

24. Nadel, "Land Tenure," 11.

25. See, for example, *Mehen Mahaza* (§§1–3) and *Mai Adgi.* It is intriguing to observe that *shehena* is called by Capomazza *ghebri* (tribute). This is strange for

a region where according to many sources tribute to the king was not paid. The Tigrinya word *nabara* is used as far as we can tell only in the *Mai Adgi*. The Saho use an identical word. We wonder if this is evidence of contamination.

26. From the Ge'ez verb *reseté:* to occupy, to conquer. Felice Ostini, *Trattato di diritto consuetudinario dell'Eritrea* (Roma: Officina Grafica, 1956), 89; Renzo Sertoli Salis, *L'ordinamento fondiario eritreo* (Padova: Cedam, 1932), 26–27.

27. Ostini, *Trattato*, 90–93.

28. Alberto Pollera, *The Native Peoples of Eritrea*, trans. Linda Lappin (Asmara: University of Asmara, 1996), 4. And unmarried women according to *Mai Adgi*, art. 14.

29. *Ghebbar* means literally, "the one who pays tribute." They are the heads of nuclear families constituting an *enda* and paying the tribute (*ghebrì*) for *resti*. *Ghebbar* who pay *ghebri* are *restegnatat* of land they possess, with a social link within the *enda*. See *Enda Fegrai* art. 9. Carlo Conti Rossini, *Principi di diritto consuetudinario dell'Eritrea* (Rome: Tip. Unione Ed., 1916), 127.

30. Trimingham, *Islam in Ethiopia*, 153.

31. To become *restegnat*, it is necessary, then, to establish habitation (*tisha*) in the village, and give evidence of being a *wedebat*, descendant of the common ancestor of the village.

32. Ilario Capomazza, *Il diritto consuetudinario dell'Acchele-Guzai*, Massimario raccolto da Ilario Capomazza (Asmara: Fioretti, 1937).

33. Nadel, "Land Tenure," 12–13.

34. *Restegnatat* organized themselves communally and nominated a representative as a guardian of common land and rights; the *chikka* was also the military commander, administrator and judge of *restegnatat*. See Pollera, *L'ordinamento*, 4.

35. There could have been a number of reasons. They are mentioned in Sertoli Salis, *L'ordinamento*, 28, and Ostini, *Trattato*, 90.

36. Nadel, "Land Tenure," 13.

37. Sandra Joireman Fullerton, "Institutional Change in the Horn of Africa: The Allocation of Property Rights and Implications for Development" (Ph.D. dissertation, University of California Los Angeles, 1995), 155.

38. Art. 16 *Mai Adgi*, Capomazza, *Il diritto*, 150. *Adgena Tegeleba*, art. 229.

39. Alberto Pollera, *Il regime della proprietà terriera in Etiopia e nella Colonia Eritrea* (Rome: Bertero, 1913), 16; Adriano Carbone, *Termini più in uso nel diritto terriero dell'Eritrea*, ed. Regio Governo dell'Eritrea (Asmara, 1940), 43.

40. Art. 20, *Mai Adgi*, Capomazza, *Il diritto*, 89–90.

41. Carlo Conti Rossini, "I Loggo e la legge dei Loggo Sarda," *Giornale della Società Asiatica Italiana* XVII (Firenze, 1904): 12–13.

42. Conti Rossini, *Principi*, 129. For further detail, see, for example, art. 26 of the *Scioatte Anseba*, Carlo Conti Rossini, "Lo statuto degli Scioattè Ansebà (Eritrea)," *Scritti Giuridici in onore di Santi Romano*, III (Padova: Cedam, 1940): 355–356; §12 of the *Fetha Mahari*, Rodén, *Le tribù*, 283–284.

43. Sertoli Salis, *L'ordinamento*, 30; Carbone, *Termini*, 92–93; Conti Rossini, *Principi*, 115–124.

44. Tom Killion, ed., *Historical Dictionary of Eritrea* (Lanham, Md.: Scarecrow Press, 1998), 233.

45. Ostini, *Trattato*, 122–123; Pollera, *L'ordinamento*, 6.

46. Conti Rossini, *Principi*, 102.

47. There were different reasons. For a clear explanation see Ostini, *Trattato*, 96.

48. Ostini, *Trattato*, 94.

49. Nadel, "Land Tenure," 11.

50. Art. 16, *Mai Adgi*, Capomazza, *Il diritto*, 150.

51. Conti Rossini, "I Loggo," 12–13.

52. Bililign Mandefro, "Agricultural Communities and the Civil Code," *Journal of Ethiopian Law* VI, no. 1 (1969): 158, 162.

53. Fullerton, "Institutional Change," 157–158.

54. For the purpose of our book we have not made any distinction between different patterns of *resti*. To be precise, *resti* could be common (*resti ʿaddi*) or be shared between a family and any individuals comprising the lineage.

55. Art. 230, *Adgena Tegeleba* substantially agrees with art. 15, *Mehen Mahaza* (in Capomazza, *Il diritto*, 83), and article 8 of *Enda Fegrai* (Capomazza, *Il diritto*, 196–197).

56. *Adgena Tegeleba*, art. 279, Different rules apply when it is sold as part of *resti tsilmi* (under which land passed down through the family mainly to the sons). The possibility of sale was restricted to this last kind of *resti*.

57. Conti Rossini "I Loggo," 9. The author does not specify nor give further details about "individual property."

58. Conti Rossini, "I Loggo," 37–38.

59. Conti Rossini, "I Loggo," 37.

60. Ostini, *Trattato*, 101–102.

61. Pollera, *Il regime*, 32–33.

62. Pollera, *Il regime*, 31–33.

63. Nadel, "Land Tenure," 16.

64. Kjetil Tronvoll, "Mai Weini: A Village in Highland Eritrea" (M.A. thesis, Oslo University, 1996), 289.

65. Tekle Abraha, personal communication, 1998.

66. Research and Documentation Center, Asmara, "Complaints from Irafaile," Awet Tewolde (trans.) Document 00537.

67. Research and Documentation Center, Asmara, Questionnaire for the Saho Speaking Areas, Document 00530.

68. *Encyclopaedia of Islam* (Leiden: E. J. Brill, 1960), 7, 125, 60–61.

69. In particular, *waqf*, which became an important part of real estate law, was adapted sometimes in a manner which did not strictly conform to *sariʿa*. Joseph

Schacht, *An Introduction to Islamic Law* (Oxford: Clarendon Press, 1964), 77, 90; *Encyclopaedia of Islam*, 10, 209–10.

70. Angelo Maiorani, *Istituzioni di diritto musulmano. Lezioni tenute nella scuola di giurisprudenza di Asmara, Fioretti, Asmara*, 1954, 63; Sertoli Salis, *L'ordinamento*, 20–21.

71. *Encyclopaedia of Islam*, 6, 496–497; Sertoli Salis, *L'ordinamento*, 19.

72. *Relazione della Commissione Generale d'Inchiesta sulla Colonia Eritrea of November 2/1891*, cited in Sertoli Salis, *L'ordinamento*, 19–21.

73. *Encyclopaedia of Islam*, 11, 60; 6, 869–870.

74. *Relazione della Commissione*, 19–21.

75. From these records it also emerges that šarī'a courts functioned as notarial authorities. Jonathan Miran, "Islamic Court Records: A Source for the Social and Economic History of Massawa in the Nineteenth Century," paper presented at the First International Conference of Eritrean Studies, Asmara, July 22–26, 2001, 3.

76. Carlo Conti Rossini, "Al Ragali," in *Estratti dal Bollettino della Societá Italiana di Esplorazioni Geografiche e Commerciali, Anni 1903–1904* (Milan: Stabilimento Tipografico Bellini, 1903), 51.

77. Schacht, *An Introduction*, 126.

78. Research and Documentation Center, Asmara, Questionnaire for the Saho Speaking Areas, Document 00530.

79. Conti Rossini, "Al Ragali," 51.

80. Miran, "Islamic Court Records."

81. Bairu Tafla, "La notion," 178–183.

82. Conti Rossini, "I Loggo," 8.

83. Carbone, *Termini*, 43.

84. Tekle Abraha agrees with this interpretation. Personal communication, 1998.

85. M. A. Mohamed Salih, "Perspectives on Pastoralists and African States," *Nomadic Peoples* 29 (1989): 3.

86. Pollera, *Il regime*, 60; Sertoli Salis, *L'ordinamento*, 40.

87. Alberto Pollera, *Relazione della Commissione Governativa Italiana per i problemi del dopoguerra, Sezione Settima (Questioni Coloniali)*, 1919, 79. And his opinion was not isolated. See the same critical position in, for example, Massimo Colucci, "Sistemi di accertamento e di pubblicità dei diritti fondiari nelle colonie," Estratto dagli *Atti del Secondo Congresso di Studi Coloniali*, Napoli, 1–5 October 1934, 16; Massimo Colucci and Giangastone Bolla, "Induzioni sugli ordinamenti fondiari nell'Africa Orientale Italiana" (Firenze: Estratto dagli *Atti del Terzo Congresso di Studi Coloniali*, 12–17 April 1937), 198.

88. Many tracts of land were temporarily vacant because of wars, epidemics, or just because of the shifting system of cultivation or cattle transhumance.

89. Sertoli Salis, *L'ordinamento*, 48–49.

90. Ambaye Zekarias, *Land Tenure*, 51, 61-70; Atti Parlamentari/Legislatura XXIII—Sessione 1909-1913, Camera dei Deputati, Doc. LXII: Relazione sulla Colonia Eritrea del Regio Commissario Civile Deputato Ferdinando Martini per gli Esercizi 1902-1907, I (Rome: Tipografia della Camera dei Deputati, 1913), 168.

91. Mesghenna, *Italian Colonialism*, 93.

92. Mesghenna, *Italian Colonialism*, 148-149.

93. Sertoli Salis, *L'ordinamento*, 51.

94. Regolamento per i Commissariati e le Residenze, approved with d.gov. 3/5/1903 and Nuovo Ordinamento della giustizia nella Colonia Eritrea, RD 2/7/1908 n.325.

95. Sertoli Salis, *L'ordinamento*, 55; Augusto Sandonà, *Il regime fondiario e la colonizzazione nell'Affrica Italiana* (Rome: Tipografia dell'Istituto Internazionale d'Agricoltura, 1917), 18.

96. RD 31/1/1909 n.378, Ordinamento fondiario per la Colonia Eritrea, in Gazz. Uff. del Regno 19/7/1909 and relative Regolamento approved with d.gov.16/9/1909, modified by 24/8/1911 n.1450. RD 7/2/1926 n.269, in Gazz. Uff. del Regno, 2/3/1926 and relative Regolamento, approved with d.gov. 9/7/1926 n. 4390, abrogating the Ordinamento of 1908 and each previous decree. For a critique of the effectiveness of both land laws, see Colucci, *Sistemi di accertamento*, 17.

97. Articles 1 and 2, RD 378/1909, while articles 1 and 2, RD 269/1926 speak of rights "existing at the time of the occupation or resulting from a preliminary investigation performed by *Direzione Affari Civili e Politici* personally or by means of *Commissari regionali*."

98. Compare articles 11 and 12, RD 378/1909, with articles 11 and 345 RD 269/1926.

99. A detailed description of which is given by Sertoli Salis, *L'ordinamento*, 90-94.

100. Sertoli Salis, *L'ordinamento*, 46-47; Sandonà, *Il regime*, 18-19. Carlo Conti Rossini, *Il regime fondiario indigeno in Etiopia ed i mezzi di accertamento della proprietà* (Rome: Sallustiana, 1936), 5-6, is of a different view.

101. Italian law tradition distinguishes between disposable and non-disposable public domain. We are not going to introduce this distinction here; we are pointing out, however, that only the land part of *demanio disponibile* could have been given in concession to private individuals. See Colucci, *Sistemi di accertamento*, 16; Colucci and Bolla, *Induzioni*, 196, 198.

102. Moreover, according to article 208 it was not possible to transfer any right that had not been previously entered into the register by the rightful holder. Thus, entering into the register on the inscription became an essential element of the ownership over the land. See Sertoli Salis, *L'ordinamento*, 85.

103. In December 2000, through the good offices of Amde Michael Kahsai,

the governor of Asmara, we were able to examine plans of urban land drawn up in Italian times.

104. Nadel, "Land Tenure," 14.

105. Siegfried Frederick Nadel, "Land Tenure on the Eritrean Plateau (Conclusion)," *Africa* XVI, no. 2 (1946): 108.

106. Haile M. Larebo, *The Building of an Empire: Italian Land Policy and Practice in Ethiopia 1935–1941* (Oxford: Clarendon Press, 1994), 146.

107. Haile M. Larebo, *The Building of an Empire*, 285.

108. Eritrea was under the authority of the British War Department until 1 April 1949 when it was transferred to the authority of the Department of State for Foreign Affairs under the same officials and administration.

109. Pateman, *Eritrea: Even the Stones Are Burning*, 159–160.

110. Sandra Joireman Fullerton, "The Minefield of Land Reform: Comments on the Eritrean Land Proclamation," *African Affairs* 95 (1996): 271–272, citing Gerald Kennedy Nicholas Trevaskis, "Notes for the Guidance of the District Officer in Eritrea," in *Trevaskis Papers* (Oxford: Rhodes House, c.1942).

111. Richard Leonard, "European Colonization and the Socio-Economic Integration of Eritrea," *Eritrea Information* 3, no. 3 (1981): 7–10.

112. Ambaye Zekarias, *Land Tenure*, 24.

113. Tesfay Abraham, *The Diesa Land Tenure System and the Land Proclamation n. 58/1994 in the Kebesa Rural Area* (Asmara: University of Asmara, 1998), 24; Killion, *Historical Dictionary*, 163.

114. Tesfay Abraham, *The Diesa Land Tenure System*, 24.

115. Paul Brietzke, "Land Reform in Revolutionary Ethiopia," *The Journal of Modern African Studies* 14, no. 4 (1976): 645.

116. Brietzke, "Land Reform," 643.

117. Book III, title VII, Individual ownership, in particular chapter 2, Section 2, Special rules regarding immovable property; and title X, registers of immovable property.

118. A. Arthur Schiller, "Customary Land Tenure among the Highland Peoples of Northern Ethiopia," *African Law Studies* 1 (June 1969): 1.

119. René David, "A Civil Code for Ethiopia: Considerations on the Codification of the Civil Law in African Countries," *Tulane Law Review* 37 (1963): 187, 202.

120. Bilillign Mandefro, "Agricultural Communities," 195–197.

121. Bilillign Mandefro, "Agricultural Communities," 175.

122. Bilillign Mandefro, "Agricultural Communities," 187.

123. Proclamation n.255 of 1967, in *Negarit Gazeta*, Year 27, n.4.

124. Brietzke, "Land Reform," 644.

125. Brietzke, "Land Reform," 645. Proclamation n.31/1975 was published in the *Negarit Gazeta*, Year 34, n.26. See in particular article 3.1, "All rural lands shall be the collective property of the Ethiopian people."

126. Articles 29 and 10, proclamation n.31/1975.

127. Articles 23 and 19, proclamation n.31/1975.

128. Articles 26 and 24, proclamation n.31/1975.

129. Brietzke, "Land Reform," 648.

130. Jason W. Clay and Bonnie K. Holcomb, *Politics and the Ethiopian Famine: 1984–1985* (Cambridge, Mass.: Cultural Survival, 1985), 139.

131. Pateman, *Eritrea: Even the Stones Are Burning*, 167.

132. Dessalegn Rahmato, *Agrarian Reform in Ethiopia* (Trenton, N.J.: Red Sea Press, 1985), 68.

133. *Liberation*, August–September 1981.

134. Pateman, *Eritrea: Even the Stones Are Burning*, 131.

135. See Appendix 3 in Bereket Habte Selassie, *Conflict and Intervention in the Horn of Africa* (New York: Monthly Review Press, 1980), 183.

136. Dan Connell, "Two Lines in Eritrea's Movement: ELF, PLF Seek Unity," in *Revolution in Eritrea: Eyewitness Reports*, Dossier préparé et réalisé conjointement par le Comité Belge de secours à l'Erythrée et Research and Information Centre of Eritrea, 1979, 75; "La réforme agraire à Azim," in *Revolution in Eritrea*, 48; "The Socio-Economic Transformations in Liberated Eritrea and its Impact on Peasant Women," *Eritrea Now*, March 1979.

137. *Memorandum* EPLF, August 1978, art. 2, a., 42–43.

138. See also Guido Bimbi, "I contadini di Medri Zien," in *Revolution in Eritrea*, 139. With regard to urban land and houses, art. 2, E. of the EPLF program aimed to "make urban land state property; to nationalize all excess urban houses in order to abolish exploitation through rent and improve the livelihood of the masses; to compensate citizens for nationalized property in accordance with a procedure based on personal income and the condition of the national economy."

139. *Liberation*, August–September 1981; *Liberation*, January–April 1982, 11.

140. Bimbi, "I contadini," 138; "The Socio-Economic Transformations," 132.

141. Tesfay Abraham *The Diesa Land Tenure System*, 27–28.

142. *Liberation*, January–April 1982, 11.

143. "La réforme agraire à Azim," 49–50 and Connell, "Two Lines," 76–77; see also "Victories Won by EPLF in 1976," *Vanguard*, March 1977, in *Selected Articles from EPLF Publications (1973–1980)*, published by EPLF, May 1982, 77–89, and "Land Reforms in the Environs of Afabet," *Dimtsi Hafash*, April 1979, in *Selected Articles*, 89. The membership of peasant assemblies was kept secret: the members of each cell formed a separate group with its own leader, who in turn was associated with the leaders of other villages in a branch which was directly linked to the nearest EPLF unit in the area—and composed for the most part of persons belonging to the poorer class. Connell, "Two Lines," 77.

144. For the reasons why there were twelve members instead of five as in the

case of the ELF, and a further discussion on the way in which the recruitment was carried out, see "La réforme agraire à Azim," 49.

145. Volker Mathies, *Der Eritrea-Konflikt: Ein "Vergessener Krieg" am Horn von Afrika* (Hamburg: Institut für Afrika-Kunde, 1981), 168.

146. Tesfay Abraham, *The Diesa Land Tenure System*, 29.

147. Peter With, "Politics and Liberation: The Eritrean Struggle, 1961–1986." (Ph.D. diss., University of Aarhus, 1987), 82.

148. Yirgalem Woldegabriel, "Women and Land Ownership System in Highland Eritrea" (LL.B. senior thesis, University of Asmara, 1998), 52–53. Citing MLWE Report in Tigrinya 9 December 1994, 12.

149. Yirgalem Woldegabriel, "Women and Land Ownership," 54–56.

150. Yirgalem Woldegabriel, "Women and Land Ownership," 61.

151. *Voice of Eritrean Women*, Special Issue, 1989, 10.

152. Proclamation 2/1991, "Transitional Civil Code," *Gazeta Awagiat Eritra* 1/91, n.1. The official text of the proclamation is in Tigrinya. It will be repealed, with other transitional codes, as soon as the new civil code comes into force.

153. In particular, articles 182 to 207 deal with local administration of land, while articles 208 to 213 contain a specific discipline for houses in rural areas.

154. Except when land is in the public domain. For the distinction between state and non-state land, see article 182.1.

155. Or by the people, if there is not a public assembly.

156. However, a major distinction is made among villagers entitled to a *"muluie gibri"* (full share) and *"ferghi gibri"* (half share). Castellani remarks that the criterion seems to penalize nuclear families. Luca Castellani, "La riforma del diritto fondiario in Eritrea," typescript, Asmara, 1998, 5.

157. For a classification of the right that goes beyond this definition, see Castellani, "La riforma," 5. Note the distinction between this and possessory rights—rights that arise from possession. This is one of three forms of property rights: property absolute; property qualified; property possessory.

158. Proclamation n.16/1991, *Gazeta Awagiat Eritra*, 1/1991, n.3. *A National Charter for Eritrea—For a Democratic, Just and Prosperous Future*, Third EPLF Congress, Nacfa, February 1994, VIII Resolution. *Gazeta Awagiat Eritra*, n IV/94 n.6.

159. Isaias Afwerki, "Interview," *Eritrea Update* June (1992): 5–6.

160. Including: customary (art. 39.1); colonial (art. 39.2); articles 182–214 of the TCCE (art. 42.1); any provisions of any existing law not in conformity (art. 42.3) are thereby repealed.

161. The Eritrean position *vis à vis* the legal system inherited from a communist regime has parallels with the experiences of post-communist states. For the issues of codifying property rights in countries in transition, see Gianmaria Ajani and Ugo Mattei, "Codifying Property Law in the Process of Transition:

Some Suggestions from Comparative Law and Economics," *Hastings International and Comparative Law Review* 19, no. 1 (Fall 1995): 117–137.

162. *Gazeta Awagiat Eritra* 7/1997, n.2.

163. A more detailed analysis of usufructuary right and duties (arts. 18–28) would go beyond the scope of this chapter. However, it seems clear that in the Eritrean legislation, the right over land is closer to an administrative concession than to usufruct as it is normally understood. For further analysis see Castellani, "La riforma," 9–10.

164. Foreigners may obtain land rights according to the special conditions described in art. 8 Procl.n.58/94 and 6.2.3. Legal Notice n.31/1997.

165. Arts. 5.3 and 50.1 Procl.58/1994. The constitution as we have seen speaks more generally of "cases of national or public interest" and specifies the criteria of due compensation and due process of law.

166. Headed by a representative of the Land Commission and constituted of members from the village assembly and various governmental bodies of the locality (arts. 10.1 and 10.2, Procl.58/94).

167. Castellani, "La riforma," 16.

168. Fullerton, "The Minefield of Land Reform," 275–276.

169. John Markakis, "Eritrea's National Charter," *Review of African Political Economy* 22, no. 63 March (1995): 127.

170. Kjetil Tronvoll, "The Process of Nation-Building in Post-war Eritrea: Created from Below or Directed from Above?" *The Journal of Modern Africa Studies* 36, no. 3 (1998): 474.

171. Mathies, *Der Eritrea-Konflikt*, 168.

172. Garrett Hardin, "The Tragedy of the Commons," in *Readings in Public Sector Economics*, ed. Samuel Baker and Catherine Elliott (Lexington, Mass.: D. C. Heath and Company, 1990).

173. Jason R. Wilson, "Eritrean Land Reform: The Forgotten Masses," *North Carolina Journal of International Law and Commercial Regulation* 24, no. 2 Winter (1999): 510–515.

174. Wilson, "Eritrean Land Reform," 515.

175. Agricultural Commission, EPLF, "Problems, Prospective Policies and Programs for Agricultural Development in Eritrea," in *Emergent Eritrea: Challenges of Economic Development*, ed. Gebre Hiwet Tesfagiorgis (Washington, D.C.: Eritreans for Peace and Democracy, 1992), 99.

176. Girmai Abraham, "The Privatization of the Diesa in Independent Eritrea: Towards an Agricultural Research and Policy Agenda," in *Proceedings of the International Conference on Eritrea*, 3–4 November 1990 (Washington, D.C.: Eritreans for Peace and Democracy, 1990), 108–112.

177. Kidane Mengisteab, "Eritrea's Land Reform Proclamation: A Critical Appraisal," *Eritrean Studies Review* 2, no. 2 (1998): 1–18.

178. Kidane Mengisteab, "Eritrea's Land Reform," 9.

179. Kidane Mengisteab, "Eritrea's Land Reform," 9.

180. See Preamble of Proclamation 58/1994.

181. Kidane Mengisteab, "Eritrea's Land Reform," 12–13.

182. Proclamation n.58/1994, art. 48.1.

183. This opinion is personal. Tigrinya society is not one of gender equality; see our chapter on this issue.

184. Kidane Mengisteab, "Eritrea's Land Reform," 13. He then makes a debatable judgment, "it is indeed not clear how the communal land tenure system can be viewed as the source of gender inequality." As an example, he cites the rule stating that in case of divorce, land was divided equally between husband and wife. The issue is more complex: he presents as a general pattern of *diesa* a very idealized model. Under the general term of *diesa* or village ownership of the land, many different regulations are involved. It would be necessary then at least to decide which among the many different regulations of *diesa* should be examined and to which the priority must be given. One example: according to art. 14 of *Mai Adgi* (Capomazza, *Il diritto*, 144) succession to the *diesa* of the father follows a strict paternal line of descent.

185. Cited by Yirgalem Woldegabriel, "Women and Land Ownership," 66.

186. Bruce, "A Perspective," 46.

187. Ajani and Mattei, "Codifying Property Law," 128–129.

188. *Gazeta Awagiat Eritra*, n.7/97, art. 3.10.

189. Wilson, "Eritrean Land Reform," 509.

190. Tesfa G. Gebremedhin, "Agricultural Development in Eritrea: Economic and Policy Analysis," in *Emergent Eritrea: Challenges of Economic Development*, ed. Gebre Hiwet Tesfagiorgis (Washington, D.C.: Eritreans for Peace and Democracy, 1992), 103.

191. Mengsteab Negash, "Investment Laws in Eritrea," 369–370.

7. Land Disputes and Conflict Resolution

1. André J. F. Köbben, "Land as an Object of Gain in a Non-literate Society: Land-Tenure among the Bete and Dida (Ivory Coast, West Africa)," in *African Agrarian Systems*, ed. Daniel P. Biebuyck (London: Oxford University Press, 1963), 252.

2. Ruffillo Perini, *Di qua dal Mareb (Mareb mellàsc)* (Firenze: Tipografia Cooperativa, 1905), 16.

3. Bilillign Mandefro, "Agricultural Communities and the Civil Code," *Journal of Ethiopian Law* VI, no. 1 June (1969): 165.

4. Yirgalem Woldegabriel, "Women and Land Ownership System in Highland Eritrea" (senior LL.B. thesis, University of Asmara, 1998), 37.

5. Belai Araia and Berhane Abraham, personal communication, Asmara, November–December 2000.

6. Siegfried Frederick Nadel, "Land Tenure on the Eritrean Plateau (Conclusion)," *Africa* XVI, no. 1 (1946): 106–107.

7. Rodolfo Sacco, *Il diritto africano* (Torino: Utet, 1995), 180–181.

8. See the debate on universalism and relativism in our chapters on FGM and land. Ulrich Beck, *What Is Globalization,* trans. Patrick Camiller (Cambridge: Polity Press, 2000), 85.

9. *Code of Customary Law of Acchele Guzai,* April 1951, Asmara, 3.

10. Carlo Conti Rossini, "I Loggo e la legge dei Loggo Sarda," *Giornale della Società Asiatica Italiana* XVII (1904): 12–13.

11. Conti Rossini, "I Loggo," 39.

12. Kurt H. Wolff, trans. and ed., *The Sociology of Georg Simmel* (Glencoe, Calif.: The Free Press, 1950), 402.

13. William A. Shack, "Open Systems and Closed Boundaries: The Ritual Process of Stranger Relations in New African States," in *Strangers in African Societies,* ed. William A. Shack and Elliott P. Skinner (Berkeley: University of California Press, 1979), 44.

14. Ilario Capomazza, *Il diritto consuetudinario dell'Acchele Guzai* (Asmara: Fioretti, 1937), 195–196.

15. Capomazza, *Il diritto,* 197–198.

16. Capomazza, *Il diritto,* 89–90.

17. After having deducted from it a part for the priest, for the *maqaderai* (the person who cuts the uvula—it was deemed that if a baby did not have his uvula cut he could die), and for the village musician. Apart from the priest, the individuals filling these posts were always foreigners.

18. In this case a fourth of the crop went to the owner of the cattle. If somebody other than the owner carried it out, the latter had the right to a fourth of the crop (art. 55§1). If a man did not possess oxen to cultivate his land, and he was already working for somebody else, he could ask for the application of the so-called *serr.* According to this rule, after he had worked for two days for his master, he could use the master's oxen on the third day to cultivate his own land. The crops belonged in this case only to him (§4).

19. The cattle owner had the right to keep for himself three crops if the land was in the highlands, and two if it was in the lowlands (§5).

20. If the crop was reaped while the owner was absent, the cultivator was not punished. But if the owner arrived in the field and affirmed that it was his property, the cultivator could be sent away, losing any right to the crop (§8). Karl Gustav Rodén, *Le tribù dei Mensa—Storia, legge e costumi. Traduzione italiana dalla lingua Tigré* (Stockholm: Nordiska Boktryckeriet, 1913), 285–286.

21. Ilario Capomazza, *Istituzioni di diritto consuetudinario del Serae—La legge degli Atchemè-Melga* (Macerata: Stabilimento tipografico Giorgetti, 1912), 84–87.

22. Capomazza, *Il diritto,* 91–92.

23. Werner Münzinger, *Studi sull'Africa Orientale-Traduzione dal tedesco per cura del Corpo di Stato Maggiore* (Rome: Voghera, 1890), 407–408.

24. Christine Obbo, "Village Strangers in Buganda Society," in *Strangers in African Societies*, ed. William A. Shack and Elliott P. Skinner (Berkeley: University of California Press, 1979), 230.

25. Capomazza, *Il diritto*, 150–152.

26. Capomazza, *Il diritto*, 197–198.

27. Asmarom Legesse, *Customary Law and Alternative Dispute Resolution (ADR)* (Asmara: Ministry of Justice, 1999), 24.

28. Sandra Joireman Fullerton, "Institutional Change in the Horn of Africa: The Allocation of Property Rights and Implications for Development" (Ph.D. dissertation, University of California Los Angeles, 1995), 159.

29. Conti Rossini, "I Loggo," 13.

30. Research and Documentation Center, Asmara, *Appeal by Hamasien Elders to Governor General*, Letter n.7/U32/62.

31. Siegfried Frederick Nadel, "Land Tenure on the Eritrean Plateau," *Africa* XVI, no. 1 (1946): 14.

32. *Code of Customary Law*, 46.

33. In the code of *Adkeme Melega* we find no mention of *shehena* or *diesa;* this is not so surprising because it was less common in Seraye than in the other regions of the *kebessa*. The three main forms of property in Seraye were *resti, medri worki*, and *moras* (art. 36); this partially explains why we find in this law a number of detailed rules about the sale of land.

34. Münzinger, *Studi sull'Africa*, 407–408.

35. Rodén *Le tribù*, 283–293.

36. Capomazza, *Istituzioni*, 69–73.

37. Capomazza, *Il diritto*, 83–84.

38. Capomazza, *Il diritto*, 150–152.

39. Capomazza, *Il diritto*, 97–98.

40. Capomazza, *Istituzioni*, 73–75.

41. Rodén, *Le tribù*, 285–286.

42. Conti Rossini, "I Loggo," 40.

43. Felice Ostini, *Trattato di diritto consuetudinario dell'Eritrea* (Rome: Officina Grafica—Corriere Eritreo, 1956), 100–104.

44. Nadel, "Land Tenure," 16–17.

45. Ostini, *Trattato*, 99. It is important to stress that in Eritrea the individual cultivates his plot of family or village land with his own implements, whereas in the parts of Ethiopia where land was also held communally (in Tigray, Begemedir, Gojjam, and the *awraja* of Lasta and Wag in Wollo) the individual would seek the aid of fellow farmers on a reciprocal basis. Bilillign Mandefro, "Agricultural Communities," 158, 164, 153.

46. *Mehen Mahaza*, arts. 18–19, 24; *Haggecti*, arts. 17–21; *Mai Adgi*, arts. 17, 21; *Zeban Serao Ennadoccò*, art. 7; *Enda Fegrai* art. 10, 12, Capomazza, *Il diritto*, 84–89, 94–96, 118–120, 152–156, 159–160, 171, 199–201, 202–203. See also, *Scioatte Anseba*, arts. 29–30, 32, 49, Carlo Conti Rossini, "Lo statuto degli Scioatte Anseba (Eritrea)," in *Scritti Giuridici in onore di Santi Romano*, III (Padova: Cedam, 1940), 356–357, 361–362; and *Adkeme Melega*, art 41, Capomazza, *Istituzioni*, 77–78.

47. Ercole Petazzi, *L'odierno diritto penale consuetudinario dell'Hamasien (Eritrea)* (Asmara: Fioretti, 1937), 65–79, articles 162–250. On the same topic, see also *Adkeme Melega*, arts. 40, 42–44, Capomazza, *Istituzioni*, 77, 81–84; *Scioatte Anseba*, arts. 50–53; Conti Rossini, "Lo statuto," 362.

48. *Eritrea Profile*, "Eritrean Traditions and Customs," 1 March 1997, 7.

49. Conti Rossini, "Lo statuto," 357.

50. Research and Documentation Center, Asmara, *Resti in Serae*, Document 00531.

51. Tom Killion, ed., *Historical Dictionary of Eritrea* (Lanham, Md.: Scarecrow Press, 1998), 166.

52. An account which, although largely sympathetic to the Ethiopian position, nevertheless contains a useful collection of appendixes is Tekeste Negash and Kjetil Tronvoll, *Brothers at War: Making Sense of the Eritrean-Ethiopian War* (Oxford: James Currey, 2000).

53. Research and Documentation Center, Asmara, *Mai Feres-Deranto*, no. 00532.

54. Dennis J. Duncanson, "Sir'at 'Adkeme Milga': A Native Law Code of Eritrea," *Africa* XIX, no. 2 (1949): 148.

55. Bilillign Mandefro, "Agricultural Communities," 154.

56. Asmarom Legesse, *Customary Law*, 19.

57. *Eritrea Profile*, "Eritrean Traditions and Customs," 31 May 1997, 7.

58. This position was highly regarded. The word of the *zera* was considered conclusive evidence in a dispute. Abraham Desta, "Establishment of Paternity under Eritrean Indigenous Laws with Particular Reference to Article 60 of the Proclamation no. 2 of 1991" (senior LL.B. thesis, University of Asmara, 1999), 12.

59. Carlo Conti Rossini, *Principi di Diritto Consuetudinario Dell'Eritrea* (Rome: Ministero delle Colonie, Tip Unione Ed., 1916), 163; Ostini, *Trattato*, 99.

60. Research and Documentation Center, Asmara, Questionnaire for the Saho Speaking Areas, Document 00530, nd.

61. Killion, "Historical Dictionary," 407.

62. *Bullettino Ufficiale della Colonia Eritrea*, n. 46, Asmara, 14 November 1903, 3.

63. *Bullettino Ufficiale*, n.46, 2–3.

64. The Tor'a clan was linked by the Italians in 1933 with the five clans of the Asaorta under a single chief. Killion, "Historical Dictionary," 90–91.

65. Killion, "Historical Dictionary," 108.

66. Alberto Pollera, *The Native Peoples of Eritrea,* trans. Linda Lappin (Asmara: University of Asmara, 1996), 95.

67. Pollera, *The Native Peoples,* 71–72.

68. Research and Documentation Center, Asmara, *Liban and Habela,* Document 00527, Asmara, n.d.

69. Conti Rossini, "I Loggo," 41–42.

70. Conti Rossini, "I Loggo," 13.

71. Roy Pateman, "Peasants and State Farms: Problems in the Transition to Socialism in Africa and Latin America," *Peasant Studies* 16, no. 2 Winter (1989): 70.

72. Daniel J. Dzurek, "The Hanish Island Dispute," *Eritrean Studies Review* 1, no. 2 (1996): 136.

73. See Annex III to the Arbitration Agreement of 3 October 1996 that establishes the joint Yemeni-Eritrean Committee for Bilateral Cooperation signed by the respective foreign ministers on 16 October 1998.

74. There are few footnotes to this section, as it has been written by one of the authors who was a participant observer of events in the Horn of Africa for more than forty years.

75. She had been married to Dan Connell, an eminent journalist writing on Eritrea. This marriage ended in divorce, and those people who favor a simplistic psychological explanation for the actions of our political masters could perhaps see a connection.

76. This is from a source that was in a privileged position to observe the very close relationship that developed between Meles Zenawi and the U.S. ambassador, David Shinn. For understandable reasons he must remain in the shadows.

77. For an anthropologist's look at this problem, with particular reference to the academy, see Paul Rabinow, *Essays on the Anthropology of Reason* (Princeton, N.J.: Princeton University Press, 1996), 3–27.

78. Alemseged Tesfai, "The Cause of the Eritrean-Ethiopian Border Conflict," *Eritrea Profile,* 19 December 1998, 3.

79. Gabriele Ciampi, "Cartographic Problems of the Eritreo-Ethiopia Border," *Africa* LVI, no. 2 (2001): 154–189.

80. Ghidewon Abay Asmerom and Ogbazgy Abay Asmerom, "A Study of the Evolution of the Eritrean Ethiopian Border through Treaties and Official Maps," *Eritrean Studies Review* 3, no. 2 (1999): 52.

81. "Joint Communique Between the State of Eritrea and Ethiopia," mimeo, Addis Ababa, 30 July 1993.

82. From 1992 onwards, Tigrayan authorities in the lower Adiabo area bordering the Eritrean Badme plains started to confiscate the property of Eritrean

farmers on the grounds that they had trespassed into Tigrayan territory. After these sorts of incidents continued into 1997, a joint meeting of high-level Tigrayan and Eritrean officials was held in Shire Tigray to talk over the problems.

83. Before the Ethiopian military offensives of 1998, there were more than ninety villages in the Badme area, all of them established in the 1960s by Eritrean agrarian refugees from the highlands and consequently inhabited by Eritreans. Many villages inside Ethiopia had also been founded and inhabited by Eritreans. Alemseged Tesfai, "The Cause of the Eritrean-Ethiopian Border Conflict."

84. *Eritrea Profile*, 4 July 1998, 5.

85. Capomazza, *Il diritto*, 161.

86. Nadel, "Land Tenure (Conclusion)," 99.

87. Tesfay Abraham, *The Diesa Land Tenure System and the Land Proclamation No 58/1994 in the Kebesa Rural Area* (Asmara: University of Asmara, 1998), 61.

88. Friederike Kemink, "The Tegreñña Customary Law Codes," *Paideuma: Mitteilungen zur Kulturkunde* 37 (1991): 58.

89. *Code of Customary Law*, 35.

90. Capomazza, *Il diritto*, 116.

91. Edward Ullendorff, *The Ethiopians: An Introduction to Country and People* (London: Oxford University Press, 1960), 186–187.

92. Ostini, *Trattato*, 31.

93. Capomazza, *Istituzioni*, 117; Capomazza, *Il diritto*, 96, 161–163; *Code of Customary Law*, 26.

94. Capomazza, *Istituzioni*, 119.

95. Kjetil Tronvoll, "Mai Weini: A Village in Highland Eritrea" (M.A. thesis, Oslo University, 1996), 311.

96. Asmarom Legesse, "Customary Law," 9–10.

97. Werner Münzinger, *Dei costumi e del diritto dei Bogos, traduzione dal tedesco a cura di A. Ostini*, con prefazione di I. M. Ziegler (Rome: Ministero degli Affari Esteri, 1891), 42–44.

98. Nadel, "Land Tenure (Conclusion)," 106.

99. *Bullettino Ufficiale*, n.46, 2.

100. Nathan Marein, *The Ethiopian Empire: Federation and Laws* (Rotterdam: Royal Netherlands Printing and Lithographing Company, 1954), 379.

101. Alan Hoben, *Social Soundness Analysis of Agrarian Reform in Ethiopia* (Washington, D.C.: USAID, 1976), 73–74; Girma Wolde Selassie, "The Impact of the Ethiopian Revolution on the Law and Legal Institutions of the Country," in *Proceedings of the Seventh International Conference of Ethiopian Studies* (Lund, Sweden: University of Lund, 1984), 565–575.

102. Cited by Bereket Habte Selassie, *Conflict and Intervention in the Horn of Africa* (New York: Monthly Review Press, 1980), 183.

103. Proclamation n.58/1994, art. 41.

104. Proclamation n.95/1997, art. 6.6.

105. Roy Licklider, "Negotiating an End in Civil Wars: General Findings," in *New Approaches to International Negotiation and Mediation: Findings from USIP-Sponsored Research*, ed. Timothy Fisk (Washington, D.C.: United States Institute of Peace, 1999), 27.

106. Simon Roberts, "Law and Dispute Processes," in *Companion Encyclopedia of Anthropology*, ed. Tim Ingold (London: Routledge, 1997), 970–973.

107. Killion, "Historical Dictionary," 135.

108. *Eritrea Update*, April 1992, 7.

109. Killion, "Historical Dictionary," 242–243.

110. See the very interesting discussion in Christopher Mitchell and Michael Banks, *Handbook of Conflict Resolution: The Analytical Problem-Solving Approach* (London: Pinter, 1996), 3–4.

111. Killion, "Historical Dictionary," 395. But Ras Tessema Asberom sometimes tried without success to alter long established and regarded practices. In the 1940s he prohibited marriage payments, but the community rejected his ruling. Zenawi Haile, "The Significance of Marriage Payments on Marriage in the Eritrean Family Law" (LL.B senior thesis, University of Asmara, 1999), 47–48.

112. Asmarom Legesse, "Customary Law," 13–14; 16.

113. Questionnaire for the Saho Speaking Areas.

114. George B. N. Ayittey, *Indigenous African Institutions* (Ardsley-on-Hudson: Transnational Publishers, 1991), 67.

115. Gebre Hiwet Tesfagiorgis, "Approaches to Resolving the Conflict between Eritrea and Ethiopia," *Eritrean Studies Review* 3, no. 2 (1999): 150.

116. Asmarom Legesse, "Customary Law," 9–10.

117. Land and Housing Commission, Consultative Workshop on Pastoralists, Land and the State in Eritrea, Keren, 10–11 May 1996, 8–11.

118. Research and Documentation Center, Asmara, *The Status of Hazemo*, Document 55147.

119. Pollera, *The Native Peoples*, 86.

120. Asmarom Legesse, "Customary Law," 18–19.

---

8. The Virgin, the Wife, the Spinster, and the Concubine

1. Robin Morgan, *The Word of a Woman* (New York: Norton & Co., 1992), 76.

2. No women were allowed to vote or stand as candidates in elections to the National Assembly held under the British administration in 1947 or under the Federation in 1952 and 1956. In the first elections held after independence in 1993, few if any women won seats in open elections. Because of this, in the

legislative field some 30 percent of seats at each level of administration were reserved for women, and they were able to compete for the other 70 percent. They sometimes won such open contests, as for example in the Asmara region in 1997.

3. Henrietta L. Moore, "Understanding Sex and Gender," in *Encyclopedia of Anthropology*, ed. Tim Ingold (London: Routledge, 1999), 813. It has been argued that both gender studies and kinship studies are premised on models that assume that the difference between woman and men is "natural" and therefore pre-social. However, Michel Foucault, *History of Sexuality, Volume I: An Introduction*, trans. Robert Hurley (New York: Random House, 1990), 154–155, argues that "sex" is an effect rather than an "origin," and is the product of specific discursive practices.

4. Cheryl Johnson-Odim, "Common Themes, Different Contexts: Third World Women and Feminism," in *Third World Women and the Politics of Feminism*, ed. Chandra Talpade Mohanty, Ann Russo, and Lourdes Torres (Bloomington: Indiana University Press, 1991), 322.

5. On this point see Charles Champetier, "Reflections on Human Rights," *Telos* 118 (2000): 77–86.

6. Moore, "Understanding Sex," 828.

7. Gayatri Chakravorty Spivak, "Can the Subaltern Speak?" in *Marxism and the Interpretation of Cultures*, ed. Cary Nelson and Lawrence Grossberg (Urbana: University of Illinois Press, 1988), 296.

8. Carlo Conti Rossini, *Principi di Diritto Consuetudinario Dell'Eritrea* (Rome: Ministero delle Colonie, Tip. Unione Ed., 1916), 567–568, 645–646.

9. Conti Rossini, *Principi*, 653.

10. *Eritrea Profile*, "Eritrean Traditions and Customs," 12 July 1997, 7.

11. Conti Rossini, *Principi*, 186–188.

12. Conti Rossini, *Principi*, 729–732.

13. Alberto Pollera, *I Baria e i Cunama* (Rome: Reale Società Geografica, 1913), 161, 174.

14. In the past fifty years the most influential account of this alliance theory has been Claude Lévi-Strauss, *The Elementary Structure of Kinship* (London: Eyre and Spottiswode, 1969).

15. Karl Gustav Rodén, *Le tribù dei Mensa. Storia, legge e costumi, traduzione italiana dalla lingua Tigré* (Stockholm: Nordiska Boktryckeriet, 1913), 189. See also article 32 of the law of *Saharti, Lamza, Uocarti*.

16. "Traditions That Oppress Women," *Voice of Eritrean Women* (Spring 1990): 5; Ercole Petazzi, *L'odierno diritto penale consuetudinario dell'Hamasien* (*Eritrea*) (Asmara: Fioretti, 1937), 38.

17. Robin Fox, *Kinship and Marriage: An Anthropological Perspective* (Harmondsworth: Penguin, 1967), 178–179.

18. Burton Pasternak, Carol R. Ember, and Melvin Ember, *Sex, Gender, and Kinship* (Upper Saddle River, N.J.: Prentice Hall, 1997), 150–151.

19. Our thanks go to Awet Tewolde for translating this for us.

20. Carlo Conti Rossini, *Ricordo di un soggiorno in Eritrea* (Asmara: Tipografia della Missione Svedese, 1903).

21. Research and Documentation Center, Asmara, "Code of Customary Law of Acchele Guzai: Adghena Tegheleba," arts. 104, 98, Document 138300, 1954.

22. *Encyclopaedia of Islam* (Leiden: E. J. Brill, 1960), 8, 26 -35.

23. Pollera, *I Baria e i Cunama*, 161, 171; Conti Rossini, *Principi*, 752-753, 755.

24. Alberto Pollera, *The Native Peoples of Eritrea*, trans. Linda Lappin (Asmara: University of Asmara, 1996), 147-148.

25. Ilario Capomazza, *Il diritto consuetudinario dell' Acchele Guzai*, Massimario raccolto da Ilario Capomazza (Asmara: Fioretti, 1937), 66.

26. For an account see Conti Rossini, *Principi*, 206, 322-323.

27. Some Bilein children were particularly disadvantaged. At one time anyone born on Wednesday was smothered at birth. Adhana Mengisteab, personal communication, Asmara, November 2000. Indeed "Wednesday's child was full of woe!"

28. Capomazza, *Il diritto*, 104.

29. For an example, see *Adkeme Melega*, art. 1. Ilario Capomazza, *Istituzioni di diritto consuetudinario del Seraè. La legge degli Atchemè Melga* (Macerata: Giorgetti, 1912), 13-14.

30. Carlo Conti Rossini, "I Loggo e la legge dei Loggo Sarda," *Giornale della Società Asiatica Italiana* XVII (1904): 7.

31. Conti Rossini, "I Loggo," 53. This is an eloquent reminder that relationships between Eritrean Tigrinya and the Ethiopian Amhara and Tigray were often as tense in the past as they are in the present.

32. Werner Münzinger, *Studi sull'Africa Orientale-Traduzione dal tedesco per cura del Corpo di Stato Maggiore* (Rome: Voghera, 1890), 402.

33. Customary Law of Akele Guzai, on file in the Law Library, Haile Selassie I University, Addis Ababa, 1945.

34. Capomazza, *Istituzioni*, 109-11.

35. Pier Giuseppe Monateri, "Running on the Horn: The Case of Beni Amer and Akele Guzai Customary Laws in Eritrea," in *New Law for New States*, ed. Lyda Favali, Elisabetta Grande, and Marco Guadagni (Torino: L'Harmattan, 1998), 154-155.

36. Pollera, *I Baria e i Cunama*, 161, 170.

37. Conti Rossini, *Principi*, 751.

38. Carlo Conti Rossini, "Lo statuto degli Scioattè Ansebà (Eritrea)," in *Scritti Giuridici in onore di Santi Romano*, III (Padova: Cedam, 1940), 350.

39. Conti Rossini, *Principi*, 197-199.

40. Conti Rossini, "Lo statuto," 351.

41. Stevan Harrell, *Human Families* (Boulder, Colo.: Westview Press, 1997), 132.

42. Luigi Luca Cavalli-Sforza, *Geni, popoli e lingue* (Milan: Adelphi, 1996), 190–194; Jared Diamond, *Guns, Germs, and Steel: The Fates of Human Societies* (New York: W. W. Norton & Company, 1997), 62–63.

43. Although sura IV. 3 does not say this, the interpretation according to which the maximum number of wives is four predominated very early in Islam. *Encyclopaedia of Islam*, 26–35; Joseph Schacht, *An Introduction to Islamic Law* (Oxford: Clarendon Press, 1964), 162.

44. Conti Rossini, *Principi*, 189–190.

45. Translated by Awet Tewolde.

46. Conti Rossini, *Principi*, 569–571, 647.

47. Pollera, *I Baria e i Cunama*, 172.

48. National Statistics Office, *Eritrea Demographic and Health Survey 1995*, 73–74.

49. Friederike Kemink, "The Tegreñña Customary Law Codes," *Paideuma: Mitteilungen zur Kulturkunde* 37 (1991): 68.

50. See for example article 743 of the Ethiopian civil code fixing this period at 300 days.

51. Abraham Desta, "Establishment of Paternity under Eritrean Indigenous Laws with Particular Reference to Article 60 of the Proclamation no. 2 of 1991" (senior LL.B. thesis, University of Asmara, 1999), 14.

52. *Encyclopaedia of Islam*, 28.

53. Pollera, *The Native Peoples*, 42.

54. Robert Harrison Barnes, "Marriage Exchange and the Meaning of Corporations in Eastern Indonesia," in *The Meaning of Marriage Payments*, ed. John L. Comaroff (London: Academic Press, 1980), 111.

55. Conti Rossini, *Principi*, 257–260.

56. Conti Rossini, "I Loggo," 25–26.

57. Conti Rossini, "I Loggo," 19–21; Conti Rossini, *Principi*, 188–189, 247–248; Petazzi, *L'odierno diritto penale*, 35, 84–85. Petazzi, however, defines as *berchi* the non-religious *qal kidan* union.

58. Kemink, "The Tegreñña," 62; Conti Rossini, "Lo statuto," 350.

59. Conti Rossini *Principi*, 252.

60. Capomazza, *Instituzioni*, 59–63.

61. Conti Rossini *Principi*, 252.

62. Conti Rossini, *I Loggo*, 21.

63. Ruffillo Perini, *Di qua dal Marèb (Marèb—mellàsc)* (Firenze: Tipografia Cooperativa, 1905), 408–409; Conti Rossini, *Principi*, 252–254.

64. Conti Rossini, "I Loggo," 28.

65. Conti Rossini, *Principi*, 251–254.

66. Capomazza, *Il diritto*, 186, 139; Conti Rossini, *Principi*, 254–255.

67. Schacht, *An Introduction*, 163.

68. *Encyclopaedia of Islam*, 28; see the entry *mutʿa* 757–759; Francesco Castro, *Materiali e ricerche sul nikah al-mutʿa* (Rome: Accademia Nazionale dei Lincei —Fondazione Leone Caetani, 1974).

69. Dwight M. Donaldson, "Temporary Marriage in Iran," *The Moslem World* XXVI, no. 4 (October 1936): 358–361.

70. Conti Rossini, *Principi*, 573–575, 649, 732–735.

71. G. J. Fleming, "Beni Amer Marriage Customs," *Sudan Notes and Records* 2, no. 1 (1919): 76; Conti Rossini, *Principi*, 732–733.

72. Conti Rossini, *Principi*, 732–735; Werner Münzinger, *Dei costumi e del diritto dei Bogos, traduzione dal tedesco a cura di A. Ostini*, con prefazione di I. M. Ziegler (Rome: Ministero degli Affari Esteri, 1891); Conti Rossini, *Principi*, 571–578 and 647–651.

73. Schacht, *An Introduction*, 163–166.

74. Conti Rossini, *Principi*, 580–584, 653–654.

75. Conti Rossini, *Principi*, 732–735.

76. John Winter Crowfoot, "Wedding Customs in the Northern Sudan," *Sudan Notes and Records* V, no. 1 and 2 (1922): 17–19.

77. Pollera, *I Baria e i Cunama*, 161–165, 171; Münzinger, *Studi sull'Africa*, 402.

78. Pollera, *I Baria e i Cunama*, 169, 173.

79. John L. Comaroff, "Introduction," in *The Meaning of Marriage Payments* (London: Academic Press, 1980), 4.

80. Comaroff, "Introduction," 36, 39; Alan Barnard, "Rules and Prohibitions: The Form and Content of Human Kinship," in *Companion Encyclopedia of Anthropology*, ed. Tim Ingold (London: Routledge, 1997), 797.

81. Alfred Reginald Radcliffe-Brown, "Introduction," in *African Systems of Kinship and Marriage*, ed. Alfred Reginald Radcliffe-Brown and Daryll Forde (London: Oxford University Press, 1950), 46.

82. Comaroff, "Introduction," 16.

83. Fox, *Kinship and Marriage*, 119.

84. It is called *kirma* in the Bilein, *semmai madharata* in Tigré, *sedaq* in the Hedareb, and as *naga* in the Rashaida. "Traditions That Oppress Women," *Voice of Eritrean Women* (Spring 1990): 6; Siegfried Frederick Nadel, "Notes on Beni Amer Society," *Sudan Notes and Records* 26 (1945): 79–80.

85. Conti Rossini, *Principi*, 569–570, 653.

86. After the times of Mohammed, the *mahr* became the legitimate compensation for a woman, it was entirely her property and remained her own if the marriage was dissolved. *Mahr* in Islamic times technically became dower, according to our classification, because property was given directly to the woman. *Encyclopaedia of Islam*, 78–79.

87. Pasternak, Ember, and Ember, *Sex, Gender, and Kinship*, 152–156.

88. So for example among the Tigré, nobles would give eleven cows and eight

MTDs from the mother, two MTDs from the grandfather along with a rug and a cloak. Serfs would give seven MTDs from the mother, one MTD from the grandfather, and a rug and a cloak. Enno Littmann, *Publications of the Princeton Expedition to Abyssinia, II* (Leiden: E. J. Brill, 1910), 124.

89. For Bilein it was fixed at ten cows for the marriage of a virgin and three for the marriage of a widow. Conti Rossini, *Principi*, 573–575, 649–651.

90. The Nabtab are direct descendants of Amer Ali, the founder of the Beni Amir; J. H. Goldsmith, "Marriage Customs of the Beni Amer Tribe," *Sudan Notes and Records* 3, no. 4 (1920): 293.

91. Fleming, "Beni Amer Marriage Customs," 76; Conti Rossini, *Principi*, 732–733.

92. Giorgio Ausenda, "Leisurely Nomads: the Hadendowa (Beja) of the Gash Delta and their Transition to Sedentary Village Life" (Ph.D. thesis, University of Michigan, Ann Arbor, 1987), 204, 217.

93. Zenawi Haile, "The Significance of Marriage Payments on Marriage in the Eritrean Family Law" (LL.B senior thesis, University of Asmara, 1999), 37.

94. Zenawi Haile, "The Significance of Marriage Payments," 23, citing Abdul Kader.

95. Pollera, *I Baria e i Cunama*, 161 162, *The Native Peoples*, 147–148.

96. Pasternak, Ember, and Ember, *Sex, Gender, and Kinship*, 152–156.

97. Richard A. Posner, *Sex and Reason* (Cambridge, Mass.: Harvard University Press, 1992), 159–160.

98. Medanie Habtezghi, "Customary Marriage and Divorce in Blin Society" (senior LL.B thesis, University of Asmara, 1999), 22, 20; Pollera, *I Baria e i Cunama*, 162.

99. Capomazza, *Istituzioni*, 37; Capomazza, *Il diritto*, 63–69,124–130, 178–184. But see article 16 of *Adkeme Melega*, leaving it undetermined. See also article 2 of *Mehen Mahaza*, article 2 of *Mai Adgi*, and article 2 of *Enda Fegrai*.

100. According to Zerehawariat Almedai, a respected Tigrinya elder, if a highland woman was unmarried or didn't receive a dowry, she had the right to a share of land. Zenawi Haile, "The Significance of Marriage Payments," 22.

101. Dennis J. Duncanson, "Sir'At 'Adkeme Milga': A Native Law Code of Eritrea," *Africa* XIX, no. 2 April (1949): 144.

102. Conti Rossini, *Principi*, 223–226.

103. Schacht, *An Introduction*, 167; J. Spencer Trimingham, *The Influence of Islam upon Africa* (London: Longman, 1980), 44–45.

104. Eritrean Assembly, "New Customary Law of the Beni Amer Tribes," typescript, Asmara, 1 June 1960; the Beni Amir used to reckon the dowry as equivalent to seven slave girls *ammat*, the actual dowry being two she-camels, ten cows, and 100 rials. A. Paul, "Notes on the Beni Amer," *Sudan Notes and Records* XXXI, pt. 2 (1950): 232.

105. Barnes, "Marriage, Exchange and the Meaning of Corporations," 111.

106. Conti Rossini, *Principi*, 209, 220–222, 237–240.

107. Conti Rossini, *Principi*, 211.

108. George Alexander Wilken, *Over de Verwantschap en het Huwelijks—er erfrecht bij de Volken van den Indischen Archipel* (Leiden: Brill, 1883), 26–28; Barnard, "Rules and Prohibitions," 797.

109. Conti Rossini, *Principi*, 219.

110. Conti Rossini, *Principi*, 231.

111. Conti Rossini, *Principi*, 251–252.

112. Conti Rossini, *Principi*, 575–578.

113. Conti Rossini, *Principi*, 649–651.

114. Pollera, *I Baria e i Cunama*, 162–163, 166.

115. In Islamic societies, an unmarried female slave was at the disposal of her owner as a concubine. A man could not have two slaves as concubines if their relationship was within the forbidden degrees of consanguinity, affinity, or fosterage. Schacht, *An Introduction*, 127, 162.

116. Perini, *Di qua dal Marèb*, 408–409.

117. Conti Rossini, *Principi*, 255.

118. Capomazza, *Istituzioni*, 60.

119. Capomazza, *Il diritto*, 78.

120. Capomazza, *La legge*, 59–63.

121. Rodén, *Le tribù*, 215.

122. Rodén, *Le tribù*, 185.

123. Alberto Sbacchi, *Ethiopia under Mussolini: Fascism and the Colonial Experience* (London: Zed Books, 1985), 172.

124. Ruth Iyob, personal communication, 1998. A legacy of this period is the unfair and insulting designation of *gual-bedama* (the child of the *madama*) still given often to maids employed by Europeans in Eritrea. Araia Tseggai, "Eritrean Women and Italian Soldiers: Status of Eritrean Women under Italian Rule," *Journal of Eritrean Studies* IV, no. 1 and 2 (1989/1990): 11.

125. Giulia Barrera, *Dangerous Liaisons: Colonial Concubinage in Eritrea, 1890–1941*, Program of African Studies Northwestern University, Working Paper 1 (Evanston, Ill.: Northwestern University Press, 1996), 3.

126. James Firebrace and Stuart Holland, *Never Kneel Down: Drought, Development and Liberation in Eritrea* (Trenton, N.J.: Red Sea Press, 1985), 157; Eritrean People's Liberation Front, *Political Report and National Democratic Programme* (The Field: EPLF, 1987), 175.

127. Tom Killion, ed., *Historical Dictionary of Eritrea* (Lanham, Md.: Scarecrow Press, 1998), 348–349. In Asmara, there are basically two kinds of prostitutes. Many of them, the poorest ones, live in an area of the city called *cerhi*. All of the area is reserved for them; very few men live there. These women are not socially integrated. The situation of the other group, women working in bars, is different. They have a better status and they are more socially inte-

grated. A "family man" can have a permanent relationship with one of these women.

128. Customary Law of Acchele Guzay, Chapter XIV, arts. 95–116.

129. Capomazza, *Il diritto*, 157–158.

130. Eritrean Assembly, "New Customary Law of the Beni Amer Tribes," art. 17, 4–5.

131. See also the code of *Saharti, Lamza, Uocarti,* art. 26. Petazzi, *L'odierno diritto penale,* 33, 35.

132. Petazzi, *L'odierno diritto penale*, 35–36.

133. Capomazza, *Il diritto*, 70.

134. Capomazza, *Il diritto*, 137.

135. Ignazio Guidi, *Il Fetha Nagast o legislazione dei re. codice ecclesiastico e civile di Abissinia*, Pubblicazioni scientifiche del R. Istituto Orientale di Napoli (Rome: Tipografia Casa Ed. Italiana, 1897), 511.

136. Conti Rossini, *Principi*, 752.

137. Pollera, *I Baria e i Cunama*, 167–168.

138. *Scioatte Anseba*, arts. 13–15; *Zeban Serao Ennadocò*, art. 8; *Adgena Tegeleba*, art. 62; *Mehen Mahaza*, art. 31.

139. But see also *Mai Adgi*, art. 19; Capomazza, *Il diritto*, 157–158; Petazzi, *L'odierno diritto penale*, 32.

140. Petazzi, *L'odierno diritto penale*, 32. We should note that the article number is according to Petazzi's abridgement of criminal rules concerning traditional laws of Hamasien and consequently does not necessarily bear any relation to the sequence in each individual code.

141. Customary Law of Acchele Guzay, arts. 95–96.

142. Capomazza, *Istituzioni*, 109–111.

143. Münzinger, *Dei costumi*, 255.

144. Customary Law of Acchele Guzay, Chapter XIV, arts. 95–116, *Adgena Tegeleba*, art. 104.

145. Rodén, *Le tribù*, 303–304.

146. Carlo Conti Rossini, "Al Ragali," *Estratti dal Bollettino della Società Italiana di Esplorazioni Geografiche e Commerciali, Anni 1903–1904* (Milan: Stabilimento Tipografico Bellini, 1903), 51–52.

147. *Eritrea Profile*, "Eritrean Traditions and Customs," 21 June 1997, 7.

148. Pollera, *The Native Peoples*, 113.

149. Wilfred Thesiger, *The Danakil Diary: Journeys through Abyssinia, 1930–43* (London: Harper Collins, 1996), 121.

150. *Eritrea Profile*, "Eritrean Traditions and Customs," 12 July 1997, 7.

151. Capomazza, *Istituzioni*, 109–111.

152. Eritrean Assembly, "New Customary Law of the Beni Amer Tribes," typescript, Asmara, 1 June 1960, 4–5.

153. Conti Rossini, "Al Ragali," 51.

154. Trish Silkin, personal communication, 22 December 1988.

155. Robert Allen Sedler, "The Development of Legal Systems: the Ethiopian Experience," *Iowa Law Review* 53, no. 3 (1967): 600. Limited protection was granted to the woman; in the case of breakdown of the union she had the right to be maintained for a certain number of months (art. 717.2). Children born or conceived pending an irregular union were assisted by a presumption of paternity similar to that of marriage (arts. 741–745).

156. Ignazio Castellucci, "Il nuovo diritto eritreo: il diritto di famiglia," Lyda Favali, Elisabetta Grande, and Marco Guadagni, eds., *New Law for New States* (Torino: L'Harmattan, 1998), 196–197.

157. Veronica Rentmeesters, "Eritrea: Will Women's Liberation Survive the Liberation Struggle?" paper presented to the Annual Meeting of the African Studies Association, Atlanta, Georgia, 1989, 4.

158. Internal EPLF document, Department of Justice, The Field, 1988.

159. Trish Silkin, personal communication, 22 December 1988.

160. Amrit Wilson, *Women and the Eritrean Revolution: The Challenge Road* (Trenton, N.J.: Red Sea Press, 1991), 134.

161. Yirgalem Woldegabriel, "Women and Land Ownership System in Highland Eritrea" (LL.B senior thesis, University of Asmara, 1998), 12.

162. Luol Ghebreab, "Interview," *Voice of Eritrean Women*, New York, September 1983, 18.

163. Wilson, *Women and the Eritrean Revolution*, 136–138.

164. Zenawi Haile, "The Significance of Marriage Payments," 30.

165. The highest in seniority being Luol Ghebreab (ranked 39 in the hierarchy) followed by Askalu Menkerios (ranked 43 in the hierarchy). Roy Pateman, "Liberté, Egalité, Fraternité: Aspects of the Eritrean Revolution," *The Journal of Modern African Studies* 28, no. 3 (1990): 465.

166. National Statistics Office, "Eritrea," 75, 45.

167. U.S. Department of State, "Eritrea."

168. The Constitution of Eritrea, ratified by the Constituent Assembly on 23 May 1997, III. Articles 14, 5, 22.

169. Bereket Habte Selassie and Richard A. Rosen, "The Eritrean Constitutional Process: An Interview with Dr. Bereket Habte Selassie," *Eritrean Studies Review* 3, no. 1 (1999): 167.

170. Bereket Habte Selassie and Rosen, "The Eritrean Constitutional Process," 157.

171. Articles 41 through 52 of the 1987 EPLF code were grafted onto the 1960 code (after art. 66). Zenawi Haile, "The Significance of Marriage Payments," 30.

172. Castellucci, "Il nuovo diritto eritreo," 208.

173. Peter Hodgin, "An Introduction to Eritrea's Ongoing Revolution: Wom-

en's Nationalist Mobilization and Gender Politics in Post-War Eritrea," *Eritrean Studies Review* 2, no. 1 (1997): 100–101.

174. Abraham Desta, "Establishment of Paternity," 29.

175. AbdulNasser Abdella, "The Institution of Family Arbitration in Eritrea" (senior LL.B. thesis, University of Asmara, 1999), 32–34, 39.

176. AbdulNasser Abdella, "The Institution of Family Arbitration," 44, 50.

177. Castellucci, "Il nuovo diritto eritreo," 204.

178. Zenawi Haile, "The Significance of Marriage Payments," 51–54.

9. Female Genital Mutilation

1. Friedrich Nietzsche, *Jenseits Von Gut und Böse* (Leipzig: Druck und Verlag, 1896), 46.

2. The choice of the appropriate word to refer to the practice has been debated at length. We are aware that the term mutilation has had a negative connotation in Western societies and is resented in societies that practice FGM. We agreed in the end to use it because "circumcision" is imprecise and can easily be conflated with the removal of the prepuce in the male, a practice which has a meaning and consequences far removed from the operation on a female. Moreover, when international organizations and even nation-states, after a long struggle, have finally decided to accept and adopt the term, it would be anachronistic not to do the same. The use of the acronym FGM (Female Genital Mutilation) has been recommended by the WHO since 1995 and is now usually used in UN documents and general discourse. WHO, *Female Genital Mutilation: Report of a WHO Technical Working Group*, 17–19 July 1995, Geneva, 1996.

3. WHO/UNICEF/UNFPA, *Female Genital Mutilation: A Joint WHO/ UNICEF/UNFPA Statement* (Geneva: WHO, 1997), 5.

4. Jane Wambui Kiragu, "Female Genital Mutilation/Female Circumcision: A Human Rights and Legal Dimension for Eradication," in *Proceedings of the Expert Meeting on Female Genital Mutilation*, ed. Els Leye, Maria de Bruyn, and Stan Meuwese, Ghent-Belgium, 5–7 November 1998, Reprinted in Rising Daughters Aware, http://www.fgm.org/ProceedExpert.html p.22.

5. Dissenting opinion of Justice Louis D. Brandeis in *Olmstead v. United States, 277 U.S. 438 (1928)*. Brandeis wrote of the framers of the U.S. Constitution: "They conferred, as against the government, the right to be let alone— the most comprehensive of rights and the right most valued by civilized men."

6. Jomo Kenyatta, *Facing Mount Kenya: The Tribal Life of the Gikuyu* (London: Secker and Warburg, 1938), 133.

7. Robyn Cerny Smith, "Female Circumcision: Bringing Women's Perspectives into the International Debate," *Southern California Law Review* 65, no. 5 (1992): 2470.

8. For a psycho-medical approach and for more details, see Michel Erlich,

La femme blessée: essai sur les mutilations sexuelles feminines (Paris: L'Harmattan, 1986), 177–182.

9. Significantly, this consideration has been expressly used to ban FGM in an official document: *The Plan of Action for Combating Violence against Women*, adopted by the Council of Europe in 1997, document EG-S-VL (97)1 (art. 10.99): "Cultural relativism often surfaces, and inaction is justified out of respect for different traditions and cultures."

10. Stanlie M. James, "Shades of Othering: Reflections on Female Circumcision/Genital Mutilation," *Signs* 23, no. 4 (1998): 1034.

11. Many scholars have shown their awareness of this problem. Among anthropological studies in particular, see Clifford Geertz, "The Cerebral Savage," *Encounter* 28 (1967): 25–32; and Edmond Leach, "Glimpses of Unmentionable in the History of British Social Anthropology," *Annual Review of Anthropology* 13 (1984): 22.

12. In Akan areas of Ghana, a potential chief's body is examined to ensure that it is free of disfigurement (including male circumcision). However, many families with no possibility of producing a chief make short incisions on the side of a boy's face beside the eyebrow—especially if an earlier child has died young—to discourage evil spirits from taking the child, thus marked as made imperfect, before his time. Richard Greenfield, personal communication, 2000.

13. See James Q. Whitman, "At the Origins of Law and the State: Supervision of Violence, Mutilation of Bodies, or Setting of Prices?" *Chicago Kent Law Review* 71, no. 1 (1996): 83 for a critical appraisal of the theory of self-help fully developed by Jhering to explain the origin of the early state.

14. Whitman, "At the Origins of Law," 79.

15. Mary Douglas, *Purity and Danger: An Analysis of Concepts of Pollution and Taboo* (New York: Praeger, 1966), 137–138.

16. Michel Erlich, *La mutilation* (Paris: Presses Universitaires de France, 1990), 10.

17. Erlich, *La mutilation*, 9–13.

18. WHO, *Female Genital Mutilation*, 6.

19. It is also known as <u>khifād</u> (reduction). In Arabic, *tahūr* means circumcision (literally, purification). It is also used to refer to excision, called *tahūra* or *tahara* in Egypt and Sudan. Asma el Dareer, *Woman, Why Do You Weep?* (London: Zed Press, 1992), 11; Erlich, *La femme blessée*, 192.

20. It is called "Pharaonic" in Sudan, because it is presumed to have its origins in Egypt, and "Sudanese" in Egypt because it is presumed to have its origins in Sudan. Séverine Auffret, *Des couteaux contre des femmes-de l'excision* (Paris: Des Femmes, 1982), 17.

21. Carl Gösta Widstrand, "Female Infibulation," *Studia Ethnographica Upsaliensia* 20 (1964): 108.

22. Lilian Passmore Sanderson, *Against the Mutilation of Women* (London: Ithaca Press, 1981), 18.

23. Maria de Bruyn, "Socio-Cultural Aspects of Female Genital Cutting"; Leye, De Bruyn, and Meuwese, *Proceedings*, 64.

24. Fran P. Hosken, Female Genital Mutilation (FGM), Women's International Network (WIN) News, 1998, Web site: http://feminist.com/fgm.htm.

25. Efua Dorkenoo, *Cutting the Rose: Female Genital Mutilation—The Practice and Its Prevention* (London: Minority Rights Publications, 1995), 32.

26. Fran P. Hosken, *The Hosken Report* (Lexington, Mass.: Women's International Network News, 1982), 239; De Bruyn, "Socio-Cultural Aspects," 63.

27. For detailed case reporting of FGM in Europe and the U.S. during the last two centuries, see Erlich, *La mutilation*, 61.

28. Abdalla Raqiya Haji Dualeh, *Sisters in Affliction: Circumcision and Infibulation of Women in Africa* (London: Zed Press, 1982), 63; Felix Bryk, *Sex and Circumcision: A Study of Phallic Worship and Mutilation in Men and Women* (North Hollywood, Calif.: Brandon House, 1967), 285.

29. Luigi Luca Cavalli-Sforza, Paolo Menozzi, and Alberto Piazza, *Storia e Geografia dei Geni Umani* (Milano: Adelphi, 1997); Merritt Ruhlen, *The Origin of the Language: Tracing the Evolution of the Mother Tongue* (New York: John Wiley & Sons, 1994).

30. R. A. Fisher, "The Wave of Advance of Advantageous Genes," *Annals of Eugenics* 7 (1936–1937): 355–369; Albert J. Ammerman and Luigi Luca Cavalli Sforza, "A Population Model for the Diffusion of Early Farming in Europe," in *The Explanation of Culture Change*, ed. Colin Renfrew (London: Duckworth, 1973), 343–357.

31. Jared Diamond, *Guns, Germs, and Steel: The Fates of Human Societies* (New York: W. W. Norton & Company, 1997), 392–393.

32. Erlich, *La femme blessée*, 198–200.

33. René Nelli, *Erotique et civilisation* (Paris: Weber, 1972), cited by Erlich, *La femme blessée*, 275.

34. Alfred Dieck, "Beschneidung von Frauen und Mannern in vorund fruhgeschichtlicher Zeit," *Curare* 4 (1981): 77–84, cited in Erlich, *La femme blessée*, 39.

35. Abdalla Raqiya Haji Dualeh, *Sisters in Affliction*, 68.

36. They are mentioned in Erlich, *La femme blessée*, 40–41.

37. See 15 Greek papyri in the British Museum; Bernardino Peyron, 1841, in Johann Jakob Bachofen, *Das Mutterecht: Eine Untersuchung Über die Gynaikokratie der alten Welt nach ihrer religiosen und rechtlichen Natur, Mutterecht* (Stuttgart: Krais & Hoffmann, 1861), 838, cited in Erlich, *La femme blessée*, 41.

38. De Mari Erythraeo, 61, cited in Erlich, *La femme blessée*, 41.

39. Strabo 16, 4.9; cited in, Erlich, *La femme blessée*, 41.

40. Erlich, *La femme blessée*, 47.

41. Otto F. A. Meinardus, *Christian Egypt: Faith and Life* (Cairo: American University Press, 1970), 327–328.

42. Heinrich Ploss and Max Bartels, *Das Weib in der Natur und Völkerkunde*, I (Leipzig: Th. Grieben's Verlag, 1895), 179.

43. *Istoria Venetiana*, cited by Widstrand, "Female Infibulation," 118 148.

44. Erlich, *La femme blessée*, 56.

45. Erlich, *La femme blessée*, 55.

46. I. Olenick, *International Family Planning Perspectives* 24, no. 1 (1998): 47–49; Dana Carr, *Female Genital Cutting* (Calverton: Macro International, September 1997), 11, 33. The survey was funded by the U.S. Agency for International Development. Of those responding to the survey, 37.6 percent were Muslim and 62.4 percent Christian. Even if we accept the Eritrean government's often-made pronouncement that 50 percent of the population is Christian, the Muslims are underrepresented by 20 percent.

47. Ninety-two percent of Tigrinya; 99 percent of Tigré; 96 percent of Saho; 100 percent of Nara; 99 percent of Bilein; 99 percent of Afar; 100 percent of Hedareb; 98 percent of Kunama.

48. Carr, *Female Genital Cutting*, 80.

49. Carr, *Female Genital Cutting*, 13.

50. Eighty percent of women and 77 percent of men with secondary education oppose FGM, compared with 24 percent of women and 18 percent of men with no formal education. See Carr, *Female Genital Cutting*, 75, 71.

51. Carr, *Female Genital Cutting*, 42, 71, 79.

52. Friederike Kemink, *Die Tegreñña-Frauen in Eritrea* (Stuttgart: Franz Steiner Verlag, 1991), 70.

53. William A. Shack, *The Central Ethiopians* (London: International African Institute, 1974), 37.

54. Esther K. Hicks, *Infibulation: Female Mutilation in Islamic Northeastern Africa* (New Brunswick, N.J.: Transaction, 1996), 256–257; Widstrand, "Female Infibulation," 105; "Traditions that Oppress Women in Eritrea," *Voice of Eritrean Women* (Spring 1989): 6; Alexander Naty, personal communication; Amrit Wilson, *Women and the Eritrean Revolution: The Challenge Road* (Trenton, N.J.: Red Sea Press, 1991), 127.

55. Hosken, *The Hosken Report*, 144.

56. Karl Gustav Rodén, *Le tribù dei Mensa—Storia, legge e costumi, traduzione italiana dalla lingua Tigré* (Stockholm: Nordiska Boktryckeriet, 1913), 223.

57. Werner Münzinger, *Ostafrikanische Studien* (Schaffhausen: Ff. Hurtersche, 1864), 143–144; Werner Münzinger, *Dei costumi e del diritto dei Bogos, traduzione dal tedesco a cura di A. Ostini*, con prefazione di I. M. Ziegler (Rome: Ministero degli Affari Esteri, 1891), 51–52.

58. Felice Ostini, *Trattato di diritto consuetudinario dell'Eritrea* (Rome: Officina Grafica—Corriere Eritreo, 1956), 126.

59. Heinrich Ploss, "Die Operative Behandlung der weiblichen Geschlechts-

theile bei verschiedenen Volkern," *Zeitschrift fur Ethnologie* 3 (1871): 381–397; Ostini, *Trattato*, 109, 167.

60. Siegfried Frederick Nadel, "Notes on Beni Amer Society," *Sudan Notes and Records* 26 (1945): 76.

61. Giorgio Ausenda, "Leisurely Nomads: The Hadendowa (Beja) of the Gash Delta and Their Transition to Sedentary Village Life" (Ph.D. dissertation, University of Michigan, Ann Arbor, 1987), 213.

62. Anders Hjort af Ornäs, *Responsible Man: The Atmaan Beja of North-eastern Sudan* (Uppsala: Nordiska Afrikainstitutet, 1991), 105.

63. Aidan W. Southall, "On Chastity in Africa," *Uganda Journal* 24, no. 2 (1960): 208; Widstrand specifies the Asaorta Saho; Widstrand, "Female Infibulation," 100. Professor Naty agrees with him. Alexander Naty, personal communication, 1999.

64. Wilfred Thesiger, *The Danakil Diary: Journeys through Abyssinia, 1930–34* (London: Harper Collins, 1996), 161.

65. Hicks, *Infibulation*, 255.

66. Thesiger, *The Danakil Diary*, 161.

67. F. Scaramucci and Enrico Hillyer Giglioli, "Notizie sul Danakil," *Archivio per l'Antropologia e l'Etnologia* 14 (1884): 17–44.

68. Denis de Rivoyre, *Aux pays de Soudan, Bogos, Mensah, Souakim* (Paris: Eplon, 1885), 17; Dr. Santelli, "Les Danakils," *Bulletin de la Societé et d'Anthropologie* 4, no. 6 (1893): 500; A. Courbon, "Observations topographiques et médicales recueillies dans un voyage à l'isthme de Suez, sur le littoral de la Mer Rouge et en Abyssinie" (Thèse de médecine 33, 1861), 53; L. Faurot, *Voyage au Golfe de Tadjoura*, extract from *Revue de l'Afrique Francaise* (Paris: Barbier, 1886), 34.

69. Kenyatta, *Facing Mount Kenya*, 46.

70. Kenyatta, *Facing Mount Kenya*, 146.

71. C. Lamb, "Female Excision: The Feminist Conundrum," *UFAHAMU* 20/3 (1992): 13–31.

72. Monika Vizedom, *Rites and Relationships*, Sage Research Papers in the Social Sciences 4 (Beverly Hills, Calif.: Sage Publications, 1976), citing Arnold van Gennep, 19.

73. Asma el Dareer, *Woman, Why Do You Weep?* 73; Wilson, *Women and the Eritrean Revolution*, 128; Alexander Naty, personal communication, 1999; M. Zaborowski, "La circoncision, ses origines et sa repartition en Afrique et au Madagascar," *Bulletin de la Societé d'Anthropologie* (18 January 1894).

74. Widstrand, "Female Infibulation," 122.

75. Meinardus, *Christian Egypt: Faith and Life*, 319–322.

76. Mircea Eliade, *The Sacred and the Profane: The Nature of Religion*, trans. Willard R. Trask (New York: Harvest, 1959), 181.

77. Edward Gibbon, *The History of the Decline and Fall of the Roman Empire*,

VI (London: The Folio Society, 1987), 83; Asma el Dareer, *Woman, Why Do You Weep?* 74; for Eritrea: Alexander Naty, personal communication, 1999.

78. In Tigrinya the same word is used for the female and male operation—*mekinshab*. In the Kunama language, *mara*, which means blood, also means leader. We might wonder if this is typical of a matrilineal society.

79. Hanny Lightfoot-Klein, *A Woman's Odyssey into Africa: Tracks across a Life* (New York: Haworth Press, 1992), 3.

80. Erlich, *La femme blessée*, 193; Edvige Bilotti, "The Practice of Female Genital Mutilation," *Mediterranean Review* 3, no. 2 (1996–1997): 6.

81. See Wilson, *Women and the Eritrean Revolution*, 128.

82. David Cohen, *Dictionnaire des racines sémitiques* (Paris: Mouton, 1976), 35.

83. Eliade, *The Sacred and the Profane*, chapter 1, in particular, 20–24.

84. Alison T. Slack, "Female Circumcision: A Critical Appraisal." *Human Rights Quarterly* 10, no. 4 (1988): 459–460.

85. Erlich, *La femme blessée*, 191–196.

86. Sanderson, *Against the Mutilation of Women*, 51; Abdalla Raqiya Haji Dualeh, *Sisters in Affliction*, 61.

87. Zaborowski, "La circoncision," 89; Erlich, *La femme blessée*, 174–177.

88. Édouard Duchenet, *Histoires Somalies: la malice des primitifs* (Paris: Larose, 1936), 165; Erlich, *La femme blessée*, 175.

89. De Bruyn, "Socio-Cultural Aspects," 69.

90. Ladislav Holy, *Religion and Custom in a Muslim Society: The Berti of Sudan* (Cambridge: Cambridge University Press, 1991), 167.

91. "Traditions that Oppress Women in Eritrea," *Voice of Eritrean Women* (Winter 1989): 8; Alexander Naty, personal communication, 1999.

92. Belkis Wolde Giorgis, *Female Circumcision in Africa* (Addis Ababa: United Nations Economic Commission for Africa, 1981), 16, citing George C. Savard, *The Population of Ethiopia II* (Addis Ababa, 1970).

93. Auffret, *Des couteaux*, 149, 155.

94. Henry Ansgar Kelly, *The Devil at Baptism: Ritual, Theology, and Drama* (Ithaca, N.Y.: Cornell University Press, 1985), 33.

95. Sanderson, *Against the Mutilation of Women*, 46.

96. Genital mutilation was universal, and usually involved the partial or total amputation of the clitoris and prepuce. It was performed on day fourteen of life by a professional female exciser—*gherazit*. When the Falasha arrived in Israel the practice was discontinued. See Nimrod Grisaru, Simcha Lezer, and Robert H. Belmaker, "Ritual Female Genital Surgery among Ethiopian Jews," *Archives of Sexual Behavior* 26 (1997): 211–215.

97. Manoel de Almeida, "The History of High Ethiopia or Abassia," in *Some Records of Ethiopia, 1593–1646*, trans. and ed. C. F. Beckingham and G. W. B. Huntingford (London: Hakluyt Society, 1954); August Dillmann, *Über die*

Regierung, insbesondere die Kirchenordnung des Königs Zar'a Jakob (Berlin: Verlag der Königlichen, Akademie der Wissenschaften, 1884), 71–72.

98. On these, see Erlich, *La mutilation*, 57–59.

99. Erlich, *La mutilation*, 61.

100. Genesis 34:14: "We cannot do this thing, to give our sister to one that is uncircumcised"; Exodus 4:25–26: "Then Zipporah took a sharp stone, and cut off the foreskin of her son . . . and said surely a bloody husband art thou to me. So he let him go: then she said, A bloody husband thou art, because of the circumcision"; Leviticus 19:23: "And when ye shall come into the land and shall have planted all manner of trees for food, then ye shall count the fruit thereof as uncircumcised: three years shall it be as uncircumcised unto you: it shall not be eaten off."

101. Erlich, *La mutilation*, 60–62.

102. Erlich, *La mutilation*, 63–64.

103. For more detail, see Erlich, *La femme blessée*, 198–200.

104. On this point, see the comment of Sami A. Aldeeb Abu-Sahlieh, "To Mutilate in the Name of Jehovah or Allah: Legitimization of Male and Female Circumcision," New Enlarged Edition, 1994.

105. Holy, *Religion and Custom*, 216, citing Ghazali.

106. According to al-Nawawi, "circumcision is compulsory, *wadjib,* according to al-Shafi'i and other doctors," while it is a *sunna* according to the majority and according to Malik. Al-Shāfiʿi deems that it is compulsory for men and women. For women, circumcision will involve only the excision of the prepuce. The *Risāla* of al-Qayrāwanī prescribes that "circumcision is a traditional obligation for the male child, while for women excision is just a recommendation." Abu Muh'ammad Abdallah Ibn Abi Zayd al-Qayrāwanī, *La Risāla,* trans. Leon Bercher (Algiers: Editions populaires de l'armée, 1983). For a detailed description, see Sami A. Aldeeb Abu-Sahlieh, "To Mutilate," Chapter II, 3 and 4. See also the same author's *Male and Female Circumcision in the Jewish, Christian, and Muslim Communities: Religious Debate* (Beirut: Riad El-Rayyes Books, 2000).

107. Joan Rosita Torr Forbes, *Women's Voices on Africa* , ed. Patricia W. Romero (Princeton: Markus Wiener, 1992), 149.

108. De Almeida, "The History of High Ethiopia or Abassia," 62; Samuel Gobat, "Journal of Three Year's Residence in Abyssinia, in Furtherance of the Objects of the Church Missionary Society," *Journal of the Royal Geographical Society* IV (1834): 271.

109. Dillmann, *Über die Regierung,* 71–72.

110. Dillmann, *Über die Regierung,* 41.

111. Arnold Hugh Martin Jones and Elizabeth Monroe, *A History of Ethiopia* (Oxford: Clarendon Press, 1968), 8.

112. James Bruce, *Travels to Discover the Source of the Nile in the Years 1768, 1769, 1770, 1771, 1772 & 1773,* Vol. 3 (Westmead: Gregg International, 1972), 348–349.

113. Dorkenoo, *Cutting the Rose*, 118. Among the Berti of Sudan, it has been observed that prolonged exposure to a media campaign that stresses the harmful medical consequences of pharaonic infibulation, and also to arguments that the practice is not part of proper Islamic religion, has led to some villages changing to *sunna* circumcision; Amna ElSadig Badri and Edith H. Grotberg, "Intellectual Women: New Approach to Sudanese Development," *The Ahfad Journal* 6, no. 2 (1989): 9. In these increasingly more fundamentalist days, a view is being promulgated that pharaonic circumcision is *šuğhūl šaytān* (the work of the devil and not permitted by the Prophet). Holy, *Religion and Custom*, 170.

114. Scilla McLean, ed., *Minority Rights Group Draft Report, No. 47, on Excision and Infibulation Operations on Female Genitals* (London: Minority Rights Group, 1980), 6.

115. François Houtart, "The Social Revolution in Eritrea," in *Behind the War in Eritrea*, ed. Basil Davidson et al. (Nottingham: Spokesman, 1980), 108.

116. Hanny Lightfoot-Klein, *Prisoners of Ritual: An Odyssey into Female Genital Circumcision in Africa* (New York: Haworth Press, 1989), 51.

117. Dorkenoo, *Cutting the Rose*, 93–94.

118. U.S. Department of State; *Eritrea Country Report on Human Rights Practices for 1997; Released by the Bureau of Democracy, Human Rights, and Labor*, 30 January 1998.

119. U.S. Department of State, *Eritrea*.

120. See also arts. 28.1 and 29.

121. National Committee on the United Nations Convention on the Elimination of Discrimination against Women: Web Page: http://www.feminist.org/research/cedawmain.html, Copyright 1996, The Feminist Majority Foundation and New Media Publishing Inc.

122. Slack, "Female Circumcision," 481.

123. Angela Gilliam, "Women's Equality and National Liberation," in *Third World Women and the Politics of Feminism*, ed. Chandra Talpade Mohanty, Ann Russo, and Lourdes Torres (Bloomington: Indiana University Press, 1991), 218–219.

124. James, "Shades of Othering," 1033.

125. Chandra Talpade Mohanty, "Cartographies of Struggle: Third World Women and the Politics of Feminism," in Mohanty, Russo, and Torres, *Third World Women*, 58.

126. WHO/UNICEF/UNFPA, *Female Genital Mutilation*, 2.

127. The *Vienna Declaration & Programme of Action*, Vienna, Third World Conference on Human Rights, 14–25 June 1993 (UN Doc. A/CONF. 157/23, 12 July 1993). See, in particular, arts. 18, 38, 49.

128. United Nations, *The Beijing International Declaration and Platform of Action*, in UN *Report of the Fourth World Conference on Women*, Beijing, 4–15 Sep-

tember 1995 (UN Doc. A/CONF.177/20, 17 October 1995 and A/CONF. 177/20/Add.1, 27 October 1995), reprinted in United Nations Department of Public Information, New York, 1996.

129. Female genital surgeries were also expressly banned in the declarations and programs of actions adopted by the UN at the Copenhagen World Summit on Social Development (1995) and the International Conference on Population and Development, held in Cairo in 1996. Documents with regional application are, for Africa, the African Charter on Human and Peoples' Rights; and for Europe, the *Final Report of Activities of the Group of Specialists for Combating Violence against Women*, adopted by the Council of Europe, which includes a Plan of Action for Combating Violence against Women (document EG-S-VL (97) 1).

130. Erika Sussman, "Contending with Culture: An Analysis of the Female Genital Mutilation Act of 1996," *Cornell International Law Journal* 31, no. 193 (1998): 208.

131. Including: the right to life; the right to protection against cruel, inhuman, and degrading treatment; the right to self-determination; the right to physical integrity; the right to health; the right to protection against discrimination.

132. United Nations, Convention on the Elimination of All Forms of Discrimination against Women, 18 Dec. 1979, U.N.G.A Res. 34/180, 34 U.N. GAOR Supp. (No.46) 194, U.N. Doc. A/34/830 (1979), entered into force 3 September 1981.

133. United Nations, Convention on the Rights of the Child, 20 Nov. 1989, U.N.G.A. Res. 44/25, annex 44 U.N. GAOR Supp. (No. 49) 167, U.N. Doc. A/44/49 (1989), entered into force 2 September 1990.

134. African Charter on the Rights and Welfare of the Child, OAU Doc. CAB/LEG/24.9/49 (1990).

135. Laws against FGM have been enacted in the U.S., Sweden, Norway, the United Kingdom, Canada, Australia, and New Zealand. Among African countries, the following have banned the practice: the Central African Republic, Senegal, Togo, Ivory Coast, Djibouti, Burkina Faso, Guinea, Tanzania, and Ghana.

136. The Banjul Declaration on Violence against Women adopted by the Symposium for Religious leaders and Medical Personnel on FGM as a Form of Violence, organized by the Inter-African Committee on Traditional Practices/ GAMCOTRAP, held in Banjul, The Gambia, 20–23 July 1998.

137. *Female Genital Mutilation Act* codified at 18 U.S.C. 116 (West Supp. 1998) and 22 U.S.C. 262K-2 (West Supp. 1998).

138. *UNESCO Proclamation of Masterpieces of the Oral and Intangible Heritage of Humanity, Eritrean Customary Laws (Southern and Central Highlands),* "Candidature from the State of Eritrea," Asmara, 2001, 8.

10. Creating Space in a Changing World for Traditional and Religious Law

1. Emma Goldman, *My Further Disillusionment in Russia* (New York: Doubleday & Page, 1924), 175–176.

2. For those readers interested in our analogy and unfamiliar with how Pirandello finishes his play; the author/director thinks about the matter for a day and decides after all that he cannot write a play for the characters. The first edition of the play ends with the curtain lines: *"E mi hanno fatto perdere una giornata!"*—"And they've made me lose a whole day." The play has much relevance to our quest; the characters have multiple personalities, and the action takes place on four levels. Eric Bentley, *The Pirandello Commentaries* (Evanston, Ill.: Northwestern University Press, 1986), 5, 64, 74.

3. For the case of socialist countries, see Gianmaria Ajani, "By Chance and Prestige: Legal Transplants in Russia and Eastern Europe," *American Journal of Comparative Law* (1995): 93–117.

4. Michael Hardt and Antonio Negri, *Empire* (Cambridge, Mass.: Harvard University Press, 2000), 18–19.

5. In Eritrea in particular it has to be recalled that during the Italian period, special codes were devised but never enacted.

6. Bereket Habte Selassie and Richard A. Rosen, "The Eritrean Constitutional Process: An Interview with Dr. Bereket Habte Selassie," *Eritrean Studies Review* 3, no. 1 (1999): 164.

7. For a detailed description, see Heinrich Scholler, "Ethiopian Constitutional Development," in *Jahrbuch Des Offentlichen Rechts Der Gegenwart* (Tübingen: J. C. B. Mohr, 1987), 502–564.

8. Isaias Afwerki, interview with Roy Pateman, Asmara, 21 September 1991.

9. A *National Charter for Eritrea* (Asmara: Adulis Printing Press, 1994), 19.

10. The G15 are all highly placed members of the PFDJ who had served as generals, ministers, and ambassadors; many were close personal friends and collaborators of the president even before the EPLF was founded in the 1970s. The group came together because of their disquiet at the president's handling of the war with Ethiopia and his opposition to the airing of alternative views in the growing independent press. The president refused to engage in dialogue with them.

11. Roy Pateman, "Eritrea Takes the World Stage," *Current History* 93, no. 83 (May 1994): 231.

12. Roy Pateman, "Liberté, Egalité, Fraternité: Aspects of the Eritrean Revolution," *The Journal of Modern African Studies* 28, no. 3 (1990): 457–472.

13. This seems particularly relevant in 2003 when both the U.S. and Israel seem consumed with this logic.

14. Bereket Habte Selassie, "Democracy and the Role of Parliament under the

Eritrean Constitution," *North Carolina Journal of International Law and Commercial Regulation* 24, no. 2 (1999): 259. He is citing an Eritrean elder.

15. Antonio Gambaro and Rodolfo Sacco, *Sistemi giuridici comparati* (Torino: Utet, 1996), 125–128.

16. Hardt and Negri, *Empire*, 147.

17. A great deal of attention was paid to customary law in the "independent homelands" of apartheid South Africa. No progressive felt comfortable in using these racist enclaves as a model; their traditional law was shunned and other traditional law systems suffered from guilt by association; Friederike Kemink, "The Tegreñña Customary Law Codes," *Paideuma* 37 (1991): 70.

18. T. W. Bennett and Jan Vermeulen, "Codification of Customary Law," *Journal of African Law* 24, no. 2 (1980): 207–208.

19. *Eritrea Profile*, "Reactivating Customary Practices on Environmental Protection and Management," 3 October 1998, 8.

20. Asmarom Legesse's team also consulted the archives of the Ministry of Local Government that include more than 30,000 pages of oral histories collected from every Eritrean ethnie by the EPLF from 1982 until 2000. The local government fighter-researchers were extremely thorough; the work on the Beni Amir alone took them three years to complete. One of us spent several hours talking with the two team leaders, Belai Araia and Berhane Abraham, and was immensely privileged to be the first outsider to have access to this material. All of the data including detailed genealogies of every Eritrean ethnie, sub-ethnie, and clan has been transferred to the computer and awaits final processing. The questionnaire included an exhaustive list of items relating to law and cultural practices and will form an incomparable resource for future Eritrean research. Belai Araia and Berhane Abraham, personal communication, Asmara, November–December 2000.

21. *Eritrea Profile*, "Promoting Efficient Court Service," 26 February 2000, 5.

22. Asmarom Legesse, personal communication, 1999.

23. Kemink, "The Tegreñña," 70.

24. Eugene Cotran, "The Unification of Laws in East Africa," *The Journal of Modern African Studies* 1, no. 2 (1963): 217–218.

25. Robert Allen Sedler, "The Development of Legal Systems: The Ethiopian Experience," *Iowa Law Review* 53, no. 3 (1967): 587, 589.

26. Jeffrey Herbst, *States and Power in Africa: Comparative Lessons in Authority and Control* (Princeton, N.J.: Princeton University Press, 2000), 183.

Selected Bibliography

Abdalla, Raqiya Haji Dualeh. *Sisters in Affliction: Circumcision and Infibulation of Women in Africa*. London: Zed Press, 1982.

Abdul Wasir Yusuf. "The Legal Status of the Shari'a Courts in Ethiopia." Senior paper, Addis Ababa University, 1971.

AbdulNasser Abdella. "The Institution of Family Arbitration in Eritrea." Senior LL.B. thesis, University of Asmara, 1999.

Abebe Kifleyesus. "Bilin: Speaker Status Strength and Weakness." *Africa* LVI, no. 1 (2000): 64–89.

Aberra Jembere. *An Introduction to the Legal History of Ethiopia: 1434–1974.* New Brunswick, N.J.: Transaction Publishers, 2000.

Abraham, Girmai. "The Privatization of Diesa in Independent Eritrea: Towards an Agricultural Research and Policy Agenda." In *Proceedings of the International Conference on Eritrea*, 100–116. Washington, D.C.: Eritreans for Peace and Democracy, November 1990.

Abu Muh'ammad Abdallah Ibn Abi Zayd al-Qayrawānī. *La Risāla.* Translated by Leon Bercher. Algiers: Editions populaires de l'armée, 1983.

Acton, Thomas, Susan Caffrey, and Gary Mundy. "Theorizing Gypsy Law." *American Journal of Comparative Law* XLV (1997): 237–250.

Adawi al I. A. "Description of the Sudan by Muslim Geographers and Travellers." *Sudan Notes and Records* 35, no. II (1954): 5–16.

Agricultural Commission, EPLF. "Problems, Prospective Policies and Programs for Agricultural Development in Eritrea." In *Emergent Eritrea: Challenges of Economic Development*, edited by Gebre Hiwet Tesfagiorgis, 91–100. Washington, D.C.: Eritreans for Peace and Democracy, 1992.

Ajani, Gianmaria. "The Supremacy of Statutory Law in Socialist Systems: Scholarly Opinions and Operative Rules." *Review of Socialist Law* 11 (1991): 123–142.

——. "By Chance and Prestige: Legal Transplants in Russia and Eastern Europe" *American Journal of Comparative Law*, 1995.

——. *Il modello post-socialista*. Torino: Giappichelli, 1996.

——. "Legal Education in Russia: Present and Future—An Analysis of the State Educational Standards for Higher Professional Instruction and a Comparison with the European Legal Education Reform Experience." *Review of Central and East European Law* 23 (1997): 267–300.

——. "Legal Transplants and Economic Performance." In *New Trends in International Trade Law*, edited by Gianmaria Ajani and Giuseppe Porro, 1–16. Torino: Giappichelli, 2000.

Ajani, Gianmaria and Ugo Mattei. "Codifying Property Law in the Process of Transition: Some Suggestions from Comparative Law and Economics." *Hastings International and Comparative Law Review* 19, no. 1 (1995): 117–137.

Alemseged Tesfai. "The Cause of the Eritrean-Ethiopian Border Conflict." *Eritrea Profile*, 19 December 1998, 3.

Almeida, Manoel de. "The History of High Ethiopia or Abassia." In *Some Records of Ethiopia, 1593–1646*, translated and edited by C. F. Beckingham and G. W. B. Huntingford. London: Hakluyt Society, 1954.

Aluffi Beck-Peccoz, Roberta. *La modernizzazione del diritto di famiglia nei Paesi Arabi*. Milano: Giuffré, 1990.

Amanuel Tesfai. "Comparative Analysis of the Customary Laws of Loggo-Chiwa, Adghena-Tegheleba, and the Transitional Civil Code of Eritrea with Particular Reference to the Law of Torts." Senior LL.B. thesis, University of Asmara, 1999.

Ambaye Zekarias. *Land Tenure in Eritrea (Ethiopia)*. Addis Ababa: Institute of Ethiopian Studies, 1966,

Ammerman, Albert J., and Luigi Luca Cavalli-Sforza. "A Population Model for the Diffusion of Early Farming In Europe." In *The Explanation of Culture Change*, edited by C. Renfrew, 343–357. London: Duckworth, 1973.

Amna el Sadig Badri and Edith H. Grotberg. "Intellectual Women: New Approach to Sudanese Development." *The Ahfad Journal* 6, no. 2 (1989): 4–20.

Anderson, Benedict Richard O'Gorman. *Imagined Communities: Reflections on the Origin and Spread of Nationalism* (London: Verso, 1991).

Arberry, Arthur J. *The Koran Interpreted*. New York: Macmillan, 1955.

Arendt, Hannah. "Communicative Power." In *Power*, edited by Steven Lukes, 59–74. New York: New York University Press, 1986.

Asma el Dareer. *Women, Why Do You Weep?* London: Zed Press, 1992.

Asmarom Legesse. *Customary Law and Alternative Dispute Resolution (ADR)*. Asmara: Ministry of Justice, 1999.

Auffret, Séverine. *Des couteaux contre des femmes—de l'excision*. Paris: Des Femmes, 1982.

Ausenda, Giorgio. "Leisurely Nomads: The Hadendowa (Beja) of the Gash Delta and Their Transition to Sedentary Village Life." Ph.D. diss., University of Michigan, Ann Arbor, 1987.

Ayittey, George B. N. *Indigenous African Institutions*, Ardsley-on-Hudson: Transnational Publishers, 1991.

Babatunde, Emmanuel. *Women's Rights versus Women's Rites.* Trenton, N.J.: Africa World Press, 1998.

Bachofen, Johann Jakob. *Das Mutterecht: Eine Untersuchung Über die Gynaikokratie der alten Welt nach ihrer religiosen und rechtlichen Natur, Mutterecht.* Stuttgart: Krais & Hoffmann, 1861.

Bairu Tafla. "La notion du pouvoir dans l'Afrique traditionnelle: le cas de l'Éthiopie." In *Introduction à la culture africaine,* 171–191. Paris: Les Presses de l'Unesco, 1977.

Barkan, Joel S., and Bruce Cronin. "The State and the Nation: Changing Norms and the Rules of Sovereignty in International Relations." *International Organizations* 48 (1994): 107–130.

Barnard, Alan. "Rules and Prohibitions: The Form and Content of Human Kinship." In *Companion Encyclopedia of Anthropology,* edited by Tim Ingold, 783–812. London: Routledge, 1997.

Barnes, John Arundel. "Class and Committees in a Norwegian Island Parish." *Human Relations* 7, no. 1 (1954): 39–58.

Barnes, Robert Harrison. "Marriage Exchange and the Meaning of Corporations in Eastern Indonesia." In *The Meaning of Marriage Payments,* edited by J. L. Comaroff, 93–124. London: Academic Press, 1980.

Barrera, Giulia, *Dangerous Liaisons: Colonial Concubinage in Eritrea, 1890–1941.* Evanston, Ill.: Program of African Studies Northwestern University, 1996.

Barrows, Richard, and Michael Roth. "Land Tenure and Investment in African Agriculture: Theory and Evidence." *Journal of Modern African Studies* 28, no. 2 (1990): 265–297.

Beck, Ulrich. *What is Globalization?* Translated by Patrick Camiller. Cambridge: Polity Press, 2000.

Beckstrom, John H. "Divorce in Urban Ethiopia Ten Years after the Civil Code." *Journal of Ethiopian Law* VI, no. 2 (1969): 283–304.

———. "Paternity Claims in Ethiopia: Ten Years after the Civil Code." *African Law Studies* X (1973): 47–65.

———. "Transplantation of Legal Systems: An Early Report on the Reception of Western Laws in Ethiopia." *American Journal of Comparative Law* 21 (1973): 557–583.

Belayneh Mamo. "Constitution as a Supreme Law with a Special Reference to the Constitution of the PDRE." Senior paper, Addis Ababa University, 1988.

Bennett, T. W., and Jan Vermeulen. "Codification of Customary Law." *Journal of African Law* 24, no. 2 (1980): 206–219.

Bent, James T. *The Sacred City of the Abyssinians: Being a Record of Travel and Research in Abyssinia in 1893.* London: Longmans Green, 1896.

Bentley, Eric. *The Pirandello Commentaries.* Evanston, Ill.: Northwestern University Press, 1986.

Bereket Habte Selassie. *Conflict and Intervention in the Horn of Africa.* New York: Monthly Review Press, 1980.

———. "Democracy and the Role of Parliament under the Eritrean Constitution." *North Carolina Journal of International Law and Commercial Regulation* 24, no. 2 (1999): 227–261.

Bereket Habte Selassie and Richard A. Rosen. "The Eritrean Constitutional Process: An Interview with Dr. Bereket Habte Selassie." *Eritrean Studies Review* 3, no. 1, 1999.

Berkowitz, Daniel, Katharina Pistor, and Jean-François Richard. *Economic Development, Legality, and the Transplant Effect.* Cambridge: Center for International Development at Harvard University, 2000.

Berman, Harold Joseph. *Law and Revolution: The Formation of the Western Legal Tradition.* Boston: Harvard University Press, 1983.

Besteman, Catherine. "Access to Land." In *Gender and Agricultural Development: Surveying the Fields,* edited by Helen K. Henderson and Ellen Hansen, 18–25. Tucson: University of Arizona Press, 1995.

Bettelheim, Bruno. *Symbolic Wounds: Puberty Rites and the Envious Male.* New York: Collier, 1962.

Bililign Mandefro. "Agricultural Communities and the Civil Code." *Journal of Ethiopian Law* VI, no. 1 (1969): 145–199.

Bilotti, Edvige. "The Practice of Female Genital Mutilation." *Mediterranean Review* 3, no. 2, 1996–1997.

Bimbi, Guido. "I contadini di Medri Zien." In *Revolution in Eritrea: Eyewitness Reports,* 137–139. Rome: Research and Information Centre of Eritrea, 1979.

Bocresion Haile. *The Collusion on Eritrea.* Asmara: Bocresion Haile, 2000.

Bohannan, Paul. "Land, Tenure, and Land-Tenure." In *African Agrarian Systems,* edited by Daniel P. Biebuyck. London: Oxford University Press, 1963.

Bonaparte, Marie. *Female Sexuality.* New York: International Universities Press, 1953.

Bousquet, Georges Henri. *L'Ethique sexuelle de l'Islam.* Paris: Maisonneuve et Larose, 1966.

Boyer, Pascal. *Tradition as Truth and Communication: A Cognitive Description of Traditional Discourse.* Cambridge: Cambridge University Press, 1990.

Brelich, Angelo. *Le iniziazioni (parte seconda).* Rome: Edizioni dell'Ateneo, 1962.

Brietzke, Paul H. "Private Law in Ethiopia." *Journal of African Law* 18, no. 2 (1974): 149–167.

———. "Land Reform in Revolutionary Ethiopia." *The Journal of Modern African Studies* 14, no. 4 (1976): 637–660.

———. *Law, Development, and the Ethiopian Revolution.* East Brunswick, N.J.: Associated University Press, 1982.

Brown, Judith K. "A Cross-Cultural Study of Female Initiation Rites." *American Anthropologist* 65, no. 4 (1963): 837–853.

Bruce, James. *Travels to Discover the Source of the Nile In the Years, 1768, 1769, 1770, 1771, 1772 & 1773.* Westmead: Gregg International, 1972.

Bruce, John. W. "A Perspective on Indigenous Land Tenure Systems and Land Concentration." In *Land and Society in Contemporary Africa,* edited by R. E. Downs and Stephen P. Reyna, 23–52. Hanover, N.H.: University Press of New England, 1988.

Bryk, Felix. *Sex and Circumcision: A Study of Phallic Worship and Mutilation in Men and Women.* North Hollywood: Brandon House, 1967.

Bullettino Ufficiale della Colonia Eritrea, XII, 45–47, Asmara, 7, 14, 21 November 1903.

Bussani, Mauro. "Tort Law and Development: Insights into the Case of Ethiopia and Eritrea." *Journal of African Law* 40, no. 1 (1996): 43–52.

Bynum, Caroline Walker. "Material Continuity, Personal Survival, and the Resurrection of the Body: A Scholastic Discussion in Its Medieval and Modern Contexts." In *Fragmentation and Redemption: Essays on Gender and the Human Body in Medieval Religion*, 239–297. New York: Zone Books, 1991.

Caffarel, William. "La legislazione dell'Eritrea." In *L'Eritrea Economica*, 461–492. Novara-Rome: De Agostini, 1913.

Capomazza, Ilario. *Istituzioni di diritto consuetudinario del Seraé—La legge degli Atchemè-Melga.* Macerata: Stabilimento tipografico Giorgetti, 1912.

———. *L'Assaorta-Saho.* Napoli: Società Africana d'Italia, 1914.

———. *Il diritto consuetudinario dell'Acchele-Guzai.* Asmara: Fioretti, 1937.

Carbone, Adriano. *Termini più in uso nel diritto terriero dell'Eritrea.* Asmara: Regio Governo dell'Eritrea, 1940.

Carr, Dana. *Female Genital Cutting: Findings from the Demographic and Health Surveys Program.* Calverton: Macro International, 1997.

Castellani, Luca "Introduzione." In *Il modello pluralista*, by Marco Guadagni. Torino: Giappichelli, 1996.

———. "La riforma del diritto fondiario in Eritrea." Typescript. Asmara, 1998.

———. "La legislazione eritrea in materia ambientale." In *New Law for New States*, edited by Lyda Favali, Elisabetta Grande, and Marco Guadagni, 223–255. Torino: L'Harmattan, 1998.

———. "Recent Developments in Land Tenure Law in Eritrea, Horn of Africa." Working Paper n. 37. Land Tenure Center, University of Wisconsin, Madison, 2000.

Castellucci, Ignazio. "Il nuovo diritto eritreo: il diritto di famiglia." In *New Law for New States*, edited by Lyda Favali, Elisabetta Grande, and Marco Guadagni, 193–223. Torino: L'Harmattan, 1998.

Castles, J. "An Alternative to Female Gender Mutilation for Kenyan Girls." *Focus* (March 1997): 23–24.

Castro, Francesco. *Materiali e ricerche sul nikah al-mut'a.* Rome: Accademia Nazionale dei Lincei—Fondazione Leone Caetani, 1974.

Caulk, Richard. "Bad Men of the Borders: Shum and Shefta in Northern Ethiopia in the 19th Century." *International Journal of African Historical Studies* 17, no. 2 (1984): 201–227.

———. "Black Snake, White Snake: Bahta Hagos and His Revolt against Italian Overrule in Eritrea, 1894." In *Banditry, Rebellion and Social Protest in Africa*, edited by Donald Crummey, 293–309. London: James Currey, 1986.

Cauvin, Jacques. *Naissance des divinité, naissance de l'agricolture. La Révolution des symboles au Néolithique.* Paris: CNRS Editions, 1994.

Cavalli-Sforza, Luigi Luca. *Geni, popoli e lingue.* Milano: Adelphi, 1996.

Cavalli-Sforza, Luigi Luca, Paolo Menozzi, and Alberto Piazza. *Storia e Geografia dei Geni Umani*. Milano: Adelphi, 1997.

Cerulli, Enrico. *Somalia: Scritti vari editi ed inediti*. Rome: Istituto Poligrafico dello Stato P. V., 1959.

Champetier, Charles. "Reflections on Human Rights." *Telos* 118 (2000): 77–86.

Chanock, Martin. *Law, Custom and Social Order: The Colonial Experience in Malawi and Zambia*. New York: Cambridge University Press, 1985.

Cheikh Gueye. "Règles de succession dans l'Islam et dans la société mouride: des articulations complexes et des effets stimulateurs de l'urbanisation toubienne," paper presented to the Second Symposium of the Islamic Law in Africa Project, Dakar, Senegal, 1 July 2001.

Chester, Bronwyn. "When the UN Comes Calling." *McGill University: Public and Media: Public Reporter*, 24 February 2000.

Ciampi, Gabriele. "Cartographic Problems of the Eritreo-Ethiopia Border." *Africa* LVI, no. 2 (2001): 154–189.

Clay, Jason W., and Bonnie K. Holcomb. *Politics and the Ethiopian Famine, 1984–1985*. Cambridge, Mass.: Cultural Survival, 1985.

Coen, Benedetto D. *Considerazioni sulla circoncisione*. Modena: Tipografia Di Andrea Rossi, 1864.

Cohen, David. *Dictionnaire des racines sémitiques*. Paris: Mouton, 1976.

Colson, Elisabeth. *The Social Consequences of Resettlement*. Manchester: Manchester University Press, 1971.

Colucci, Massimo. "Sistemi di accertamento e di pubblicità dei diritti fondiari nelle Colonie." Estratto dagli *Atti del Secondo Congresso di Studi Coloniali*, 12–22. Napoli, 1–5 October 1934.

———. *Il regime fondiario indigeno in Etiopia ed i mezzi di accertamento della proprietà*. Rome: Sallustiana, 1936.

Colucci, Massimo, and Giangastone Bolla. "Induzioni sugli ordinamenti fondiari nell'Africa Orientale Italiana." Firenze: *Estratto dagli Atti del Terzo Congresso di Studi Coloniali*, 12–17, 195–202, April 1937.

Comaroff, Jean, and John L. Comaroff. *Of Revelation and Revolution: Christianity, Colonialism, and Consciousness in South Africa*. Chicago: University of Chicago Press, 1991.

Comaroff, John L. "Introduction." In *The Meaning of Marriage Payments*. London: Academic Press, 1980.

Connell, Dan. "Two Lines in Eritrea's Movement: ELF, PLF Seek Unity." In *Revolution in Eritrea: Eyewitness Reports*, 75–78. Rome: Research and Information Centre of Eritrea, 1979.

Constitutional Commission of Eritrea. *Information on Strategy, Plans, and Activities*. Asmara, October 1995.

Conti Rossini, Carlo. "Al Ragali." *Estratti dal Bollettino della Societá Italiana di Esplorazioni Geografiche e Commerciali, anni 1903–1904*. Milano: Stabilimento Tipografico Bellini, 1903.

———. *Ricordo di un soggiorno in Eritrea*. Asmara: Tipografia della Missione Svedese, 1903.

———. "I Loggo e la legge dei Loggo Sarda." *Giornale della Società Asiatica Italiana* XVII (1904).

———. "Schizzo etnico e storico delle popolazioni eritree." In *l'Eritrea Economica*, edited by Ferdinando Martini, 61–90. Roma, 1913.

———. *Principi di diritto consuetudinario dell'Eritrea*. Rome: Ministero delle Colonie, Tip. Unione Ed., 1916.

———. *Il regime fondiario indigeno in Etiopia ed i mezzi di accertamento della proprietà*. Rome: Sallustiana, 1936.

———. "Lo statuto degli Scioattè Ansebà (Eritrea.)" In *Scritti Giuridici in onore di Santi Romano, III*, 345–366. Padova: Cedam, 1940.

Cooper, Barbara. "Ambiguities of Laicité: Reflections on Women and the Christian Minority in Colonial and Post-Colonial Niger," paper presented to the Second Symposium of the Islamic Law in Africa Project, Dakar, Senegal, 29 June 2001.

Costanzo, Giuseppe Aurio. *Le fonti del diritto abissino delle popolazioni cristiane*. Rome: Ferraiolo, 1940.

Cotran, Eugene. "The Unification of Laws in East Africa." *The Journal of Modern African Studies* 1, no. 2 (1963): 209–220.

Council of Europe. *Activities of the Council of Europe: 1997 Report*. Strasbourg: Council of Europe Publishing, 1997.

Courbon, A. "Observations topographiques et médicales recueillies dans un voyage à l'isthme de Suez, sur le littoral de la Mer Rouge et en Abyssinie." Thèse de médecine 33, 1861.

Crawford, R. James. *The Creation of States in International Law*. Oxford: Clarendon, 1979.

Crowfoot, John Winter. "Wedding Customs in the Northern Sudan." *Sudan Notes and Records* V, no. 1 and 2 (1922): 1–28.

Cumming, D. C. "The History of Kassala and the Province of Taka." *Sudan Notes and Records* XX, pt. 1 (1937): 1–45.

David, René. "Les Sources du Code Civil Ethiopien." In *Revue de droit international et droit comparé* (1962): 497–506.

———. "A Civil Code for Ethiopia: Considerations on the Codification of the Civil Law in African Countries." *Tulane Law Review* 37 (1963): 187–204.

———. *Les grandes systèmes de droit contemporains*. Paris: Précis Dalloz, 1992.

D'Avray, Anthony. *Lords of the Red Sea: The History of a Red Sea Society from the Sixteenth to the Nineteenth Centuries*. Wiesbaden: Aethiopistische Forschungen, 1996.

De Bruyn, Maria. "Socio-cultural Aspects of Female Genital Cutting." In *Proceedings of the Expert Meeting on Female Genital Mutilation*, edited by Els Leye, Maria de Bruyn, and Stan Meuwese, 62–75. Ghent-Belgium, 5–7 November, 1998.

De Rivoyre, Denis. *Aux pays de Soudan, Bogos, Mensah, Souakim*. Paris: Eplon, 1885.

De Stefano, Giuseppe. *I costumi penali abissini Fethà Neghest*. Firenze: Bemporad & Figlio, 1906.

Dessalegn Rahmato. *Agrarian Reform in Ethiopia*. Trenton, N.J.: Red Sea Press, 1985.

Desta, Abraham. "Establishment of Paternity under Eritrean Indigenous Laws with Particular Reference to Article 60 of Proclamation 2/91." Senior LL.B. thesis, University of Asmara, 1999.

Diamond, Jared. *Guns, Germs, and Steel: The Fates of Human Societies*. New York: W. W. Norton & Company, 1997.

Dieck, Alfred. "Beschneidung von Frauen und Mannern in vorund frühgeschichtlicher Zeit." *Curare* 4 (1981): 77–84.

Dillmann, August. *Über die Regierung, insbesondere die Kirchenordnung des Königs Zar'a Jakob: Verlag der Königlichen*. Berlin: Akademie der Wissenschaften, 1884.

Dimtsi Hafash, "Land Reforms in the Environs of Afabet." In *Selected Articles from EPLF Publications (1973–1980)*, 89. Eritrean People's Liberation Front, May 1982.

Dines, Mary. "The Social Transformation of Eritrean Women under the E.P.L.F." In *The Eritrean Case*, 267–269. Rome: Research and Information Center on Eritrea, 1984.

———. "Ethiopian Violation of Human Rights in Eritrea." In *The Long Struggle of Eritrea for Independence and Constructive Peace*, edited by Lionel Cliffe and Basil Davidson, 139–161. Nottingham: Spokesman, 1988.

Dingwall, Eric John. *Male Infibulation*. London: John Bale, Sons & Danielsson, 1925.

Dobkin de Rios, Marlene, and Brian Hayden. "Odors Differentiation and Variability in the Sexual Division of Labor among Hunter/Gatherers." *Journal of Human Evolution* 14 (1985): 219–228.

Dolphyne, Florence Abena. *The Emancipation of Women: An African Perspective*. Accra: Ghana Universities Press, 1991.

Donaldson, Dwight M. "Temporary Marriage in Iran," *The Moslem World* XXVI, no. 4 (1936): 358–364.

Dorkenoo, Efua. *Cutting the Rose: Female Genital Mutilation—The Practice and Its Prevention*. London: Minority Rights Publication, 1995.

Douglas, Mary. *Purity and Danger: An Analysis of Concepts of Pollution and Taboo*. New York: Praeger, 1966.

Duchenet, Édouard. *Histoires Somalies: la malice des primitifs*. Paris: Larose, 1936.

Duncanson, Dennis J. "Sir'At 'Adkeme Milga'—A Native Law Code of Eritrea," *Africa* XIX, no. 2 (1949): 141–149.

Dupret, Baudoiun, Maurits Berger, and Laila Al-Zwaini. *Legal Pluralism in the Arab World*. The Hague: Kluwer Law International, 1999.

Dupuis, Jacques. *Storia della paternità*. Milano: Tranchida Editori Inchiostro, 1992.

Dzurek, Daniel J. "The Hanish Island Dispute." *Eritrean Studies Review* 1, no. 2 (1996): 133–152.

Earle, Timothy. "Political Domination and Social Evolution." In *Companion*

Encyclopedia of Anthropology, edited by Tim Ingold, 940–961. London: Routledge, 1997.

Eliade, Mircea. *Le mythe de l'éternel retour.* Paris: Gallimard, 1949.

———. *Forgerons et alchimistes.* Paris: Flammarion, 1956.

———. *The Sacred and the Profane: The Nature of Religion.* Translated by Willard R. Trask. New York: Harvest, 1959.

———. *Myth and Reality.* New York: Harper and Row, 1963.

———. *Aspects du mythe.* Paris: Gallimard, 1963.

Eritrean Assembly. "New Customary Law of the Beni Amer Tribes." Typescript, Asmara, 1 June 1960.

Eritrean People's Liberation Front. *Memorandum (the Correct and Just Solution).* The Field: EPLF, 1978.

———. *Political Report and National Democratic Programme.* The Field: EPLF, 1987.

———. *A National Charter for Eritrea: For a Democratic, Just and Prosperous Future.* Asmara: Adulis Printing Press, 1994.

Eritrean Women's Association-Europe. *Women and Revolution in Eritrea.* Rome: EWAE, 1979.

Erlich, Michel. *La femme blessée: essai sur les mutilations sexuelles feminines.* Paris: L'Harmattan, 1986.

———. *La mutilation.* Paris: Presses Universitaires de France, 1990.

Escarra, Jean. "Exposé des Motifs." Unpublished typescript. Addis Ababa: Law Faculty Library Haile Selassie I University, 1954.

Evans-Pritchard, Edward Evan. *The Nuer: A Description of the Modes of Livelihood and Political Institutions of a Nilotic People.* Oxford: Clarendon Press, 1940.

Fabietti, Ugo, and Francesco Remotti, eds. *Dizionario di antropologia, etnologia, antropologia culturale, antropologia sociale.* Bologna: Zanichelli, 1997.

Fasil Nahum. "Socialist Ethiopia's Achievements as Reflected in its Basic Law: The Law Making Process in Ethiopia Post 1974, Part One." *Journal of Ethiopian Law* 4, no. 1 (1989): 122–127.

———. "The Enigma of Eritrean Legislation." *Journal of Ethiopian Law* IX, no. 2 (1973): 307–345.

Fassil Abebe and Stanley Z. Fisher. "Language and Law in Ethiopia." *Journal of Ethiopian Law* V, no. 3 (1968): 553–559.

Faurot, L. *Voyage au Golfe de Tadjoura.* Paris: Barbier, 1886.

Favali, Lyda. "La legittimazione e i suoi protagonisti (una premessa allo studio delle fonti in Eritrea)." In *New Law for New States,* edited by Lyda Favali, Elisabetta Grande, and Marco Guadagni, 159–182. Torino: L'Harmattan, 1998.

Firebrace, James, and Stuart Holland. *Never Kneel Down: Drought, Development, and Liberation in Eritrea.* Trenton, N.J.: Red Sea Press, 1985.

Fisher, R. A. "The Wave of Advance of Advantageous Genes." *Annals of Eugenics* 7 (1936–37): 355–369.

Fleming, G. J. "Beni Amer Marriage Customs." *Sudan Notes and Records* 2, no. 1 (1919): 74–76.

Foley, Robert. "A Reconsideration of the Role of Predation on Large Mammals in Tropical Hunter/Gatherers Adaptation." *Man* 17, no. 3 (1982): 393–402.

Forbes, Joan Rosita Torr. In *Women's Voices on Africa*, edited by Patricia W. Romero, 123–157. Princeton: Markus Wiener, 1992.

Fortes, Meyer, and Edward Evan Evans-Pritchard. *African Political Systems*. London: Oxford University Press, 1958.

Foucault, Michel. *The History of Sexuality, Volume I: An Introduction*. Translated by Robert Hurley. New York: Random House, 1990.

Fox, Robin. *Kinship and Marriage: An Anthropological Perspective*. Harmondsworth: Penguin Books, 1967.

Freeman, Derek. *The Fateful Hoaxing of Margaret Mead: A Historical Analysis of Her Samoan Research*. Boulder, Colo.: Westview Press, 1999.

French, Thomas R. "Legal Literature of Eritrea: A Bibliographic Essay." *North Carolina Journal of International Law and Commercial Regulation* 24, no. 2 (1999): 417–449.

Fullerton, Sandra Joireman. "The Minefield of Land Reform: Comments on the Eritrean Land Proclamation." *African Affairs* 95 (1996): 269–285.

———. "Institutional Change in the Horn of Africa: The Allocation of Property Rights and Implications for Development." Ph.D. diss., University of California Los Angeles, 1995.

Gambaro, Antonio, and Rodolfo Sacco. *Sistemi giuridici comparati*. Torino: Utet, 1996.

Gebre Hiwet Tesfagiorgis. "Approaches to Resolving the Conflict between Eritrea and Ethiopia." *Eritrean Studies Review* 3, no. 2 (1999): 139–165.

Gebrehiwot. "Foreword." In *The Code of Customary Law of Acchele Guzay*. Asmara, April 1951.

Gebremedhin, Tesfa G. "Agricultural Development in Eritrea: Economic and Policy Analysis." In *Emergent Eritrea: Challenges of Economic Development*, edited by Gebre Hiwet Tesfagiorgis. Washington, D.C.: Eritreans for Peace and Democracy, 1992.

———. *Beyond Survival: The Economic Challenges of Agriculture and Development in Post-Independence Eritrea*. Lawrenceville, N.J.: Red Sea Press, 1996.

Geertz, Clifford. "The Cerebral Savage." *Encounter* 28 (1967): 25–32.

———. *Local Knowledge: Further Essays in Interpretive Anthropology*. New York: Basic Books, 1983.

Geraghty, Thomas. "People, Practice, Attitudes and Problems in the Lower Courts of Ethiopia." *Journal of Ethiopian Law* VI, no. 2 (1969): 427–489.

Ghebil Temnewo. "Murder and Blood Money under the Fit'ha Megarh." LL.B. senior thesis, University of Asmara, 1999.

Ghidewon Abay Asmerom and Ogbazgy Abay Asmerom. "A Study of the Evolution of the Eritrean Ethiopian Border through Treaties and Official Maps." *Eritrean Studies Review* 3, no. 2 (1999): 43–88.

Giannini, Amedeo. *Nuove costituzioni di stati del Vicino Oriente e dell'Africa*. Milano: Giuffré, 1954.

Gibbon, Edward. *The History of the Decline and Fall of the Roman Empire*, VI. London: The Folio Society, 1987.

Giddens, Anthony. *Central Problems in Social Theory.* Berkeley: University of California Press, 1979.

Gilliam, Angela. "Women's Equality and National Liberation." In *Third World Women and the Politics of Feminism,* edited by Chandra Talpade Mohanty, Ann Russo, and Lourdes Torres , 215-236. Bloomington: Indiana University Press, 1991.

Gimbutas, Marija Alsekaite. *The Language of the Goddess.* San Francisco: Harper & Row, 1995.

Giorgis, Belkis Wolde. *Female Circumcision in Africa.* Addis Ababa: United Nations Economic Commission for Africa, 1981.

Glenn, H. Patrick. "The Capture, Reconciliation, and Marginalization of Custom." *American Journal of Comparative Law* 45 (1997): 613-620.

———. *Legal Traditions of the World.* Oxford: Oxford University Press, 2000.

Gobat, Samuel. "Journal of Three Year's Residence in Abyssinia, in Furtherance of the Objects of the Church Missionary Society." *Journal of the Royal Geographical Society* IV (1834): 268-277.

Goldman, Emma. *My Further Disillusionment in Russia.* New York: Doubleday & Page, 1924.

Goldsmith, J. H. "Marriage Customs of the Beni Amer Tribe." *Sudan Notes and Records* 3, no. 4 (1920): 293-295.

Goody, Jack. *Literacy in Traditional Societies.* Cambridge: Cambridge University Press, 1968.

Gordley, James. "Common Law v. Civil Law: Una distinzione che va scomparendo?" In *Scritti in onore di Rodolfo Sacco.* Milano: Giuffré, 1994.

Gow, J. J. "Law and the Sudan." *Sudan Notes and Records* XXXIII, pt. 2 (1952): 299-309.

Gramsci, Antonio. *Quaderni dal carcere.* Torino: Einaudi, 1948-51.

———. "Osservazioni sul folklore." *Letteratura e vita nazionale.* Torino: Einaudi, 1950.

Grande, Elisabetta. "Transplanting Alternative Dispute Resolution in the Horn of Africa: Some Issues of Law and Power." In *New Law for New States: Politica del Diritto in Eritrea,* edited by Lyda Favali, Elisabetta Grande, and Marco Guadagni, 109-122. Torino: L'Harmattan, 1998.

Grassivaro Gallo, Pia. *Figlie d'Africa Mutilate: Indagini epidemiologiche sull'escissione in Italia.* Torino: L'Harmattan, 1998.

Graven, Jean. "The Penal Code of the Empire of Ethiopia, Part 1." *Journal of Ethiopian Law* I, no. 2 (1964): 267-298.

Griaule, Marcel. *Dieu d'eau: Entretiens avec Ogotemmeli.* Paris: Fayard, 1966.

Griffiths, John. "What is Legal Pluralism?" *Journal of Legal Pluralism* 24, no. 1 (1986): 1-55.

Grisaru, Nimrod, Simcha Lezer, and Robert H. Belmaker. "Ritual Female Genital Surgery among Ethiopian Jews." *Archives of Sexual Behavior* (1997): 211-215.

Grossi, Paolo. *L'ordine giuridico medievale.* Roma-Bari: Laterza, 1995.

Guadagni, Marco. "Note sulle fonti del diritto etiopico, con particolare riferimento all'istituto del divorzio." *Africa* 28, no. 3 (1973): 369-388.

——. "Eritrean Law between Past and Future: An Introduction." In *New Law for New States: Politica del Diritto in Eritrea*, edited by Lyda Favali, Elisabetta Grande, and Marco Guadagni, 11–19. Torino: L'Harmattan, 1998.

——. "Legal Pluralism." In *The New Palgrave: A Dictionary of Economics and the Law*, edited by Peter Newman. London: Macmillan, 1998.

Guidi, Ignazio. *Il Fetha Nagast o legislazione dei re: codice ecclesiastico e civile di Abissinia*. Rome: Tipografia Casa Ed., Italiana, 1897.

Gunning, Isabelle R. "Arrogant Perception, World Traveling, and Multi Cultural Feminism: The Case of Female Genital Surgeries." *Columbia Human Rights Law Review* 23, no. 2 (1992): 189–248.

Gwyther, Moore D. "Notes on the Legislation of the Anglo-Egyptian Sudan." *Journal of Comparative Legislation and International Law* VI, no. 1 and 4 (1924): 131–134.

Hale, Sondra. "A Question of Subjects: The 'Female Circumcision' Controversy and the Politics of Knowledge." *Ufahamu* XXII, no. 3 (1994): 26–35.

Hammond, Jenny, ed. *Sweeter Than Honey: Ethiopian Women and Revolution*. Trenton, N.J.: Red Sea Press, 1990.

Hardin, Garrett. "The Tragedy of the Commons." In *Readings in Public Sector Economics*, edited by Samuel Baker and Catherine Elliott. Lexington, Mass.: D. C. Heath and Company, 1990.

Hardt, Michael, and Antonio Negri. *Empire*. Cambridge, Mass.: Harvard University Press, 2000.

Hardy, Michael James Langley. *Blood Feuds and the Payment of Blood Money in the Middle East*. Leiden: E. J. Brill, 1963.

Harrell, Stevan. *Human Families*. Boulder, Colo.: Westview Press, 1997.

Hawkesworth, D. "The Nuba Proper of Southern Kordofan." *Sudan Notes and Records* XV, no. 2 (1932): 159–199.

Hayes, Rose Oldfield. "Female Genital Mutilation, Fertility Control, Women's Roles and Patrilineage in Modern Sudan: a Functional Analysis." *American Ethnologist* 2, no. 4 (1975): 617–632.

Held, David. *Democracy and Global Order: From the Modern State to Cosmopolitan Governance*. Stanford: Stanford University Press, 1995.

Herbst, Jeffrey. *States and Power in Africa: Comparative Lessons in Authority and Control*. Princeton, N.J.: Princeton University Press, 2000.

Hicks, Esther K. *Infibulation: Female Mutilation in Islamic Northeastern Africa*. New Brunswick, N J.: Transaction, 1996.

Highin Siratin Nay MeretAdebo: Codes and Bylaws of Eritrean Regions and Countries, compiled and published by ZeraYacob Estifanos, WoldeMariam Abraham, and Gherima GhebreMeskel (West Germany, 1990).

Hirsch, Susan F., and Mindie Lazarus-Black. *Contested States: Law, Hegemony and Resistance*. New York: Routledge, 1994.

Hjort af Ornäs, Anders. *Responsible Man: The Atmaan Beja of the Eastern Sudan*. Uppsala: Nordiska Afrikainstitutet, 1991.

Hoben, Alan. *Social Soundness Analysis of Agrarian Reform in Ethiopia*. Ethiopia: USAID, 1976.

Hobhouse, Leonard Trelawny. *Morals and Evolution: A Study in Comparative Ethics.* London: Chapman and Hall, 1951.

Hobsbawm, Eric, and Terence Ranger, eds. *The Invention of Traditions.* Cambridge: Cambridge University Press, 1983.

Hodgin, Peter. "An Introduction to Eritrea's Ongoing Revolution: Women's Nationalist Mobilization and Gender Politics in Post-war Eritrea." *Eritrean Studies Review* 2, no. 1 (1997): 85–110.

Hogue, Arthur R. *Origins of the Common Law.* Bloomington: Indiana University Press, 1966.

Holy, Ladislav. "The Segmentary Lineage Structure and its Existential Status." In *Segmentary Lineage Systems Reconsidered,* edited by Ladislav Holy, 1–22. Belfast: The Queen's University of Belfast, 1979.

———. *Religion and Custom in a Muslim Society: The Berti of Sudan.* Cambridge: Cambridge University Press, 1991.

———. *Anthropological Perspectives on Kinship.* London: Pluto Press, 1996.

———, ed. *Comparative Anthropology.* Oxford: Blackwell, 1987.

Hosken, Fran P. *The Hosken Report.* Lexington: Women's International Network, 1982.

Houtart, François. "The Social Revolution in Eritrea." In *Behind the War in Eritrea,* edited by Basil Davidson et al., 83–110. Nottingham: Spokesman, 1980.

Hughes, Austin L. *Evolution and Human Kinship.* New York: Oxford University Press, 1988.

Hutchinson, John, and Anthony D. Smith, eds. *Ethnicity,* Oxford: Oxford University Press, 1996.

Huxley, Aldous. "A Note on Dogma." In *Proper Studies.* London: Chatto & Windus, 1927.

Ikenberry, G. John. "Introduction." In *American Foreign Policy: Theoretical Essays,* edited by G. John Ikenberry, 1–12. New York: Longman, 1999.

Ivinson, Duncan. "Decolonising the Rule of Law: Mabo's Case and Post Colonial Constitutionalism." *Oxford Journal of Legal Studies* 17, no. 2 (1997): 253–279.

Iyob, Ruth. "The Ethiopian-Eritrean Conflict: Diasporic vs Hegemonic states in the Horn of Africa, 1991–2000." *Journal of Modern African Studies* 38, no. 4 (2000): 651–682.

James, Stanlie M. "Shades of Othering: Reflections on Female Circumcision/Genital Mutilation." *Signs* 23, no. 4 (1998): 1032–1048.

Janis, Irving L. "Escalation of the Vietnam War: How Could It Happen?" In *American Foreign Policy: Theoretical Essays,* edited by G. John Ikenberry, 533–560. New York: Longman, 1999.

Jervis, Robert. *Perception and Misperception in International Politics.* Princeton, N.J.: Princeton University Press, 1976.

———. "Hypothesis on Misperception." In *American Foreign Policy: Theoretical Essays,* edited by G. John Ikenberry, 483–504. New York: Longman, 1999.

Jhering, Rudolph von. *Geist des römischen Rechts.* Leipzig: Breitkopf und Härtel, 1878.

Johnson-Odim, Cheryl. "Common Themes, Different Contexts: Third World Women and Feminism." In *Third World Women and the Politics of Feminism*, edited by Chandra Talpade Mohanty, Ann Russo, and Lourdes Torres, 314–327. Bloomington: Indiana University Press, 1991.

Jones, Arnold Hugh Martin, and Elizabeth Monroe. *A History of Ethiopia*. Oxford: Clarendon Press, 1968.

Jonsen, Albert R., and Stephen Toulmin. *The Abuse of Casuistry: A History of Moral Reasoning*. Berkeley: University of California Press, 1988.

Kassamali, Noor J. "When Modernity Confronts Traditional Practices: Female Genital Cutting in Northeast Africa." In *Women in Muslim Societies: Diversity with Unity*, edited by Herbert C. Bodman and Nayereh Tohidi, 39–61. Boulder, Colo.: Lynne Rienner, 1998.

Kelly, Henry Ansgar. *The Devil at Baptism: Ritual, Theology, and Drama*. Ithaca, N.Y.: Cornell University Press, 1985.

Kemink, Friederike. *Die Tegreñña-Frauen in Eritrea*. Stuttgart: Franz Steiner Verlag, 1991.

———. "The Tegreñña Customary Law Codes." *Paideuma: Mitteilungen zur Kulturkunde* 37 (1991): 55–72.

Kennedy, Duncan. *Legal Education and the Reproduction of Hierarchy: A Polemic against the System*. Cambridge: Afar, 1983.

Kenyatta, Jomo. *Facing Mount Kenya: The Tribal Life of the Gikuyu*. London: Secker and Warburg, 1938.

Kéré, Lucy Aimée, and Isabelle Tapsoba. "Charity Will Not Liberate Women: Female Genital Mutilation in Burkina Faso." In *Private Decisions, Public Debate: Women, Reproduction, and Population*, 43–56. London: Panos, 1994.

Kertzer, David I., and Tom Fricke, eds., *Anthropological Demography: Toward a New Synthesis*. Chicago: University of Chicago Press, 1997.

Khazanov, Anatoly Michailovich. *Nomads and the Outside World*. Translated by Julia Crookenden. Cambridge: Cambridge University Press, 1984.

Kidane Mengisteab. "Eritrea's Land Reform Proclamation: a Critical Appraisal." *Eritrean Studies Review* 2, no. 2 (1988): 1–18.

Killion, Tom, ed. *Historical Dictionary of Eritrea*. Lanham, Md.: Scarecrow Press, 1998.

Kiragu, Jane Wambui "Female Genital Mutilation/Female Circumcision: A Human Rights and Legal Dimension for Eradication " In *Proceedings of the Expert Meeting on Female Genital Mutilation*, edited by Els Leye, Maria de Druyn, and Stan Meuwese. Ghent-Belgium, 5–7 November 1998.

Köbben, André J. F. "Land as an Object of Gain in a Non-literate Society: Land-Tenure among the Beté and Dida (Ivory Coast, West Africa)." In *African Agrarian Systems*, edited by Daniel P. Biebuyck, 245–266. London: Oxford University Press, 1963.

Krapf, Lewis J. *Travels, Researches, and Missionary Labors*. London: Frank Cass, 1968.

Krzeczunowicz, George. "A New Legislative Approach to Customary Law." *Journal of Ethiopian Law* I, no. 1 (1964): 111–117.

——. "Code and Custom in Ethiopia." *Journal of Ethiopian Law* II, no. 2 (1965): 425–439.

——. "Putting the Legal Clock Back? The Law and Its Sources." *Journal of Ethiopian Law* III, no. 2 (1966): 623–629.

Lamb, C. "Female Excision: The Feminist Conundrum." *UFAHAMU* 20, no. 3 (1992): 13–31.

Land and Housing Commission, State of Eritrea. *Consultative Workshop on Pastoralists, Land and the State in Eritrea.* Keren, 10–11 May 1996.

Larebo, Haile M. *The Building of an Empire: Italian Land Policy and Practice in Ethiopia 1935–1941.* Oxford: Clarendon Press, 1994.

Lawson, Frank. "A Common Lawyer Looks at Codification: Further Reflections on Codification." In Frank Lawson, *Selected Essays,* Oxford: North Holland, 1997.

Leach, Edmond. "Glimpses of Unmentionable in the History of British Social Anthropology." *Annual Review of Anthropology* 13 (1984): 1–23.

Leonard, Richard. "European Colonization and the Socio-Economic Integration of Eritrea." *Eritrea Information* 3, no. 3 (1981): 7–10.

Lévi-Strauss, Claude. *The Elementary Structure of Kinship.* London: Eyre and Spottiswode, 1969.

Levine, Donald N. "Simmel at a Distance: On the History and Systematics of the Sociology of the Stranger." In *Strangers in African Societies,* edited by William A. Shack and Elliott P. Skinner, 21–36. Berkeley; University of California Press, 1979.

Lewis, Ioan M. "South of North: Shamanism in Africa: A Neglected Theme." *Paideuma, Mitteilungen zur Kulturkunde* 35 (1989): 181–188.

——. *Peoples of the Horn of Africa: Somali, Afar and Saho.* London: Haan Associates, 1994.

Licklider, Roy. "Negotiating an End in Civil Wars: General Findings." In *New Approaches to International Negotiation and Mediation: Findings from USIP-Sponsored Research,* edited by Timothy Fisk, 24–27. Washington, D.C.: United States Institute of Peace, 1999.

Lightfoot-Klein, Hanny. *Prisoners of Ritual: An Odyssey into Female Genital Circumcision in Africa.* New York: Haworth Press, 1989.

——. *A Woman's Odyssey into Africa: Tracks across a Life.* New York: Haworth Press, 1992.

Lindsey, Linda L. *Gender Roles: A Sociological Perspective.* Upper Saddle River, N.J.: Prentice Hall, 1997.

Littmann, Enno. *Publications of the Princeton Expedition to Abyssinia, II.* Leiden: Late E. J. Brill, 1910.

Llewellyn, Kurt Nickerson, and Edward Adamson Hoebel. *The Cheyenne Way: Conflict and Case Law in Primitive Jurisprudence.* Norman: University of Oklahoma Press, 1941.

Lombardi Satriani, Luigi M. *Antropologia culturale e analisi della cultura subalterna.* Messina: Pletoriana, 1968.

Longrigg, Stephen H. *A Short History of Eritrea.* Westport, Conn.: Greenwood Press, 1974.

Lowenstein, Steven. "Ethiopia." In *African Penal Systems*, edited by Alan Milner. New York: Praeger, 1969.

M. A. Mohamed Salih. "Perspectives on Pastoralists and African States." *Nomadic Peoples* 29 (1989): 3–19.

McLean, Scilla, ed. *Minority Rights Group Draft Report on Excision and Infibulation Operations on Female Genitals.* London: Minority Rights Group, 1980.

Mahmoud Ahmed Sherifo. "Why a New Administrative Structure?" *Eritrea Profile*, 2, 12, 3 June 1995.

Maine, Henry Sumner. *Ancient Law: Its Connection with the Early History of Society and Its Relation to Modern Ideas.* London: John Murray, 1930.

Maiorani, Angelo. *Istituzioni di diritto musulmano.* Asmara: Fioretti, 1954.

Mansfield, Parkyns. *Life in Abyssinia; Being Notes Collected during Three Years' Residence and Travels in That Country.* New York: Appleton, 1854.

March, Kathryn S. "Deer, Bears, and the Blood: A Note on Nonhuman Animal Response to the Menstrual Odor." *American Anthropologist* 82 (1980): 125–127.

Marein, Nathan. *The Ethiopian Empire: Federation and Laws.* Rotterdam: Royal Netherlands Printing and Lithographing Company, 1954.

Markakis, John. "Eritrea's National Charter." *Review of African Political Economy* 22, no. 63 (1995): 126–129.

Marshall, Peter. *Demanding the Impossible: A History of Anarchism.* London: Fontana, 1993.

Martini, Ferdinando. *Nell'Africa italiana.* Milano: Treves, 1892.

———. "Relazione sulla Colonia Eritrea per gli esercizi 1902–7." Rome: Tipografia della Camera dei Deputati, 1913.

Mathies, Volker. *Der Eritrea-Konflikt: Ein "Vergessmer Krieg" am Horn von Afrika.* Hamburg: Institut für Afrika-Kunde, 1981.

Mattei, Ugo. *Common law—Il diritto anglo-americano.* Torino: Utet, 1992.

———. "Three Patterns of Law: Taxonomy and Change in the World's Legal Systems." *American Journal of Comparative Law* 45 (1997): 5–44.

———. "Patterns of African Constitution in the Making." Paper presented at the International Conference on African Constitutions held at the University of Bologna, 27 November 1999.

Mattei, Ugo, and Pier Giuseppe Monateri. *Introduzione breve al diritto comparato.* Padova: Cedam, 1997.

Mead, Margaret. *Sex and Temperament in Three Primitive Societies.* New York: William Morrow and Co., 1935.

Medanie Habtezghi. "Customary Marriage and Divorce in Blin Society." LL.B. senior thesis, University of Asmara, 1999.

Meinardus, Otto F. A. *Christian Egypt: Faith and Life.* Cairo: American University Press, 1970.

Mengsteab Negash. "Anthropology, Law, and Transnational Processes." *Annual Review of Anthropology* 21 (1992): 357–379.

———. "Investment Law in Eritrea." *North Carolina Journal of International Law and Commercial Regulation* 24, no. 2 (1999): 313–380.

Merry, Sally Engle. "Legal Pluralism." *Law and Society Review* 22, no. 5 (1988): 869–896.

———. "Anthropology, Law, and Transnational Processes." *Annual Review of Anthropology* (1992): 357.

Mesghenna, Yemane. *Italian Colonialism: A Case Study of Eritrea, 1869–1934— Motive, Praxis, and Result.* Lund: Skrifter utgiva av Ekonomisk-historiska föreningen, 1988.

Meuwese, Stan, and Annemieke Wolthuis. "Legal Aspects of FGM: Legislation on International and National Level in Europe." In *Proceedings of the Expert Meeting on Female Genital Mutilation,* edited by Els Leye, Maria de Bruyn, and Stan Meuwese, 52–75. Ghent-Belgium, 5–7 November 1998.

Middleton, John, and David Tait. *Tribes without Rulers: Studies in African Segmentary Systems.* London: Routledge & Kegan Paul, 1958.

Miller, Daniel, Michael Rowlands, and Christopher Tilley. "Introduction." In *Domination and Resistance,* edited by Daniel Miller, Michael Rowlands, and Christopher Tilley. London: Unwin Hyman, 1989.

Ministry of Justice. *Human Resources Development Strategies Report.* Asmara: Eritrea, 1998.

Miran, Jonathan. "Islamic Court Records: A Source for the Social and Economic History of Massawa in the Nineteenth Century." Paper presented at the First International Conference of Eritrean Studies, Asmara, 22–26 July 2001.

Mitchell, Christopher, and Michel Banks. *Handbook of Conflict Resolution: The Analytical Problem-Solving Approach.* London: Pinter, 1996.

Mohamed El-Awa. "The Place of Custom (ʿurf) in Islamic Legal Theory." *Islamic Quarterly* XVII, no. 3 and 4 (1973): 177–182.

Mohammed, Abdul Kader Saleh. "Die Afar-Saho Nomaden in Nordost-Afrika." Ph.D. diss., Universität zu Münster, 1984.

Mohanty, Chandra Talpade. "Cartographies of Struggle: Third World Women and the Politics of Feminism." In *Third World Women and the Politics of Feminism,* edited by Chandra Talpade Mohanty, Ann Russo, and Lourdes Torres, 51–80. Bloomington: Indiana University Press, 1991.

Monateri, Pier Giuseppe. "Running on the Horn: The Case of Beni Amer and Akele Guzai Customary Laws in Eritrea." In *New Law for New States,* edited by Lyda Favali, Elisabetta Grande, and Marco Guadagni, 149–158. Torino: L'Harmattan, 1998.

———. *The Weak Law: Contaminations and Legal Cultures, Italian National Report to the XVth International Congress of Comparative Law,* Bristol, 1998.

———. "Black Gaius: A Quest for the Multicultural Origin of the 'Western Legal Tradition'." *Hastings Law Journal* 51, no. 3 (2000): 479–555.

Monateri, Pier Giuseppe, and Rodolfo Sacco. "Legal Formants." In *The New Palgrave Dictionary of Economics and the Law,* edited by Peter Newman. London: Macmillan, 1998.

Mondaini, Gennaro. *La legislazione coloniale italiana nel suo sviluppo storico e nel suo stato attuale (1881–1940) I.* Milano: Istituto per gli Studi di Politica Internazionale, 1941.

Moore, Henrietta L. "Understanding Sex and Gender." In *Encyclopedia of Anthropology*, edited by Tim Ingold, 813–830. London: Routledge, 1997.

Moore, Sally Falk. *Law as a Process: An Anthropological Approach*. London: Routledge and Kegan Paul, 1978.

Moreno, Martino Mario. "Le popolazioni dell'Eritrea." In *L'Italia in Africa, I, Il territorio e le popolazioni*, 121. Rome: Ministero degli Affari Esteri, Roma, n.d.

Morgan, Robin. *The Word of a Woman*. New York: Norton & Co., 1992.

Morris, Henry Francis, and James S. Read. *Indirect Rule and the Search for Justice: Essays in East African Legal History*. Oxford: Clarendon, 1972.

Münzinger, Werner. *Ostafrikanische Studien*. Schaffhausen: Fr. Hurtersche, 1864.

———. *Studi sull'Africa Orientale. Traduzione dal tedesco per cura del Corpo di Stato Maggiore*, Rome: Voghera, 1890.

———. *Dei costumi e del diritto dei Bogos. Traduzione dal tedesco a cura di A. Ostini*. Rome: Ministero degli Affari Esteri, 1891.

Musa Naib. "The Applicability of the Civil Procedure Code to the Muslim Courts." Senior thesis, University of Addis Ababa, 1974.

Nadel, Siegfried Frederick. *Races and Tribes of Eritrea*. Asmara: British Military Administration, 1944.

———. "Notes on Beni Amer Society." *Sudan Notes and Records* 26 (1945): 51–94.

———. "Land Tenure on the Eritrean Plateau." *Africa* XVI, no. 1 (1946): 1–21.

———. "Land Tenure on the Eritrean Plateau (Conclusion.)" *Africa* XVI, no. 2 (1946): 99–108.

Nader, Laura. "Controlling Processes: (Tracing the Dynamic Components of Power)." *Current Anthropology* 38, no. 5 (1997): 711–737.

National Statistics Office [Eritrea] and Macro International Inc. *Eritrea Demographic and Health Survey 1995*. Calverton, Mo., 1995.

National Union of Eritrean Women in North America. *Changing Roles: Women in Eritrea*. New York: National Union of Eritrean Women, n.d.

Negash, Tekeste, and Kjetil Tronvoll. *Brothers at War: Making Sense of the Eritrean-Ethiopian War*. Oxford: James Currey, 2000.

Nelli, René. *Erotique et civilisation*. Paris: Weber, 1972.

Nietzsche, Friedrich. *Jenseits Von Gut und Böse*. Leipzig: Druck und Verlag, 1896.

———. *Nachlass*. Frankfurt am Main: Fischer Bücheri, 1959.

Nonet, Philippe, and Philip Selznick. *Law and Society in Transition: Toward Responsive Law*. New York: Harper & Row, 1978.

Obbo, Christine. "Village Strangers in Buganda Society." In *Strangers in African Societies*, edited by William A. Shack and Elliott P. Skinner, 227–241. Berkeley: University of California Press, 1979.

Obeid Hag Ali. "The Conversion of Customary Law to Written Law." In *Folk Law: Essays in the Theory and Practice of Lex Non Scripta*, edited by Alison Dundes Renteln and Alan Dundes, 351–365. New York: Garland, 1994.

Okwubanego, John Tochukwu. "Female Circumcision and the Girl Child in

Africa and the Middle East: The Eyes of the World Are Blind to the Conquered." *International Lawyer* 33, no. 1 (1999): 159–187.

Olenick, I. *International Family Planning Perspectives* 24, no. 1 (1998): 47–49.

Ortner, Sherry B., and Harriet Whitehead, "Introduction." In *Sexual Meanings: The Cultural Construction of Gender and Sexuality*, edited by Sherry B. Ortner and Harriet Whitehead, 1–27. Cambridge: Cambridge University Press, 1981.

Ostini, Felice. *Trattato di diritto consuetudinario dell'Eritrea*. Rome: Officina Grafica—Corriere Eritreo, 1956.

Ostrom, Vincent. *The Meaning of Democracy and the Vulnerability of Democracies: A Response to Toqueville's Challenge*. Ann Arbor: University of Michigan Press, 1997.

Parkyns, Mansfield. *Life in Abyssinia, II*. London: John Murray, 1853.

Pasternak, Burton, Carol R. Ember, and Melvin Ember. *Sex, Gender, and Kinship*. Upper Saddle River, N.J.: Prentice Hall, 1997.

Pateman, Roy. "Peasants and State Farms: Problems in the Transition to Socialism in Africa and Latin America." *Peasant Studies* 16, no. 2 (1989): 69–86.

———. "Liberté, Egalité, Fraternité: Aspects of the Eritrean Revolution." *The Journal of Modern African Studies* 28, no. 3 (1990): 457–472.

———. "Eritrea Takes the World Stage." *Current History* 93, no. 583 (1994): 228–231.

———. "Eritrea: W(h)ither the Jihad?" *Journal of Contingencies and Crisis Management* 3, no. 4 (1995): 241–246.

———. "Structure and Functions of the Eritrean Government." Paper commissioned by the Eritrean Institute of Management, Embatkalla, 1997.

———. *Eritrea: Even the Stones Are Burning*. Trenton, N.J.: Red Sea Press, 1998.

Paul, A. "Notes on the Beni Amer." *Sudan Notes and Records* XXXI, pt. 2 (1950): 223–245.

Paulos Zaid. *Eritrea Profile*, 1 January 2000, 2.

Perini, Ruffillo. *Di qua dal Marèb (Marèb mellàsc)*. Firenze: Tipografia Cooperativa, 1905.

Petazzi, Ercole. *L'odierno diritto penale consuetudinario dell'Hamasien (Eritrea)*. Asmara: Fioretti, 1937.

Peters, E. L. "The Proliferation of Segments in the Lineage of Bedouin of Cyrenaica." *Journal of the Royal Anthropological Institute* 90 (1960): 29–53.

Pirandello, Luigi. *Sei personaggi in cerca d'autore*. Firenze: Bemporad, 1921.

Ploss, Heinrich. "Die operative Behandlung der weiblichen Geschlechtstheile bei verschiedenen Volkern." *Zeitschrift fur Ethnologie* 3 (1871): 381–397.

Ploss, Heinrich, and Max Bartels. *Das Weib in der Natur und Völkerkunde, I*. Leipzig: Th. Grieben's Verlag, 1895.

Pollera, Alberto. *I Baria e i Cunama*. Rome: Reale Società Geografica, 1913.

———. *L'ordinamento della giustizia e la procedura indigena in Etiopia e in Eritrea*. Rome: Tipografia Bertero e C., 1913.

———. *Il regime della proprietà terriera in Etiopia e nella Colonia Eritrea*. Rome: Bertero, 1913.

——. "Relazione della sottocommissione eritrea." *Relazione Governativa Italiana per i problemi del dopoguerra, Sezione Settima (Questioni Coloniali).* Rome, 1919.

——. *La donna in Etiopia.* Rome: Grafia, 1922.

——. *Lo stato etiopico e la sua chiesa.* Rome-Milan: S.E.A.I., 1926.

——. *Le popolazioni indigene dell'Eritrea.* Bologna: Manuali Coloniali, 1935.

——. *The Native Peoples of Eritrea.* Translated by L. Lappin. Asmara: University of Asmara, 1996.

Pollock, Frederick. "Introduction." In Henry Sumner Maine, *Ancient Law: Its Connection with the Early History of Society and its Relation to Modern Ideas.* London: John Murray, 1930.

Posner, Richard A. *The Economics of Justice.* Cambridge, Mass.: Harvard University Press, 1983.

——. *Sex and Reason.* Cambridge, Mass.: Harvard University Press, 1992.

Pospisil, Leopold. *The Anthropology of Law: A Comparative Theory of Law.* New York: Harper and Row, 1971.

Publications du Comité d'Études Historiques et Scientifiques de l'O.A.F. *Coutumiers Juridiques de l'Afrique Occidentale Française* (Paris: Larose, 1939).

Rabinow, Paul. *Essays on the Anthropology of Reason.* Princeton, N.J.: Princeton University Press, 1996.

Radcliffe-Brown, Alfred Reginald. "Introduction." In *African Systems of Kinship and Marriage,* edited by Alfred Reginald Radcliffe-Brown and Daryll Forde, 1–85. London: Oxford University Press, 1950.

Rav A. Somekh. *Brit Milà–Circoncisione.* Milan, 1995.

Raz, Shlomo. *Tigré Grammar and Texts.* Malibu: Undena Publications, 1983.

Redden, Kenneth R. *The Legal System of Ethiopia.* Charlottesville, Va.: The Michie Company, 1968.

Redden, Kenneth R., ed. *Modern Legal Systems Cyclopedia, V 6A Part II.* Buffalo: William S. Horn, 1990.

Reid, J. A., and J. F. P. Maclaren. "Arab Customary Procedure and Customary Law." *Sudan Notes and Records* XIX, pt. 1 (1936): 158–161.

Reimann, Mathias, ed. *The Reception of Continental Ideas in the Common Law World, 1820–1920.* Berlin: Duncker and Humblot, 1993.

Reinisch, Leo. *Texte der Saho Sprache.* Vienna: Alfred Hölder, 1889.

Rentmeesters, Veronica. "Eritrea: Will Women's Liberation Survive the Liberation Struggle?" Paper presented to the Annual Meeting of the African Studies Association, Atlanta, 1989.

Research and Documentation Center, Asmara. "Appeal by Hamasien Elders to Governor General." Letter 7/u37.

——. "Code of Customary Law of Acchele Guzai: Adghena Tegheleba, arts. 104, 98," Document 138300.

——. "Highi Endaba BetTarge Bogos." Box #4/07007.

——. "Highi Engana'a: Sira'at Astmi Harmaz." Document 00519.

——. "Highin Siratin Nay MeretAdebo Codes and Bylaws of Eritrean Regions and Countries." Document 00504.

——. "Irafaile." Document 00537.

——. "Kile' Mensa'e: Dighem, wa Fitih, wa'Aotat." Document 00495.

——. "Liban and Habela." Document 00527.

——. "Mai Feres-Deranto." Document 00532.

——. "Questionnaire for the Saho Speaking Areas." Document 00530.

——. "Resti in Serae (Adkeme Melega)." Document 00531.

——. "Sir'at nay Habslus, nay GhebreKristos nay DegiTeshim." Document 00494/ 00500.

——. "Sir'at Karneshim." Document 00492.

——. "Sira'at LogoChewa." Document 00502.

——. "Siraat Dembezan." Box #4/07008.

——. "Siraat Highitat Endaba ab Hamassien." Box #4/07006.

——. "The Status of Hazemo." Document 55147.

——. "Wa'ela Shewa'te Anseba." Box #4/07006.

——. "Warsa Bet." Document 00534.

Reyntjens, Filip. "Note sur l'utilité d'introduire un système juridique 'pluraliste' dans la macro-comparaison des droits." *Revue de Droit International et de Droit Comparé* 68 (1991): 41–50.

Risse, Thomas. "The Power of Norms versus the Norms of Power: Transnational Civil Society and Human Rights." In *The Third Force: The Rise of Transnational Civil Society*, edited by Ann M. Florini, 177–209. Washington, D.C.: Carnegie Endowment for International Peace, 2000.

Roberts, Richard. "Custom and Muslim Family Law in the Native Courts of the French Soudan, 1905-1912," paper presented to the Second Symposium of the Islamic Law in Africa Project, Dakar, Senegal, 30 June 2001.

Roberts, Simon. "The Recording of Customary Law: Some Problems of Method." In *Folk Law: Essays in the Theory and Practice of Lex Non Scripta*, I, edited by Alison Dundes Renteln and Alan Dundes, 331–337. New York: Garland, 1994.

——. "Law and Dispute Processes." In *Companion Encyclopedia of Anthropology*, edited by Tim Ingold, 962–982. London: Routledge, 1997.

Rodén, Karl Gustav. *Le tribù dei Mensa—Storia, legge e costumi. Traduzione italiana dalla lingua Tigré.* Stockholm: Nordiska Boktryckeriet, 1913.

Rose, Paul Lawrence. *Revolutionary Antisemitism from Kant to Wagner.* Princeton, N.J.: Princeton University Press, 1990.

Rosen, Richard A. "Constitutional Process, Constitutionalism and the Eritrean Experience." *North Carolina Journal of International Law and Commercial Regulation* 24, no. 2 (1999): 263–311.

Rosenfeld, Michel. "A Pluralist Critique of the Constitutional Treatment of Religion." In *The Law of Religious Identity: Models or Post-Communism*, edited by Andras Sajo and Shlomo Avineri, 44–45. The Hague: Kluwer Law International, 1999.

Rubinstein, Robert A. "Collective Violence and Common Security." In *Companion Encyclopedia of Anthropology*, edited by Tim Ingold, 983–1009. London: Routledge, 1997.

Ruhlen, Merritt. *The Origin of the Language: Tracing the Evolution of the Mother Tongue.* New York: John Wiley & Sons, 1994.

Russell, F. F. "Eritrean Customary Law." *Journal of African Law* 3 (1959): 99–104.

Sacco, Rodolfo. "Di alcune singolari convergenze fra il diritto ancestrale dei Berberi e quello dei Somali." *Africa* 44, no. 3 (1989): 341–368.

———. "Legal Formants: A Dynamic Approach to Comparative Law." *American Journal of Comparative Law* 39, no. 1 (1991): 1–34; 39, no. 2 (1991): 343–401.

———. *Introduzione al diritto comparato.* Torino: Utet, 1994.

———. *Il diritto africano.* Torino: Utet, 1995.

———. "Perché l'armato ubbidisce all'inerme (Saggio sulla legittimazione del diritto e del potere.)" *Rivista Diritto Civile* 1 (1997): 1–18.

Sami A. Aldeeb Abu-Sahlieh. "To Mutilate in the Name of Jehovah or Allah: Legitimization of Male and Female Circumcision," New Enlarged Edition, 1994.

———. "Islamic Law and the Issue of Male and Female Circumcision." *Third World Legal Studies* (1994–1995): 73–101.

———. *Male and Female Circumcision in the Jewish, Christian and Muslim Communities: Religious Debate.* Beirut: Riad El-Rayyes Books, 2000.

Sanday, Peggy Reeves *Female Power and Male Dominance: On the Origins of Sexual Inequality.* Cambridge: Cambridge University Press, 1991.

Sanderson, Lilian Passmore. *Against the Mutilation of Women.* London: Ithaca Press, 1981.

Sandonà, Augusto. *Il regime fondiario e la colonizzazione nell'Affrica Italiana (Colonia Eritrea, Somalia, Libia).* Rome: Tipografia dell'Istituto Internazionale d'Agricoltura, 1917.

Santelli, Dr. "Les Danakils." *Bulletin de la Societé d'Anthropologie* 4, no. 6 (1893): 479–501.

Sarubbi, Francesco. "Di alcune consuetudini delle popolazioni del bassopiano occidentale in Eritrea." In *Atti del terzo congresso di studi coloniali,* III, II, 92–298. Firenze-Roma: Centro di Studi Coloniali, Istituto Coloniale Fascista, 1937.

Savard, George C. *The Population of Ethiopia, II.* Addis Ababa, 1970.

Sbacchi, Alberto. *Ethiopia under Mussolini: Fascism and the Colonial Experience.* London: Zed Books, 1985.

Scaramucci, F., and Enrico Hillyer Giglioli. "Notizie sul Danakil." *Archivio per l'Antropologia e l'Etnologia* 14 (1884): 17–44.

Schacht, Joseph. *An Introduction to Islamic Law.* Oxford: Clarendon Press, 1964.

———. "Notes sur la sociologie du droit musulman." *Revue Africaine* 93, 1952.

Schaeffer, George. "After Office Hours: Female Circumcision." *Obstetrics and Gynecology* 6, no. 2 (1955): 235–238.

Schapera, Isaac. *A Handbook of Tswana Law and Customs.* London: Oxford University Press, 1938.

Schiller, A. Arthur. "Legislation." *The American Journal of Comparative Law* 2 (1953): 375–383.

———. "Customary Land Tenure among the Highland Peoples of Northern Ethiopia." *African Law Studies* (1 June 1969): 1–22.

Scholler, Heinrich. "Ethiopian Constitutional Development." In *Jahrbuch Des offentlichen Rechts der Gegenwart*, 502–564. Tübingen: J. C. B. Mohr, 1987.

Scott, James C. *Domination and the Arts of Resistance: Hidden Transcripts.* New Haven, Conn.: Yale University Press, 1990.

Sedler, Robert Allen. "The Development of Legal Systems: The Ethiopian Experience." *Iowa Law Review* 53, no. 3 (1967): 562–635.

Selassie, Girma Wolde. "The Impact of the Ethiopian Revolution on the Law and Legal Institutions of the Country." In *Proceedings of the Seventh International Conference of Ethiopian Studies*, edited by Sven Rubenson, 565–575. Lund, Sweden: University of Lund, 1984.

Selznick, Philip. *Law, Society, and Industrial Justice.* New York: Russell Sage Foundation, 1969.

Semere, Haile. "The Roots of the Ethiopia-Eritrea Conflict: The Erosion of the Federal Act." *Journal of Eritrean Studies* 1, no. 1 (1996): 1–18.

Seneca, Lucius Annaeus. *Epistulae Morales ad Lucilium*, Libri XX [Seneca's Letters to Lucilius, letter 20]. Translated by E. Phillips Barker. Oxford: Clarendon, 1932.

Sertoli Salis, Renzo. *L'ordinamento fondiario eritreo.* Padova: Cedam, 1932.

Shack, William A. *The Central Ethiopians.* London: International African Institute, 1974.

——. "Open Systems and Closed Boundaries: The Ritual Process of Stranger Relations in New African States." In *Strangers in African Societies*, edited by William A. Shack and Elliott P. Skinner, 37–47. Berkeley: University of California Press, 1979.

Sheleff, Leon Shaskolsky. *The Future of Tradition: Customary Law, Common Law and Legal Pluralism.* Ilford: Frank Cass, 2000.

Sherfey, Mary Jane. *The Nature and Evolution of Female Sexuality.* New York: Random House, 1972.

Shipton, Parker. "The Kenyan Land Tenure Reform: Misunderstandings in the Public Creation of Private Property." In *Land and Society in Contemporary Africa*, edited by R. E. Downs and Stephen P. Reyna, 91–135. Hanover, N.H.: University Press of New England, 1988.

Singer, J. David. "The Level-of-Analysis Problem in International Relations." In *The International System: Theoretical Essays*, edited by Klaus Knorr and Sidney Verba, 77–92. Princeton, N.J.: Princeton University Press, 1961.

Singer, Norman J. *Governmental Recognition of Non-governmental Laws and Legal Institutions in Ethiopia.* Addis Ababa: Law Library Haile Selassie I University, n.d.

Singer, Philip, and Daniel E. Desole. "The Australian Subincision Ceremony." *American Anthropologist* 69 (1967): 355–358.

Sklar, Richard L. "The Nature of Class Domination in Africa." *The Journal of Modern Africa Studies* 17, no. 4 (1979): 531–552.

Slack, Alison T. "Female Circumcision: A Critical Appraisal." *Human Rights Quarterly* 10, no. 4 (1988): 437–486.

Smith, Clarence J. A. "Human Rights in Eritrea." *Modern Law Review* 18, no. 5 (1955): 484–486.

Smith, M. G. "On Segmentary Lineage Systems." *Journal of the Royal Anthropological Institute* 86, no. 2 (1956): 39–80.

Smith, Robyn Cerny. "Female Circumcision: Bringing Women's Perspectives into the International Debate." *Southern California Law Review* 65, no. 5 (1992): 2449–2504.

Smith, W. Robertson. *Kinship and Marriage in Early Arabia.* Oosterhout, The Netherlands: Anthropological Publications, 1966.

Snyder, Francis G. *Capitalism and Legal Change: An African Transformation.* New York: Academic Press, 1981.

Soumarè, Diop Aida. "Un voto contro la violenza delle donne." *Internazionale* (March 1999): 275.

Southall, Aidan W. "On Chastity in Africa." *Uganda Journal* 24, no. 2 (1960): 207–217.

Spivak, Gayatri Chakravorty. "Can the Subaltern Speak?" In *Marxism and the Interpretation of Culture,* edited by Cary Nelson and Lawrence Grossberg, 271–313. Urbana: University of Illinois Press, 1988.

Stolz, Joelle. "Putting a Stop to Excision in Burkina Faso." *Le Monde Diplomatique,* translated by Lorna Dale (October 1998): 6–7.

Stone, Linda. *Kinship and Gender: An Introduction.* Boulder, Colo.: Westview Press, 1998.

Strathern, Marilyn. "Self-Interest and the Social Good: Some Implications of Hagen Gender Imagery." In *Sexual Meanings: The Cultural Construction of Gender and Sexuality,* edited by Sherry B. Ortner and Harriet Whitehead, 166–191. Cambridge: Cambridge University Press, 1981.

Sussman, Erika. "Contending with Culture: An Analysis of the Female Genital Mutilation Act of 1996." *Cornell International Law Journal* 31 (1998): 193–251.

Taba, A. H. "Female Circumcision." *Tropical Doctor* (January 1980): 21–23.

Taddia, Irma. *L'Eritrea-Colonia 1890–1952: paesaggi, strutture, uomini del colonialismo.* Milano: F. Angeli, 1986

Talhami, Ghada H. *Suakin and Massawa under Egyptian Rule, 1865–1885.* Washington, D.C.: University Press of America, 1979.

Teame Beyene. "The Eritrean Judiciary: Struggling for Independence." Paper submitted to the International Conference of Eritrean Studies, Asmara, July 2001.

Tesfay Abraham. *The Diesa Land Tenure System and the Land Proclamation n. 58/1994 in the Kebesa Rural Area.* Asmara: University of Asmara, 1998.

Thesiger, Wilfred. *The Danakil Diary: Journeys through Abyssinia, 1930–34.* London: Harper Collins, 1996.

Thompson, Virginia, and Richard Adloff. *Djibouti and the Horn of Africa.* Stanford, Calif.: Stanford University Press, 1968.

Tie, Warwick. *Legal Pluralism: Toward a Multicultural Conception of Law.* Brookfield, Vt.: Dartmouth, 1999.

Trevaskis, Gerald Kennedy Nicholas. "Notes for the Guidance of the District Officer in Eritrea." In *Trevaskis Papers.* Oxford: Rhodes House, c.1942.

——. *Eritrea: A Colony in Transition, 1941–52.* Westport, Conn.: Greenwood Press, 1975.

Trimingham, J. Spencer. *Islam in Ethiopia.* London: Oxford University Press, 1952.

——. *Islam in the Sudan.* London: Frank Cass and Co., 1965.

——. *The Influence of Islam upon Africa.* London: Longman, 1980.

Tronvoll, Kjetil. "Mai Weini: A Village in Highland Eritrea." M.A. thesis, Oslo University, 1996.

——. "The Eritrean Referendum: Peasant Voices." *Eritrean Studies Review* 1, no. 1 (1996): 23–67.

——. "The Process of Nation-Building in Post-war Eritrea: Created from Below or Directed from Above?" *The Journal of Modern African Studies* 36, no. 3 (1998): 461–482.

——. *Mai Weini: An Highland Village in Eritrea.* Lawrenceville, N.J.: Red Sea Press, 1998.

Tseggai, Araia. "Eritrean Women and Italian Soldiers: Status of Eritrean Women under Italian Rule." *Journal of Eritrean Studies* IV, no. 1 and 2 (1989/1990): 7-12.

Twining, William, and Jennifer S. Uglow, eds. *Legal Studies in Small Jurisdictions: A Report of a Conference Held at Osgoode Hall Law School.* Donsview, Ontario: York University, 1978.

Tzehainesh Tekle. "Eritrea: il processo di formazione di uno stato africano." In *Transplants Innovation and Legal Tradition in the Horn of Africa*, edited by Elisabetta Grande. Torino: L'Harmattan, 1995.

——. "Prime osservazione sul sistema gudizario eritreo: la fase della transizione." In *New Law for New States*, edited by Lyda Favali, Elisabetta Grande, and Marco Guadagni, 183-192. Torino: L'Harmattan, 1998.

U.S. Department of State. *Eritrea Country Report on Human Rights Practices for 1997.* 30 January 1998.

Ullendorff, Edward. *The Ethiopians: An Introduction to Country and People.* London: Oxford University Press, 1960.

UNICEF/UNFPA. *Female Genital Mutilation.* Geneva: World Health Organization, 1997.

United Nations. *Report of the International Conference on Population and Development: The UN International Conference on Population and Development.* Cairo, 5-13 September 1994.

——. Department of Public Information. *The United Nations and the Independence of Eritrea.* New York, 1996.

Van Caenegem, Raoul Charles. *Judges, Legislators and Professors.* New York: Cambridge University Press, 1987.

Van Doren, John M. "Positivism and the Rule of Law: Formal Systems or Concealed Values—A Case Study of the Ethiopian Legal System." *Journal of Transnational Law & Policy* 3 (1994): 165-204.

Van Gennep, Arnold. *Les rites de passage.* Paris: Nourry, 1909.

Vanderlinden, Jacques. "An Introduction to the Sources of Ethiopian Law from the 13th to the 20th Century." *Journal of Ethiopian Law* III, no. 1 (1966): 227-255.

——. "A Further Note on an Introduction to the Sources of Ethiopian Law." *Journal of Ethiopian Law* III, no. 2 (1966): 635-640.

——. "Le pluralisme juridique: essay de synthèse." In *Le pluralisme juridique*, edited by J. Gilissen. Université de Brussels: Bruxelles, 1971.

——. "Ethiopia." In *National Reports E/F of the International Encyclopaedia of Comparative Law, I*, edited by Viktor Knapp, E.23-35. Tübingen: J. C. B. Mohr, 1973.

——. "À propos des familles de droit en droit civil comparé." In *Hommages à René Dekkers*. Brussels: Bruylant, 1982.

——. "Return to Legal Pluralism: Twenty Years Later." *Journal of Legal Pluralism* 28 (1989): 149-157.

Verdier, Raimond. *La vengeance: études d'ethnologie, d'histoire et de philosophie.* Paris: Cujas, 1980.

——. "Coutume et loi dans drois parental et foncier (Afrique de l'Ouest francophone)." In *Dynamiques et finalités des droits africains*, edited by Gérard Conac. Paris: Economica, 1980: 312-313.

——. "Customary Family Law." In *International Encyclopaedia of Comparative Law IV*, edited by René David et al., 11.221-289. Tübingen: J. C. B. Mohr, IV, 1983.

Viljoen, Frans. "*Supra*-national Rights Instruments for the Protection of Children in Africa: The Convention on the Rights of the Child and the African Charter on the Rights and Welfare of the Child." *Comparative and International Law Journal of Southern Africa* (July 1998): 199-212.

Villari, Salvatore. *Le consuetudini giuridiche dell'Albania.* Rome, 1944.

Vizedom, Monika. *Rites and Relationships.* Sage Research Papers in the Social Sciences, 4. Beverly Hills, Calif.: Sage Publications, 1976.

Waelde, Thomas W., and James L. Gunderson. "Legislative Reform in Transitional Economies: Western Transplants: A Short-Cut to Social Market Economy Status." *International Comparative Law Quarterly* 43, no. 2 (1994): 347-378.

Waltz, Kenneth N. "Anarchic Orders and Balance of Power." In *American Foreign Policy: Theoretical Essays*, edited by G. John Ikenberry, 67-90. New York: Longman, 1999.

——. *Man, the State, and War.* New York: Columbia University Press, 1959.

Watson, Alan. *Legal Transplants: An Approach to Comparative Law.* Edinburgh: Scottish Academic Press, 1974.

Whitman, James Q. "At the Origins of Law and the State: Supervision of Violence, Mutilation of Bodies, or Setting of Prices?" *Chicago Kent Law Review* 71, no. 1 (1996): 41-84.

WHO. "Female Genital Mutilation." Report of a WHO Technical Working Group. Geneva, 17-19 July 1995.

Widstrand, Carl Gösta. "Female Infibulation." *Studia Ethnographica Upsaliensia* 20 (1964): 95-124.

Wilken, George Alexander. *Over de Verwantschap en het Huwelijks—er erfrecht bij de Volken van den Indischen Archipel*. Leiden: Brill, 1883.

Wilson, Amrit. *Women and the Eritrean Revolution: The Challenge Road*. Trenton, N.J.: Red Sea Press, 1991.

Wilson, Jason R. "Eritrean Land Reform: The Forgotten Masses." *North Carolina Journal of International Law and Commercial Regulation* 24, no. 2 (1999): 497–520.

Wilson, Wendy Pitcher. "The Deportation of 'Eritreans' from Ethiopia: Human Rights Violations Tolerated by the International Community." *North Carolina Journal of International Law and Commercial Regulation* 24, no. 2 (1999): 451–496.

With, Peter. "Politics and Liberation: The Eritrean Struggle, 1961–1986." Ph.D. diss., University of Aarhus, 1987.

Wolff, Kurt H., trans. and ed. *The Sociology of Georg Simmel*. Glencoe, Calif.: The Free Press, 1950.

Woodman, Gordon R. "Legal Pluralism and the Search for Justice." *Journal of African Law* 30, no. 2 (1996): 152–167.

———. "Ideological Combat and Social Observation: Recent Debate about Legal Pluralism." *Journal of Legal Pluralism* 42 (1998): 21–59.

World Bank (Africa Region). *Indigenous Knowledge Notes*, 3 December 1998.

Yahya Ould El-Bara. "Le statut personnel de la femme entre droit musulman et droit coutumier dans la Mauritanie post-coloniale," paper presented to the Second Symposium of the Islamic Law in Africa Project, Dakar, Senegal, 29 June 2001.

Yirgalem Woldegabriel. "Women and Land Ownership System in Highland Eritrea" LL.B. senior thesis, University of Asmara, 1998.

Young, Arthur. *Travels in France*. Edited by Matilda Betham-Edwards. London: Bell, 1892.

Yuzbashi Negib Eff. Yunis. "Notes on the Baggara and Nuba of Western Kordofan." *Sudan Notes and Records* 5, no. 4 (1922): 200–207.

Zaborowski, M. "La circoncision, ses origines et sa repartition en Afrique et au Madagascar." *Bulletin de la Societé d'Anthropologie* (18 January 1894): 654–675.

Zaki Mustfa. "The Substantive Law Applied by Muslim Courts in Ethiopia." *Journal of Ethiopian Law* IX, no. I (1973): 138–148.

Zenawi Haile. "The Significance of Marriage Payments on Marriage in the Eritrean Family Law." LL.B. senior thesis, University of Asmara, 1999.

Index

335

Index

Index

Lyda Favali is a lawyer and researcher at the University of Turin, Italy. She teaches African and private comparative law, and is the author of *Fra legge e modelli ancestrali: prime osservazioni sulle mutilazioni genitali in Eritrea.*

Roy Pateman is Professor Emeritus of Political Science at the University of California, Los Angeles. He is author of *Eritrea: Even the Stones Are Burning* and *Chaos and Dancing Star*. He was in British Army counterintelligence and has also worked for the Australian government and British public interest groups.